HISTORY AND SOCIETY

Noah Edward Fehl

CHUNG CHI PUBLICATIONS
CHUNG CHI COLLEGE
THE CHINESE UNIVERSITY OF HONG KONG

Published by Chung Chi College
March 1964

Made in Hong Kong

by

CHUNG LUEN PRINTING CO., 232, MA TAU WEI RD., KOWLOON

History and Society

Chung Chi Philosophy of Life
Publication Series

IN MEMORIAM

Laura H. Fehl
Emiline Wolf
Harriet Hatton
Joachim Wach
Winfred Donovan

✝

Rest in peace and light
perpetual shine upon you

FOREWORD

In the summer of 1963, I came to Hong Kong on the invitation of the University of Hong Kong to give a series of lectures. This lecture tour gave me a chance to observe the way of life of the people of Hong Kong. It is a staggering thought that when Hong Kong was first ceded to the British it was only a port inhabited by a small number of fishermen, and it has now grown into a large city with a population of over three million. One must remember that most of the present inhabitants are refugees who have come to Hong Kong at various stages as results of numerous civil wars in China, the Boxer trouble, the Revolution in 1911, the "Northern Expedition", the war with the Japanese and the retreat of the Kuomintang from the mainland. It is almost true to say that the prosperity of Hong Kong is derived from all the fightings and disturbances in China. This is a lesson which the Chinese here should not forget.

After my arrival I was introduced to the academic circle at a banquet given by P.M. Liu, C.I. Tang, C.S. Mou and Y.W. Hsieh. At this and other banquets I was amazed at the luxury of the food. There were dishes such as bird's nest from Manila, sharksfin from Karachi or Mexico, fish from Cambodia, sea-gurkel from Japan, crabs from the lakes of Soo-chow, water melon from Hawaii, pears from Tientsin and frozen chicken from the United States. I soon discovered that, not only in matters of food but in other respects, Hong Kong is probably the first city in the world for material comfort because it is an international market of consumer goods from many countries.

At the same time, there is no lack of spiritual foods, the nature of which is rather more complicated. In politics, there are many anti-communist journals such as the *United Voice* and those published by Union Research. In education there is the recently established Chinese University and also various religious centres for translation and research work. One of the movements with which I am closely connected is the revival of the philosophy of the Confucian school. This revival movement is a much thought-over activity which had its beginnings in the reaction to the impact of Western philosophy on the minds of Chinese intellectuals. Since about a century ago, Chinese returned students have been expounding in China what they learned from their teachers abroad. Yen Fo translated the works of Adam Smith, Thomas Huxley, J.S. Mill, Spencer and others; those who returned from France tried to do the works of the Encyclopaedists; V. K. Ting preached the positivism of K. Pearson; Dr. Hu Shih spread the philosophy of John Dewey; others translated the works of Henri

Bergson. Some adopted the philosophical view of Hegel and some of Kant. In the post war years, there was a general realization of the futility of the perpetual search for foreign philosophy, and a movement for the revival of Confucian philosophy was started. The aim was to put the Confucian and Neo-Confucian systems on a broader basis in order to incorporate Western concepts. The Neo-Confucian school which was founded on Confucian and Mencian systems had a treasury of fundamental concepts such as *Ri* (form), *Chi* (matter), *Sin* (mind), *Hsin* (human essence), *Ssu* (thinking) and *Pien-ti* (reality), which are rich enough for forming the basis of modern Chinese philosophy.

Another important work which is done at the Chung Chi College in Hong Kong, whose members are on friendly terms with the Neo-Confucian Revival Movement, is the Philosophy of Life Programme. Under this programme, which is in the charge of Dr. Fehl, five books have been written: *A Guide to the Study of Plato's Republic, The Spiritual Roots of Western Culture; The University East and West; Science and Culture* (Part I *Space and Time*; Part II *Mass, Motion and Machines*; Part III *Process and Life*); and the present work, *History and Society*. The common purpose behind the writing of these books is to make the younger Chinese generation familiar with the traditions of both East and West. Bearing this in mind, I think Dr. Fehl's *History and Society* is of special importance as it is probably the first attempt ever made to bring historiography in China, Israel, Ancient Greece and Europe together in one single comparative study for Chinese students. The present age is one of uncertainty, when people are becoming more and more eager in their search for knowledge of the past and the present and the future of the human race. In other respects, we can compare the world today to that of Europe in the age of the Enlightenment when there were great changes in the views and conditions of life. The following works which appeared in the period of the Enlightenment bore witness to the changes which contributed to the making of modern Europe. J.B. Boussuel's *Discours sur l'historie Universelle;* Vico's *Scienza Nuova;* J.D. Herder's *Ideen zur Philosophie der Geschichte der Menschheit,* and Kant's *Ideen zu einer allgemeinen Geschichte in Weltbürglicher Absicht.* Similarly, in the Han Dynasty in China, Ssu-ma Chien's *Shih Chi* put on record China's change from the feudal system to the universal empire of the Ch'in and Han Dynasties. The next turning point in Chinese history occurred from the division of North and South to the re-unification under Sui and T'ang and the blossoming of the arts and philosophy in the Sung period. Liu Chi, a critic of histories in the T'ang Dynasty, reviewed all the historical works known in his time. Contemporary with Liu Chi was

Tu Yu, the author of *T'ung-tien* (通典) a historical record of Chinese social institutions. Following Liu and Tu, there were many historical works such as Ssu-ma Kuang's (司馬光) *Tzu-chih t'ung-chien* (資治通鑑) and Ma Tuan-ling's (馬端臨) *Wen-hsien t'ung-kau* (文獻通攷) and Cheng Tsao's (鄭樵) *T'ung Chih* (通志). These are books of Chinese greatness which was on the point of passing-by. Dr. Fehl's book gives also a summary of Western theories of history from Herodotus down to Vico, Herder and Comte and of present writers including Bertrand Russell. Excerpts from the writings of these authors are also included in the book which university students should find useful.

Finally, I must say that at a time of cultural exchanges between East and West, it will be a great benefit to the peoples of both sides if they can find an understanding of the meaning of life based on the knowledge and proper appreciation of the histories of the human race in different parts of the world. In *History and Society* Dr. Fehl supplies us with an outline of the views of historiographers on both sides. This may prove to be the beginning of an important branch of human studies in Chinese higher education.

Carsun Chang

PREFACE

A preface is usually to warn the reader. It is like the label on a medicine bottle which, while not frankly advising the reader not to touch the stuff at all, lays down the fairly restricted use from which some benefit might be expected. I propose to be equally candid with anyone who has already bought this book.

It is not a book that contains any historical knowledge. What few 'facts' there are in it point not to events but to ideas, i.e. not to history but to the writing of history. Nor is this book a history of historiography in the sense that it attempts to re-create the inner side of the development of historical writing. I have attempted only a sketch of the story of man as historian. Large and important sequences have not even been noted: Persian, Hindu and Islamic. Of the Far East, there is only the barest outline of traditional Chinese historiography and one sampling from the modern era. So much of critical study and of the 'philosophy of history' lies ahead before anything comparable to Collingwood's *Idea of History* can be done in Sinology. Some Chinese scholars, like Lin Yu-tang some years ago and Chan Wing-tsit at present, are still pre-occupied with the task of introducing a popular version of Chinese historical writing to the West. And there is still a measure of ambivalence in many Chinese scholars with respect to the bearing of Western Sinology. One has only to compare what is said in English on one side of the Pacific with what is said in Chinese on the other side to appreciate the profound tensions of the Chinese scholar in this decade. Yet this very restlessness reveals the liveliness of the contemporary 'meeting of East and West.'

The simple *apologia* for this kind of comparative study in historiography is to invite Chinese and Western university students to consider the role of historical thought in their own specialities—whether these may lie in the sciences, commerce, or the arts, and whether they may be approached from the Eastern or from Western traditions. Every university subject has an historical context. One approach to all kinds of knowledge is historical. Indeed, it is doubtful whether we can approach any important problem in any faculty apart from its historical context.

Moreover, as persons, as well as students, we live and move and have our being in an historical existence. The story of man as historian is *our* story in a broader and deeper sense than can be comprehended in our academic endeavours. Man as historian means man as self interpreter. For all of us—the scientist, the sociologist and the poet— there is an existential dimension to Lord Acton's insight that the real point of history is the history of history.

N. E. F.

Hong Kong
The Feast of St. Paul, 1964

ACKNOWLEDGEMENTS

Apart from my somewhat daring suggestion that *The Book of Isaiah* may have been the work of a single editor-author at the end of the Fifth Century B.C., there is very little that is original in this book.

For the chapter on Chinese Historiography I have followed, in the dating of dynasties and reigns, Tung Tso-ping, *Chronological Tables of Chinese History*, vols. I & II. For other materials I have consulted with profit Duyvendak, *The Book of Lord Shang*, Derk Bodde, *China's First Unifier* (A Study of the Ch'in Dynasty as Seen in the Life of Li Ssu), Burton Watson, *Records of the Grand Historian of China*; Yang Lien-sheng, *Topics of Chinese History* and 'The Organization of Chinese Official Historiography' in Beasley and Pulleyblank, *Historians of China and Japan*; Reischauer and Fairbank, *East Asia, The Great Tradition*, A.F.P. Hulsewe, 'Notes on the Historiography of the Han Period' also from Beasley and Pulleyblank; C.S. Gardner, *Chinese Traditional Historiography*; the translations by Chan Wing-tsit and Y. P. Mei in T. de Bary, *Sources of Chinese Tradition*; and Achiles Fang, Ssu-ma Kuang's *Tzu-chih t'ung-chien* (*Harvard Yenching Institute Studies VI*). The Selection from Aeschylus' *Agamemnon* in the chapter on 'Greek Historical Writing' is a fairly free new translation. I have followed for the most part the themes of Toynbee's *Greek Historical Thought* and *Greek Civilization and Character* in the selected readings for this chapter.

It is a pleasant duty to remark the encouragement and practical helpfulness of my colleagues. Our whole department has taken an active part in this project. Dr. Philip Shen did a major job for the first mimeographed text in the editing of selections for Part III. Joan Ho has done the same for this printed edition, and contributed the essay on 'History and the Social Sciences.' I am most grateful to Dr. Carsun Chang and to Professor Kramers for their kindness in reading the chapter on 'Chinese Historiography' and for their helpful corrections and suggestions. I am indeed grateful for the kind Foreword of Dr. Chang. It is an honour to have this word from a Chinese scholar, now in his 76th year, who is not only an historian but also a maker of history. Dr. Kramer's essay on a modern Chinese historiographer reminds us of his active interest in Chung Chi and in the dialogue between East and West in this area of Chinese studies.

Lee Tsu-wei paced us all in her help with research, translations, editorial assistance, art work and proof reading. Mr. Peter Suttmeier took on the unenviable task of simplifying my Germanic style to make it more readable for Chinese students. Under his expert hand many qualifying clauses completely disappeared and semi-colons became periods. Mrs. Peter Suttmeier helped her husband with the proof and the index, and Mr. John Barr did the reading of the final proofs, thereby giving much work to the printer and peace of mind to me.

I am particularly grateful for the competent services of Mrs. Amy Wong Ng who typed in season and out of season, often after hours, and for the help of Miss Amy Chan who came to our assistance in meeting several printer's deadlines.

For a book such as this so much depends upon the generous response of publishers. We have been particularly fortunate, perhaps because Chung Chi as a member of the recently established Chinese University of Hong Kong, is an exciting new venture in higher education. Many of our excerpts are abstracts, simplified in some instances for the student who reads English as a second language. I am sure that our students will consider my efforts in this the height of charity, believing that I have given priority to minor surgery on the writing of others over the major surgery needed on my own. Where abstracts have been made, I have used parenthesis. Characters have been used where Romanization might confuse the Cantonese student.

For the kind permission to reprint excerpts, acknowledgement is gratefully made to the following publishers:

International Publishers Company, Inc., for Mao Tse-tung, *The Chinese Revolution and the Chinese Communist Party*, Vol. III (c. 1954), pp. 73-78, and 81-83. And for Mao Tse-tung, *On New Democracy in Selected Works of Mao Tse-tung*, Vol. III, p. 115.

Simon and Schuster, Inc., and George Allen and Unwin, Ltd., for Bertrand Russell, *The Basic Writings of Bertrand Russell 1903-1959*. Edited by Robert E. Egner and Lester E. Denonn (c. 1961), pp. 500-510.

Rathbone Books Ltd., and Doubleday and Company, Inc., for Bertrand Russell, *Wisdom of the West* (1959), pp. 272-273.

World Publishing Co., for Leopold von Ranke, Preface to *History of the Germanic Nations from 1494-1514*, translated by Fritz Stern in *The Varieties of History*, edited by Fritz Stern (c. 1956), pp. 57-59.

Macmillan and Company, Ltd., and St. Martin's Press, Inc., for Acton, *Lectures on Modern History* (c. 1952) pp. 315-318.

George Allen and Unwin Ltd., for *Meaning in History: W. Dilthey's Thoughts on History and Society*, edited and translated by H. P. Rickman (c. 1961), pp. 68-69, 71-72, 79-82, 163, 167-168.

Hutchinson and Company (Publishers) Ltd., for W. H. Walsh, *An Introduction to Philosophy of History* (c. 1958), pp. 14-25.

G. Bell and Sons, Ltd., for Herbert Butterfield, *Christianity and History* (c. 1949).

Oxford University Press, for Gilbert Highet, *People, Places and Books,* 'Sailing to Byzantium.'

Penguin Books, Ltd., for Sir Bernard Pares, 'Russia—East or West?' in *Russia.*

Oxford University Press for Arnold Palmer, 'Dinner at Four' in *Movable Feasts.*

Oxford University Press, for paragraphs from R. G. Collingwood, *The Idea of History* (1951).

Alfred A. Knopf, Inc., for C. W. Ceram, 'The Rediscovery of the Assyrian Empire' in *Gods, Graves and Scholars.*

Alfred A. Knopf, Inc., for Perry Miller, 'The Puritans and Democracy' in *America in Crisis* edited by Daniel Aaron.

Charles Scribner's Sons, for George Santayana, 'Santayana in Greece' in *My Host and the World,* Vol. III *Of Persons and Places.*

Alfred A. Knopf, Inc., for Frederick B. Artz, 'The Origins of Modern Drama' in *The Mind of the Middle Ages.*

Sinica Leidensia, for the translation by Derk Bodde of Ssu-ma Chien's *Li Ssu* in Derk Bodde, *China's First Unifier,* Sinica Leidensia Vol. III (Leiden: E. J. Brill, c. 1938) and Arthur W. Hummel, *The Autobiography of a Chinese Historian (Ku Shih Pien).*

As in all things temporal as well as spiritual, a man stands deeply in debt to his wife, I should mention in addition to such general aid, the specific contribution of proof reading which was done with the same painstaking precision as is befitting any scrutiny of a husband's work in accordance with a tradition as ancient as the ark.

The publication of this book has been made possible by the generous gift of Harvard Yenching funds through the United Board for Christian Higher Education in Asia. I am most grateful for this grant and for the interest in this project of Dr. William P. Fenn and the Harvard Yenching Foundation.

Finally, I am grateful to Mr. Shing-lam Yip of the Chung Luen Printing Co. for his patience and cooperative assistance in the making of this book.

N. E. F.

CONTENTS

PART ONE
THE STUDY OF HISTORY

PART TWO
ANCIENT HISTORIOGRAPHY

PART FOUR
READINGS IN HISTORY

Part One

The Study of History

HERODOTUS
THE FATHER OF HISTORY

HISTORY AS A DISCIPLINE OF HUMAN KNOWLEDGE

The Origins of History: *1. Myth and Saga*

OUR WORD HISTORY comes from the Greek (*h*)*istoria* which means learning by enquiry or the report of an investigation. Like all other departments of human knowledge, history had its beginnings in myth. Myths supplied the first accounts of the origins of tribes, clans and families against the background of primitive science and ancestral deities. Myth deals with the dateless past. It is, in this sense, pre-historical. Not all fanciful stories are necessarily mythical. We may define myth as the serious, religious or philosophical attempt to grapple with the high issues of human destiny. It is different from those fantasies, legends, sagas and tales which serve chiefly as amusement for the storyteller and his hearers.

Susanne Langer (*Philosophy in a New Key*) suggests that there are three levels of symbolic expression which may be characterized as the 'subjective,' the 'social,' and the 'religious.' The lowest level, that of the dream narrative, is expressed by fantasy. Its symbols are images taken from life but related to each other by an unempirical law of subjective wish fulfillment. A modern example would be *The Private Lives of Walter Mitty*. In Chinese literature there is the Tang story by Li Fu-yen of *The Man Who Became A Fish*.

Midway between fantasy and myth are the animal fable, the story of the tricksters, the ghost and fairy tale. These reflect the demand of public appeal, and they induce in us the dream of a better world. In this dream world, barriers of wealth and class, and limitations even of time and space are overcome by a super animal, a fairy prince or a semi-saviour and deliverer. Anthropologists call this figure the 'cultural hero.' Examples would be Manibozo (North American Indian), Maui

(Polynesian), Hermes (Greek), Krishna (Hindu), Legban (Dahomey, West Africa), and the pseudo-Buddhist monkey (China). In these stories the gallant hero is the champion of the villager's cause against unreasonable kings and naughty dragons. An irresponsible attitude pervades these tales in contrast to the religious seriousness of myth.

The myth, unlike the fantasy and animal fable, is in no way intended to gratify private or public desires. Rather it reflects the supremely earnest attempts of early man to face reality and to catch universal and mystical truth in the subtle web of language. Tragedy here replaces wish fulfillment. The somber and the serious, touched now and then with tenderness, dominates mythic thought. In the myth there is no fairy prince or 'cultural hero' to fight against fate and the gods on behalf of his followers. Instead, the bright visions of fantasy are replaced by the representative symbols of man. The myth presents such basic conflicts as the individual against society, or the eternally perishing against the constant and abiding. The hero seeks a resolution that will go beyond the seemingly arbitrary denial of human values. What is found, therefore, in myth is not escape but moral re-orientation. What emerges from the true myth is thus a view of the world, a more or less total perspective, a normative understanding of life, and a right attitude toward its tasks and resources.

The mythic representation of reality cannot yield itself to analysis and critical re-interpretation. Its mode is exhausted in its gift of a tone, a direction, a spiritual atmosphere. It must at last pass into limbo, making place for the rise of the discursive mode which is history, science and philosophy. The transition from myth to philosophy can be seen as a gradual change, first to epic generalization (Homer) and lyric sensitivity (Pindar, Theognis), then to speculation (Heraclitus, Anaxagoras) and finally to reconception (Plato). Though generalized and disenchanted, the symbols of philosophy retain some vestige of their mythic origins. Each people lives within the magic circle of its own language. Language encloses its users within a culture, and forbids trespass from without except upon penalty of much labour and effort. Myth bequeaths to history a cultural perspective, a special way of looking at things and also particular qualities of feeling and relationship. The seminal ideas of mythology are part of the conceptual heritage of the historian.

2. Chronology

A later source of history may be traced to the chronologies devised by ancient civilizations. These were records of the names of kings, their regnal years and their mighty deeds. Chronology has been defined as the corpse of the past. Actually, it is less than the corpse, because a corpse still has flesh and can 'look natural'. Perhaps it would be more accurate to call chronology the 'skeleton' of the past, rather than its corpse. The skeleton does not even suggest the corpse let alone the living body.

The first of the precursors of history (myth, legend, saga, fable) was interpretive. The second (chronology) was merely factual without any attempt to relate events or to show their meaning.

The Purposes of History

History has served many masters. 1. It has provided satisfaction for man's profound curiosity and his capacity for wonder and amusement. It has been the near ally of poetry. 2. It has been one of man's basic responses to his recognized duty to his ancestors, to his own past. Tacitus said that it was the duty of the historian to ensure that 'noble actions shall not pass away in silence.' 'History,' said Cicero, 'gives life to remembrance . . . (it is) the messenger of antiquity.' History can, therefore, hardly avoid the strong force of patriotism or the call to enshrine heroes. And two further uses of history are herein indicated: *a.* polemics which defends the glory and grandeur of the nation's past, and *b.* the eulogy of heroes whose lives are presented as models of moral excellence. 'Teach us how we ought to live,' the Medieval chronicler, Ordericus Vitalis, asks of history, 'by taking the heroic figures of the past as models and profiting thereby.' That 'history is a philosophy that teaches by examples' is a saying so ancient and so often quoted that its author cannot be identified. History from its beginning has been in some measure a division of moral science. St. Augustin observes that 'it is one thing to record events and quite another to teach people what they ought to do.' History is properly the latter: 'to record events in a serviceable manner.' Even so objective an historian as Lord Acton emphasizes this use of history as 'the record of truths revealed by experience.'

3. Equally practical is the notion that the value of history lies in the light it may throw upon the future. 'Those who have a clear picture of past events will thereby be able to predict the recurrence of

similar events under similar circumstances in the future. It is therefore an important discipline for those who aspire to public office. So Polybius urges the study of history as 'the most satisfactory training for public life.' So also did Ssu-ma Kuang (司馬光) in his *Tung Chien* (通 鑑): 'To view antiquity as through a mirror is an aid in the administration of government.'

Grounded in historical wisdom, the statesman may serve his God as well as his country. By employing the lessons of history he may 'enjoy the honour of being a servant of Divine Providence.' Several English statesmen have been credited with the saying: 'It is a good thing to know what God plans to do in the next fifty years.' Some colonial statesmen have appeared to exercise a notable patience in waiting to see!

4. Beginning at least as early as Thucydides (471-400 B. C.) in the Greek world—earlier among the Israelites—there was a serious concern for accuracy in the recording of events. This was an interest in history as a trustworthy account of the past quite apart from its practical values. Polybius, the last of the great Greek historians (205-120 B. C.) insisted that it was the 'function of history to ascertain what words were actually spoken, and next to find out the reason why what was done or said resulted in failure or success.' Josephus, the great Jewish historian of the First Century, and Origen, the Christian theologian of the Third, stress the need for a faithful use of canons of textual and conceptual criticism. In modern times, however, as well as in antiquity, facts may easily become 'ventriloquists' dummies, uttering the wisdom of the man upon whose lap they sit.'

A concise and inclusive view of the purpose of history was suggested by the late Professor R.G. Collingwood. It serves to attain, he wrote, to 'human self knowledge . . . . The clue to what man can do is what he has done.'

The History of History

We may assume that history developed as a separate science after it had gained its independence from mythic and ritual representation. A transitional stage is to be found in the epics of Homer and in the Yahwist epic of the earliest days (from Adam to Abraham, *Gen.* chs. 1-11).

Greek Historical Writing

The first Greek historian of whom we have any knowledge was Hecataeus of Miletus (born c. 550 B.C.). He boldly began his comparative study of Egyptian and Greek legends with the opinion that before his time nearly everyone who had offered information about the early days of Greece was a liar. He was deeply impressed by Egyptian culture and the evidences of its ancient past and so was led to examine critically the claims of Greek antiquity. He is said to have influenced Herodotus, the first of the great Greek historians (485-425 B.C.).

The history of Herodotus is still entertaining and informative. It was probably originally in ten volumes or scrolls. The purpose of the work was at least twofold: 1. to undertake a critical examination of local versions of the ancient legends, and, by a rational critique, to suggest the possible basis of truth underlying the several variants; 2. to present as a drama the conflicting forces which he traces in his nation's past from the beginning to the Persian War.

Collingwood finds in the work of Herodotus the essential elements of history as a special science or discipline. First, the basis of his work is a seeking of answers to questions. History is not simply a repetition of what is known, it is an enquiry into matters concerning the past that are not known. Second, the history of Herodotus is humanistic, i.e. it is concerned with things *men* have done. Actions of the gods are only of secondary importance. The historian's interest is in what man does in response to what he understands to be the work of the gods. Finally, Herodotus is rational. His concern is to reconstruct a reasonable picture of the past. He appeals to evidence and he deals with his evidence in a rational manner. Collingwood sums up the greatness of Herodotus by the comment that he elicited knowledge (*episteme*) from the opinions (beliefs—*doxa*) of his informants.

From Herodotus onward the ideal in Greek historical writing was the account of eye-witness testimony. Such testimony was dealt with by the historian according to the rules of evidence acceptable in court. The historian thus acts as a judge who makes careful notes of the documents of eye–witnesses, and then proceeds to evaluate all the testimony available. He then tries to reconstruct, in an impartial way, the events as they actually happened. A description of this method was written by Polybius whose rule of evidence became the model of Roman historiography. The limitations of this method reflect the

limitations of the view of history involved: original research can deal
only with the recent past—the past that is still within the memory of
living persons. Further it can deal only with what has been remembered
by living eye–witnesses. The historian is thus bound not only to a
narrow time but also to a narrow range of materials within that time.

Thucydides (471-400 B.C.) was inspired by the notion that future
events could be predicted on the basis of the course of events in the
past. He found in history a pattern: the working out of an inexorable
judgment upon pride and arrogance. Wealth, he saw, led to an indulgence
in luxury, which in turn fed the flames of pride. People and nations,
at the height of their pride, seemed almost to be driven by a power
outside themselves (*Ate*) to consider themselves exceptions to all laws
of human behaviour and even to the limitations of mortality.   Hence
they committed deeds of excessive cruelty and insolence, defying even
the gods. They, therefore, became guilty of usurping divine honours.
They were then met by retribution (*Tisis*) and finally destroyed (*Nemesis*).
The clear illustration of this pattern for Thucydides was the Persian
Empire. By the same token, Athens, he saw, was doomed to a similar
fate. In a sense Thucydides' strong conviction of an inexorable pattern
in the lives of men and of nations led him away from history to poetry
or philosophy. He did, however, bring a new interest into the portraiture
of individuals.   C.N. Cochrane has observed that his real mentor was
not Herodotus but Hippocrates. Like that great man of medicine,
Thucydides is intrigued by abnormal psychology—psychopathology. He
studied the way the neuroses of Greek city-states and the obsessions of
individuals affected the course of history as a parallel to the predictable
etiology and cycle of disease.

With the conquests of Alexander the Great, and the experiment of
the cosmopolitan city (Alexandria in Egypt), the Hellenistic historian
was forced to enlarge his horizons. Alexandria became the center of the
writing of polemic, national histories. These supported in each instance
the superior antiquity and glory of the writer's own nation. But in so
far as they were national histories, written for the enlightenment of
foreigners, Alexandria provided the arena for comparative study and
criticism. An excellent example of the critical stage of nationalist
polemics is the work of the great Jewish historian of Alexandria,
Josephus. His work, *Contra Apionem* (*Against Apion*) deals critically
with the Egyptian historian, Manetho, the Phoenician, Dius, the Ephesian,
Menander, and the Chaldean, Berosus. History in the Hellenistic
Age (325 B.C. to A.D. 300—that is from Alexander the Great to

Constantine) had of necessity to deal with empires. The expansion of the Roman Empire widened the scope of history. This expansion brought with it trade, military conflict and cultural and religious intercourse. Polybius, the last of the great Greek historians, undertook to record the conquest of the world (European and Middle Eastern) by Rome. Significantly he prefaces his study with an outline of Roman history (political, cultural, and moral) going back one hundred fifty years before the Empire. Hellenistic history was by the very nature of the times broadened horizontally (a wider scope) and deepened vertically (going further back into the past). The former extension was a demand of the times and the latter had been made possible by the surviving documents from earlier historians.

Empires tend to justify themselves on the superior antiquity and culture of the ruler in contrast to the ruled. The greatest of the Roman historians, Livy, attempts such an apology for the Roman people. He wrote of the glory of the Roman past, the simplicity, honour, purity, and integrity of early Roman society. These were the qualities, he urged, that had made Rome great and justified her growth to empire. Livy's work is the classical example of Roman history, and its vertical deepening of the task of the historian illustrates the major contribution of Rome to historiography.

The Historiography of Israel

One of the blind spots in European education since the Renaissance has been the 'one root' theory of Western culture. The Renaissance was a revival of the capacity to respond to the mind and spirit of ancient Greece and Rome. The West could and did respond to Greek civilization as to its own past, its own cultural heritage. It had not that capacity with respect to the other root of its past: Hebrew civilization. Students in England and Germany prepared for their university careers with Greek and Latin. Greek and Latin were needed to study literature, science, history and philosophy. But this was the study of only one cultural tradition (from Homer onwards). They studied Bible (and particularly the Old Testament) as a separate discipline outside the main course of Western civilization. New Testament studies could be fitted into the pattern of that one channel development but Old Testament was regarded as an elective, a course to be chosen from the specialists' offerings in the fields of oriental

studies or theology. The result was an almost complete neglect of
Hebrew historiography. This was true in the Nineteenth Century
and is even true in our own time. Collingwood exhibits an admirable
capacity for sensitive response to Homer, Herodotus, Thucydides and
Polybius. But he writes his *Idea of History* like a man who had
never read the Yahwist's history of the Hebrew People from Abraham to David, or the Deuteronomist's history of the Israelite Monarchy.
He deals with Christian historiography as though he were unaware of
the fact that Clement of Alexandria, Eusebius, Origen, Jerome and
Augustin were building upon the broad foundation of Jewish historiography. He can observe that the Greek mind tended to be anti-
historical, to regard the actions of men as predetermined by fate, and
the life of nations as bound to a cyclical pattern. Yet he seems
ignorant of the source of that new perspective in the Hellenistic Age
which enabled Christian historians to regard history as linear.

The history of the ancient Israelites covers a span of seventeen
centuries. It reaches back much further than the beginnings of Greek
civilization. It continues on far beyond the twilight of Greek genius.
Again the Israelites were *the* historians of antiquity as the Greeks
were *the* philosophers. The *J* narrative of history from Abraham to
Moses was completed by the middle of the Tenth Century B.C. The
E Document was probably completed by the middle of the next
century, and a highly significant synthesis and editing of the two as
JE was begun before the time of Hesiod (750 B.C.). A careful history
of the Israelite Monarchy and its antecedents (i.e. from the settlement
in Palestine c. 1200-1100 B.C. to the Monarchy under David c. 1004-965
B.C., and from the division of the kingdom in 926 to the fall of Samaria
in 722-721 and the fall of Jerusalem in 587-586 B.C.) known as the *D*
Document was added to *JE* and circulated probably in the same years
that Hecataeus of Miletus was collecting his materials in Egypt (550
B.C.)—nearly five hundred years before Ssu-ma Chien (司馬遷).

The Greeks viewed the pattern of history as cyclical. The Israelites
saw it as linear, the work of a divine providence guiding events toward
the fulfillment of a final purpose in creation. According to the
Yahwist tradition in the Pentateuch, God had chosen certain individuals
to be His agents in guiding Israel toward the destiny ordained for her.
This notion of providence left room for human freedom. God worked
through men. He dealt with them as a parent deals with a child,
permitting them to make mistakes, to exercise their freedom even to
the extent of rebellion against Him. And, like a parent, God so

guided their lives and shaped the events through which they lived that a fruitful alternative was always possible. The heart of the Hebrew idea of history was that it was subject to divine direction. It was directed in such a way that men could not by their evil completely destroy their own opportunities for reform, redemption and growth. God's providence was a power within history which re-created the conditions of freedom, challenge and spiritual growth.

Concern for systematic writing of history began for the Israelites at least as early as the synthesis of *J* and *E* (760-650 B.C.). Josephus (A.D. 37-100), criticized the laxity of the Greeks with respect to accuracy and the strict sifting of evidence. He presents the principles of integrity that were claimed as the canons of trustworthy recording from the earliest days of Jewish historiography. In part the rules urged by Josephus emerged only with the threat of criticism by foreign historians. It is probably true that the concern for accuracy grew out of the controversial nationalistic writing carried on in centers where the encounter of peoples of various traditions occurred. As has been noted in Alexandria, Greeks, Egyptians and Jews became acquainted with each other's traditions. Where these involved events common to two or more nations, questions of evidence and interpretation were bound to arise as in the dispute between Manetho's account of the flight of the Israelites from Eygpt and the record of the Exodus in the Pentateuch. A sober estimate of the debates between the Alexandrian historians, leading to a systematic presentation of criteria for trustworthy historical writing, may be found in Origen's *Contra Celsum*.

The Early Christian View

A new dimension was added to Western historiography with the advent of the Christian era. The Gospel of the Reign of God was regarded by Christians as a gospel for the whole world, and the fulfillment of the destiny of all peoples. The history of Israel was then interpreted as a preparation for the coming of the Christ. Similarly other histories were so interpreted. Clement of Alexandria suggested that Greek philosophy was a preparation for the Christ in the Gentile world just as the Mosaic Law was the preparation within Judaism. St. Augustin (*City of God*) fitted the history of Rome into the same 'pattern of purpose' in the past. Julius Africanus (c. A.D. 180-240) attempted a universal history to show that 'World History' was a unity, and that it was linear—pointing toward a goal. In his *Preparation for the Gospel*, Eusebius (260-340) describes all history as leading to the crucial event of the Christ and the founding of the Christian Church. Augustin, in his *City of God* (A.D. 426), applies this viewpoint to the problem of the collapse of the Roman Empire. Orosius in a comprehensive world history tried to prove that the decay of pagan empires was simply part of the working out of the divine plan. They were not simply repetitions of the cycle of civilization (the rise, rule and ruin of empires) but a working out of a pattern of divine judgment and grace: judgment in terms of the tribulation of peoples (war, disease, earthquake, flood, fire, etc.), and grace in terms of a leading through judgment to the Christian era which he found to be marked by a gentleness of nature and a new humanitarian spirit in society.

Biblical realism demanded a more adequate notion of human nature than that of the Greeks. The Greeks viewed man as essentially rational. The Israelites knew something of the depths of the irrational in man. The Greeks could not fully appreciate the irrational as a force in human life and in society. Thus the Christian doctrine of original sin provided for a more realistic treatment of human nature in history and a perspective that could deal more fairly with all nations and cultures. The doctrine of original sin was a universal principle. Moral evil in history could thus be seen as a function of distorted human nature and not as simply the characteristic of one nation or of one culture (e.g., the Greek view of the Persians).

Again, the Christian view of nature, based on the Old Testament, took the form of a doctrine of creation *ex nihilo* (from or out of nothing) rather than the notion of the shaping of an 'eternal primordial stuff' out of which all things were made. Creation out of something (vase out of clay) involves two metaphysical principles: mind and matter. The Judeo-Christian view could give a much greater place to life and freedom in the idea of history than could the Graeco-Roman. Christians emphasized the *Living* God of the Old Testament and of the experience of the early church. The Greeks and Romans emphasized the notion of changeless, immutable, impassive and remote God of Pure Reason. Over against the eternally fixed ideas in Plato's philosophy or the eternal forms in Aristotle, the Christians emphasized the free, creative activity of the Living God. Nature too has a *biography*. Here there is nothing apart from God—not even potentiality. Creation *ex nihilo* rejects the notion of matter as a second metaphysical principle.

Christian historiography with its roots in Hebrew culture may be summarized in terms of the following perspectives. 1. The notion of universal history: all history—the whole of the past is seen as related to God's purpose. All previous history constituted a preparation for the coming of Christ. But not all human experience is on the same level. Some, including the history of the Israelites, exhibits the judgment of God. Some, including the history of the Greeks, exhibits the gracious guiding of God in preparation for the coming of the Christ. All history is part of the fulness of time for the coming of the Gospel. 2. Therefore history is to be written not in terms of years or centuries or reigns of kings or even of civilizations. History is seen as certain periods (seasons) characterized by promise or judgment. The New Testament word is *Kairos*—crucial or meaningful time. The central point in history is the coming of the Christ. This is the pivot of all history. What happened before belongs to one great era. What happened after belongs to another· This is the significance of B.C. (Before Christ) and A. D. (in the year of the Lord). 3. History is not cyclical but linear. It moves toward an event and it moves through that event to fulfillment. 4. History is dynamic, not static. It deals with the action of God and the action of man, not with eternal, fixed ideas or with eternal, fixed patterns. As Gregory of Nyssa wrote: Christian history starts with beginnings and moves through new beginnings to beginnings that have no end. History, from the Christian perspective, bears the mark of novelty and of adventure. 5. Reason is only one aspect of it as order is only one aspect of process. Man must be viewed as an actor in history in terms of his whole being—the irrational as well as the rational. The dynamics of history cannot be fitted into the neat schemes of rationalism. The dynamic involves something of the demonic even as it involves the free and responsive creativity of the Living God.

The Medieval View

Medieval historians for the most part were imitators and commentators upon the Christian histories of the late Hellenistic Age. Augustin had divided his history into seven periods: 1. the infancy of the human race —from Adam to Noah, 2. the childhood—from Noah to Abraham, 3. the adolescence—from Abraham to David, 4. early manhood—the Kingdom of David, 5. later manhood—the scattering of the Hebrew people among the nations after the destruction of Samaria (722 B.C.) and of Jerusalem (586 B.C.), 6. old age—the coming of the Messiah, and 7. the last days

—the waiting for the consummation of history in the return of the Christ in glory as the judge of creation. These ages also corresponded to the six days of creation and the 'resting of God' on the seventh day, the Sabbath: first, creation (bestowal of light—promise given to the first disobedient parents of the human race); second day, separation of the firmament—separation of the chosen people from the nations of the world; third day, separation of the land and the waters—elect race further separated from the heathen nations; fourth day, creation of the sun and stars— the rising star of the people of God—the star of David; fifth day, creation of fish and birds—scattering of the chosen people upon the wide seas of the nations where they found no resting place; sixth day, the creation of man—the coming of the New Adam who is given authority over all creation: seventh day, the day of perfection when God rested from all his labours. Contemporary man lives in the seventh and last age waiting for the return of the Christ who will establish the eternal Sabbath. No new thing may be expected in this age. All that is of importance has gone on. It is as the last days of an old man who waits for the peace of his final sleep. The New Testament writers had expected the imminent return of the Christ and the final judgment. Their counsel was to watch and to pray: to watch for the second Advent and to keep themselves in readiness for the final judgment. No new ventures were to be attempted; the world was soon to come to an end.

Two aspects of Augustin's writing of history dominate the historiography of the Middle Ages: 1. the interest in listing and classifying (the seven days of creation, the seven periods of the life of the individual) and 2. the notion that the present age is the last age, an age of waiting for the end of the world and the final judgment. The first of these had several implications. It led to the development of elaborate typologies based upon the Bible. The Bible became the 'realm of ideas' in a Platonic sense for the Middle Ages. Everything, every experience, every type of human temperament, every point of view, every aspect of nature, every thing in history was a type—a copy, a fulfillment, a parallel of something found in the Bible, especially in the Old Testament. The Bible became a parable for all of life, and not always in terms of its profound and spiritual doctrines. Mostly it was in terms of details out of context: Balaam's ass, Noah's ark, Aaron's beard. Scholarship, therefore, turned to the discovery of analogies, types and far fetched parallels, rather than to an enquiry into contemporary experience and the phenomena of nature and society. Medieval scholars searched the Fathers of the Hellenistic Age for such typologies as well as for authoritative statements on all subjects of human knowledge. This prodigious study of commentaries led to the compilation of huge indices and collections of the sayings of the Fathers according to author, subject and point of view.

Early Medieval scholars were cataloguers. They listed and they classified. They did not ask new questions. They did not seek new knowledge. All that was valuable and significant had already happened, and all that was essential had already been thought. They watched the Fathers and they waited for the end of the world. This then is the second dominant aspect of Medieval historiography: civilization was universally believed to be under sentence of death but with an indefinite, though short, reprieve. The writing of history was therefore largely for the purpose of warning the careless and reminding the frivolous of approaching judgment. The last days were days of sifting the wheat from the chaff, the good from the evil, the serious and sober from the careless and frivolous. A prominent aspect of the age was then seen to be the contest between the Church and the devil for the souls of men. The means of salvation was at hand—the Church was the 'Ark of Salvation,' the sanctuary to which men could flee for their lives from the world and the wiles of the devil. History in the Middle Ages is in this respect not too different from Thucydides. It is a series of stories with a moral. In Thucydides the moral was the inevitable judgment of pride. For the Medieval historian it was the drama of the contest between the Church and the devil for the souls of men. It was the drama of judgment like the morality play. It was also the drama of salvation, like the miracle play. History illustrates the plot. Like Aristotle, the Medieval man believed that poetry was more real than history.

For these reasons there was little incentive to probe the complexity of historical events or to preserve any real feeling for history. Christian theology tended to move in the direction of Platonic and Aristotelian notions of eternal and universal truths. Therefore, it neglected the concrete and unique which are of the stuff of history. Credulity rather than criticism, for the most part, characterized Medieval historiography. The Middle Ages were not entirely 'dark' ages. They were also a contemplative time. The Middle Ages developed the seeds that were later to take root in the new-plowed fields of the Renaissance. Among these seeds must be recognized the emphasis upon experience found in Anselm; the vision of the unity of knowledge, the unity of truth (the idea of a university), Abelard and Aquinas; the practice of contemplation among the great Platonists and mystics; the painstaking, though at times seemingly trivial, scholarship of the monastics; the feeling after a unity of truth and goodness with beauty in painting, music, literature and architecture. Above all, the Medieval preoccupation with the world to come had its tremendous import for the modern world. Those who neglected the world to think about heaven were thinking about perfection, about ideals, goals, ultimate values. The Middle Ages took seriously the destiny of man. The Greek enquiry into the nature of things and the nature of man can never be more than half the story. The question of destiny is equally, if not more, important as a fruitful enquiry. The Medieval blueprint of the eternal city was not all childish and crass fantasy. It dealt as well with basic human aspiration. It too was an enquiry, as scientific, in a real sense, as what we have prized in the Greek study of nature. It was an enquiry, enriched by the Christian tradition, into the constitution of a new republic, a republic not only of pragmatic values, but also with a vision of an ultimate: the City of God.

All these creative aspects of the Medieval mind are found in a prophetic writer whose influence upon the modern world has only recently begun to be appreciated. Joachim of Fiore (1132-1202) was the abbot of a Cistercian monastery and was known in his own age as a man of remarkable piety and as a mystic. Up to his time in nearly all cultures except Judaism one can find the pervasive power of the myth of a golden age in the past. This myth is found in Greek literature (Homer, Hesiod, Plato) and in Chinese literature. It is found also among many contemporary primitives as, for example, among the Arunta of Australia. There is an echo of it in the Old Testament in the Yahwist revision of the Sumerian myth of a perfect primeval garden. Joachim appears to have been the first to devise and popularize the myth of the third age—the notion of a golden age in the future.

In three books Joachim developed the notion of three ages and three orders of society. The first was the 'Age of the Father' under the order of the patriarchal family. It began with Adam and continued through the lifetime of John the Baptist (c. A.D. 30). The second was the 'Age of the Son' which began from the reign of King Uzziah of Judah (c. 750 B.C.) and would continue until the middle of the Thirteenth Century. Joachim computed this age as covering forty-two generations of thirty years each. The order of this age was the hierarchical structure of the Church. The third age was that of the 'Holy Spirit' which had begun with the monastic rule established by Benedict of Nursia

(c. A.D. 500) and would come into its fruition in the golden age of the future. In the first age man was under the Law and the authority of a patriarchal society. In the age of the church, society was feudal according to the pattern of the ecclesiastical hierarchy. Joachim describes it as a monarchy limited by a constitution and by the new law of Christianity which had replaced the law of Moses. Mankind is pictured as an adolescent under this order. It is now that the human race enters upon its advanced training with the disciplines of the sacraments and the virtue of intentional obedience to priests, bishops, abbots, and the pope. In the golden age of the future neither law nor authority will be necessary, and both sacraments and church orders, will be superseded by the life of the spirit in which each person will participate directly. Petrarch's new society was based upon this vision of a new kind of fraternal community.

Joachim had the keen insight to see that historical periods, movements and ages overlap. Between his first and second ages there is an overlapping of almost eight hundred years. For the second period the overlap is six hundred years. The seeds of a new age are sown and begin to germinate long before the powers of the present age are in decline. One age does not end at midnight, and the next begin at 12:01 a.m. Equally significant is the fact that Joachim's theory of history points to the future. History is the record of a preparation for a destiny yet to be realized, and its true values will not be of the kind that are imposed. They will be such as emerge out of man's own experience as a redeemed creature witnessing to the Holy Spirit. Augustin also had a notion of three ages: 1. before the fall, 2. under the law and 3. under Christ. But in his schema man was living in the third age, and the end of history was shortly to come. Joachim points to the future as the time of fulfillment within history. The golden age will not be in another world but in this one, and it will be a new age of justice and freedom.

Joachim's theory has become one of the most pervasive and controlling myths of the modern world. It was taken over first of all by the 'spiritual Franciscans' and then by both the Rationalists and the Romantics of the Enlightenment. It became a leading motif both of liberal Protestantism and of Marxism. It passed into modern historiography through Vico of Naples in the Eighteenth Century. From Vico it was appropriated by August Comte who secularized Joachim's ages into those of the mythico-religious, the philosophical-speculative and the scientific. Comte was convinced that the West had by the middle of the Nineteenth Century entered upon the third and glorious age of a scientific culture. G.E. Lessing in his *Education of the Human Race* described the three ages as: 1. that in which man was prodded toward goodness by the fear of punishment (Old Testament times), 2. that in which man was urged toward goodness by the promise of reward (the age of the Christian Church) and finally, 3. the golden age of the future when men should do good for the sake of goodness itself without either the fear of punishment or the hope of reward. Karl Marx, following Hegel, was also an apostle for the myth of the third age. His periods were those of 1. primitive communism, 2. the age of the class society marked by struggle, and 3. the glorious age of the intentionally and scientifically communist society.

Most of these third age theories seem to imply that the coming of a golden age is inevitable because the passing away of the first age has occurred and the collapse of the present age is about to occur.

The myth of the third age of the future expresses a basic concept upon which modern history is built: the notion of periodicy involving pivotal events. History, if it is to have meaning, must, like a sentence, have punctuation. Otherwise it is just a jumble of events. The ordering of events in a meaningful way demands the notion of periods: a series of events that constitutes in some sense a unity of time and a continuity of development. A period must also have significance both in terms of itself and in terms of other unities that came before it and followed it. Both the art and the science of the historian are involved in the divining of pivotal events which illumine what came before them and what happened afterward.

Collingwood rightly observes that the Renaissance man was more Christian than Classical. The Renaissance comes as an answer to some of the problems raised by the Middle Ages. Once basic questions are being asked a Renaissance is inevitable. It was in the latter part of the Middle Ages that such questions were asked. Some of them were concerned with—law: the development of international trade required new laws. What should be the relationship between Church law and civil law? Do the old laws apply to the new situations? Questions were asked also about the responsibility of the Christian West to the Moslem East. They stimulated the study of other languages and other cultures. Questions were asked in the field of education. Abelard had already demonstrated in his *Sic et Non* (*Yes and No*) the inadequacy of the simple compilation type of scholarship, and had suggested new methods of dealing with the knowledge of the past. Thomas Aquinas saw that this knowledge, even as critically studied, was inadequate. He insisted that the various branches of human knowledge must be related—that there should be a cross fertilization of studies in the arts, law, philosophy and theology. Aquinas was a daring thinker and a creative methodologist. Both Abelard and Aquinas made fundamental contributions to the idea of a university. Both emphasized the life of the university as a dialogue between masters in different fields of learning. Abelard, particularly, explored the values of a dialogue between different cultures, the comparative study of basic perspectives: Jewish, Moslem, and Christian. Aquinas re-stated the problem of the relation of religion to culture. He saw that relation as organic: cultural institutions are like the organs of a body. They are energized by religion which is the soul of a civilization. This notion had vast implications for law, education and government. His major concern was the organization of human science on a theoretical basis in terms of first principles. It issued in the third major work on education in the West. The first was Plato's *Republic*. The second was a body of Christian literature in the Hellenistic period that would include Clement of Alexandria, Origen and Augustin. The third was the great synthesis of St. Thomas Aquinas in the Thirteenth Century. The contributions of the Renaissance, particularly with respect to history, were an answer to Aquinas' syllabus of university studies.

Renaissance Historiography

Both Bacon and Descartes attempted a new organization of autonomous disciplines as the foundation of Renaissance learning. Bacon thought in terms of three realms of knowledge: 1. poetry, 2. history and 3. philosophy. He regarded these as fundamental divisions since he found them to correspond with the three faculties of the human mind: 1. imagination, 2. memory, and 3. understanding. Descartes added a fourth discipline: Divinity (Theology). For both Bacon and Descartes the physical sciences were included under philosophy. Thus Descartes described the departments of philosophy as 1. mathematics, 2. physics, and 3. metaphysics. Despite the humanism of the Renaissance, its interest in man and his life and deeds, its interest in what had been thought and written in the past, this age produced no great history or historiography. In part this was due to the anti-historical mind of the Greeks. What Descartes wrote of history could have been said by

Aristotle; history is not a trustworthy account of man, it has little
practical value. In many ways the Renaissance was not a return to
classical culture nearly so much as it was a revival of man's interest
in himself as scholar, artist, inventor and statesman. It was also a
rediscovery of the importance of the present age and a hope for the
years to come.   Men had ceased to wait for the end of time and for
another world.   They had rediscovered the unrealized possibilities of
this world and were optimistic about its future. So Descartes could
accuse historians of retreating into the past rather then meeting the
challenge of the present.

The major contribution of the Renaissance to historiography is to
be sought in its critical re-evaluation of Medieval and Classical historians.
Jean Bodin attacked the rigid and artificial schemes and typologies of
the Medieval writers.   His critique was directed against the notion that
universal history could be fitted into four empires (Persian, Greek, Roman
and Christian—the Holy Roman Empire).   He traced this typology
back to the book of *Daniel*, and observed that it was pressed upon the
data of history rather than arising from historical study itself.   Lorenzo
Valla (1406-1457) was able to prove that the famous *Donation of
Constantine* was a forgery.   Later Tillemont and the Bollandists
suggested canons of criticism that would avoid the errors of past
historians: 1. Reason rather than authorities must be the ultimate tribunal
of historical judgment. This is the principle of the possible. What
cannot happen now could not have happened in the past. 2. Probability
is the second law of historical judgment. The writers of the past often
disagree in their accounts of the same event.   Conflicting authorities
must be compared and harmonized according to the principle of probability.
3. Literature should not be the only source of historical knowledge.
Stones may be more reliable than scribes. Ancient documents must,
as far as possible, be verified by other evidences, especially those of
archaeology. The historian must check whatever he can of the written
testimony. When it is said that cities or historical shrines were located
so many miles from other cities or from the sea he must check these
statements against contemporary geographical knowledge.

The Reformation led to a new interest in the text and interpretation
of the Bible and in early Christian history. It was the Protestant claim
that the Roman Church had, during the Middle Ages, been subject to
the influence of paganism while the religion of the Reformers was a
return to the true faith of the apostles and the early church. A
monument of this Protestant polemic is the *Magdeburg Centuries* of

Flacus Illyricus (1520-1575). Flacus and his colleagues traced the history of Christianity from its origins through progressive stages of degeneration to the year 1300. A Roman Catholic answer was made by Cardinal Caesar Baronius (1538-1607) in his *Annales Ecclesiastici* which sought to prove that the Roman Church was enriched by a development of the faith through the ages.

Modern Historical Writing

It was not until the Eighteenth Century that the spirit of the Renaissance bore fruit in a major historian and historiographer, Vico of Naples. His aim was to formulate principles of historical method to parallel the principles of scientific method devised by Bacon. Vico substantially altered Bacon's notion of the divisions of human knowledge. Like Bacon's, his schedule of knowledge comprised three faculties, but, for Vico, these were: 1. art, 2. religion and 3. philosophy. Further, he noted that they represented the evolution of human enquiry and were logically consecutive, that is, each was built upon the former. It was from Vico that Comte learned of Joachim di Fiore's notion of the three ages of mankind which after radical alteration became the mythological, philosophical and scientific. Vico, however, regarded history as fundamental to philosophy. His Renaissance heritage may be seen in his warning against a bias in favour of past achievements and the glories of past civilizations. But he is a post-renaissance man in his recognition of other prejudices to be avoided in the writing of history. He warns well against the conceit of nations (nationalistic and patriotic bias), the conceit of the learned, and the fallacy that knowledge of the past decreases with the march of time. He denies that the Greeks knew more about ancient Greece than contemporary historians could possibly learn. One can be too close as well as too far from the events he studies. Further, enquiry, whenever it is pursued, is likely to yield results by which even the ancients could have profited. Finally, he warns against the notion that the culture of civilization must be explained in terms of transmission—that all similar ideas and institutions must have had a common origin. As God created the world, so Vico sees history as the creation of man. Vico's two major interests were the investigation of origins and the formulation of laws of historical development. With respect to the former he saw the task of the historian as an exposure of the pedigree of contemporary society. History should deal with the problem of the genesis and development of societies and institutions. History, to be meaningful, must in some way be the story of *our* past. It must contribute to our understanding of ourselves, our society and our institutions.

Vico did not initiate the theory of universal stages in the development of civilization, but he did provide one of the more persuasive and influential schedules of advance and decline. Actually he combines several former notions: 1. the Greek notion of the stages in the cycle of the rise and fall of nations, 2. the Christian Medieval notion of typology, and 3. the Christian Renaissance notion of progress. He notes that periods as stages tend to follow the same order in all societies He came to this conclusion from his studies of Homeric Greece and Medieval Europe. Each society, he believed, had passed through three stages: 1. the Heroic (Homeric Greece and Medieval Europe), 2. the Classical (Pericles' Athens), and 3. Decline and Barbarism. But this did not mean for Vico that history was cyclical. He noted that Christian barbarism was not on the same level as pagan barbarism, and the Heroic age of the Middle Ages in Europe was not on the same level as that of the Homeric Age in Greece. History, he concluded, was not cyclical but spiral.

Finally, Vico represents a mellowing of the negatively critical spirit of the Renaissance. His method derives from a weighing of critical method and a broadening of the spirit behind it. He commends without qualification the emphasis upon language study. He sees, as the Renaissance did not, the historical value of mythology, sagas, fables and legends. In these, the past speaks to us of its spirit. Tradition cannot be discarded or neglected by the historian simply because it distorts. Within tradition is the kernel of truth which the historian seeks. But even the husk is important. It reveals both self interpretation and also the accepted interpretation of a later age with respect to past events.

Though he flourished early in the century, Vico was unequalled as a historiographer with balance and insight by the many contributors who came later in the Eighteenth Century. Neither Rationalism nor Romanticism produced a comparable figure. Rationalism was an intellectual movement in the late Seventeenth and Eighteenth Centuries. It stressed the use of science and reason as the guides to understanding and was skeptical of traditional knowledge. Romanticism came as a reaction to the coldness of rationalism. Voltaire, the rationalist, now seems almost obsessed to the point of blindness with his insistence that historical study has one goal: to combat superstition, to lay bare the follies and deceits of the past. Rousseau, the Romantic, never fully overcame his youthful prejudice against all civilization. He accepted, apparently as a revealed truth, the notion that earliest man was good and free. Civilization was for him the corruption of the natural and good man, fettering his spirit and driving him to unnatural meanness and error.

Hume was undoubtedly a more brilliant and more critical thinker than his Rationalist contemporaries in France. He was no more prepared to accept such modern myths as Rousseau's notion of the magnificent savage and the claims of the infallibility of scientific theory than he was to accept the ancient ones. He was, however, as much as the French, a child of his age, dedicated to the new rationalism, critical to the point of cynicism with respect to the wisdom of the past. His programme of studies is similar to that of Bacon. However, Hume does not allow for imagination. He, therefore, proposes the three faculties of mathematics, natural philosophy (science and history) and natural religion (a rational man's notion of value). In some respects he is the champion of Christian realism with respect to man as sinner. History is self criticism; it enables man to look back upon his past and observe his errors. While he was a librarian at Edinburgh he improved his time at his post by writing a *History of Great Britain* from James I through Charles I. He demonstrated his impartiality by offending everyone.

With Montesquieu and Gibbon a new notion of periodicy in history is introduced. The former sees the past as ignorant armies clashing by night. The past is the age of irrationality. The rationalism of the Eighteenth Century Enlightenment becomes the pivot of history, replacing the birth of Christ. Gibbon has three ages: 1. the golden age of classical civilization (the Antonine period in Roman history), 2. the Age of Barbarism—the Christian period, and 3. the future, a second golden age of reason and sophisticated sensitivity. Basically, however, Gibbon viewed history as the irrational triumph of barbarism and religion over the truth, goodness, and beauty of noble Roman paganism. In general, the Enlightenment saw itself as the pivot of a slanted see-saw. The past was tilted downward to the wretched ages of superstition. The future pointed upward towards man's unlimited future, supported by an invincible rationalism.

The Romantic Movement in the latter part of the Eighteenth Century was equally sure of the golden age of the future, but it rejected the notion that it would be built upon the foundations of Rationalism. As the Rationalist theory was an inversion (perversion) of the Christian in which the Enlightenment took the place of the Gospel, so the Romantic theory was an inversion of the Hebrew linear view of history in which the historical process as Divine Providence was replaced by the process of man's own self development. Romantic history is the record of man's irrepressible forward thrust—the progressive expression of his creative spirit. Rationalism had related man to nature. Montesquieu saw man as purely biological. Romanticism, on the other hand, distinguished man from his physical environment. Man was seen in contrast to nature, and history in contrast to science. Nature was the realm of necessity and science was an account of nature's rigid laws. History was, on the other hand, the description of the realm of freedom—the diary of the human spirit. Romantic interest centered upon the *unique moment* and the passionate enjoyment of the passions of the past. The official past (the documents of state and church) was of value only in so far as it gave a setting to the life of the people. Von Schlegel explored the origins of German literature. Tiech published his research into the origins of folk music. Arnim and Brentano sought the soul of the nation in its songs and ballads. Herder directed historians to listen to 'the voices of the people.'

Hegel was unwilling to distinguish so sharply between the reason of the Rationalists and the spirit of the Romantics. He accepted a doctrine of progress, a faith in the golden age of the future, an appreciation of the contributions of the past. But he insisted that history was rational, a part of the self realization of the Absolute as Mind. The history of philosophy, he affirmed, is the philosophy of history. He saw the past as the expression of *subjective mind,* the present (especially the German State) as *objective mind,* and the future as having its consummation in the self realization of Absolute mind. All history is a pattern of forces involving *thesis, antithesis,* and a *synthesis,* which in turn becomes a new thesis. This is Hegel's famous 'dialectic'. The grandeur of Hegel's philosophy of history continued long into the Twentieth Century to fascinate men with its all inclusive embrace of art, science, and religion. It was a truly universal history, and Hegel's own encyclopedic knowledge of ancient civilizations, classical antiquity, medieval Europe, and even of the Middle East and the Orient seduced his readers toward the belief that history was philosophy and that philosophy was history. History proper, however, remained for Hegel political history—the history of the state as the true expression of humanity. Bauer's famous work in church history followed not only the Hegelian dialectic of progress (thesis, antithesis, and synthesis); it followed also Hegel's valuation of the universal institution as the fullest expression of human experience. Bauer simply substitutes the Church for the State. Karl Marx was in some ways far more faithful to the Hegelian philosophy of history but in others his views are a negation of Hegel. In the place of the state as the highest expression and dynamic of human culture, Marx put the economic system. He is more political than Bauer but he cuts off the head of the Hegelian system (the notion of the Absolute—history as the Divine self realization), and he cuts out the heart, the humanity of Hegel. Economic law functions as blindly and as inexorably as nature. Collingwood has observed that Marxism is really an anti-historical naturalism. When everything in history from a child's dream to a Shakespearean sonnet, and from personal friendship to international conventions, is reduced to economics, man is reduced to something less than even the biological.

A contemporary of Hegel who tempered Romantic historiography with a new and scientific criticism of evidence was Berthold Georg Niebuhr (1776-1831). He was convinced that the present is to be understood only from the past. He explored the roots of European culture in the records of classical antiquity. His great work was the *History of Rome* wherein he sought to present Roman history as a living reality in the light of modern equivalents while at the same time maintaining a faithfulness to ancient documents subjected to the thoroughgoing analysis both of textual and historical criticism. The task of the historian, he suggested, was to reconstruct a complete picture of the past from the fragments available and a 'complete figure from the torso.' Niebuhr put great emphasis upon the faculty of intuition and upon the unity of history. For him this meant that contemporary situations could throw light upon the past as the large patterns of the past could alone give an adequate background to the events of the present.

From about the middle of the Nineteenth Century many new disciplines were developed which provided the historian with better tools for his trade. Among these were archaeology, anthropology, sociology, philology and psychology. Darwin's studies in comparative morphology and anatomy leading to his hypothesis of organic veolution was but one of the many breakthroughs attributed to the comparative method of study. Schleiermacher and Herder had earlier pointed the way to a phenomenology of culture in religion and art. Gustav Hugo related the growth of law to other social institutions and was a precursor of H. Maine's work on *Ancient Law* as was also Karl Friedrich Eichorn's *History of German Institutions.* From the new point of view 'law was a living thing like language, growing out of the life of the people.' Its origin was custom springing from the fundamental instincts of a nation and developing for the most part unconsciously and without effort.

The Recent Past

The father of modern scientific history was Leopold von Ranke (1795-1886) whose *History of the Germanic Peoples 1495-1514* is mainly important for its appendix in which the author sought to spell out the canons of a scientific historiography. The demand was first of all to discover what actually happened. The historian must approach his task without presuppositions. He must write history for its own sake, not to prove a point or to defend a belief. 'I am first an historian.' he wrote on one occasion, 'then a Christian.' But it may have been the other way around, at least so far as his own development was concerned. He spoke as a young man of his new found interest in history as 'the works of God displayed in the history of the human race.' All through his career he kept firm hold of the belief that the goal of the historian's task is universal history. Butterfield has pointed up the error of some of his followers in their aim to associate him almost exclusively with the motto 'presuppositionless history.' But his 'eye for generalities' and his 'passion for humanity' were as great as his 'joy in detail.' Von Ranke was convinced that understanding is more than knowledge. The historian must, he said, be endowed with the mature judgment that enables him to 'mark the place of men and nations in the development of civilization.'

A younger contemporary of von Ranke's was Dilthey who shared his elder's feeling for the 'spirit of the age.' His own contribution was a serious and systematic attempt to compare the method and study of history with the method and purpose of physical science. Dilthey saw clearly the dominance of these two great disciplines in the modern quest for knowledge and the necessity to understand the place of both in the modern university. He distinguished the subject matter of history, as the study of concrete individuals (events), from that of natural science, as the search for abstract generalizations; and the knowledge of history, as an inward experience, from the knowledge of science which has to do with objects that are external.

One decade after the publication of Dilthey's work (*Introduction to the Science of Mind*, 1883) the Italian philosopher, Croce, published his essay *History Subsumed Under the Concept of Art*. It might have been entitled 'The Portrait of the Historian as a Young Artist.' Croce, like Dilthey, was concerned to see the two great branches of modern knowledge (history and science) in perspective. Art he defined as 'the intuitive vision of individuality,' and 'knowledge of the individual.' Science, on the other hand, is the knowledge of the general. Again, history like art is not basically descriptive; it is contemplative. Science, on the other hand, is analytical for the purpose of generalization and abstraction. History is a division of art in that art in general narrates the possible while history narrates what has really happened.

Sixteen years later Croce was led to distinguish history from art. The dividing line is logic, the theory of thought. To think is to make judgments, and history is a judgment of the shape of past events. He rejects the Kantian distinction between apriori, universal judgments and aposteriori empirical and individual judgments. He views this distinction as implying a divorce between universal truths and matters of fact. 'The universal,' he had come to believe, 'must be incarnate in the individual.' Historical fact (not the occurrence itself but the historian's narrative) is a judgment with a predicate. The predicate involves a concept, a universal. Philosophy, which is built upon the widest range of human knowledge, develops the concepts which are the framework within which the historian mounts his history. History thus becomes the Queen of the Arts. 'All reality is history.' 'All knowledge is historical knowledge.' Croce was inclined at this stage of his thought to regard science not as knowledge but as action, as occurrence or the record of the evidence of occurrence. Nature then is also a part of history. 'Scientific facts are historical facts viewed practically.'

Eight years later Croce published his *Theory and History of Historiography* in which he further clarified the relation of history and science. Science is based on history. A scientific experiment is an event. Its report is the record of an event. Croce's discussion of the relation of science to history concludes in almost the very words used by Collingwood at the end of his study of *The Idea of Nature*: 'Natural science is a form of thought that depends for its existence upon some other form of thought—history. A scientific fact is an event in the world of nature. A scientific theory is an hypothesis about that event....I conclude that natural science as a form of thought exists and always has existed in a context of history.'

A second major aspect of Croce's final work on historiography was his conclusion that 'all history is contemporary history.' That is to say that the Past is always viewed from the present and in terms of the life of the present. History is the meaning of the past for the present, i.e., the meaning of the past as intentionally recognized. Only in a remote sense are ostraka (fragments of pots with writing on them) or bone inscriptions the stuff of history. They become the stuff of history only at the point that they contribute to some aspect of man's concern for his past as significant for the present. Scholarship of and for itself is not history. It may be economics! If you get paid for it! Nor is scholarship in and of itself a true science. Neither is it art. It is only when scholarship is a servant of the insistent present—when scholarship is joined to religion, that is, when it is seen to serve some ultimate concern, however instrumentally and indirectly, that it becomes history or science or art.

The English historian, Michael Oakeshott, comes to a similar conclusion but by a different route. He too was concerned to see the two basic faculties of the modern university (history and science) in perspective. Both, he observed, are a viewing of the world. History sees the world under the aspect of the past. Science sees the world under the aspect of measurement. But when it is said that history sees the world under the aspect of the past, it must be understood that 'history is a seeing of the world from a fixed point in experience.' It is the latter phrase that is important (point in experience). There is no objective history in terms of what happened. Every object is seen from a perspective. Perspective is as ingredient in history as is past event. 'We cannot separate what has come to us from our interpretation of it.' History then is what the past means to *us* at *this* moment and from *our* perspective. Thus there is no 'fixed and finished past.' Facts of history are present facts. In some sense something of the past must die in order to live. It is a matter of a past event's becoming a living symbol which in turn is ingredient in present event.

One fairly certain conclusion that we may draw from this brief survey of histories and historians of the past was pencilled on a file card by the Cambridge historian of modern history, Lord Acton, at the turn to this century: 'The great point is the history of history.'

Part Two

Ancient Historiography

CHINESE
HISTORICAL WRITING

The Ancient Tradition: *1. The Cosmological Order*

EARLY CHINESE HISTORIOGRAPHY was closely related to the concepts of nature and of society. These had their source in the notion of an all embracing order of things. On earth that order was manifest in a social structure, the regular succession of the seasons, and the relation of the elements in the rhythms of nature. In the heavens the same order was found in the society of the stars and the daily, monthly and annual processions of the sun and moon.

The legends of the past were fitted into the framework of this cyclical order in terms of the metaphysical relations of Yin (陰), and Yang (陽) the five agents (elements), colours, stems (sounds), animal powers and the eight trigrams (*Pa Kua* 八卦). The pattern of the succession of events could then be explained either in terms of progression or of conquest. Winter proceeds from summer, or summer overcomes winter. Wood produces fire, and fire produces earth, and earth produces metal, and metal produces water; or wood is overcome by fire, fire by earth, earth by metal, and metal by water. Virtues are included in the properties of the elements: benevolence in wood, wisdom in fire, faithfulness in earth, righteousness in metal, and decorum in water. Colour and season also were related to the elements: green and spring to wood, red and summer to fire, white and autumn to metal, black and winter to water. Wood then was characterized as the Green Dragon, fire as the Scarlet Bird, earth as the Yellow Dragon, metal as the White Tiger and water as the Black Tortoise. Culture had its source and pattern in the eight trigrams (*Pa Kua*) and so was related to the metaphysical forces determining nature—rather than to history, i.e. to human discovery or invention based on experience.

I Ching (易經), Hsi Tz'u (繫辭) (The Great Appendix) proclaims: Heaven is high, earth is low; thus the ch'ien (乾) and the k'un (坤) are fixed. As high and low are thus ordered, honourable and humble have their places. Movement and rest have their constancy; according to these strong and weak are differentiated. Ways coincide according to their species and things fall into classes. Hence good fortune and bad fortune come about. In the heavens phenomena appear; on earth shapes occur. Through these, change and transformation become manifest. Therefore the strong and the weak (lines of the trigrams) interplay, and the eight trigrams act and react upon each other. Things are roused by thunder and lightning; they are fertilized by wind and rain. Sun and moon revolve on their courses with a season of cold and then a season of heat. The way of the ch'ien constitutes the male, the way of k'un constitutes the female. The ch'ien knows the great beginning; the k'un gives things their completion. The ch'ien knows through the easy; the k'un accomplishes through the simple.

Therefore the gentleman dwells securely in the emblems of the *Book of Changes* (易經) and delights in studying its explanation of the lines. When the gentleman is living quietly he observes the emblems and studies the explanations, and when he is about to act he observes their changes and studies their predictions. Therefore help comes to him from Heaven: good fortune and nothing that is not beneficial . . . .

The successive movement of Yin and Yang constitutes what is called the Way. What issues from it is good, and that which brings it to completion is the individual nature. The man of humanity recognizes it and calls it humanity; the wise man recognizes it and calls it wisdom. The people use it daily and are not aware of it, for the Way of the gentleman is but rarely recognized. It manifests itself as humanity but conceals workings. It rouses all things, but is free from the anxieties of the sage. Its glorious power and great reserve are perfect indeed! It possesses everything in abundance: this is the great reserve. It renews everything daily; this is its glorious power. It produces and reproduces, and hence it is called the Changes. As creator of the primal images, it is called ch'ien. As giver of the forms in imitation of the images, it is called k'un. Because it enables one to explore the laws of number and know the future it is called divination. Because it affords the element of coherence in change it is called the course of affairs. That aspect of it which cannot be fathomed in terms of the Yin and Yang is called Spirit . . . .

Therefore in the Changes there is the Supreme Ultimate. This generates the two primary forms (Yin and Yang). The two primary forms generate the four modes (major and minor, Yin and Yang). The four modes generate the eight trigrams. The eight trigrams determine good and bad fortune . . . .

I Ching, Hsi Tz'u, 2 explains: 'When in ancient times Fu Hsi (伏羲) ruled the world, he looked up to observe the phenomena of the heavens and gazed down to observe the contours of the earth. He observed the markings of birds and beasts and how they were adapted to their habitats. Some ideas he took from his own body, and went beyond this to take other ideas from other things. Thus he invented the eight trigrams in order to comprehend the virtues of spiritual beings and represent the conditions of all things of creation. He knotted cords and made nets for hunting and fishing. This idea he probably adopted from the hexagram *li* (離).

After Fu Hsi died Shen Nung (神農氏) arose. He carved a piece of wood into a plowshare and bent another piece to make a handle, and taught the world the advantages of plowing and weeding. This idea he probably took from the hexagram *i* (益). He set up markets at midday and caused the people of the world to bring all their goods and exchange them and then return home so that everything found its proper place. This he probably took from the hexagram *Shih-ho* (噬嗑).

After Shen Nung died, the Yellow Emperor (黃帝), Yao (堯), and Shun (舜) arose. They comprehended change and caused the people to be unwearied, transforming them with spirit so that they were rightly ordered. When the Changes has run one course to its extreme, then it changes, and by changing it is able to continue, and by continuing it achieves longevity. Thus the Changes receives help from good fortune and nothing that is not beneficial.

The Yellow Emperor, Yao and Shun allowed their upper and lower garments to hang down and the world was ordered. This they probably took from the hexagrams ch'ien (乾) and k'un (坤). (This may be either a note on the invention of the proper dress, the traditional costume, or a reference to wisdom of ruling without stirring.) They hollowed out logs to make boats and shaved pieces of wood for rudders and by the advantages of boats and rudders opened up new roads of communication to distant places for the profit of the world. This they probably took from the hexagram *huan* (渙). They yoked oxen to pull heavy loads and mounted horses to go long distances, thus benefiting the world. This they probably took from the hexagram *sui* (隨). They provided double gates and watchmen with wooden clappers to guard against robbers, and this they took from the hexagram *yu* (豫). They split wood to make pestles and scooped hollows in the ground for mortars and thus benefited all mankind by the advantage of mortar and pestle. This they probably took from the hexagram *hsiao-kuo* (小過). They strung a piece of wood for a bow and whittled arrows of wood and introduced the benefits of bow and arrow to awe the world. This they took from the hexagram *k'uei* (睽).

In the earliest times men dwelt in caves and lived out in the open. But the sages of later times substituted houses with ridgepoles and roofs to protect them from wind and rain. This they probably took from the hexagram *ta-chuang* (大壯). In the earliest burials the dead were covered thickly with brushwood and buried in the fields with neither mound nor trees to mark the grave, and there was no set period of mourning. But the sages of later times substituted inner and outer coffins. This they probably took from the *ta-kuo* (大過). In the earliest times knotted cords were used in government but the later sages substituted written documents . . . so that officials were kept in order and the people had a clear idea of their duties. This they probably took from the hexagram *kuai* (夬).

2. *Moral Implications*

The cosmological order had also its moral elements. In the first place the natural order established the proper relationships among things and between men. To ignore these proprieties is to act impiously; for apart from the established order there is only the chaos of individual willfulness. When the ruler departs from the established and proper order he will then be subject to the passions of a private person. He will incur heaven's indignation. There is in the *T'ai shin* (泰誓) The Great Declaration [The first of the 'Books of Chou' in the *Shu Ching*] a 'distinctively prophetic and moral tone, which it would be wrong to bury completely under a naturalist explanation.'

The formal order guards virtue. Wherever it is strictly observed the moral life within will be secure. Like a shell, formal propriety envelops and protects the moral kernel. While the shell holds, the kernel will be sound and whole. One aspect of the moral order is then the propriety of correct relations. This is illustrated in the *Spring and Autumn Classic* (春秋) which was taken as the model for historical writing by the three schools Kungyang (公羊), Kuliang (穀梁) and Tso (左傳). Their commentaries trace the final editions of the *Ch'un Ch'iu* (春秋) to Confucius. In the fulfillment of this task, Confucius stands as a spiritual successor to the saintly emperors Yao and Shun in that he preserves the ideals of the ancient society. In editing the text of these annals, Confucius applied the principle of *wet yen ta i* (微言大義), 'great significance behind insignificant words.' 'Thus, on one occasion, the *Ch'un Ch'iu* records that 'the king (of Chow 周) went on a hunting expedition in the west.' The real reason for the king's expedition was that he had been summoned by the leader of his powerful vassals to an important meeting; the power of the Chou kings had by that time dwindled to insignificance. Yet, it is improper for a feudal lord to summon his king, so the historian, in stating that the king went hunting, implied blame on the feudal lord for losing the true sense of propriety.

This is the historian's task of judgment in the selection of facts recorded and also, as in this instance, often in the very phrasing of the record.

In the office of the Emperor these several orders of the divine, the natural, and the human were united. As early as the Ch'in (秦) Dynasty, the interrelations of astronomy, ritual, the social structure, and the varied tasks of each class and office constituted an all-important cultural motif. The historian's task was seen to be in large measure the demonstration of the wholeness of the Empire in terms of these interrelations of the three orders in the person and function of the Emperor. A full expression of this ideal characterized Han (漢) historiography. We can, however, see a clear instance of that ideal in an earlier encyclopedic document of the Ch'in—the *Lü-shih ch'un-ch'iu* (呂氏春秋)—Spring and Autumn of Lu Pu-wei, (呂不韋) the predecessor of the famous Li Ssu. (李斯) It, too, is an important link between the older classics *Shu Ching* (書經) and *I Ching* (易經) and the rise of history as a special imperial discipline in the time of the Han Emperor Wu Ti (漢武帝) with the work of Ssu-ma T'an (司馬談) and his son Ssu-ma Chien (司馬遷). The *Lü-shih ch'un-ch'iu* was a compilation of the work of a number of philosophers and scholars who had been attracted to the Ch'in court by the prime minister. Its immediate importance is indicated by its title which bears official sanction in the name of the prime minister himself, and also, by using the characters *ch'un-ch'iu* (*Spring and Autumn*), points back to the older chronicle which had taken on a new and normative significance when it was attributed by Mencius to Confucius. In the use of *ch'un-ch'iu* in the title of this Ch'in document we may see a claim to associate its perspective with the normative pattern of historiography in the Confucian tradition. In the following excerpt the tie with the metaphysical pattern underlying the processes of succession and of conquest together with the interrelation of astronomy, nature, ritual, ethics and politics is clearly in evidence.

Lü-shih ch'un-ch'iu (*Spring and Autumn of Lü Pu-wei*), I:1a-4a: In the first month of spring, the sun is in the constellation *Ying-shih* (營室). The constellation *Shen* (參) (Orion) reaches the zenith at dusk, the constellation *Wei* (尾) (Scorpio), at dawn. The first two days of the month are *chai* (甲) and *i* (乙) its divine ruler is T'ao Hao (太皞), its attendant spirit, Kou Mang (句芒). Its creatures are scaly, its musical note *chueh* (角), its pitch-pipe *t'ai-ts'ou* (太蔟), its number 8. Its taste is sour, its smell goatish; its sacrifice is at the inner door for which the spleen of the victim is essential.

The east wind dispels the cold, the hibernating insects and reptiles begin to stir, the fish rise up under the ice where the otter catches them to eat, and the wild geese fly north in season.

The Son of Heaven shall live in the apartment on the left side of the Green Bright Hall. He shall ride in a great belled chariot drawn by dark green dragon horses and bearing green flags. He shall wear green robes with pendants of green jade. His food shall be wheat and mutton, his vessels coarse and open to represent a coming forth. In this month, spring begins. Three days before spring begins the Grand Astrologer shall report to the Son of Heaven, saying: 'On such and such a day spring will begin. The agent of wood is in ascendance.' The Son of Heaven shall then fast and purify himself and on the first day in person lead the chief ministers and feudal princes and officials to the eastern suburbs to greet the spring. On his return he shall hold court and bestow rewards upon them. He shall order the three chief ministers to publish abroad his good teachings and to relax the prohibitions of winter, to present awards and bestow alms to all down to the common people so that everyone who is deserving shall receive awards and gifts.

He shall order the Grand Astrologer to cherish the laws and publish the ordinances, to observe the sun and moon, the stars and zodiacal signs so that there will be no error in the calculations of their movements and no mistake in their courses, taking as a model the astronomical laws of ancient times.

In this month, on a favourable day, the Son of Heaven shall pray to the Lord-on-High for abundant harvests. Then, selecting a lucky day, he shall himself bear a plowshare and handle in his carriage, attended by the charioteer and the man-at-arms and, leading the chief ministers, feudal princes, and officials, shall personally plow the Field of God. The Son of Heaven shall plow three furrows, the three chief ministers five, the feudal princes and officials nine. On their return, they shall assemble in the Great Hall where the emperor shall take a chalice and offer it to each of them, saying: 'This is wine in recompense for your labours.'

In the month this vital force of Heaven descends, the vital force of earth arises; Heaven and earth are in harmony and the grass and trees begin to burgeon.

The ruler shall order the work of the field to begin. He shall order the inspectors of the field to reside in the lands having an eastern exposure, to repair the borders and boundaries of the fields, to inspect the paths and irrigation ditches, to examine closely the mounts and hills, the slopes and heights and the plains and valleys to determine what lands are good and where the five grains should be sown, and they shall instruct and direct the people. This they must do in person. When the work of the fields has been well begun, with the irrigation ditches traced out correctly beforehand, there will be no confusion later.

In this month, the Chief Director of Music shall be ordered to open school and train the students in dancing.

The rules for sacrifices shall be reviewed and orders given for offerings to the spirits of the mountains, forests, rivers, and lakes, but for these sacrifices no female creature may be used.

It shall be forbidden to cut down trees, to destroy nests, to kill young insects, the young yet in the womb or new born, or fledgling birds. All young of animals and eggs shall be spared.

Multitudes of people shall not be summoned for any service, nor shall any construction be done on walls or fortifications.

All bones and corpses of those who have died by the wayside shall be buried.

In this month it is forbidden to take up arms. He who takes up arms will surely call down Heaven's wrath. Taking up arms means that one may not initiate hostilities, though if attacked he may defend himself.

In all things one must not violate the way of Heaven, nor destroy the principles of earth, nor bring confusion to the laws of man.

If in the first month of spring the ruler carries out proceedings proper to summer, then the wind and rain will not come in season, the grass and trees will soon wither and dry up, and the nations will be in great fear.

If he carries out the proceedings proper to autumn, then a great pestilence will strike the people, violent winds and torrential rains will come in abundance, and the weeds of orach and fescue, darnel and southernwood will spring up together.

If he carries out the proceedings of winter, the rains and floods will cause great damage, frost and snow will wreak havoc, and the first seeds sown will not sprout.

Each year had its own set of associations characterized by an animal power, and each reign came to be known in terms of the vast complex of relationships of time, colour, agent and animal power. Dynasties followed each other according to the inexorable order, and reigns within each dynasty bore also these recognizable features.

Shih Chi (史記) 74:1b-3a: In the state of Ch'i (齊) there were three scholars named Tsou (騶) .... The second of the Tsou scholars was Tsou Yen (騶衍), who came after Mencius (孟子). He saw that the rulers were becoming ever more dissolute and were not disposed to exalt virtue, like (those ancient rulers recorded in) the *Ta Ya* (大雅) (section of the *Book of Odes* 詩經), embodying it themselves and diffusing it among the common people. Thereupon he scrutinized the operations of the yin and yang and increase and decrease, and wrote about the strange ways of the processes of change ....

He claimed that from the time of the separation of heaven and earth onward, the five powers (of the five agents) had been in the processes of mutual production and mutual overcoming, and that each temporal reign was in exact correspondence with one of the powers, like parts of a tally....

Thus Ch'in Shih-huang (秦始皇) at the threshold of Empire chose for his element, water, and adopted black as the royal colour. Actual time was made to accord with conceptual time. Years were shortened or lengthened to fit the presupposed or desired pattern. Dynasties had their essential meaning as exhibiting their elemental nature, and individual reigns were not so much units of history as stages in the fixed order of procession or conquest.

The following diagram which was adopted by Wang Mang (王莽), is one of the several systems contrived by different scholars at various times, and is typical of the emphasis on the interrelatedness of nature and society.

Wood: Fu Hsi (伏羲), T'ai Hao (太皥)　　Fire: Emperor Yao (堯帝)
(Water): Kung Kung (公工)　　　　　　　Earth: Emperor Shun (舜帝)
Fire: Shen Nung (神農)　　　　　　　　　Metal: Emperor Yu (虞帝) (Hsia 夏)
Earth: Yellow Emperor (黃帝)　　　　　　Water: Shang Dynasty (商朝)
Metal: Shao Hao (少昊)　　　　　　　　　Wood: Chou Dynasty (周朝)
Water: Chuan Hsu (顓頊)　　　　　　　　(Water): Ch'in Dynasty (秦朝)
Wood: Ti K'u (帝嚳)　　　　　　　　　　Fire: Han Dynasty (漢朝)
(Water): Ti Chih (帝摯)　　　　　　　　　Earth: Wang Mang (王莽)

The *Shih Chi*, quoting the *Shu Ching*, (書經), provides us with a typical mandate for seizing the power of rule because the old ruler neglects the elements and so has forfeited his mandate. The passage refers to the speech of the second king of the Hsia Dynasty.

There was a great battle in Kan (甘). The six minister-generals of his hosts were assembled. The King said: 'Oh, all ye of my six armies. I have a solemn announcement to make to you. The Lord of Hu (扈氏)

violates and despises the five agents (metal, wood, water, fire and earth),
and he neglects and discards the three proper spheres (heaven, earth, and
man). Heaven is about to cut off his mandate; and I am reverently executing
the punishment appointed by Heaven.'

With the above text on the mandate of heaven we should compare
the passage from the 'Great Declaration' (泰誓) of the *Shu Ching*
(V.I i 3-i i 5) 'Heaven and Earth is the parent of all creatures; and, of
all creatures, man is the most highly endowed. The sincere, intelligent
and wise among men becomes the great sovereign; and the great sovereign
is the parent of the people. But now....the King of Shang does not
reverence Heaven above, and inflicts calamities on the people below.
He has been abandoned to drunkenness, and is reckless in lust. He
has dared to exercise cruel oppression. Along with criminals he has
punished all their relatives. He has put men into office on the hereditary
principle....Great Heaven was moved with indignation....and still he says,
'the people are mine: the decree is mine....The iniquity of Shang is
full. Heaven gives command to destroy it....The innocent cry to heaven.
The odour of such a state is plainly felt on high. Heaven loves the
people, and the sovereign should reverence this mind of heaven.' Mencius
commented on this passage in answer to the question of his disciple,
Wan Chang (萬章), who asked: 'Is it true that Yao gave the kingdom
to Shun?' Mencius replied: 'Heaven gave it to him. He was placed in
charge of public affairs, and they were well administered and the people
were at peace. That indicated his acceptance by the people. Heaven
thus gave him the kingdom, the people thus gave him the kingdom.
That is why I said the emperor cannot give the empire to another
—This is what is meant in the *Great Declaration* where it is said:
'Heaven sees as my people see, Heaven hears as my people hear."
(*Mencius* V.A:5)

Here the moral aspect of the mandate of Heaven is explicit as a
prophetic oracle against the sin of the ruler who has oppressed the
people.

Professor Eric Voegelin in his *Order and History* points up the
relevance of the concepts of the *teh* (德), virtue, and *ming* (命), the
heavenly decree, to the notion of cosmological order: '—the rule of a
dynasty depends on its possession of a specific virtue, the *teh*. Like
all things under the heavens, the *teh* is exhaustible; and when it has
weakened to the point of causing suffering to the people and revolutionary
unrest, a new possessor of the *teh* with his family will succeed in

overthrowing the declining dynasty. The rise and fall of dynasties, then, is integrated into the order of the cosmos in so far as a heavenly decree, the *ming* ordains the rule of a family that possesses the *teh*, and also ordains its overthrow when it has lost the *teh*; and also attunement of society to the cosmos depends on the son of heaven and his dynastic *teh*, while the power of heaven, the *t'ien* (天), will provide for the rise and fall of dynasties. Hence political events, though partaking of the nature of cosmic forces, remain strictly in the sphere of a human struggle for power; heaven preserves its majesty of undisturbed order, while society is engaged in its struggle for attunement. In Chinese civilization political order is symbolized as due to the operation of impersonal cosmic forces....The cosmological symbolism in China left sufficient freedom in the human sphere to allow, in the breakdown of the Chou dynasty, for a conception of social order as dependent, not on the son of heaven alone, but on councillors and an administration formed by the spirit of Confucius. This was a step in the anthropological direction, but not a complete breakthrough. The intermediate position of Confuciansm is reflected in the debate on the question whether Confucianism was a 'religion.' It was not a 'religion' because it did not go beyond the conception of the Confucian sage as a man who was so well attuned to the *tao* (道) of the cosmos that he could be an ordering force in society, supporting, if not supplanting, the dynastic *teh*. But since Confucianism was a discovery of the order of the soul, in its autonomy and immediacy under divine order, it was a revolutionary break with cosmological collectivism, and contained the seeds of a 'religion' that might have flowered under more favourable circumstances.'

What seems most impressive in the historical literature before Ssu-ma Chien is the understanding of relationship. The Greeks had by Homer's time (c. Tenth Century B. C.) found an order in the heavens based upon an analogy to the structure of human society. Natural law was at first an interpretation of nature in terms of tribal custom. For the Israelites the determinative idea of history developed from their concept of covenant—the covenant with a Sovereign Lord in whose purpose their destiny was fixed. The seminal notion in early Chinese historiography was that of the complex relationships and qualities of social experience. For this pattern of relationship, as was also the case of the Greek concept of order in society, nature furnished the symbol but not the notion itself.

Love of order, the valuation of neatness, stability and dependability, led the early historians to fit all ancient lore into a pattern which illustrated relationship. Since 'relationship' was the comprehensive and fundamental principle, it followed that propriety should be the first commandment.

The mandate of heaven (*t'ien ming* 天命) was the demand to fulfill the obligations of propriety. Never could too much emphasis be placed upon that mandate. All religion was exhausted in fulfilling it. Beyond it nothing else was needful. The kings of Shang had forfeited their right to rule by their lack of propriety—(their disregard of relationships). Therefore, the Chou chieftains were justified by the mandate of heaven to overthrow them. In the institution of a new dynasty the mandate was vindicated.

The Shih Chi (史記)

Ssu-ma Chien (145-85 B.C.) is often regarded as the father of Chinese historiography. He himself insisted that his work was simply the completion of his father's task. And so by filial piety he justified the vocation of the historian. It is significant that his father, Ssu-ma T'an, held the office of Grand Astrologer in the court of Han Wu Ti. Historiography was thus one of the applied arts of astrology. In Ssu-ma T'an we have the transition from the sage's knowledge of ancient lore to the historian's pursuit of records. It is a transition from the all embracing wisdom of astrology (relationship plotted on the screen of the heavens) to history as an independent discipline — a subject of investigation in its own right with a claim to its own methods and a promise of its own proper contribution to knowledge and empire.

Ssu-ma Chien succeeded his father in the traditional office, and is known to have continued the function of that office for at least six years after Ssu-ma T'an's death in 110 B.C.; for he is credited with the reform of the calendar in 104 B.C. From that time onward, however, his main concern appears to have been the writing of history. We have in his own words the explanation of his devotion to this new profession. It was an expression of his filial piety and that piety had its reward at least by the circumstance that he found the task itself agreeable to his own purposes. It suited his spirit and fitted his powers.

Shih Chi 130: 8a-b, 30b-32a: The Grand Astrologer (Ssu-ma T'an) grasped my hand and said weeping: 'Our ancestors were Grand Astrologers for the House of Chou (周室). From the most ancient times they were eminent and renowned; for in the days of Yu and Hsia they were in charge of astronomical affairs. In later ages our family declined. Will this tradition end with me? If you in turn become Grand Astrologer, you must continue the work of our ancestors ...When you become Grand Astrologer, you must not forget what I have desired to expound and write. Now filial piety begins with the serving of your parents; next you must serve your sovereign; and finally you must make something of yourself, that your name may go down through the ages to the glory of your father and mother. This is the most important part of filial piety. Everyone praises the Duke of Chou, saying that he was able to expound in word and song the virtues of King Wen (文王) and King Wu (武王), publishing abroad the Odes of Chou and Shao; he set forth the thoughts and ideals of T'ai-wang (太王) and Wang Chi (王季), extending his words back to King Liu (公劉) and paying honour to Hou Chi (后稷) (ancestors of the Chou dynasty). After the reigns of Yu (幽) and Li (厲) the way of the ancient kings fell into disuse and rites and music declined. Confucius revived the old ways and restored what had been abandoned, expounding the *Odes* and *History* and making the *Spring and Autumn Annals*. From that time till today men of learning have taken these as their models. It has now been over four hundred years since the capture of the unicorn (481 B.C., end of the Spring and Autumn Period 春秋時代). The various feudal states have merged together, and the old records and chronicles have become scattered and lost. Now the House of Han (漢室) has arisen and all the world is united under one rule. I have been Grand Astrologer, and yet I have failed to make a record of all the enlightened rules and wise lords, the faithful ministers and gentlemen who were ready to die for duty. I am fearful that the historical materials will be neglected and lost. You must remember and think of this!'

I bowed my head and wept, saying: 'I, your son, am ignorant and unworthy, but I shall endeavor to set forth in full the reports of antiquity which have come down from our ancestors. I shall not dare to be remiss!'

This our house of Han has succeeded the descendants of the Five Emperors (五帝) and carried on the task of unification of the Three Dynasties (三代). The ways of Chou fell into disuse and the Ch'in scattered and discarded the old writings and burned and destroyed the *Odes* and the *History*. Therefore the plans and records of the Illustrious Hall and the stone rooms, of the metal caskets and jade tablets, became lost or confused.

Then the Han arose and Hsiao Ho (蕭何) put in order the laws and commandments; Han Hsin (韓信) set forth the rules of warfare; Chang Ts'ang (張蒼) made the regulations and standards; and Shu-sun T'ung (叔孫通) settled questions of rites and ceremonies. At this time the art of letters began again to flourish and advance and the *Odes* and *History* gradually reappeared. From the time when Ts'ao Ts'an (曹參) put into practice Master

Kai's (蓋公) teachings of the Yellow Emperor and Lao Tzu (老子), when Chia Sheng (賈生) and Ch'ao Ts'o (晁錯) expounded the doctrines of the Legalist philosophers Shen (申) and Shang (商), and Kung-sun Hung (公孫弘) achieved eminence for his Confucian learning, a period of some one hundred years, the books that survived and records of past affairs were all without exception gathered together by the Grand Astrologer. The Grand Astrologers, father and son, each in turn held and carried on the position.

I have sought out and gathered together the ancient traditions of the empire which were scattered and lost. Of the great deeds of kings I have searched the beginnings and examined the ends; I have seen their times of prosperity and observed their decline. Of the affairs that I have discussed and examined, I have made a general survey of the Three Dynasties and a record of the Ch'in and Han, extending it all back as far as Hsien Yuan (軒轅 the Yellow Emperor) and coming down to the present, set forth in twelve Basic Annals. After this had been put in order and completed, because there were differences in chronology for the same periods and the dates were not always clear, I made the ten Chronological Tables. Of the changes of rites and music, the improvements and revisions of the pitch-pipes and calendar, military power, mountains and rivers, spirits and gods, the relationships between heaven and man, the economic practices handed down and changed age by age, I have made the eight Treatises. As the twenty eight constellations revolve about the North Star, as the thirty spokes of a wheel come together at the hub, revolving endlessly without stop, so the ministers, assisting like arms and legs, faithful and trustworthy, in true moral spirit serve their lord and ruler: of them I made the thirty Hereditary Houses. Upholding duty, masterful and sure, not allowing themselves to miss their opportunities, they made a name for themselves in the world: of such men I made the seventy Memoirs. In all one hundred and thirty chapters, 526,500 words, this is the book of the Grand Historian, compiled in order to repair omissions and amplify the six Disciplines (六藝). It is the work of one family, designed to supplement the various interpretations of Six Classics (六經) and to put into order the miscellaneous sayings of the hundred schools.

At least until the time of the T'ang Dynasty (唐朝) there is the fascinating parallel between the personages of the Classical Greek and the Chinese historians. They were men who had once been officials in high position who were forced by circumstance to retire from action to the contemplation of action. In 98 B.C. Ssu-ma Chien drew upon himself Imperial disfavour and was condemned to dishonour. The ignominy of his punishment (castration) traditionally obliged a man of spirit to make an honourable exit from the dark countenance of his Emperor by passing through the door of death. Honour beckoned at that door, but piety restrained. This was the filial piety which led

Ssu-ma Chien to fulfill the wishes of his father, even at the risk of
dishonour. To this we shall add the 'testament' of the historian as
prophet: 'woe is me if I pass on in silence!'

Ssu-ma Chien has been credited with the expansion of chronology
into history. Several notable developments do appear to go back beyond
his own efforts. We may accept his filial witness to his father's grand
conception of a comprehensive history of China—a continuous annal
of imperial deeds and words from Yao, Shun and Yu to the reign of
Han Wu Ti. We may also suppose that so grand a scheme had been
iaccompanied in his father's mind with an interest as well in method
.e. with a concern for accuracy, at least for inclusiveness with respect,
to different traditions. The concise prose style of Ssu-ma Chien
together with the sweep of his ambitious undertaking probably had its
source, at least in part, in his father's conception of a new history. It is
equally probable that his essays on institutions and the brief biographies,
no less than the annals, set the pattern for most, including some of the
best, later historical writing. It has been suggested that the *Spring
and Autumn Classic* was the proto-type of the basic (Imperial) annals
and that the 'Three Traditions' similarly furnished the proto-type for
the treatises and biographies (*lieh-chuan*列傳). Ssu-ma Chien had also
at hand important materials from the traditions of the clan cults. Much
of this survives only in his work. He was perhaps more of a compiler
and preserver than a creator of new forms or theories. His greatness
lies in the grand sweep of his plan, and in the carefulness of its
execution. He did see the value of biography and of collateral essays,
and his own work in these areas made a substantial contribution to the
later development of Chinese historiography. They introduced narrative
as an essential aspect of historical writing. The biographies explain
the annals in a way which no commentary could do. With them the
bones of annalistic records are given flesh and life. Spirit that abides in
the concrete event and in the unique individual is thus breathed into
the body of historical fact.

Like the first Greek historians Ssu-ma Chien was also interested
in geography. He was among the first to see the importance of the
information of the traveler both to test ancient traditions and to expand
contemporary knowledge. The following brief excerpt from the 123rd
Chapter of the *Shih Chi* illustrates the use he made of the experience
of a contemporary (Chang Chien 張騫) who had reached Turkestan
as an envoy of the Emperor.

Shih Chi 123: 21a-b: The Basic Annals of Emperor of Yu records that the source of the Yellow River is in the K'un-lun (崑崙) Mountains, some 2,500 *li* (里) high, the place where the sun and the moon in turn go to hide when they are not shining.   It is said that on their heights are to be found the Fountain of Sweet Water and the Pool of Jade.   Now since Ch'ien (騫) visited Bactria, the Yellow River has been traced to its source, and no one has found any such K'un-lun Mountains as the 'Basic Annals' records. Therefore, what the *Book of History* (尚書) states about the mountains and rivers of the nine provinces of China is nearer the truth, while when it comes to the wonders mentioned in the 'Basic Annals of Emperor Yu' or the *Classic of Hills and Seas,* I cannot accept them.

Much has been written in recent years of the bearing upon our knowledge of the Ch'in and the early Han of the official editing of the *Shih Chi* after the completion of the *Han Shu* (漢書).   Tradition suggests that the imperial censor deleted a substantial portion of the original work in respect of the Han.   Later these chapters of the *Shih Chi* were reconstructed from the *Han Shu,* and hence may not provide an independent account of the Han history.   It might, however, be argued that it is the *Han Shu* that is not an independent source, since on the matters in question, its own immediate source was probably Ssu-ma Chien and its deviations from his original MS may have gone little further than a judicious editing of his material.

The major selection chosen from the *Shih Chi* is taken from the Ch'in biographies—the life of Li Ssu who has been called 'China's first unifier.' He is at once the villain and the hero of antiquity—the man who envisioned and engineered, not always by peaceful means, a centralized Chinese Government.   He was also the man who was prepared in principle as well as in action to sacrifice classical tradition in the interests of the efficiency and strength of centralized rule.

Few men could have been involved so decisively in the two most pervasive ideals of China—Empire and Classical culture—as was Li Ssu.   We are in recent years more sensitive to the importance of Ch'in to the normative development of the imperial concept and the imperial ideal.   It was a transitional dynasty between the venerated Chou and the grandeur of the Han.   It was an upstart dynasty—brief, violent, lacking the time and conditions for the cultivation of mind and manner.   As Socrates' life spanned the golden age of Greece from the expulsion of the Persian invasion in 470 B.C. to the defeat of Athens by the Spartan General Lysander in 404 B.C., so also Li Ssu's life measured the rise of the Ch'in to imperial power over all China, the centralization of the bureaucratic system, the standardization of writing, a new system of education, the building of cities, and the beginning of the tradition of the grand imperial court. Socrates lived on for a few years after the fall of Athens. Li Ssu was executed two years before the fall of Ch'in. He was born, to the year, a century after Plato had written his *Republic,* two centuries after the collection of the Pentateuchal sources under Ezra. He lived during the century of the final editing of the prophetic literature, the last of which had been written over a hundred years before his birth. Socrates drank his hemlock nearly two centuries before Li Ssu suffered the five tortures of execution. Jeremiah, Ezekiel and Isaiah, the last of the great Hebrew prophets survived and interpreted the last days of Jerusalem and the aftermath of Judah's destruction a quarter of a millennium before the birth of Li Ssu. All that we know of this man is presented in the *Shih Chi* which Ssu-ma Chien completed a century and a quarter after Li Ssu's death.

Ssu-ma Chien's history is all speech and action. It included what was said in memorials to the emperor, the imperial action taken, and finally the significance of the event in terms of praise and blame. We should not of course expect either direct speech or memorial to be precisely what was said or what was written. Like Thucydides, Ssu-ma Chien had a fine sense of the dramatic and the artist's touch in the construction of his mosaic of speech and action. His *Biography of Li Ssu* is a drama—observing the essential limits demanded of the dramatic unities. There is a specific plot: the rise and fall of Li Ssu as the power behind the first truly imperial throne of all China and the rise and fall of the Ch'in as dominant over all China. The two processes coincided and were concluded within the brief span of forty years. There are four acts tracing the rise of Li Ssu's authority and Ch'in power. The climax is the feast given by the lordly grand councillor at the height of Ch'in's achievements. But it forebodes in the speech of Li Ssu himself the downward plunge of fortune—both for himself and the throne. 'Alas!' he sighs, 'I have heard Hsun Ching (荀卿) (Confucian scholar known also as Hsun Tsu 荀子) say: 'Things should not be allowed to become too flourishing. I was a commoner, an ordinary village fellow. The Emperor, not knowing my lowly origins, has promoted me to my present position of which none is higher. It is indeed the peak of wealth and honour. But when things have reached their peak they decline. I do not now know where I shall be led when my harness is finally removed.'

Ssu-ma Chien has called our attention to this scene as the turning point in his drama by having informed us at each of the four previous stages of the new honours granted the rising Li Ssu. First he rose from retainer to scribe, then to alien minister of justice and finally to grand chancellor.

Like a meteor he has risen from the horizon to the height of heaven —but the sky path from the horizon to the center is always up and the way thence across the sky is always downward. Acts I-IV measure the upward movement from horizon to apex—from 247 to 212 B.C., the date of Li Ssu's grand banquet. The last four—in a sense only one—describe the sudden plunge like the sinking of the polar sun into the winter night's early darkness. Four distinct events are dealt with as examples of the issues involved in the rise of Li Ssu. They reflect also the rise and growth of the power of Ch'in. All four are prefigured in the story of the rats which serves also as a parable of Li Ssu's notion of kingdom. He is brought before us as a product of a single-minded and ruthless dynasty. Its parallel in the Greek world would have been Sparta. Indeed the Ch'in appears to have had a universal conscription. Women carried provisions, and the aged and infirm guarded the cattle and gathered herbs during war time. Rank in the army was based not upon heredity, education, or even years of service, but rather upon the number of enemy heads brought back from the battlefield.

Hsun Tzu visited Ch'in c. 264 B.C., and reported: 'I saw that its people are simple and unsophisticated. Their music is not corrupting or licentious, their clothing is plain. Their officials do not engage in private business, indulge their personal fancies nor join parties... Nevertheless Ch'in also has its disturbing features. Granted that it possess all these estimable qualities, yet it is not truly royal. It has no scholars. It is said that a thoroughgoing Confucianism will make a true king; partial will make a Lord protector; while when there is not one particle, there comes disaster.'

The barbarous realism of Ssu-ma Chien's tale of the rats tells us immediately the kind of man and the kind of state at which, in the following pages we are invited to look. The first word we hear from Li Ssu is the bald comment: 'A man's ability is similar to the condition of the rats. It merely depends upon where he places himself.'

The first thematic event opens with the speech of the youthful adventurer. It is his farewell speech to his Confucian teacher, Hsun Tzu. Here we see the young opportunist. One eye is focused on the weakness of his superiors and the other is on his personal ambition.

He tells us that one should feel shame only for poverty and the lowliness of his position. The action taken is his application to the councillor of the king, Lü Pu-wei for a position at court. The result of the action is his appointment as a retainer.

The second thematic event is his speech addressed to the new king Ch'in Shih-huang (秦始皇). Here the counsel of opportunism is repeated. The way of rule is an inflexible pursuit of the advantage offered by the weakness of one's opponents. But there is an end in view: the creation of one government of all China—one world. Li Ssu, by imperial appointment, becomes a senior scribe. The action of intrigue by bribery, deception, and even pre-meditated assassination leads on to fortune. State after state is annexed to the victorious Ch'in. Li Ssu reaches the status of Alien Minister.

The third thematic event is introduced with the memorial presented to the Emperor by his ministers on the expulsion of aliens. Li Ssu's answering memorial develops the theme of universal empire. Strength and unity are inclusive. Bigotry and mean patriotism are both symbol and source of weakness. Empire must embrace all talents if it is to enjoy all benefits. What is useful should be used. By imperial action the alien act is revoked. Li Ssu is elevated to Minister of Justice. With the annexation of Chi (齊 221 B.C.) all China is unified. Feudalism is abolished and Li Ssu becomes the Grand Chancellor of the Left.

The final thematic event in the rise of Ch'in and of Li Ssu is introduced by the memorial expressing the dissatisfaction of the Ch'in court with the abolition of feudalism. The king has adopted the title of Emperor Ch'in Shih-huang (秦始皇帝), yet true political unity and internal order have still to be established. Conquest has led to crisis. Here is the highest point of the drama of imperial power and the highest point of the career of Li Ssu. The memorial of the disaffected lords and princes is answered by Li Ssu's infamous memorial on the Burning of the Books. Now the decisive contest is joined between two philosophies of life and two ways of rule.

The older way looked in awe upon an ancient golden age. For the Confucians and Mohists, the ideal was the mythical glories of the sage rulers Yao, Shun and Yu. For the Taoists, it was the mythical period when men lived in the state of nature. All that belonged to the past could thus be urged in the finding of a way of return to that golden era of peace and happiness. The new way was in part the philosophy of the Legalists: law in place of traditional morality or manners (li 禮), and a strong, efficient, centralized empire replacing feudalism. Both Taoists and Legalists opposed the Confucian ideal of education based upon the wisdom of the past. The Legalists opposed that ideal because they feared its effect upon the vigour of the state. The Taoists opposed it because they were concerned about its effect upon the well being of the people.

Li Ssu is neither Taoist nor Confucian, and he is Legalist only in so far as this more realistic ideal serves the need of Ch'in at this moment of its crucial testing. He is the Thrasymachian ruler *par excellence*, the strong man with the singleness of the simple ambition to guide the destiny of a unified and powerful Empire. We may suppose that he feared most the activist philosophy of the Confucians, and that he saw the intellectual who was revered for his learning and who wore the badge of approved orthodoxy, as the greatest threat to what had been achieved and to what must yet be won. He, therefore, plunges immediately into the heart of the matter: the Confucian worship of antiquity to the detriment of the present. Even antiquity has its several voices—the voice of each self-styled interpreter. But the imperial voice can be one and only one, and that voice must prevail. Let the hundred flowers be nipped in the bud and the source of their dissenting counsels (classical literature) be confiscated by the state. Science and practical knowledge may still be privately pursued, but it must lie solely within the right of the state to formulate and expound doctrine. It is nowhere stated that the Emperor repudiated the treasures of the past, nor that the classics in the imperial library were destroyed. The issue is the removal of these documents from private use and abuse.

Ssu-ma Chien, in a rare instance of personal comment, interrupting the terse report of the action taken, remarked this was done 'for the purpose of making the people ignorant.' What is this ignorance? We are almost led to surmise that Ssu-ma Chien means moral ignorance and is, therefore, constrained by conscience, to indict the Ch'in with that crime which he believes must for all time discredit that dynasty —the destruction of the roots of righteousness for the sake of unrighteous rule.

Contemporaneous comment, however, gives some justification to Li Ssu. We have a revealing opinion expressed by Han Fei Tzu (韓非子) who had been a fellow disciple with Li Ssu under the instruction of the Confucian scholar, Hsun Tsu: 'In the state of an intelligent ruler, there is no literature of books and bamboo tablets, but the law is the only doctrine; there are no sayings of early kings, but the officials are the only models.' We can in fact build upon the questionable *Book of*

Lord Shang (商君書), the traditions of which go back at least as far as the Ch'in Legalists, and upon Han Fei Tzu as well as the late Ch'in and early Han Mohists and Taoists a fairly strong case for a general suspicion of Confucian conspiracy against the centralization of Government under the Ch'in.   And this evidence points clearly to Confucian sympathies with feudalism.

Li Ssu is certainly not the only supporter of the strong and centralized military state based upon a rugged and frugal peasantry, a formidable and ruthless military machine, and a bureaucratic organization of inflexible efficiency in meting out punishment and reward.   In rejecting the traditional virtues of Confucianism, Li Ssu is the spokesman for his age and for the court he served.   His memorial on the Burning of Books is simply a summary of the pervasive realism of his time.   Han Fei Tzu puts the legalist case more sharply:

> Now that Yao and Shun cannot come to life again, who is to determine the genuineness as between Confucianism and Mohism, if one should want now to scrutinize the ways of Yao and Shun which prevailed three thousand years ago, I should imagine it would also be impossible for him to achieve any certainty.   To claim certainty without corroborating evidence is stupid; to refer to anything that one cannot be certain of is self-deceptive. Therefore, those who explicitly refer to the ancient kings and dogmatically claim the authority of Yao and Shun must be either stupid or deceitful....The scholars of the land have neither any definite theory to expound nor any constant standard for their conduct....Now that heretical teachings are equally listened to and contradictory talk is absurdly acted upon, how can there be anything else but chaos? Since such is the way the ruler listens to advice, it will also, of course, be the way he will govern the people.. Suppose there again is someone who collects books, practices the art of speaking, gathers a band of pupils, wears an appearance of culture and learning, and discusses the principles of all things.   The ruler of the time will respect him for this, saying: 'To show respect to worthy scholars is the way of the ancient kings.' Now, those who are taxed by the magistrates are the farmers, while those who are maintained by the sovereign are the learned gentlemen.   As long as heavy taxes are collected from the farmers while rich rewards are given to the learned gentlemen, it will be impossible to expect the people to work hard and talk little....As long as the merit of beheading the enemy in war is not rewarded, while bravery in family quarrels is celebrated with honours, it will be impossible to expect the people to fight hard against the enemy but refrain from having private feuds.   In time of peace the literati and the cavaliers are patronized; in time of war uniformed warriors are employed. Thus neither are the ones patronized the ones used, nor are the ones used the ones patronized.   This is the reason why there is disorder....When the sage rules the states, he does not count on people doing good of themselves but employs such measures as will keep them from doing any evil....When

the Confucianists of the present day counsel the rulers they do not discuss the way to bring about order now, but the achievement of good order in the past....The reason for the ruler to look for wise and well-informed men is that the intelligence of the people is not such as to be respected or relied upon. For instance, in ancient times, when Yu (禹) opened the rivers and deepened them, the people gathered tiles and stones (to hit him); when the prime minister of Cheng (鄭), Tsu Ch'an (子產), cleared the fields and planted mulberry trees, the people of Cheng slandered and reviled him. Yu benefited the whole empire and Tzu Ch'an preserved the state of Cheng, but each incurred slander thereby. Clearly the intelligence of the people is not to be relied upon. Therefore, to seek for the worthy and the wise in selecting officials and to endeavor to suit the people in administering the government are equally the cause of chaos and not the means for attaining order.' (*Han Fei Tzu*, 50)

Taoist realism was also critical of a reactionary Confucian orthodoxy. 'Banish wisdom, discard knowledge, and the people will be benefited a hundred fold.' (*Tao Te Ching* 道德經, 19). 'The difficulty of ruling the people is commensurate with the amount of their knowledge. Therefore those who rule by giving knowledge are despoilers of their state. Those who rule without giving knowledge, are the state's good fortune.' (*Tao Te Ching* 65).

Li Ssu, as Grand Chancellor, must have considered the Confucian critics who supported the feudal reaction as burdens which the new empire could not afford to carry. Legalists, Taoists and even Mohists were all critics of the sterile reactionary position of the late Ch'in Confucians. All others were sensitive to the blowing of the winds of change, alert to the values of a new China, unified, vigorous and progressive. Confucian insistence upon the genteel tradition must have seemed less than candid to other scholars as well as to the hard pressed Grand Chancellor. It was a time that called for rugged virtues and pioneer values. *The Book of Lord Shang* exhorts:

If music and fine clothing do not penetrate to all the districts, the people, when they are at work, will pay no attention to the latter, and, when they are at rest, will not listen to the former. If, at rest, they do not listen to the one, their spirits will not become licentious, and if, at work, they pay no attention to the other, their minds will be concentrated ...A Sage knows what is essential in governing a country, and so he induces the people to devote their attention to agriculture. If their attention is devoted to agriculture, then they will be simple, and being simple, they may be made correct ... Indeed, the people will love their ruler and obey his commandment even unto death, if they are engaged in farming from morning to evening. But they will be of no use, if they see that glib—tongued itinerant scholars

succeed in being honoured through serving the ruler, that merchants succeed
in enriching their families, and that artisans have plenty to live upon. If
the people see the comfort and advantage of these three walks of life, they
will certainly shun agriculture ...and will not protect (their homes) and
fight for their rules.

Ssu-ma Chien makes full use of this dramatic encounter—the contest
which he appears to have believed would prove decisive between Empire
and the intangible heritage of the Chinese Spirit. The Deuteronomic
editor's treatment in *I Kings* 18 of the contest on Mount Carmel between
the claim and promises of empire and the demands of the prior commitment to Yahweh offer a striking parallel.

Li Ssu and the Ch'in ideal of Empire won the day against the
Confucian ideal. Li Ssu's banquet given a few months later is a
celebration of victory. We see in Li Ssu's premonition of retribution
the hand writing on the wall! We hear the echo of Hsun Tzu's witness
against the Ch'in: 'Nevertheless, it has disturbing features...When there
is not one particle of Confucian humanism there comes disaster.'

As inexorable as the grinding of the mills of the gods in Aeschylus
or Thucydides the judgment of Ch'in and of Li Ssu follows the feast.
A new figure appears, the Eunuch, Chao Kao (趙高), ruthless as Li Ssu
but degenerate: the answer which providence seems so often to give to
Thrasymachus and to Shang Yang (商鞅). With fine poetic irony Li
Ssu is the victim of his own counsel of opportunism and ruthless realism. As in Plato's *Republic,* the degenerate state under tyranny flees
to sensualism, and rules by fear. In six short years Li Ssu is victim
of his own philosophy, and two years later Ch'in falls. The drama which
began with the rats—bold opportunists, clever shameless rascals—ends
with a wistful reference to rabbits. To his son, as they go together
from prison to the place of execution, he addresses his last speech:
'Even if I and you wished once more to lead a yellow dog and go
together out of the East Gate of Shang-ts'ai (上蔡) to hunt rabbits,
could we indeed do so?'

Did Ssu-ma Chien take an historical event as the basis of a parable:
the story of the man and the dynasty that lost their own souls to
gain Empire? If so, we may see in this biography one of China's eternal
tensions, the tension between Confucian humaneness and the urge
toward Empire and national strength. In Confucian humaneness, you
find tolerance of all ills, as long as they are part of the pursuit of the
good life. In the latter, you find a healthy and progressive state, with

authority coming from the strong central government.

Did Ssu-ma Chien construct this drama on the basis of the witness of two scholars and a few bare facts? The scholars were the Confucian, Hsun Tzu, and the Legalist, Han Fei Tzu. The facts were the meteoric rise and fall of Ch'in, the Anti-Alien Act, and the Burning of the Books. Even the precipitating cause of the Alien Act may have been misunderstood by Ssu-ma Chien. If so, then we have the drama of ideals: the philosophy of Han Fei Tzu put into the speeches and memorials of Li Ssu, against the background of Hsun Tzu's ideology. Legalism appears to conquer. But then as Ssu-ma Chien saw it, the reversal scene comes as the judgment of history: the swift decay of Ch'in, its plunge into degeneracy with the second generation, and the poetic irony of Li Ssu's fall.

The Biography Of Li Ssu In The Shih Chi

Li Ssu was a native of Shang-ts'ai in Ch'u. When a young man, he became a petty clerk of his district. In the toilet room belonging to his official quarters, he noticed that there were rats that ate the filth, and that the approach of man or dog would repeatedly frighten them. But upon entering the granary, he observed that the rats there were eating the stored up grain. They lived beneath the great side-galleries, and did not evidence any un-easiness from man or dog. Thereupon Li Ssu sighed and said: 'A man's ability or non-ability is similar to (the condition of) these rats. It merely depends upon where he places himself.' He thereupon became a follower of Hsün Ch'ing in studying the methods of emperors and kings.

Upon completing his studies, he judged that the King of Ch'u was of insufficient worth to be served, and that as the Six States were all weak, there were none who would give the opportunity of performing great deeds (in their service). Hence he wished to go westward to enter Ch'in. Upon taking his departure from Hsün Ch'ing, he said: 'I have heard that when one obtains the opportune moment one should not be tardy. Now is the time when ten thousand chariots are at war, and when the travelling (politicians) control affairs. At present the King of Ch'in desires to swallow up the world and to rule with the

title of Emperor. This is the time for the commoners to be busy, and
is the golden age of the travelling politicans. One who (at such a
time), abiding in a mean position, decides to remain passive, is like
a bird or deer that will merely look at meat (but not touch it). But
one who possesses a human countenance can act vigorously. Hence
there is no greater shame than meanness of position, nor deeper grief
than poverty. To remain long in a mean position or in a condition of
privation, criticizing the world, despising profit, and committing oneself
to the principle of Non-activity—such is not the nature of a gentleman.
Therefore I intend to go westward to give counsel to the King of Ch'in.'

Arriving just at the death of its King, Chuang-hsiang (249—247), Li
Ssu sought to become a member of the establishment of the Ch'in
Councillor, the Marquis of Wen-hsin, Lu Pu-wei. (Lu) Pu-wei esteemed
him and gave him the title of *lang*, and it was in this way that Li
Ssu obtained speech (with the successor of King Chuang-hsiang).

In advising the King of Ch'in, he said: 'The small man is one who
throws away his opportunities, whereas great deeds are accomplished
through utilizing the mistakes (of others), and inflexibly following them
up. Why is it that in ancient times Duke Mu of Ch'in (659—621), as
Lord Protector, did not in the end annex the Six States in the east? It
was because the feudal lords were still numerous, and the power of
Chou had not yet decayed. Hence the Five Princes who arose one
after the other, still continued to honour the House of Chou. But from
the time of Duke Hsiao of Ch'in (361—338) onward, the House of Chou
declined, and the feudal lords have been annexing one another's
(states). East of the pass lie the Six States, and Ch'in, availing itself
of its victories, has now indeed for six generatons brought the feudal
lords into servitude.

'The feudal lords at the present time are paying allegiance to Ch'in,
as if they were its commanderies and prefectures. With Ch'in's might
and its great King's ability, (the conquest of the other states would be)
like sweeping (the dust) from the top of a kitchen stove. (Ch'in's
power) is sufficient to obliterate the feudal lords, bring to reality the
imperial heritage, and make of the world a single unity. This is the
one time of ten thousand generations. If now you are negligent and
do not press to a finish, the feudal lords will return to strength, and
will combine to form north-to-south alliances against you, so that
although you had the ability of the Yellow Emperor, you would be
unable to bring them into unity.'

The King of Ch'in now conferred upon (Li) Ssu the office of Senior

Scribe. He listened to his plans, and secretly commissioned plotters, bearing gold and precious stones, to travel about and advise the feudal lords. They were liberally to reward and thus ally those of the feudal lords and the officers of note whose submission could be won by material lucre; as for those who were unwilling, these were to be stabbed with sharp swords. They were (also) to create rifts in policy between ruler and subject. The King of Ch'in moreover sent able generals to follow in their rear.

The King of Ch'in had conferred upon (Li) Ssu the title of Alien Minister just at the time when a man of Han, named Cheng Kuo, had come to sow dissension in Ch'in by constructing a drainage and irrigation canal. This had already (been completed) when (the plot) was discovered, and the members of the Ch'in royal house and the great dignitaries all spoke to the King of Ch'in, saying: 'The men of the feudal lords who come to serve Ch'in are for the most part acting on behalf of their own rulers, and merely travel to Ch'in to sow dissension. We request that there be a complete expulsion of all aliens.' Li Ssu, whose inclusion among those to be expelled had also been decided upon, thereupon submitted a memorial which said:

'I, your minister, have heard the officials deliberating about the expulsion of aliens. Your unworthy servant considers that this would be a mistake. Of old, when Duke Mu was seeking for officials, he procured Yu Yü from the Jung in the west, and obtained Po-li Hsi, from Yuan, in the east. He welcomed Chien Shu from Sung, and sought P'ei Pao and Kung-sun Chih from Chin. These five men had not been reared in Ch'in; yet Duke Mu, by using them, united twenty states, and so became Lord Protector over the western Jung.

'Duke Hsiao used the laws of Shang Yang to modify the usages and change the customs. The people thereby became prosperous and flourishing and the state became wealthy and powerful. The clans served with joy, and the feudal lords concluded marriage alliances and offered their allegiance. He captured the armies of Ch'u and Wei and snatched up a territory of one thousand li, so that until the present day the government has remained powerful.

'King Hui used the plots of Chang I to seize the territory of San-ch'uan and annex Pa and Shu in the west. In the north he acquired the commandery of Shang and in the south obtained Hanchung. He enveloped the nine I and imposed his rule on Yen and Ying. In the east he seized the strategic point of Ch'eng-kao and annexed fertile territories. Subsequently he dispersed the north-to-south alliance of the

Six States and forced them to face westward and serve Ch'in. His merit has extended down to the present time.

'King Chao, having obtained Fan Sui, suppressed the Marquis of Jang and expelled Hua Yang. He strengthened the Ducal House and blocked up private doors. He made gradual inroads upon the feudal lords, and brought to realization for (the House of) Ch'in the imperial heritage.

'These four rulers have all made use of the signal deeds of aliens. Looked at from this viewpoint, how have aliens been ungrateful to Ch'in? Let us suppose that in the past these four rulers had sent aliens away instead of receiving them, and had discarded these officials instead of employing them. The result would have been that the state would be without the actualities of wealth and profit, and Ch'in would be without the name of power and greatness.

'At present, Your Majesty causes the jade of the K'un mountains to come to him, and possesses the treasures of Sui and Ho. (From his girdle) he hangs pearls brilliant as the moon and wears the T'ai-o sword. He rides Hsien-li horses and puts up banners (decorated with) green phoenixes. He sets up drums (made from the skin) of the 'divine crocodile'. Of these numerous treasures, Ch'in does not produce one; (why then,) does Your Majesty delight in them?

'If they must needs be products of the state of Ch'in before they become permissible, then these jewels that make bright the night would not ornament the court, and there would be no utensils of rhinoceros horn and ivory as delightful playthings. The women of Cheng and Wei would not fill the rear palaces, and good horses and rapid coursers would not occupy the outer stables. The gold and tin of Chiang-nan would not find any use, and the cinnabar and blue of western Shu would not be utilized for painted decoration. If those things which ornament the rear palaces, fill the lower ranks (of the palace women), divert the mind and delight the ear and eye, must needs be produced in Ch'in before they become permissible: then the hairpins decorated with Yüan pearls, the ear buckles of long pearls, the woven clothing of O, and embroidery decorations, could not be presented before you; while the women of Chao, agreeably adapting themselves to fit every custom, beautiful, gracious and elegant, would not stand at your side.

'Now the beating on earthen jugs, knocking on jars, plucking of the *cheng*, and striking on thigh bones, the while singing and crying 'Wu! Wu!' as means of delighting the ear and eye: such indeed was the music of Ch'in. The Sangchien of Cheng and Wei, the Shao of Yü, and the Wu and the Hsiang are music of other states. But today (the people of Ch'in) have done away with this beating on earthen jugs and knocking on jars, and have introduced (the music of) Cheng and Wei. They refuse to pluck the *cheng* and accept instead the Shao of Yu. Why is this so? It is simply that whatever pleases us we must have before us, and that (these are the things that) meet our taste.

'Yet when at the present time it comes to selecting men, this is not the case. Without asking whether they will do or not, and without discussing whether they be deceitful or not, persons not of Ch'in are to be sent away and aliens are to be expelled. This being the case, it is feminine charms, music, pearls and jade that are held as weighty, whereas human beings are esteemed lightly. Such is not the policy by which to straddle (what lies) within the seas and to rule over the feudal lords.

'I, your minister, have heard it said that it is in the extensive land that grain is abundant, and in the large state that the people are numerous. When the weapons are strong, then the soldiers will be courageous. This is why Mount T'ai does not reject the dust (which blows upon it), and so is able to attain its greatness, and why the Yellow river and the sea do not make preference between the tiny rivulets, and so are able to attain their deepness. (In like manner) a King does not repulse the masses of the people, and so is able to make his power illustrious. This is why (when such a ruler exists), the earth has no four quarters, the people have no foreign countries, the four seasons are prosperous and beautiful, and spiritual beings bestow their blessings. This (is the way) in which the Five Emperors and Three Kings had no equals.

'But now you throw away your people, thus enlarging the enemy states. You send away outsiders so that they may serve the feudal lords. And you cause the gentlemen of the world to retire without daring to face westwards, and to halt their feet without entering Ch'in. This is what is known as offering weapons to brigands and presenting provisions to robbers.

'Now there are many articles not produced in Ch'in and yet valuable, and numerous gentlemen who were not reared in Ch'in and are yet desirous of being loyal. If at present you expel aliens so as to give increment to opposing states, and decrease your people so as to make addition to the enemy, then you will find yourself depopulated at home and will have established (sowers of) enmity against you among the feudal lords abroad. Should you then wish to have the country without danger, you could not obtain it.'

The King of Ch'in thereupon removed the order for the expulsion of aliens and returned Li Ssu to office. Unto the end he used his counsels, and his office was advanced to that of Minister of Justice (t'ing wei). After more than twenty years the world was united. The King was honored by becoming Sovereign Emperor (huang ti), and he made Li Ssu his Grand Councillor (ch'eng hsiang). He established commanderies, prefectures and townships, and melted up the weapons of these, with a view that they should not again be used (against Ch'in). He caused Ch'in to be without a single foot of territory of feudal investiture, and did not establish his sons and younger brothers as Kings; but meritorious ministers were made nobles. This was done to ensure that later on there should be none of the miseries of warfare.

In the thirty-fourth year of Shih-huang (213 B.C.), while a feast was being held in the palace at Hsien-yang, a scholar of wide learning, the p'u-yeh, Chou Ch'ing-ch'en, together with others, extolled Shih-huang upon his majesty and virtue. (Thereupon) a native of Ch'i, Shun-Yu Yueh, advanced to remonstrate, saying:

'Your servant has heard that the reason why the Yin and Chou kings (held the empire) for more than a thousand years, was because they gave fiefs to their sons, younger brothers and meritorious ministers, as branches and supporting props to themselves. At present Your Majesty possesses all within the seas, yet his sons and younger brothers remain common men. If eventually there should occur such disasters as those of T'ien Ch'ang or of the Six High Dignitaries, and your subjects were without means of assistance, how could they save you? Of affairs which, unless modelled on antiquity, can endure for long, I have never heard. At present (Chou) Ch'ing-ch'en, together with his associates, nevertheless, flatters you to your face, thus aggravating Your Majesty's error. Such are not loyal subjects.'

Shih-huang submitted this criticism to the Grand Councillor. The Grand Councillor, (Li Ssu,) regarded this advice as misleading and rejected its expressions. He thereupon submitted a memorial which said:

'Of old, the empire was scattered and in confusion, and there was none able to unite it into one. Therefore the feudal lords all became active together, and in their discussions they harped on the past so as to injure the present, and made a display of empty words so as to confuse the truth. Men valued what they themselves privately studied, thus casting into disrepute what their superiors had established.

'At present Your Majesty possesses a unified empire, has laid down the distinctions of right and wrong, and has consolidated for himself a single (position of) eminence. Yet there are those who with their private teachings mutually abet each other, and who discredit the decrees (*chih*) of laws and instructions. When they hear orders promulgated, they criticize them in the light of their own teachings. Within (the court) they mentally discredit them, and outside they criticize them upon the streets. To cast disrepute on their ruler they regard as a thing worthy of fame; to accept different views they regard as high (conduct); and they lead the people to create slander. If such conditions are not prohibited, the imperial power will decline above, and partisanships will form below. It is expedient that these be prohibited.

'Your servant requests that all persons possessing works of literature, the *Shih*, the *Shu*, and the discussions of the various philosophers, should destroy them with remission of all penalty. Those who have not destroyed them within thirty days after the issuing of the order, are to be branded and sent to do forced labor. Books not to be destroyed will be those on medicine and pharmacy, divination by the tortoise and milfoil, and agriculture and arboriculture. As for persons who wish to study, let them take the officials as their teachers.'

Shih-huang approved this recommendation. The confiscation and destruction of the *Shih*, the *Shu*, and the discussions of the various philosophers, done for the purpose of making the people ignorant, and of bringing it about that none within the empire should use the past to discredit the present; the clarification of the laws and the fixation of the regulations: all this began with Shih-huang. He made the systems of writing uniform, established palaces and country villas, and extensively travelled throughout the empire. In the next year he again made a tour of inspection, and expelled the four I tribes beyond (the borders). In all these affairs (Li) Ssu exerted himself.

(Li) Ssu's eldest son, Yu, became Administrator of San-ch'uan, and all (Li's) sons became allied with the daughters of the Ch'in royal family, while his daughters all became affianced with the princes of the House of Ch'in. On the occasion when the Administrator of San-ch'uan, Li Yu, announced his return to Hsien-yang, Li Ssu held a feast at his home. The heads of the various offices all came before him to wish him long life, and the chariots and horse-men at his door could be counted by the thousand. Li Ssu, heaving a sigh, exclaimed: 'Alas! I have heard Hsun Ch'ing say, 'Things should not be allowed to become too flourishing.' I was a commoner of Shang-ts'ai, an ordinary man from the village. The Emperor did not realize that his nag was inferior, and so finally promoted me to this (position), Among the ministerial posts of the present time, there is none higher than mine, which may indeed be called the peak of wealth and honor. But when things have reached their peak they decline. I do not yet know where I shall unharness.'

In the tenth month of the thirty-seventh year of Shih-huang, (the Emperor) made a tour to Kuei-chi, then along the border of the sea, and northward to Lang-ya. The Grand Councillor, Li Ssu, and Chao Kao, Keeper of the Chariots, who was concurrently in charge of the sending of letters and of sealed orders, accompanied him.

Shih-huang had more than twenty sons, of whom the eldest, Fu-su, because he had several times frankly remonstrated with His Majesty, was sent by the latter to oversee the soldiers at the commandery of Shang, of which Meng T'ien was the commandant. The youngest son, Hu-hai, was the one (Shih-huang) loved, and when he begged to accompany him, His Majesty granted him permission. None of the other sons, however, accompanied (the expedition).

In the seventh month of this year, when Shih-huang-ti arrived at Sha-ch'iu, he fell severely ill. He commanded Chao Kao to write a letter to be sent to Fu-su, saying: 'With the soldiers belonging to Meng T'ien, accompany my funeral cortege to Hsien-yang, and bury me there.' The letter was already sealed, but had not yet been delivered to the messenger, when Shih-huang died. The letter and the imperial seal were at that time both in the quarters of Chao Kao. Only the son, Hu-hai, the Grand Councillor, Li Ssu, and Chao Kao, together with five or six of the favourite eunuchs, knew that Shih-huang had died, and none of the other officials knew about it.

Because the Emperor had died outside (of the capital), and because there was no definite crown prince, Li Ssu concealed the matter and pretended that Shih-huang was keeping to his sleeping chariot. The various officials continued to submit their affairs, and (a pretence was kept up that) the Emperor ate food as before. The eunuchs who directly accompanied the sleeping chariot, pretended to transmit the royal approval on the affairs that were submitted.

Chao Kao, using the fact that he had retained the letter and seal which were to have been sent to Fu-su, spoke to Prince Hu-hai, saying: 'The Emperor has died, without giving instructions as to the enfieffing of his sons as Kings, and has only given a letter for his eldest son.

When this eldest son arrives, he will become established as Sovereign Emperor, while you will remain without a foot or inch of territory What are you going to do about this?'

Hu-hai replied: 'I have certainly heard that the intelligent ruler knows his subjects, and the intelligent father knows his sons. If my father has departed this life without enfieffing his sons, what can I say about it?'

'Not so,' said Chao Kao. 'At the present time the salvation or ruin of the empire depend only upon you, myself, and the Grand Councillor. I beg you to consider this. Moreover, when it comes to making others one's subjects, or being the subject of others; ruling over others, or being ruled over by others, how can the two be discussed in the same breath?'

Hu-hai said: 'To remove an eldest brother and establish a younger one, is contrary to what is right. Not to transmit a father's edict, being afraid of death, is against the duties of a son. When one's ability is limited and one's talents shallow, to make forcible use of other men's achievements is to be lacking in ability. These three acts are the very opposite of (a ruler's) proper qualifications (teh), and the empire would not submit to them. I myself would fall into peril, and the spirits of the soil and grain would not accept my sacrifices.'

(Chao) Kao said: 'your servant has heard that when T'ang and Wu assassinated their rulers, the empire called them righteous and did not consider them disloyal. The Prince of Wei murdered his father, and the state of Wei recorded his virtue, while Confucius made note of him and did not consider him unfilial. Great conduct does not consist in petty caution, nor does admirable virtue lie in polite refusal. Each village has its own propriety, and in the various offices merit is not acquired in the same way. Therefore if you pay attention to what is small and forget what is great, later, harm must result. If you are hesitating and uncertain, later must result regret. But one who is decisive and dares to act, him even spiritual beings avoid, so that eventually he accomplishes something of merit. I beg you to agree with this.'

Hu-hai heaved a sigh and exclaimed: 'At present the great event has not yet been revealed, and the mourning rites have not come to a conclusion. How would it be proper to approach the Grand Councillor in this matter?'

Chao Kao said: '(Now) is the time! (Now) is the time! By remaining idle we shall not attain to our plans. We have abundant provisions and swift horses, and need only fear to fall behind the proper time.'

After Hu-hai had given his approval to (Chao) Kao's words, the latter continued: 'If we do not make plans with the Grand Councillor, I fear lest the business may not succeed. I request to deliberate on your behalf with the Grand Councillor myself.'

(Chao) Kao then spoke to the Grand Councillor, saying: 'The Emperor has died, leaving a letter with orders for his eldest son to accompany the funeral cortege to Hsien-yang, and establish himself as his successor. The letter, however, has not yet gone, and at present there is none who knows of the Emperor's death. The letter for the eldest son, together with the imperial seal, are both in Hu-hai's quarters. The decision as to who is to be Crown Prince depends upon the say of Your Lordship and of myself. What is to be done in the matter?'

(Li) Ssu said: 'How can you speak words that would destroy the state? This is not a fit affair for subjects to discuss.'

(Chao) Kao replied: 'If Your Lordship will make an estimate of ability, who compares with Meng T'ien? In worthiness, who compares with Meng T'ien? In the making of far reaching and unfailing plans, who compares with Meng T'ien? In freedom from the resentment of the empire, who compares with Meng T'ien? In enjoying the intimacy and trust of the eldest son, who compares with Meng T'ien?'

'In all these five respects,' replied (Li) Ssu, 'I indeed do not come up to Meng T'ien. How deeply, sir, do you reprove me!'

(Chao) Kao said: 'I am indeed but a menial of the inner offices, who through the writings of his pen has been fortunate to obtain entry into the Ch'in palace. I have conducted affairs for more than twenty years, and have not yet seen a Grand Councillor or meritorious minister whom Ch'in had dismissed and who has retained his feudal investiture down to the second generation. All have eventually died by execution.

'You, sir, are acquainted with all of the twenty odd sons of the Sovereign Emperor. The eldest son is firm, resolute, warlike and and courageous. He is a sincere man and a spirited gentleman, and when he succeeds to the throne it is inevitable that he will use Meng T'ien as his Grand Councillor. Hence it is evident that Your Lordship will not possess an entire lifetime your seal as Marquis of the highest rank, but will some day be returning to your village.

'When I received the order to instruct Hu-hai, I had him study legalistic matters for a number of years, but I have never seen him commit an error. He is kind, human-hearted, sincere and liberal. He regards wealth lightly, and esteems gentlemen deeply. He is discriminating in mind, but compliant in speech. He is the fullest exemplification of good manners, and a courteous gentleman. Among the sons of the House of Ch'in, none is equal to this one. He may properly become the successor. Consider the matter, sir, and decide it.'

(Li) Ssu replied: 'Return, sir, to your position. I have received our (late) monarch's decree, and listen obediently to the Will of Heaven. What doubts can there be as to what should be decided?'

(Chao) Kao said: 'What is secure may become perilous, and what is perilous may become secure. If what are secure and perilous is not decided upon, what means is there of honouring the Sages?'

(Li) Ssu replied: 'I was but a commoner of the lanes and byways of Shang-ts'ai, who through the imperial favour have attained to the position of Grand Councillor, and been ennobled as Marquis of the highest rank. My sons and grandsons all hold the most honourable positions and greatest revenues. Therefore the measures pertaining to the salvation or the ruin (of the dynasty), its security or peril, have fallen upon me. How then can I turn my back (upon my duty)? For the loyal subject does not hope to reach perfection while shunning death, nor does the filial son take heed of peril while he is exerting himself. Each subject should simply keep to his own duties. Do not repeat your words, for you would be causing me to do evil.'

'And yet,' (Chao) Kao replied, 'I have heard that the Sage shifts his course without having an infallible rule. He accords with changes and follows the time. When he sees the branches, he knows their root, and when he observes the finger he sees where it points. Things (all) certainly have (this law of change). How can there be unchanging rules (for conduct)?

'At the present moment the fate of the empire hangs on Hu-hai, and I am able to have my way with him. Moreover, from without to regulate what is central, may be called a delusion; from below to regulate what is above, may be called injurious. For with the descent of autumn dew, plants and flowers wither, while with the stirring of (spring) waters, all things become active. This is an invariable law, and why, sir, are you so slow in seeing it?'

(Li) Ssu said: 'I have heard that when Chin changed its crown prince, for three generations there was no peace. Huan of Ch'i contested for the throne with his brother, and his body when he died was desecrated. When Chen killed his relative and did not listen to those who remonstrated, the country became a desert waste, and finally its altars of the soil and grain fell into danger. These affairs were contrary to Heaven, and in the ancestral temples (the spirits) did not accept the sacrifices. (If I were to do as you wish,) I should be like these men. (With their example before me,) how can I make plots?'

(Chao) Kao said: 'When superior and inferior are harmonious, they may endure for long. When the internal and the external are like one, affairs are without (the distinction of) outer and inner. If you, sir, will listen to my plan, you will long hold your title as a marquis, and for generation on generation (your descendants) will designate themselves as 'The Orphan', and will surely have the longevity of a stately pine, and the wisdom of a Confucius or a Mo. But now if you renounce this plan and do not follow it, disaster will overtake your descendants. sufficient to chill your heart. He who is skilful makes good fortune out of disaster. What, sir, is your position?'

(Li) Ssu then looked up to Heaven and groaned. Dropping some tears, he exclaimed with a great sigh: 'Alas! Since I alone, (of all my line,) should encounter this unsettled age, if I cannot bring myself to die, on what am I to rely for life?' After this (Li) Ssu listened to (Chao) Kao.

The latter now reported to Hu-hai saying: 'I requested to transmit the illustrious decree of (you), the Crown Prince, and announce it to the Grand Councillor. How would the Grand Councillor, (Li) Ssu, dare to disobey the order?'

Having (all three) deliberated together, they thereupon pretended that they had received an edict from Shih-huang, ordering the Grand Councillor to establish the son, Hu-hai, as Crown Prince. They composed a letter as a substitute (to the former one) to be sent to the eldest son, Fu-su, which said: 'We (i.e., the Emperor, Shih-huang) have traversed the empire, and have sacrificed to the divinities of the famous mountains, in order to prolong our life. At the present time Fu-su stays with the army Commandant, Meng T'ien, who for more than ten years has had charge of several hundred thousands of troops along the military posts of the frontier. There he (i.e., Fu-su) has been unable to come before us (with news of) his advance, and many soldiers have been destroyed, without the winning of a foot or inch (of territory). But he has been repeatedly sending frankly worded letters, speaking evil of what we have been doing. Because he has not obtained his return (from exile) as Crown Prince, day and night he has viewed us with resentment.

'As a son, Fu-su has been unfilial, and herewith is presented with a sword with which he may cut short his existence. The Commandant of the army, (Meng) T'ien, who has been staying with Fu-su along the outer frontiers, has been lacking in rectitude, and it is fitting that we should have become acquainted with his plots. As a subject he has not been loyal, and so it is hereby granted to him to die. As for his soldiers, let them be attached to Lieutenant—General Wang Li.'

They sealed the letter with the imperial seal, and commissioned one of Hu-hai's followers to take the letter and give it to Fu-su in the commandery of Shang. When the emissary arrived and produced the letter, Fu-su wept and entered his inner apartment, wishing to kill himself. But Meng T'ien stopped Fu-su, saying: 'When His Majesty lived outside (the capital) and had not yet established a Crown Prince, he employed me to command a host of three hundred thousand to protect the frontier, and you, his son, to be Overseer. This is a weighty responsibility in the empire, and yet now, upon the coming of a single emissary, you are about to kill yourself. How do you know that this is not a trickery? I beg of you to send back a request (for confirmation of this letter). If after sending back the request you should then die, it would not be too late. The emissary will hasten the message.'

Fu-su was a man of true virtue and said to Meng T'ien: 'When a father allows his son to die, how can there be any question about sending back a request?' With this he killed himself. Meng T'ien was unwilling to die, however, so that the emissary had him, together with his retaining officers, imprisoned at Young-chow.

When the emissary returned and made his report Hu-hai (Li) Ssu and (Chao) Kao were greatly delighted. Having arrived at Hsien-yang, they proclaimed the mourning. The (new) Crown Prince was established (on the throne) as Erh-shih-huang-ti, and he made Chao Kao his Palace Chamberlain, so that the latter constantly waited upon him on matters within (the palace).

When Erh-shih was once taking his ease, he summoned (Chao) Kao to discuss matters with him, and said during the conversation: 'Man's life in this world is but an instant; it is like the pressing onward of six chargers which instantaneously pass by a crack (in a wall). Now that I govern the empire, I desire everything which the ear and eye enjoys, and the utmost of whatever my heart's desire delights in. Thus shall I bring repose to my ancestral temple and give pleasure to the myriad. (But at the same time I wish) long to hold the empire, and to bring my span of years to a natural conclusion. Is such a course possible?'

'Such,' replied (Chao) Kao, 'is what the capable ruler is able to pursue, but is forbidden to the confused and disordered ruler. I beg to speak out, without daring to avoid execution from the axe. I am anxious that Your Majesty pause a little in his ideas. For indeed all the princes and great ministers are suspicious about the consultation at Sha-ch'iu. At the same time every one of the princes is an older brother of Your Majesty, besides which the great ministers are men who were established by the former Emperor. At present Your Majesty has just been enthroned, for which reason they are dissatisfied in their attachment. None of them pays allegiance, and they may, I fear, make some disturbance.

'Moreover, now that Meng T'ien is dead, Meng I leads the soldiers posted along the outer (frontiers). I am trembling and alarmed, and fear only that there may not be a (peaceful) conclusion. How then can Your Majesty still pursue these pleasures?'

'What is to be done about this?' Erh-shih asked.

Chao Kao replied: 'Make the laws more severe and the punishments more rigorous. Command that when a man has committed a crime, punishment be meted out on a basis of mutual responsibility, and let this extend to include his clan. Exterminate the great ministers and exile your own flesh and blood. Enrich the poor, give honour to the humble, and completely do away with the old ministers of the former Emperor. Appoint, furthermore, those with whom Your Majesty is intimate, and bring near those whom you trust. When this is done, all the hidden influences will turn to Your Majesty. What is injurious will be eradicated, and villainous plots will be cut short. Among the ministers there will be none who does not receive your beneficent kindness, nor who will not be the gainer from your abundant virtue. Your Majesty will then (recline peacefully) on a lofty pillow, giving free vent to his desires, and favouring what he takes pleasure in. No plan can surpass this one.'

Erh-shih approved of (Chao) Kao's words, and began making the laws anew. Thereupon officials and princes (accused of) guilt were all examined and judged under Chao Kao's orders. The great minister, Meng I, and others, he had executed; twelve of the royal princes died and had their bodies exposed on the market-place of Hsien-yang; and ten of the princesses of the royal family were killed at Tu by being torn limb from limb. Their riches and belongings went to the offices of the prefectures (in which they lived), while (the number of) those who were implicated (and punished) with them surpasses all estimation.

Prince Kao wished to flee, but fearing lest his family might be seized, he submitted a memorial which said: 'When the former Emperor was in good health, I was granted food upon entering (the palace), and on leaving, I rode in a chariot. Clothing from the imperial storehouse and valuable horses from the stables were bestowed upon me. (When the Emperor died,) I should have followed him in death, but was unable. As a son I have been unfilial, and as a subject have been disloyal. Being disloyal, I have no renown to establish in this world, and so request that I may follow him in death and be buried at the foot of Mount Li. May Your Majesty but have the kindness to pity me.'

When the memorial was submitted, Hu-hai, greatly pleased, summoned Chao Kao and showed it to him, saying: 'This may indeed be called prompt!'

Chao Kao said: 'If (all) the ministers would thus die from grief without delay, who would there be to plot disturbances?'

Hu-hai granted the memorial and presented one hundred thousand (ounces) of money for the funeral. Daily the laws and punishments were made more severe, so that among the officials, each man felt himself in danger, and there were many who wanted to revolt. (Erh-shih,) furthermore, constructed the palace of O-pang, and laid out imperial highways in straight lines. The collection of taxes became ever more burdensome, and there were exactions of forced military service without ceasing.

At the time the frontier guards of Ch'u, (led by) such men as Ch'en Sheng and Wu Kuang, revolted and arose east of the mountains. Men of ability established each other, set themselves up as Marquises and Kings, and revolted against Ch'in. Their soldiers arrived as far as Hung-men before halting.

Li Ssu several times wished to ask for a private opportunity to give advice, yet Erh-shih would not grant it, but made reproving enquiries of Li Ssu and said:

'Among the confidential councils which I have, there is one which has been heard from Han (Fei) Tzu as follows: 'When Yao held the empire, his reception platform was (but) three feet high, his oak roof-beams were unsmoothed, and his reed thatch was not trimmed. Even a travellers' inn could not be more miserable than this. In winter he wore deerskins and in summer clothing of dolichos fiber. The unhusked kernels of pannicled millet were his food, and the li and huo plants made his broth. He ate from earthen containers and drank from earthen vases. Were it the nourishment of a gatekeeper, it could not be worse than this.

'Yu pierced Lung-men and penetrated Ta-hsia. He made the nine rivers passable, and separated their nine watercourses by dams. He released the stagnant waters and led them to the sea. (So hard did he labour that) his thighs were without fat and his shanks worn off of all hair. His hands and feet were calloused and hardened, and his face and eyes became blackened. In the end he died away (from home) and was buried at Kuei-chi. The labours of a servant or slave could not be more arduous than this.

'This being so, why should he who is honoured by holding the empire wish to distress his frame and weary his spirit? His body resting in a travellers' inn, his mouth eating the sustenance of a gatekeeper, his hand holding the labours of a slave! Such is what an unworthy man may constrain himself to; it is not what a man of ability need concern himself with. When an able man possesses the empire, he does nothing else but use the empire exclusively so that it will accord with his own (desires). This is the value of possessing the empire. Now, he who is considered a man of ability must be one able to pacify the empire and govern its various peoples. But if at the present time I am even unable (to obtain) what is profitable for myself, how shall I be able to rule the empire? This is why I should like to give free play to my impulses and to broaden my desires, so as long to enjoy the empire without harm (to myself). How shall I do this?'

Yu, the son of Li Ssu, was Administrator of San-ch'uan, and when the bandit hordes of Wu Kuang and his associates had overrun the territory on their way toward the west, he had been unable to prevent them from passing by. After Chang Han had broken up and expelled the soldiers of (Wu) Kuang and his followers, an emissary who had made an investigation of the regions attached to San-ch'uan, reproached (Li) Ssu, (asking him) why, when he held the position of (one of) the Three High Dignitaries, he had allowed the bandits to act like this? Li Ssu became alarmed and increased (the man's) rank and revenue. Not knowing how to get out (of his difficulties), he now assented to Erh-shih's ideas, wishing in this way to obtain favour. He replied (to Erh-shih's speech) in a memorial which stated:

'The able ruler must needs be one able in his every act to carry out the methods of supervising and holding responsible. When one supervises them and holds them responsible, subjects dare not but exert their ability to the utmost so as to devote themselves to their ruler. If thus the distinction between subject and ruler is made certain, and the (respective) relationships of superior and inferior made manifest, then among both the virtuous and the unworthy in the empire, there will be none who will dare not to exert their strength to the utmost, and to strain at their duties, so as to devote themselves to their ruler. In this way the ruler alone will rule in the empire, and will be ruled by none. He will succeed in reaching the apex of pleasure. Can the able and intelligent ruler afford, then, not to examine this matter?

'Therefore Shen Tzu has said: 'To possess the empire, and yet not throw off all restraints, is called making shackles (for oneself) out of the empire.' There is no other reason for this than the failure (of rulers) to supervise and hold responsible, and thus watch over (the empire). They are men who labour with their own bodies for the people of the empire, as did Yao and Yu and therefore (the empire) is called their shackles.

'Now if one is unable to practise the intelligent methods of Shen (Pu-hai) and Han (Fei Tzu), and to follow the way of supervising and holding responsible, so that the empire will suit one's own pleasure; and if on the contrary one busies oneself to no purpose with distressing one's body and wearying one's spirit, in order that one may devote oneself to the hundred clans; then one is but a servant of the black headed ones, and not one who rears the empire. What is there valuable (in such a position)? For when others devote themselves to oneself, then oneself is illustrious and the others are humble, whereas when one devotes oneself to others, oneself is humble and the others are illustrious. Therefore he who devotes himself to others is humble, and he to whom others devote themselves is illustrious. From antiquity till today, there has never been a case which was not like this.

'All men of old who were considered respectable and virtuous, were so because of their illustrious (position), whereas those who were considered despicable and unworthy, were so because of their humble (position). And so if we, because Yao and Yu devoted themselves to the empire, are on that account to follow and to honour them, then we are indeed losing the mind (that can distinguish) respectability and ability. Such may be called a great delusion, and is it not fitting to speak of it as one's shackles? It is a fault resulting from incapacity to supervise and hold responsible.

'Therefore Han (Fei) Tzu has said: 'It is the affectionate mother who has the prodigal son, while the severe household is without fierce slaves.' What does this mean? It means that one should be able, in the application of punishments, to keep them definite.

'Therefore according to the laws of Lord Shang, there was corporal punishment for those who scattered their ashes into the streets. Now, the scattering of ashes is a small offense, whereas corporal punishment is a heavy penalty. Only he who is capable of conducting far-reaching supervision for light offenses is an intelligent ruler. For supervision is far reaching even for light offenses, how much more will it be so when there is a serious offense! And thus the people will not dare to violate (the laws).

'Therefore Han (Fei) Tzu has said: 'Even an ordinary piece of cloth, the common man will not leave aside (if he has the opportunity of stealing it), while one hundred *i* of molten gold, even Robber Chih would not snatch. It is not that the mind of the common man puts a heavy estimate on the value of an ordinary thing, or that the desires of Robber Chih are slight. Nor again is it that the conduct of Robber Chih is to regard the heavy (value) of one hundred *i* but lightly. But it is because if the act of seizing be inevitably followed by immediate retribution, Robber Chih would not seize even one hundred *i*, whereas if punishment do not necessarily follow, even a common man would not leave aside an ordinary thing.'

'Therefore a city wall fifty feet high, even Lou Chi would not lightly transgress, whereas even a lame shepherd will herd (his flock) on top of Mount T'ai's height of one hundred *jen*. Now when Lou Chi finds a fifty foot barrier difficult, how is it that a lame shepherd will make light of a height of one hundred *jen?* It is because the conditions (*shih*) of steepness and depression are different.

'There is no other way for the intelligent ruler and Sage-king to remain long in a position of honour, to maintain long the major power (*shih*), and to take sole possession of what is advantageous in the empire. It consists in passing judgment, and in supervising and holding responsible, and in one's own person. If you make definite the severe punishments, . . . then the empire will not dare to transgress (the laws). If at present you do not busy yourself with what will lead to such non-transgression, but conduct yourself in the manner which makes the affectionate mother have the prodigal son, you have certainly not looked into the discussions of the Sages. As for him who is unable to practise the methods (*shu*) of the Sages, what else does he do but make himself the servant of the empire? Can we do aught but pity him?

'Furthermore, when men who are abstemious, self-controlled, virtuous (*jen*) and righteous (*i*), stand in the court, then wild and unrestrained revels are cut short. When remonstrating ministers who prate of 'reason' appear at one's side, then abandoned and reckless aims become curbed. When 'patriots' whose actions are those of men ready to die for their principles, appear in the world, all thought of dissolute pleasures becomes obliterated.

'Therefore the intelligent ruler is one able to expel these three classes of men and to hold the methods (*shu*) of the ruler in his own hands alone, issuing his decrees to ministers who will listen and follow him, and thus practising his clear laws. Therefore being venerated in his own person, his power (*shih*) is weighty. All talented rulers must necessarily be able to oppose the world and to grind the usages (to their own liking), destroying what they dislike and establishing what they desire. During life, in consequence, they hold a power (*shih*) that is honourable and weighty, and after death they receive a posthumous title that speaks of ability and intelligence.

'This is why the intelligent ruler makes decisions solely himself, and hence his authority does not lie in the hands of his ministers. Only when this is so can he obliterate the path of 'virtue' (*jen*) and 'righteousness' (*i*), close the mouths of irresponsible speakers, hinder the activities of the 'patriots', and bottle up 'wisdom' and 'intelligence', so that within (the palace) he alone sees and listens. Then outside (the palace) he cannot be overthrown by the actions of the 'virtuous' and 'righteous' patriots, and within he cannot be carried away by debates of remonstration and by angry wrangling. Therefore he is able for himself alone to follow a mind of complete unrestraint, and no one dares to oppose him. Only in this way can one be said to be capable of under standing the methods (*shu*) of Shen (Pu-hai) and Han (Fei Tzu), and of practising the laws of Lord Shang. I have never heard that if one practised these laws and understood these methods, the empire would be in disorder.

'Therefore it is said that the Way of the King (*wang tao*) consists in maintaining restraint and keeping easily in hand. It is only the intelligent ruler who is able to follow this, and it is when conditions are like this that there may be said to be supervision and holding responsible. Then will one's subjects be without depravity.

'When one's subjects are without depravity, the empire will be at peace. When the empire is at peace, its ruler will be awe-inspiring and venerated. When the ruler is awe-inspiring and venerated, supervision and holding responsible are definite. When supervision and holding responsible are definite, what is sought for will be obtained. When what is sought for is obtained, the nation will be prosperous. When the nation is prosperous, its ruler's joy will be abundant. Therefore when the methods (*shu*) of supervising and holding responsible are instituted, there is nothing wished for that is not obtained, officials and the hundred clans have no way of remedying their wrongs and what disturbances can they then dare to plan? Under these conditions the way of the Emperor (*ti tao*) is made complete, and one may be said to be able to understand the methods (*shu*) of ruler and subject. Though Shen (Pu-hai) and Han (Fei Tzu) were to return to life, they would be unable to add to this.'

When this memorial was presented, Erh-shih was delighted, and from then on the carrying out (of the policy) of supervising and holding responsible was increased in severity. Those who taxed the people heavily were regarded as intelligent officials, Erh-shih saying: 'Such as these may be considered capable of supervising and holding responsible.' Persons who had suffered corporal punishment made up half of those to be seen on the roads, and the men who died, daily formed a heap in the market-place. Those who executed the people in large numbers were regarded as loyal ministers, Erh-shih saying: 'Such as these may be considered capable of supervising and holding responsible.'

When Chao Kao had first become Palace Chamberlain, those whom he had executed and on whom he had requited private hatred were very numerous. Hence he feared that the great ministers who entered the court might submit matters that would vilify him, and so he spoke to Erh-shih, saying:

'What makes the Son of Heaven noble (in the eyes of his people is that they hear only the sound (of his voice), and none of the subjects can obtain a view of his countenance. Therefore he designates himself as *chen*. Moreover, Your Majesty is rich in his years (to come), and is not yet necessarily conversant with all affairs. If now he were to sit in court, and some error were to occur in the criticisms or recommendations (that were submitted), he would show his shortcomings to the great ministers, which would not be the way to display spirit-like intelligence to the empire. Moreover, if Your Majesty were to keep himself in reserved dignity within the forbidden (part of the palace), and leave it to me and to palace attendants practised in the laws, to attend to matters, then when matters came up, there would be someone to decide them. In this way the great ministers would not dare to bring up doubtful affairs, and the empire would acclaim you as a sage ruler.'

Erh-shih used this counsel, and now no longer sat in court to give audience to the great ministers, but stayed within the forbidden precincts. Chao Kao and the eunuch attendants had charge of affairs, all of which were decided by Chao Kao.

Hearing that Li Ssu had made some remarks about this, (Chao) Kao paid a visit to the Grand Councillor and said: 'There are many bands of brigands east of the pass, and yet at present the Emperor impresses more and more forced labour for the building of the O-pang palace. He collects dogs, horses and useless things. I should like to remonstrate, but my position is lowly. Really this is a matter for Your Lordship. Why do you not see him?'

Li Ssu replied: 'As a matter of fact, I have wished to speak about this for a long time, but at present the Emperor no longer sits in court, but stays within the inner palaces. When I have something to speak about, I am unable to transmit it, and when I wish to see him, he has no leisure.'

Chao Kao said: 'You, sir, are certainly one who should be able to remonstrate with him. I beg to arrange a time for Your Lordship when the Emperor will have leisure for discussion with you.'

Chao Kao then waited until Erh-shih was in the midst of feasting and merriment, with women before him, to send a man to tell the Grand Councillor that at that moment the Emperor was free, and that he (Li Ssu) might submit his business. On arriving at the palace gate, the Grand Councillor had the announcement of his visit sent up. This happened three times, until Erh-shih angrily said: 'I have many days of leisure when the Grand Councillor does not come, but as soon as I am feasting in private, the Grand Councillor straightway comes requesting business. Why does the Grand Councillor slight and force me in this way?'

Chao Kao took this opportunity to say: 'If he is like this, he is dangerous. The Grand Councillor was a participant in the Sha-ch'iu plot, and now Your Majesty has already been established as Emperor, whereas the dignity of the Grand Councillor has not been advanced. His idea is one looking forward toward becoming a king by making a partition of the country. Furthermore, since Your Majesty did not ask me, I did not dare to tell you that it is the Grand Councillor's eldest son, Li Yu, who is Administrator of San-ch'uan, and that the Ch'u brigands, including Ch'en Sheng and others, are all fellows of the prefecture adjacent to (that of the birthplace of) the Grand Councillor. On this account the Ch'u bandits have acted quite openly, and when they traversed San-ch'uan, the Administrator in the city was unwilling to attack them. I have heard that letters pass back and forth between them, but having been unable to make an investigation, I have not ventured (until now) to tell about it.

'The Grand Councillor, moreover, dwells outside (the palace), where his authority is more weighty than that of Your Majesty.'

Erh-shih agreed with what he said, and wished to have the Grand Councillor tried. Fearing, however, lest (the case against him) might not stand investigation, he sent a man to investigate concerning the Administrator of San-ch'uan, as to whether there was ground for the charge of holding communication with the brigands.

At the time when Li Ssu heard of this, Erh-shih was at Kan-ch'uan, where he was witnessing contests of strength and theatricals. Li Ssu failed to obtain an interview, and therefore presented a memorial in order to speak of Chao Kao's shortcomings, saying:

'Your servant has heard that there is no case of a minister deceiving his ruler which has not endangered the state, or of a concubine deceiving her master which has not endangered the home. At the present time there is a great minister who has usurped from Your Majesty both what may be advantageous and disadvantageous, so that between him and Your Majesty there is no distinction. This is extremely inexpedient.

'Of old, when the Minister of Public Works, Tzu Han, was minister of Sung, he administered the punishments himself, applying them with severity. One year later he expelled his prince.

'T'ien Ch'ang was the minister of Duke Chien. His rank was without match in the state, and the wealth of his private household was equal to that of the ducal house. By scattering his favors and exhibiting kindness, he obtained (the goodwill of) the clans below, and of the officials above, and thus secretly gained control of the state of Ch'i. He then killed Tsai Yu in the court and murdered Duke Chien in his audience chamber, so that ultimately he possessed the state of Ch'i. These things are well known in the empire.

'(Chao) Kao's will is at present bent upon evil, and his actions are dangerous and subversive, like those of Tzu Han when he was minister of Sung. The wealth of his private household is like that of the T'ien clan in Ch'i. He is following the seditious ways of T'ien Ch'ang and Tzu Han at the same time, and has snatched from Your Majesty, Your Majesty's awe-inspiring trust. His purpose is similar to that of Han Chi, who became minister of An of Han. If Your Majesty does not take consideration of the matter, your servant fears this man will cause revolt.'

'How can this be!' said Erh-shih. 'It is true that (Chao) Kao was formerly (a mere palace) eunuch; yet he did not exert his ingenuity (merely) with a view to his own peace, nor did he, in face of danger,

By keeping his conduct pure and by practising, he brought himself to this point. He obtained approach to us because of his loyalty, and exercised his position with good faith. We truly esteem him, yet you, sir, doubt him. How is this?

'Moreover, when still being young, we lost our forbear, we were without wisdom and were unaccustomed to ruling the people, whereas you, sir, were old, and, as we feared, out of contact with the empire. So if then we had not attached Lord Chao to ourselves, whom could we have employed? Lord Chao, furthermore, is a man of incorruptible spirit and strong vitality. He understands the natures of the men below and is able to accord with us above. Be you, sir, without doubt on that score.'

'Not so,' replied Li Ssu. 'For (Chao) Kao comes of mean origin. He has no understanding of reason, and his avaricious desires are without satiation. He seeks for profit unceasingly, his rank and power are only second to the ruler, and the pursuit of his desires is without limit. I therefore say that he is dangerous.'

Since Erh-shih had already earlier put his trust in Chao Kao, and since he feared that Li Ssu would kill him, he privately informed Chao Kao. The latter said: 'It is only I whom the Grand Councillor fears. Were I once dead, the Grand Councillor would forthwith wish to do what T'ien Ch'ang did.'

Erh-shih then said: 'As to Li Ssu, let the matter be referred to the Palace Chamberlain.'

Chao Kao then had Li Ssu brought to trial, and Li Ssu was seized and bound and thrown in prison. Raising his eyes to Heaven, he exclaimed with a groan: 'Alas! For an unprincipled ruler, how can one make any plans? Of old, Chieh killed Kuan Lung-feng; Chou killed the King's son, Pi Kan; and Fu Ch'a, King of Wu, killed Wu Tzu-hsu. How were these ministers not loyal? Yet they did not escape death, and when they died their loyalty proved of no avail. My wisdom at the present day does not equal that of these three men, whereas Erh-shih's lack of principle exceeds that of Chieh, Chou and Fu Ch'a. Fitting it is that I should die on account of my loyalty.

'In what, besides, is Erh-shih's government not disordered? Up till now he has already exterminated his elder and younger brothers and established himself. He has executed loyal ministers and honoured base men. For the making of the O-pang palace he has exacted taxes throughout the empire. It is not that I have not remonstrated with him, but he would not listen to me. The Sage-kings of old all had definite rules for their drinking and eating; had a fixed number for their chariots and utensils; and maintained a measure for their palaces and apartments. The issuing of orders for building activities, if they entailed increases in expenditures which would be of no advantage to the public weal, was forbidden. Therefore they were able to govern in peace for a long time.

'But now he has run counter to his elder and younger brothers, without examining if they had guilt, and has executed his loyal ministers one by one, without taking thought of their misfortunes. He has carried out great constructions of palace buildings, and has heavily taxed the empire, without regard for the expenditure. (Because) these three things have gone on, the empire no longer obeys him, and the rebels at the present time already possess half the empire. Yet still his mind has not awakened, so that he makes Chao Kao his assistant. Therefore I shall certainly see the outlaws arrive at Hsien-yang, and deer wandering through the (palace) courts.'

Erh-shih now ordered (Chao) Kao to try the case of the Grand Councillor and determine his offense. (The latter) accused (Li) Ssu and his son, Yu, on the charge of plotting revolt, and he had the kindred and pensioners of both arrested. He ordered (Li) Ssu to be given a flogging of more than one thousand strokes, so that (the latter), unable to endure the pain, falsely confessed (his guilt).

So as not to die, (Li) Ssu undertook to give an exposition of his merits, and to say that he was in truth without seditious intent, thus hoping that with good fortune he might yet be able to submit a memorial of self exposition, and by good grace Erh-shih might yet waken (from his blindness) and pardon him. Hence Li Ssu from within his prison now submitted a memorial which said:

'Your servant has become Grand Councillor, and has administered the people for more than thirty years. When he arrived within Ch'in's narrow confines, during the time of the former King, Ch'in's territory did not exceed one thousand li, and its soldiers did not number more than a hundred thousand. Your servant used his meagre talents to the utmost, carefully establishing laws, secretly sending out plotters, giving them gold and precious stones, and causing them to travel about and advise the feudal lords, and secretly to prepare armor and weapons. He spread the teachings of (imperial) government, gave position to men of arms, honoured meritorious officials, and enriched their ranks and revenues. In this way it was ultimately possible to seize Han, weaken Wei, destroy Yen and Chao, raze Ch'i and Ch'u, and so finally annex the Six States, make captives of their kings, and establish (the King of) Ch'in to be Son of Heaven. This is his crime number one.

'(Although thus Ch'in's) territory was certainly not lacking in extent, he also expelled the Hu and Ho along the north, and imposed rule upon the various Yüeh in the south, thus manifesting Ch'in's power. This is his crime number two.

'He honoured the great ministers and enriched their ranks and positions, so as to strengthen their attachment. This is his crime number three.

'He established the altars of the soil and grain, and repaired the ancestral temple, in order to make his ruler's merit illustrious. This is his crime number four.

'He reformed harmful policies, equalized the *tou* and *hu* measures, the measures of weight and size, and the written characters (*wen chang*), and made these universal throughout the empire, thus crime number five.

'He laid out imperial highways and inaugurated (imperial) tours of inspection, in order to show (to the people) that their ruler had attained to his every desire. This is his crime number six.

'He relaxed the punishments and reduced the collection of taxes, in order to further his ruler's (efforts to) win the hearts of the masses, so that the people might honour their ruler and not forget him after death. This is his crime number seven.

'The crimes of one who, as a minister, behaved as (Li) Ssu had done, would certainly have merited death already long ago; yet the Emperor has been gracious enough to make use of his ability to the utmost even unto the present time. May it please Your Majesty to look into the matter.'

When the memorial was sent up, Chao Kao sent a clerk to reject it (as not fit) to be presented, saying: 'How can a prisoner be allowed to submit a memorial?' Chao Kao then sent from among his pensioners some ten odd men who pretended to be assistants of visiting imperial secretaries, come again to conduct (Li) Ssu's interrogation. And when (Li) Ssu again replied with the truth, (Chao Kao) immediately ordered men to flog him anew.

Later when Erh-shih sent men to examine (Li) Ssu, the latter believed that it would go as before, and so to the end he did not dare to alter his statements, but admitted his guilt. When this fact was submitted to the emperor, Erh-shih said delightedly: 'If it were not for Lord Chao, I should nearly have been sold by the Grand Councillor.'

By the time the person sent by Erh-shih to examine the Administrator of San-ch'uan had arrived there, Hsiang Liang had already arrested and executed him. On his return, the delegate, together with officials who had served under the Grand Councillor, and with Chao Kao, all falsely made a report of sedition (against Li Yu).

In the seventh month of the second year of Erh-shih (July 30 to August 27, 208 B.C.), they prepared the five punishments for Li Ssu and he was condemned to be cut in two at the waist upon the market-place of Hsien-yang. While Li Ssu was being taken out from the prison together with his second son, he looked at him and said: 'Even if I and you wished once more to lead a yellow dog and go together out of the east gate of Shang-ts'ai in pursuit of the crafty hare, could we indeed do so?' Thereupon father and son both wept. (Their execution was followed by) the extermination of their kindred to the third degree.

Once Li Ssu was dead, Erh-shih conferred on Chao Kao the post of Grand Councillor, and all affairs both big and small were decided by the latter. (In order to) find out how far his authority carried, (Chao) Kao now presented a deer (to Erh-shih), the while calling it a horse. Erh-shih then inquired of those about him, 'But this is a deer.' His entourage all replied: 'It is a horse.' Believing that he was suffering from some delusion, Erh-shih became alarmed and summoned the Great Diviner to prognosticate the matter.

The Great Diviner said: 'When performing the suburban sacrifices in spring and autumn, and making offerings in the ancestral temple and to spiritual beings, Your Majesty has not been pure in his fasting, and that is why he has come to this. He should rely upon his abundant virtue and be pure in his fasting.'

(Erh-shih) then went to Shang-lin to fast. There he every day went out hunting. Once there happened to be a traveller who entered Shang-lin, and Erh-shih shot an arrow and killed him. Chao Kao thereupon instructed his son-in-law, the prefect of Hsien-yang, Yen Yo, to prosecute, no matter how, the person who had killed the man passing through Shang-lin. (Chao) Kao then reproved Erh-shih, saying: 'The Son of Heaven has killed an innocent man without cause. Such is forbidden by God (*Shang ti*), and (is reason enough for) spiritual beings not to accept (your sacrifices). Moreover, Heaven will be sending down calamities for this. You must go far away from the palace in order to make a sacrifice so as to ward off the evil.'

Erh-shih then went to stay in the Wang-i palace. After he had been there three days, Chao Kao deceitfully summoned the guard, and commanded the soldiers to put on ordinary clothes, take their weapons, and enter the palace. He (then) entered to report (the matter) to Erh-shih, saying: 'The bandit-forces from east of the mountains have all come!' Erh-shih, having mounted a pavilion, saw them, and was smitten with terror. (Chao) Kao seized the opportunity to force him to commit suicide. Then he took the imperial seal and hung it from his own girdle. But of the officials around him, none would follow him, and when he ascended the audience hall, three persons there wished to do him harm. (Chao) Kao himself realized that Heaven refused to grant him (the empire), and that the body of officials would not consent. Hence he summoned a younger brother of Shih-huang, and conferred on him the imperial seal.

Having acceded to his position, Tzu-ying was afraid of (Chao Kao). Hence, saying that he was ill, he did not attend to (state) matters, but together with a eunuch named Han T'an, and his sons, plotted to kill Chao (Kao). When the latter came on a visit to ask about his illness, he invited him to enter. Then he commanded Han T'an to stab him to death. (Chao Kao's) kindred were exterminated to the third degree.

Tzu-ying had held the throne for three months when the soldiers of the Duke of P'ei arrived at Hsien-yang from the Wu pass. The ministers and officials all threw off their allegiance and did not resist, and Tzu-ying, accompanied by his wife and sons, bound his neck with a silken cord and made his submission near Chih-tao. Thereupon the Duke of P'ei handed him over to the officials (to be tried), but King Hsiang, on his arrival, decapitated (Tzu-ying). And thus it is that (Ch'in) lost the empire.

The Great Astrologer says:

'Li Ssu went forth from his simple hamlet among the feudal lords, and entered the service of Ch'in. He used their mistakes to assist Shih-huang, and eventually brought to realization for him the imperial heritage. (Li) Ssu himself became one of the Three High Dignitaries, which may be called honourable employment. Although he knew what the purport was (of the teaching) of the Six Disciplines, yet he paid no attention to enlightened government, with which to patch up the defects of his ruler. He seized the greatest of positions and revenues for himself, gave his assent to immoral associations, and was relentlessly severe and tyrannical in his punishments. He paid heed to (Chao) Kao's evil words, voided the proper succession, and established on the throne a prince of the second rank. Then when the feudal lords had

already revolted, (Li) Ssu wished to remonstrate. Was this not late?
Men all think that (Li) Ssu underwent the five punishments and died
because he was the acme of loyalty. On examining the fundamentals
of the matter, however, I find myself at variance with the common
criticism. But for this (lack of loyalty), (Li) Ssu's merit would have
been in a class with that of Chou and Shoa.'

From Ssu-ma Chien to Ssu-ma Kuang

We must conclude that the work of Ssu-ma Chien made a deep
impression even upon his own generation. His success assured that
the record in consecutive narratives of succeeding reigns would be
continued. Pan Piao (班彪) (A.D. 3-54) at first planned to do a second
universal history of China, but, the work he planned was mostly done
by his son Pan Ku (班固) (A.D. 32-92) and daughter Pan Chao (班超).
They believed that the task of the historian should be the record of
one dynasty. The Pan family may be credited with the model of the
dynastic history. That model became the standard of historiography
for almost two thousand years. In part the ideal of the dynastic history
was based upon their criticism of Ssu-ma Chien's reconstruction of
ancient times. Pan Ku describes his writing of the *Shih Chi* as 'a
treading of his way through the classics and commentaries, and as
galloping up and down from the past to the present,' covering a period
of several thousand years. He adds that Ssu-ma Chien at times strayed
rather far from the judgment of Confucius (*Han Shu* 62:22a).
Here are the clues to the concept of a 'Standard' dynastic history:
1. It should be the record of a particular dynasty. It should be written
immediately after the end of the dynasty so that all the necessary
information will be available. 2. It should preserve the history of a
dynasty as a unit. Therefore it will avoid the dangerous generalizations
which Ssu-ma Chien was supposed to have made. 3. Its form should
be based upon the *Spring and Autumn Classic* interpreted as a
Confucian document. This would insure a standard form and provide
the proper basis for criticism (praise and blame). The Pans, therefore,
avoided the evils of 'universal history' and the subjectivity of the
historian. In so doing, they bound Chinese historiography to the notion
of the repetitive dynastic cycle which tended to conceal the dynamics

of Chinese experience. Dynastic histories tended to ignore the cultural vitalities which are not confined to the limits of a particular dynasty. The style of writing tended to conform to the concept of the task, and hence lost the liveliness of narrative. Events were reduced to items to be listed as separate units related to the seasons and days of the *Spring and Autumn Classic*. Therefore the sequence and interrelations of events came to be fixed in time and ordered in significance by the pattern of metaphysical elements rather than to follow the natural historical relation and significance of the events themselves. In the worst of the dynastic histories we have little more than chronology superimposed upon an astrological chart. Even in the best, astrology and the 'standard' forms, based on *Spring and Autumn Classic,* are given too much importance. They inhibit the use of narration as a vehicle of meaningful historical expression.

Though Ssu-ma Kuang (司馬光) revived the concept of 'universal history' and produced the second great general history of China, his *Tzu Chih T'ung Chien* (資治通鑑) often betrays the strong tradition of dynastic formalism. In the record of the romantic age of the Three Kingdoms at the point of the highly dramatic abdication by the Han emperor in favour of Wen-Huang-ti (文皇帝) we find this lifeless passage which is typical of the whole body of official historiogaphy.

> 69:13. Second month. On *ting-wei* (丁未) the sun was eclipsed.
> 14. On *jen-hsu* (壬戌), Chia Hsu (賈詡) was appointed to be Grand Marshal.
> 15. On *ting-mao* (丁卯), King Wu (武王) was buried in the tomb of Kao-ling (高陵).

For the most part the *Han Shu* reproduced the material of the *Shih Chi*. There is, however, one important source of dynastic history that appears to have had its beginning in the later Han. This was the institution of the court recorder who kept the *Diaries of Action and Repose*, the day to day records of the words and action of the Emperor. It is explained centuries later that the official historian sometimes stood in relation to the emperor as did the Hebrew prophet to his king. In other words, the historian was the conscience of the court. He made note of the daily words and deeds of the Emperor, summing up sometimes in somber fulness the grounds of Heaven's indignation which justified the transfer to other hands of the mandate to rule. In China the voice of conscience was seldom as articulate as the prophetic word in Israel. It was, however, powerful. It would

remind later generations of the failures and accomplishments (the folly
and wisdom) of a particular emperor. From the later Han through the
T'ang (唐), these records were probably not subject to imperial censor.
Two passages from *Tzu-chih t'ung-chien* support the thesis that
historians in the Sung Dynasty (宋朝) still jealously guarded the integrity
of their office against imperial interference:

> 196:8a: The year 642, Summer, 4th month.   The Emperor T'ai-tsung
> (太宗) spoke to the Imperial Censor Ch'u Sui-liang (褚遂良), saying: 'Since
> you, Sir, are in charge of the *Diaries of Action and Repose,* may I see what
> you have written?' Sui-liang replied: 'The historiographers record the
> words and deeds of the ruler of men, noting down all that is good and
> bad, in hopes that the ruler will not dare to do evil.   But it is unheard of
> that the ruler himself should see what is written.'   The emperor said: 'If
> I do something that is not good, do you then also record it?' Sui-liang
> replied: 'My office is to wield the brush.   How could I dare not record it?'
> To the Gentleman of the Yellow Gate Liu Chi (劉洎) added: Even if Sui-liang
> failed to record it, everyone else in the empire would; to which the emperor
> replied: 'true.'

> 246:6b: The year 839, Winter, 10th month, The Emperor Wen-tsung
> (文宗) went to the Official in Charge of the *Diaries of Action and Repose,*
> Wei Mo (魏謩), picked up his notes and began looking at them.   Wei Mo
> objected, saying: 'The *Diaries of Action and Repose* record both good and
> bad in order to warn and admonish the ruler of men.   Your Majesty should
> only strive to do good.   It is not necessary that Your Majesty see the
> records.'   The emperor said: 'Once before I looked at them.'   'That,' replied
> Wei Mo, 'was the fault of the official in charge of history at that time. If
> Your Majesty were to examine the records personally, the historiographers
> would be forced to distort or alter their accounts.   Then how could we
> expect later ages to put any faith in them?'   With this the emperor desisted.

A brief, I think, could be made for a check-and-balance relation
between the court and the historian. For the most part dynastic history
was made by emperors, empresses, and chancellors of the Legalist
stamp.   These were strong men and women whose dream of empire
and whose realistic design of action were bound to collide with Confucian
conservatism. The historians on the other hand were committed to
the Confucian criterion of 'praise and blame,' Shang Yang, Ch'in
Shih-huang-ti, Han Wu Ti, Wang Mang, Kuang Wu Ti (光武帝) Chin
Wu Ti (晉武帝), T'ang Tai-tsung, (唐太宗) Empress Wu (武則天) and Wang
An-shih (王安石) were all rulers who acted, if they did not speak, in
agreement with the political philosophy of Han Fei Tzu.   These made
history. Those who judged that history were Confucian.   The historians

lived by a kind of faith in the orderliness of all things under Heaven. They believed in the rightness of the virtues of antiquity, of that golden age in the beginning, whose ways would be vindicated in each dynastic cycle. Thus the record of the triumphs of these virtues was sacred history. So Wang O (王鶚) wrote: 'Since antiquity, a state can be destroyed but not its history.' T'ai-tsu (太祖), the first Ming (明) emperor, also agreed that, 'History marks success and failure and offers a lesson of encouragement or warning.'

This is the heart of Chinese historiography—a veritable record of the past as sacred and immortal, and a vindication of propriety as the proper relation of man to man according to the relation of earth to Heaven, and of man to earth and to Heaven. For the writing of history there is this mandate: that the record shall be veritable and that it shall be clear.

The first of the few who were primarily concerned with the 'theory of historical method' was Liu Chih-chi (劉知幾 A.D. 661-721). He was blessed with the curse of genius—the curse of seeing those things to which his contemporaries were blind. Professor Pulleyblank points up his youthful conviction that important scholarship lay along the lines of historical studies rather than the classics. The following is Pulleyblank's translation of an autobiographical section of the *Shih-t'ung* (史通).

When I was a child I received instruction from my father and early began to make excursions into the field of letters. When I was still of an age to wear an embroidered jacket and white silk trousers I was given the Book of Documents in Ancient Characters (*Ku-wen Shang-shu* 古文尚書) to read but I always had trouble with its difficult phrases and found it hard to recite. Though I was frequently beaten I did not master it. When I used to hear my father expounding for my brothers the *Spring and Autumn Annals* with the Tradition of Tso (Tso chuan 左氏傳), I would put aside my own book and listen. After the lesson was over I would explain it to my brothers. I sighed to myself and said, 'If all books were like this I would not be lazy any more.' My father thought this unusual and thereupon began to teach me the Tso Tradition. In a year he had expounded it all and I could recite it. At that time I was just 12 years old. Although I had no deep understanding of it, yet I could roughly give the main sense. My father and brothers wished me to study all the subcommentaries and explanations and become perfect in the words of this one classic. I declined because I had not learned of matters later than the Capture of the Unicorn (the end of the *Spring and Autumn Annals*) and I begged to be allowed to read the other books of this category in order to broaden my knowledge. Next I read the Records of the Historian (*Shih-chi*), the History of the

Former Han Dynasty (*Han-shu* 漢書) and the History of the Three Kingdoms (*San-kuo chih* 三國志). When I wished to know the continuities and changes and how successive events had followed one another from ancient times to the present, I attacked the whole class (of historical writing) and without instruction down to the Veritable Records of the present dynasty. By the time I was seventeen my reading was fairly comprehensive. The books I read were largely borrowed or hired. Though some of the rolls were imperfect and there were missing portions, I knew fairly well the main course of events andt he outline of the words. (*Shih-t'ung t'ung-shih* 史通通釋 10.11a.b)

Historians appear to be people who prefer action but are relegated to the duller task of thought—the contemplation of action. Liu Chih-chi was an unhappy youth. He found himself bound to the tedious duties of registrar of Huo-chia (獲嘉) county in the Huai Prefecture (懷州). Like clerks in London who write letters to the Times, he wrote memorials to the Empress. Confucius was his model, and he desired to emulate the sage by collecting and editing all that had been written from the beginning of the later Han to his own time. But he had not Confucius' courage:

I feared that if I were rashly to carry out the example of Confucius without having Confucius' reputation I would startle vulgar opinion and be blamed by my contemporaries, receiving no thanks for my trouble. Whenever I took my writing brush in hand I would sigh irresolutely, and so it went on. It was not that I wanted to do something beyond my powers. It was really within my powers, but I did not dare to do it. (*Shih-t'ung t'ung-shih* 10.12b)

We are indebted to Liu Chih-chi for his deeply personal insight into the difficulties of an official dynastic record. He gave five good reasons why he could not continue as a member of the official team of historians who were charged with the task of writing the record of the reign of Empress Wu.

1. Whereas the great histories of former times were written by one man, now the practice of collective compilation has grown up. Everything has to be scrutinized and passed back and forth and nothing is ever decided.

2. In the Former Han Dynasty all documents from provincial authorities went first to the archivist before being sent to the Chief Minister; but nowadays it is very difficult for historians to get access to any government documents.

3. In ancient times historians made their words public and were not

afraid to risk the displeasure of the mighty. More recently it has been customary to write histories in secret within the palace in order to avoid importuning by interested persons; but in fact, with the large number of those engaged in history, this has meant that it has become impossible to write anything critical of a person in authority without his immediately knowing and objecting.

4. In ancient times historians writing privately had a free hand in establishing their own working standards. Now high-placed officials jointly supervise and give contradictory instructions.

5. If there must be overseers their proper function should be to divide up and allocate tasks; but not even this is being done and the historians are left to idle away their time doing nothing.

Liu Chih-chi was searching for a way to insure the writing of accurate records. He wanted an approved system that would be safe from the influences of the emperor, his officials, the other historians, or any other enemies of truth.

When man takes from between heaven and earth his life is brief as a mayfly in the world, as the white colt crossing the gap (i.e. the sun crossing the sky—a single day). Yet he is ashamed not to achieve meritorious deeds during his lifetime and hates to perish without leaving a name. From emperors and kings down to poor commoners, from courtiers near the throne to distant wayfarers in the mountains and forests, there is none that does not work and strive for merit and fame. Why is this? It is that they think to create an imperishable thing. And what is it that can be called imperishable? It is only to have one's name recorded on bamboo and silk. If formerly the world had been without bamboo and silk, if there had been no history officers at the time, then whether it was a question of sages such as Yao and Shun, Yin I and Chou Kung, or of villains such as Chieh (桀), Chou (紂), Wang Mang and Tung Cho (董卓), whether virtuous men like (Po) i (夷) and Liu-hsia Hui (柳下惠) or bandits such as Tao (Chih) (跖) and Chuang (Ch'iao) (蹻), whether parricides such as Shang (Ch'en) (商) and Mao (Tun) (冒) or filial sons such as Tseng (Shen) (曾) and Min (Sun) (閔), once they had followed the mutability of things, even before the earth had dried on their grave mounds, good and bad would have been indistinguishable, beautiful and ugly would have perished forever. But if history officers are not lacking, if bamboo and silk survive, then though the man himself has perished, vanished into the void, his deeds are as if present, bright as the Milky Way. So scholars who come after can open the wrappers and boxes (which hold the books) and meet in spirit the men of antiquity, without leaving their own houses they can exhaust a thousand ages. When they see a worthy example they think of emulation, when they see an unworthy one, they examine themselves within—just as unruly sons were afraid when the *Spring and Autumn Annals* were completed, and the deeds of rebellious subjects were recorded when *Nan-shih* (南史) came. Such is the way in which deeds and words are recorded, such is the way in which they encourage good and reprove evil. From this we see that the advantages of history are very great. For that which living men strive for marks out the vital path for the state. Can those who have the governance of states neglect it? (*Shih-t'ung t'ung-shih* 11.1a,b)

Liu Chih-chi was no radical who desired to write a new kind of history. Thoroughly Confucian, thoroughly imbued with the spirit of dynastic historiography, thoroughly committed to the ideal of empire and to the responsibility of meting out praise and blame, he strove against the grain to insure an accurate record.

In the 'Chinese renaissance' (T'ang and Sung) we find a revival of interest in the writing of topical historical essays. These were in some respects the most valuable, and to the modern scholar the best, historical writing of that period. Such special studies had a distinguished model in the 'treatises' and 'biographies' of Ssu-ma Chien. We should recall that Pan Ku also added to his annals a number of such essays and that the dynastic histories were frequently topical in outline. Probably the most valuable collection of 'monographs' is found in the *T'ung Tien* (通典) of Tu Yu (杜佑 A.D. 735-812). This extensive collection (200 chapters), known in the West as *The General Institutions*, might be called an institutional history of China or an encyclopedia of Chinese political and social science. It is interesting to note that Tu Yu was influenced by the Legalists and that his purpose seems to have been to provide a useful manual on the kind of information that he deemed essential to the well informed discussion of practical statecraft. Somewhat more conventional and formal was the definitive reference work of 'the thousand chapters'—the *Encyclopedia of 977*. Quite in contrast to Tu Yu's work were the two great compilations of On-yang Hsiu (歐陽修) in the eleventh century. On-yang was the ideal figure of the Confucian statesman. He was both scholar and successful man of affairs, His devotion to antiquity led him to write in the ancient *ku-wen* (古文) style. Perhaps the most valuable contribution of his historiography was his concern for inclusiveness. He believed that history must extend beyond politics to literature, including fiction. Serious historical writing need not exclude the 'gossip of the past.' He valued anecdotes that relieved the sheer monotony of the orthodox annalistic 'chronologies'. But he remained in the tradition of the Confucian historian, the retrospective judge of the court and the scholar, according to their measure of conformity to classical virtues as the reflection of a past perfection.

Ssu-ma Kuang

The greatest work of the Sung historians, probably the best known Chinese history in the West, was Ssu-ma Kuang's comprehensive *Tzu-chih t'ung-chien* (General Mirror). The work begins with the Warring States (戰國 403 B.C.) and concludes with the events of the inauguration of the Sung (A.D. 959). This huge labour grew out of Ssu-ma Kuang's own suggestion that there was a need for a comprehensive history to be used by the emperor himself. Former monographic treatises and even the standard histories did not present a clear picture of the course of past dynasties, the problems encountered and the decisions taken. They lacked the power to impress by the long sweep of the whole political and cultural past, and they did not provide the facility of easy reference. It was this long sweep of China's past, and the pattern of dynastic succession, confirming the Confucian notion of the character of importance, that inspired the work. Ssu-ma Kuang first submitted a kind of prospectus, the *Li-nien t'u* (曆年圖 *The Chart of Successive Years*) to Ying-tsung (英宗) in 1064. Two years later (1066) the order was given to fulfill the monumental task of compiling from the vast literature of annals, treatises and biographies one accurate record. In his reply to the order, Ssu-ma Kuang underlines the purpose and philosophy of history.

> *Hsü tzu-chih t'ung-chien ch'ang-pien* (資治通鑑長編續) 208:2: Since I was a child I have ranged through all the histories. It has appeared to me that in the annal-biography form the words are diffuse and numerous so that even an erudite specialist who reads them again and again cannot comprehend and sort them out; how much the more, though a prince amid his ten thousand daily concerns must wish to know comprehensively the merits and demerits of former ages, will it be difficult for him to accomplish his desire. Disregarding my inadequacy I have constantly wished to write a chronological history roughly in accordance with the form of the Tso Tradition, starting with the Warring States and going down to the Five Dynasties, drawing on other books besides the Official Histories and taking in all that a prince ought to know——everything pertaining to the rise and fall of dynasties and the good and ill fortune of the common people, and good and bad examples that can furnish models and warnings.

It is said that the Emperor himself supplied the full title of the work. It was both descriptive of the plan of the project and supported

its purpose: *The Comprehensive Mirror for Aid in Government.* Two
points underlying Ssu-ma Kuang's manifesto on historiography show
how far history as a separate discipline had progressed from astrology.
They highlight the contrast of the Han and the Sung historians: 1.
History is not a subdivision of astrology. It has its own internal
pattern and its own laws. 2. It is the task of the historian to record,
in so far—and no further—than he is able on the basis of the evidence,
what did happen, when it happened and what was the result. It is
the duty of the historian to render judgment but it should not be
private judgment and it must derive from universally accepted norms
of Confucian orthodoxy. Such judgment is the purpose of history, the
lesson of history, but it is not a justification for re-writing history in
order to make the lesson clearer.

> *Tzu-chih t'ung-chien* 69:7-8: your servant Kuang observes: Heaven gave
> birth to the multitudes of people. But conditions make it impossible for
> them to govern themselves, so that they must have a ruler to govern over
> them. Anyone who is able to prevent violence and remove harm from the
> people so that their lives are protected, who can reward good and punish
> evil and thus avoid disaster—such a man may be called a ruler. Thus before
> the Three Dynasties the feudal lords had a countless number of states, and
> anyone who had subjects and possessed altars to the soil and grain went
> by the name of ruler. But he who united all these countless states and who
> set up laws and issued commands which no one dared to disobey was called
> king. When the power of the king declined, there were rulers of strong
> states who were able to lead the other feudal lords and enforce respect
> for the Son of Heaven and such were called 'overlords.' Thus since ancient
> times there have been instances when the world was in disorder and the
> feudal lords contended with each other for power, and for a number of
> generations there was no king at all.
>
> After Ch'in had burned the books and buried the Confucianists alive,
> the Han arose, and at this time scholars first began to propound the theory
> of how the five agents produce and overcome each other according to
> which the Ch'in was an 'intercalary' reign coming between those of wood
> (Chou) and fire (Han), ruled by an overlord and not by a true king. Thus
> began the theory of legitimate and intercalary dynasties. After the House
> of Han was overthrown, the Three Kingdoms ruled simultaneously like the
> legs of a tripod. Then the Chin (晉) lost its control of the empire and
> the five barbarian tribes swarmed in. From the time of the Sung and the
> Northern Wei (北魏), north and south were divided politically. Each had
> its own dynastic histories which disparaged the other, the south calling the
> north 'slaves with bound hair,' the north calling the south 'island barbarians.'
> When Chu Ch'uan-Chung (朱全忠) succeeded to the T'ang the empire was
> once again rent to pieces, but when the Chu-yeh (朱邪) clan entered Pien

〈汴〉and overthrew him they compared him to the ancient usurpers YL and Wang Mang and discarded completely the chronology of his dynasty. All these are examples of biased phraseology based on personal interest and do not represent enlightened and just opinions.

Your servant, being stupid, is surely not qualified to know anything about the legitimate and intercalary dynasties of former times. But he would be bold enough to consider that unless rulers were able to unite the nine provinces under one government, although they all bore the name of Son of Heaven there was no reality behind it. Although distinctions may be made on the basis of the fact that one dynasty was Chinese and another foreign, one humane and another tyrannical or that they differed in size and power, yet essentially they were just the same as the various feudal states of ancient times. How can we single out one state for honour and call it the legitimate successor, and consider all the rest as false or usurpers?

Or are we to make virtuous ways the criterion of legitimacy? But even the tiniest state must sometimes have its good sovereigns while in the declining days of the Three Dynasties there were surely unrighteous kings. Thus from ancient times to the present these theories of legitimate dynasties have never possessed the kind of logic sufficient to compel men to accept them without question.

Now your servant in his narrative has sought only to trace the rise and fall of the various states and make clear the people's times of joy and sorrow so that the reader may select for himself what is good and what is bad, what profitable and what unprofitable, for his own encouragement, and warning. He has no intention of setting up standards of praise and blame in the manner of the *Spring and Autumn Annals* which could compel a disorderly age to return to just ways.

As the work progressed, once again there arose a contest between the Legalist and progressive minister (Wang An-shih) and the Confucian historian. Again for the moment the scholar was driven from the field of action into the retirement from which he contemplated the action of the past. But the last word in this contest also was that of the historian. For good or ill the reforms of Wang An-shih were judged to have been contrary to that precept for the 'renewal of the people' which was the lesson of history and, hence, the ultimate weapon of the historian—the weapon the historians themselves had forged and, over the long course from Ssu-ma Chien to Ssu-ma Kuang, had themselves perfected.

Tzu-chih-t'ung-chien 69 [Chronicle of Wei (魏)]: Shih Tsu Wen-Huang-ti (世祖文皇帝):

First Year of Huang-ch'u (黃初) (A.D. 220) Twelfth month.

42. The imperial palace was being built in Lo-yang (洛陽). On the day wu-wu (戊午) the Emperor went to Lo-yang.

43. The Emperor said to the Grand Chamberlain Su Tse (蘇則): 'Some time ago, after Chiu-ch'uan (酒泉) and Chang Yeh (張掖) were conquered, the Western Regions sent envoys to Tun-huang (燉煌) to offer me a large pearl, one inch in diameter. Do you think I can get some more of them through purchase?'

Tse replied: 'If Your Majesty's benign influence pervades China and your virtue overflows to the desert, they will come to you without your ever seeking for them. There is no glory in obtaining them through seeking after them.' The Emperor did not answer a word.

44. The Emperor summoned the Commandant of the Eastern Guard Chiang Chi (蔣濟) to the capital and appointed him Chamberlain. At that time he had addressed to the General of the Forces for Southern Expedition Hsia-hou Shang (夏侯尚) an edict which read: 'Because you are my trusted and esteemed general, I empower you with special privileges. Your benevolent heart is ample for my service; your affection for me is worth my cherishing. You may display terrors or confer favours, you may kill or let live.' Shang showed the edict to Chi.

When Chi came, the Emperor asked what he had recently heard and seen. He replied: 'Nothing good, certainly. On the contrary I have heard words that could bring doom to the dynasty.'

The Emperor coloured and grew angry, demanding an explanation. Chi told him the details and went on to expostulate: 'The *Shu* expressly warns against displaying terrors and conferring favours. The ancients saw to it that 'a son of Heaven does not speak playfully.' I beg Your Majesty to reflect on this.'

Thereupon the Emperor sent a messenger to retrieve the edict in question.

45. The Emperor wished to move a hundred thousand households of soldiers from Chi-chou (冀州) to Ho-nan (河南). At this time, due to drought and a plague of locusts, the people were suffering from famine. Various officials of the Court disapproved of this measure, but the Emperor's mind was set on it. The Grand Chamberlain Hsin P'i (辛毗), together with other court officials, requested an audience with the Emperor. Knowing well that they intended to remonstrate with him on this score, the Emperor wore a vexed expression when he received them. No one else dared to speak; P'i, however, said, 'Your Majesty intends to move the

households of the soldiers. What is your aim?'

The Emperor asked him, 'Do you mean to say that you disapprove my moving them?' P'i affirmed, 'I definitely disapprove.' The Emperor said, 'I am not going to discuss the matter with you.'

To this P'i said, 'Your Majesty, not considering me unworthy, has made me one of your attendants and appointed me one of your counsellors. How can you now be unwilling to discuss the matter with me? It is not of private nature, but concerns the dynasty itself. Why should you be vexed at me?'

Without answering, the Emperor rose from his seat and went inside. P'i followed him, pulling him back by the lapel of his coat; the Emperor shook himself loose and would not return. After a long while he finally came out and said: 'Tso-chih (佐治), how you did harass me!'

P'i said: 'Should you move these households, you will lose their affection; and besides, you cannot feed them. That is why I could not help braving your vexation and contended as hard as I could.'

In the end the Emperor moved half the original number.

On one occasion, when the Emperor went out of his palace to shoot pheasants, he turned to his attendants and exclaimed, 'How delightful this pheasant shooting is!' P'i replied, 'Delightful indeed to your Majesty, but very burdensome to all your subjects.' The Emperor did not utter a word, but thereafter did not go out so frequently, because of him.

Seventh Year of Huang-ch'u (A.D. 226)

11. Summer, fifth month. The Emperor was gravely ill, and appointed Jui (叡) as the Crown prince.

12. On the day *ping-ch'en* (丙辰) the Emperor summoned to his presence Ts'ao Chen (曹眞), Ch'en Ch'un (陳羣), Ts'ao Hsiu (曹休), and Ssu-ma I (司馬懿). All these received an imperial testament appointing them to serve as guardian regents.

13. On the day *ting-ssu* (丁巳) the Emperor passed away.

14. Ch'en Shou's (陳壽) commentary reads: 'Wen-ti was endowed by nature with literary talent; to compose, he had only to apply his writing-brush. He was widely read and had a strong memory; his talents and accomplishments were equally comprehensive. Had he added to these a quality of breadth and greatness, and given encouragement through sincere

fairness, and given encouragement exerting his will to preserve the Way and broaden his power and heart, he would hardly have been far removed from the worthy sovereigns of antiquity.'

15. The Crown prince ascended the imperial throne and issued a general amnesty. He honoured the Empress Dowager as Grand Empress Dowager and the Empress as Empress Dowager, and conferred various ranks and enfeoffments on the different officials.

16. Now while in the Eastern Palace, Ming-ti (明帝) did not make friends with the court officials, nor inquire into politics, but devoted himself solely to books. After he mounted the throne the officials were all eager to know more about him. After some days he received singly in audience Liu Yeh (劉曄). They conversed the whole day, the crowd listening outside. When Yeh came out, they asked what he was like. Yeh said: 'He is on a par with Ch'in Shih-huang and Han Hsiao-Wu (漢孝武); his talent and capacity are in no way inferior to theirs.'

17. When the Emperor first took charge of the government, Ch'en Ch'un sent up a memorial saying, 'The *Shih* (詩) says,

> Take your pattern from King Wen (文王).
> And the myriad regions will repose confidence in you.

It also says,

> And his example acted on his wife,
> Extended to his brethren,
> And was felt by all the clans and states.

'The Way begins with the close by, and the transformation to good permeates the whole empire. Now, war gear and weapons have not been laid down since the disorders, and the people are unacquainted with the foundation of royal instruction; I am much afraid it will fall into decay. Your Majesty finds himself in the midst of the greatness of the flourishing Wei dynasty (魏朝), having inherited the work of your two ancestors. The whole empire looks to you to bring about good government. You have only to revere virtue to spread moral transformation, and show benevolence toward the people as a whole; then all will be surpassingly fortunate for the multitudes.

Now if officials but echo each other's opinion, right and wrong will become confused, and this will be a great calamity for the state. If they are not in harmony with each other, there will be enmity among them; if there is enmity among them, slander and praise will be indiscriminate. If slander and praise are indiscriminate, true and false will be confused, These are things which must be looked into thoroughly.'

3

ISRAELITE

HISTORIOGRAPHY

Historical Outline

ONE WAY OF LOOKING at the historiography of the ancient
Israelites would be like looking at Hong Kong from a space ship one
hundred miles above the earth.   You would see so much—almost all
of China, Japan, the Philippines, Taiwan, Malaysia, Thailand, Burma
and Indonesia. Hong Kong would be a tiny dot, just like a dot on a
map.   Some 'world historians' give us that kind of view of ancient
Israel—a tiny country 150 miles from North to South and about 70
miles from East to West not nearly as large in population as Hong
Kong.   From this viewpoint it was only a small nation involved for
a brief period in the golden age of the Ancient Near East.   Egypt
was a great nation with a substantial empire from 3000 to 300 B.C.
Mesopotamia with its Sumerian, Akkadian, Assyrian and Babylonian
Empires was a great political and cultural power center for three
thousand years.   The Israelite Monarchy lasted less than five hundred
years, from 1004 to 586 B.C.   At its height, under David and Solomon
from 1004 to 926 B.C. during a brief political vacuum in the Near
East, it had a tiny empire 200 by 150 miles, including the smaller
states of Aram, Ammon, Moab and Edom.   In Toynbee's history, Israel
is just an insignificant and passing ripple upon the small ocean of Near
Eastern history.

Israelite-Philistine Invasion of Palestine	1250-1175
Growth of Syriac Civilization	1150- 926
Syriac Time of Troubles (Age of the Prophets)	926- 538
Syriac Universal State (Persia)	538- 332

Another way of looking at Israel is to see it as a part of the remote

past. Roughly the Age of the Patriarchs (Abraham to Moses) was that
of the Shang Dynasty (商朝). Moses lived before or during the Yin
(殷). David and Solomon were contemporaries of Chou Mu Wang (周穆王).
Jehu overthrew the Omri Dynasty in the North the same year that
Chou Li Wang (周厲王) died. The fall of Samaria (end of the Northern
Kingdom) came in the first year of the Spring and Autumn Period.
Confucius wrote and taught after the destruction of Jerusalem. The
reconstruction of Israel as a cultural and religious, though non-political,
community under Ezra occurred just at the beginning of the Period of
Warring States. The whole course of Israel's monarchial history fits
into the span of the Western and Eastern Chou (西周及東周). The Old
Testament books had received their final editing by the time of Han
Wu Ti, when Chinese historiography began with Ssu-ma Chien. The
final arrangement of books in the sacred canon of the Old Testament
received conciliar authorization during the reign of Han Ho Ti (漢和帝),
at the Council of Jamnia (c. A.D. 100).

Israelite history has two great portals supported like a suspension
bridge in the center by the historical fact of the monarchy of David
(1004-961) and Solomon (961-929). The first of these portals was the
experience of Israel under Moses. At this time the several Jacob clans
were bound together as a people of the covenant with Yahweh at Sinai.
They had thereby become a special people—the people of God (*Kahal
Yahweh*). They became Yahweh's agent, through whom he would
accomplish his purpose in history. The other portal was the new covenant
proclaimed by Ezra to the returned exiles in Jerusalem. According to
this covenant, a New Israel, no longer as a nation, but as a new
community of priests should let its light of devotion shine before the
nations that all might see its good works and glorify the king of Heaven.

Sinai was the portal not only to the future but also to the past.
It made clear God's purpose in the creation of man, and it was the
interpretive experience that made the whole past meaningful — not
only Israel's past but the whole of human history. It was the event
for which all history had been the preparation.

The futility of human experience (the long story of the tragedy of
man's existence, the mythic apologies for man's failure to create meaning
and win through to permanence, the cycles of the rise and fall of men
and societies, the mythic theme of the eternally perishing) is not the
last word in history. It is indeed not history but the prelude to history.
It is the record of the progressive self destruction of man going apart
from God, and hence from his fellowmen and from the meaning of

human existence. This is the record from Adam to Noah. There was the rebellion of the first man, Adam, and then the brokenness between the vicious cycles of brute force spending itself in sensualism. History begins with God's decision to redeem his creation by creating a history, by choosing and training one people to accomplish his purpose. The meaningless cycles go on, but within them now appeared the bearers of promise. Against the background of the ethnic divisions of mankind (Ham's descendants—African Peoples, Japheth's descendants—European Peoples, and Shem's descendants—Oriental-Semitic Peoples), and of the brokenness of culture in the diversity of language, there is the emergence of order, the order of history, the order of purpose. From Noah to Abraham the order is seen in selection: ethnic—Shem, clan—Peleg, family—Terah, and finally the chosen individual—Abraham, who was thus selectively bred to respond to God's calling and command. Abraham is the father of a new people, and the patriarchal period from Abraham to Moses is the story of a training under the conditions of nomadic existence and of a testing in the period of enslavement in Egypt. The Moses Saga is the story of a renaissance, being born anew. The Israelites were delivered from Egypt to serve Yahweh as his people, instructed by his law (The Ten Commandments). In *Joshua* and *Judges* is the story of conquest, the mighty act of Yahweh by which he gave Palestine into the hand of Israel. Now Israel is a people with a law and a land. Under Samuel, Saul and David it won the peace as it won the war. Now as a true monarchy it had an historical existence rooted both in a land, and in a political and cultural unity. Its triumph is visibly proclaimed in the palace and temple built by Solomon. But it is a people of the *covenant*, not a nation like other nations; for it is Yahweh who is King. Israel's kings are only agents of Yahweh. The People are servants appointed, not to please themselves, but to serve Yahweh's purpose. Tutored by the Law, Israel can continue as Yahweh's people only in so far as it does the good work for which it was chosen. Empire and land are gifts of Yahweh, and they will be taken away when they are regarded as ends in themselves rather than the instruments of service. From Solomon to the end of Jerusalem is the story of Israel's failure to serve her God. The rise of the great powers of Assyria (745-612 B.C.) and Babylon (612-540 B.C.) is Yahweh's answer to the transgressions in which Israel proved herself unfaithful, so that she no longer knew nor understood her Lord. From civil discord (division of the kingdom in 926 B.C.) and trust in monarchy and in treaties with other nations rather than faith in Yahweh and loyalty to

the Covenant, Israel plunged into the meaningless whirlpool of cyclical
civilization. The monarchy ceased to be an organ of the covenant. To
redeem Israel, Yahweh raised up Assyria and Babylon as rods to be
picked up and used to destroy her monarchy, but then to be broken and
discarded. In 722 B.C. Samaria fell, and in 586 Jerusalem was destroyed.
Israel, now only a band of survivors, was forced to go as an exile into
Babylon as the Jacob clans had centuries before gone into Egypt.
Exile, like Egypt, was a tutor. It was the harsh and humiliating
'unlearning' of the ways of monarchy. It was a time for the people to
remember the wilderness and Sinai.

The portal of the further span was a new beginning (*Isaiah* 40)
for a new Israel. It now looked toward a new kind of kingdom, not
of this world, yet *in* this world, a kingdom of righteousness. Ezra is
the new Moses, but now the law is made plain. It is written into the
fabric of life, expressed in the simple and humble duties of the daily
round. But the kingdom is yet to come. Ezra, no more than Moses,
enters the new land of promise; for that lies beyond, waiting for God's
own mighty acts even as in the conquest of Canaan. It waits for the
new Joshua and the new David, but it waits with patience, confident in
the covenant; for Israel's God is now known as Creator, Maker of
heaven and earth and of all things visible and invisible, Lord of all
nations. Looking backward, Israel saw the past as history. Even in
failure was fulfillment. By her dying as a nation she had come to
know what it meant to live as the people of God. By her suffering
she was to become a light to the nations. Her God had survived his
nation.

Israelite Historical Literature

The whole of the *Old Testament* can be said to be historical
literature. Even its laws are presented in the context of historical
narrative, associated with historical events, and interpreted in the light
of history. Herder was one of the first modern historians to note what
a large place the *Old Testament* gives to the 'voices of the people'—
the love ballads of the *Song of Songs*, the folk wisdom and popular
philosophy of *Proverbs* and *Ecclesiastes*, the simple patriotism of *Esth-
er*, the critical drama of *Job*, and the poetry of liturgy in the *Psalms*.
All of these as the *I Ching* and *Shih Ching* are prime documents

for the historian. But the major part of the *Old Testament* is intentionally historical. The Israelites, as no other people, lived by their history. Their religion was a history. Their political philosophy was a history. Their law, festivals, family life, worship and recreation were a rehearsal of history.

Old Testament literature was traditionally divided into three collections: the *Law*, the *Prophets* and the *Writings.* The first was called the *Torah* or the *Pentateuch* (the five scrolls) or the *Five Books of Moses: Genesis, Exodus, Leviticus, Numbers* and *Deuteronomy.* It was the first collection to be accepted as Scripture. It is the official record and interpretation of events from creation to the death of Moses, compiled from several traditions. The *Prophets* was the second collection to be canonized. It was divided into two parts: 1. The *Former Prophets* comprising the books of *Joshua* (conquest of Canaan), *Judges* (the settlement of the Israelite tribes in Palestine), *Samuel* (the transition from tribal federation to monarchy in the face of the Philistine compaign for Palestine), and *Kings* (the history of the monarchy from David to the fall of Jerusalem). 2. The *Latter Prophets* are no less history. They are commentary and commandment based upon the demands of the covenant in concrete situations. Four scrolls comprised this division: *Isaiah, Jeremiah, Ezekiel,* and the *Book of the Twelve Prophets.*

The structure of the *Old Testament* is historical rather than systematic. Historical sense dictated the arrangement of books to form a continuous account of Israel's history regardless of theme or time of writing. The Five Books, *Genesis* through *Deuteronomy,* trace world history from creation to the death of Moses. *Joshua, Judges, Samuel* and *Kings* carry the story onward from Moses to the end of the monarchy. *Chronicles* is a summary of that history from a later perspective. *Ezra* and *Nehemiah* interpret the events of the exile under Babylonian rule and the rehabilitation of Jerusalem and its temple under the Persian Empire. The folk literature, philosophy and liturgical documents come next. They reflect the cultural life of Israel from the early days of the monarchy into the Hellenistic Age (1000 to 200 B.C.). The Latter Prophets (*Isaiah* to *Malachi*) preserve the Yahwist tradition from 750 to 400 B.C., and its running commentary upon Israel's history as it was made and lived from the time of Jeroboam II (King of Israel) and Uzziah (King of Judah) through the age of Ezra (c. 400 B.C.). Israelite historiography begins with the monarchy and expands backward to creation. But it took its final form at the 'portal of Ezra.'

Yet it is not unusual to find a fragment of verse from the Seventeenth Century B.C. fitted into the framework of a Tenth Century narrative that was edited by a theologian in the Fifth or even as late as the Second Century.

The Sources of Israelite Historiography: *The Oral Tradition*

Behind all ancient historiography lies a long oral tradition. The Near East like China depended for centuries upon a living oral tradition before anything was written down. What was important of the past was known by the whole people, rehearsed in carefully guarded form by priest and chieftain in tribal assembly, celebrated in song and story, and enacted in ritual. Israelite oral tradition can be traced back to the Seventeenth Century before Christ. And long after the written code of the law appeared, it is commanded that the law shall still be preserved in oral transmission from father to son (*Deut.* 6:4-7). The writing down of law and tradition usually comes at the point that a 'crisis of confidence' has occurred. At such a time new ways would threaten the continuity of the oral tradition. The heart of that tradition was the covenant at Sinai, the word (Law) that was given to Moses and the events surrounding the covenant (*Ex.* 20:23-19). From this center the oral tradition expanded backwards through the stories which told how Israel had been guided to Sinai, the wondrous deliverance from Egypt, the night of escape, and the disaster that overtook Pharoah's army at the Reed (Red) Sea. But these mighty acts of Yahweh had their roots in an earlier past: the ancestral memory of the race—the bondage of the Rachel tribes under Egypt, the heroic days of the patriarchs, and then backward to the ultimate beginning in the mythic stories of the birth of civilization and of creation. And then from that center (Sinai) the oral tradition reached toward the present in the stories of the fulfillment of the promise made to Moses of a land and a destiny.

That present was the glorious kingdom of David and Solomon. With the establishment of the monarchy, Israel was keenly conscious of Yahweh's fulfillment of the covenant. The Kingdom of David was seen as the crowning event of the whole course of Yahweh's mighty acts. In achieving monarchy, Israel had gained a new and profound sense of its own historical existence. It had become a people whose past was important. It was now a true community about which a history could be written.

The J Document

Sometime during the reign of Solomon, probably at the height of his success in diplomacy and internal organization (c. 950 B.C.), the first history of Israel was composed. It began with the call of Abraham (*Gen.* 12:1-4a) and recounted the patriarchal tradition, the sojourn in Egypt, Moses' encounter with Yahweh, the great exodus, and the giving of the law at Sinai. It was an epic of heroic accomplishments beyond expectations. Beyond all hopes, the Jacob clans (Israel) had successfully broken out of Egypt, made their way across Sinai in a hazardous journey through the desert, and won through to a settlement in Palestine. Against the superior forces of the Canaanites, Philistines, Moabites, Amorites and Aramaeans, Israel had carved out under David an empire of its own. The *J* document explains the real source of Israel's strength, the real power behind the Empire. Its strength was Yahweh who had chosen Abraham to become the father of a nation. Israel had triumphed because it was the people of Yahweh. The real foundation of empire was the covenant. We do not know who wrote this history, committing to writing the oral tradition, and giving to the whole the form of a continuous narrative that explained the sources of the Davidic Monarchy. That document is now part of the Pentateuch. In the Nineteenth Century, scholars distinguished this source from others in the Pentateuch and gave it the name of *J*. *J* is the initial of *Jahweh* (Yahweh or Jehovah) and also of Judah, and so appropriately distinguished this document from the other sources in the Pentateuch since it uses the name *Jahweh* for God, and reflects the pride of Judah in the Davidic Monarchy. David was of the tribe of Judah, and Jerusalem, which he chose for his capital, was geographically and culturally bound to Judah. The monarchy provided the peace and leisure for the writing of history. The references to the capture of Edom (*Gen.* 27:40) and to the high position of Judah in the monarchy suggest a date sometime after Solomon had succeeded to the throne. The generally accepted date is c. 950 B.C. Sometime later, possibly as early as the Ninth Century, *J* was expanded backwards to include the ancient myths that were now revised in the light of the Mosaic religion: the stories of creation, the beginnings of culture, of the tower of Babel (*Gen.* 1-11).

As a whole *J* could be entitled *The Glorious History of Yahweh and His People.* It achieved an epic quality not only in terms of the breadth of its canvas (from creation to Joshua) but also in its style which maintains the fine balance of 'nobility and simplicity.' Although its main theme is the story of Yahweh's mighty acts, it is also a warmly patriotic, national epic, telling the story of the people that Yahweh chose to be 'his people' and hence the bearers of his promise. It is a vivid epic with lyric intensity in the description of events and of persons. The patriarchs are heroes, men of faithfulness and valour, but they are men, not symbols in bas relief of virtue.   Each is a personality, a character in the round: the faithful Abraham, the crafty Jacob, the forgiving Joseph and the titanic Moses, are also quite human, betraying weakness, deceit and passion. To *J*, Yahweh is the most vivid character of the story.   His vitality dominates the narrative and suggests the winds of the wilderness: the hot wind of wrath, the fierce wind of irresistible force, the merciful breezes of the dawn and sunset. Yahweh is above all else, the Living God, in intimate relationship to his people. He is a faithful God of inflexible purpose. Yet he, too, lives in history with the openness of a wise chief who acts with sensitive and imaginative appreciation of the persons and factors in each concrete situation.

The E Document

A second written source of the *Pentateuch* is called *E* because it is the initial of *Elohim* (the word used for God in *E* before he revealed his name to Moses), and also because the document probably originated in the North (Ephraim). *E* could be entitled *The Religious History of Israel.* It is more concerned with the purity and proprieties of worship than *J*, i.e., with Yahwism in contrast to the religious practices of other peoples. *E* is the first writing to condemn idolatry (*Ex.* 32), the first to recognize that Israel could so easily be unfaithful to her God, so easily compromise the covenant in her compromises with other cultures. It reflects the tradition of the covenant renewal ceremony of New Year at Shechem, and echoes the great contest between Elijah, as the champion of Yahwism, and King Ahab who had less faith in the covenant than in the ways of the great civilizations. *E* provides the better, and perhaps earlier, tradition of the covenant and the decalogue.

When the Northern provinces seceded from the United Kingdom in 926 B.C. they would naturally become more keenly interested in their own patriarchal tradition. *J* recalled the Abraham or Amorite source of Hebrew culture which had come to fulfillment in the great Judah tribe, and in David, its first king. As an independent kingdom, the North now recalled its own heritage in the Jacob or Aramaean stream of Hebrew Culture. *E* preserves that heritage. These circumstances point to a date for *E* under the historical conditions of the northern kingdom following the religious crisis of Ahab's reign, and an identification of its theme with the position of the prophet Elijah (c. 850 B.C.).

Deuteronomy and the Deuteronomic Historiography

Monarchy supplied a further source or series of sources for Israelite historiography: the court memoirs. Explicit reference is made to these in a later history of the monarchy: *The Acts of Solomon* (*I Kings* 11:41), *The Acts of the Kings of Israel* (*I Kings* 14:10) and *The Acts of the Kings of Judah* (*I Kings* 14:29). It must be supposed that a full account was kept of the deeds of Samuel, Saul and David, and that, in the case of the kings both of Israel and Judah, a court historian recorded the events of each reign in a manner similar to the keeping of the *Diaries of Action and Repose*. However, even these court records appear to have been in narrative form, memoirs rather than chronologies. They were the material of which was built the great Deuteronomic history of the monarchy, *The Book of the Kings of Judah and Israel*.

Deuteronomy means 'second law,' and it is the title of the last book of the Pentateuch. The core of this book (chs. 5-28) is known as the *D Code*, a third source of the Pentateuch and the perspective which inspired the writing of the history of Israel from the death of Moses to the fall of Jerusalem. *D* itself had an interesting history. It was at first a liturgical rehearsal of the law, associated with *E*, in yearly use at the patriarchal shrine of Shechem as a central feature of a New Year's ritual. Then, following the religious crisis under Ahab, that liturgical creed may have been expanded to sharpen the distinctive features of Yahwism in contrast to foreign cults as a written witness to the faith of Elijah. It served the double function of an affirmation of faith in the covenant and of a manifesto of Yahwist nationalism, i.e. the point of view that led to the Jehu revolt and overthrow of the Omri Dynasty. Then, during the latter half of the Eighth Century, the prophetic theology of the Covenant (*Amos* and *Hosea*) and the re-interpretation of the law, making it relevant to the prosperous though corrupt reign of Jeroboam II, added to this creed the note of judgment. When the northern kingdom was conquered by Assyria in 722 B.C. and its cities destroyed, the document was rescued along with *E* and came to be deposited in the archives of the temple in Jerusalem. It may have inspired the reform instituted by Hezekiah (715-687), and it would have given some support to his attempted revolt against Assyria. The Shechem document was of course revised by the Jerusalem Deuteronomists in line with their desire to purify Yahweh worship by making the Jerusalem temple the exclusive center of ritual action, and destroying the shrines corrupted by Canaanite and other foreign cultic practice. During the reign of Manasseh (687-642), the Deuteronomists were driven underground, but in the prophetic and priestly reaction against the pagan excesses and foreign influences of his reign, the *D* perspective gained substantial favour. When Josiah (640-605) was able, during a period of internal trouble in Assyria, to rebel against that Empire and to suppress foreign culture in Judah, the Deuteronomic book was 'found' (621 B.C.) in the temple by the priest Hilkiah, and presented to the king as Moses' final interpretation of the Law given at Sinai. *D* does not purport to be direct, divine revelation. It is Moses who speaks to Israel. So *Deut.* 1:5: 'Moses undertook to explain the law.' It was the duty of the messengers of Yahweh (Moses, Joshua, the Judges, Samuel, Nathan, Elijah and the great prophets of the Eighth to the Sixth Centuries) to remind Israel of its covenant, and, in the name of Yahweh, to witness against the king when he turned from the covenant to do what he pleased as though he ruled by his own authority, not recognizing that it was Yahweh who was king.

The messenger of Yahweh presented the covenant law in vivid relevance to the contemporary situation. Moses is described in *Deuteronomy* as doing precisely this toward the end of his life. The earliest core of the document was a covenant renewal liturgy. Then in the last days of the Kingdom of Judah, the prophetic priestly champions of the covenant as the ground of the monarchy urged *D* upon their king and people as a last, crucial warning: 'Yahweh cut a covenant with us in Horeb (Sinai), not with our fathers did Yahweh cut this covenant, but with us—we—here—this day—all of us who are alive.'

(*Deut.* 5:2-3) The Covenant, if it were to be kept, had to be understood by the people as a living, present reality—not just an ancient treaty between Yahweh and their ancestors.

D in 621 in Judah was a *prophetic manifesto,* a kind of last word on the mandate of monarchy. *D* in Israelite historiography became a perspective, a philosophy of history. The Deuteronomic school survived the fall of Jerusalem. It continued its historical studies of the monarchy and collected the royal, prophetic and priestly records to produce a continuous narrative account of the whole course of events to the fall of Jerusalem. *D* was its clue to the all important question of the relation of the faith (covenant) and the land (monarchy). The writing of this history was the pivotal point at which the order of Israel as a monarchy under God turned toward the order of a Jewish 'church' with its historical present and the basis of its historical existence in a religious community under the law, the written law of the *Torah*.

Looking backward from *D*, the prophetic-priestly historians in exile attempted a comprehensive and systematically ordered account of Israel under the covenant. Earlier sources similar to *J* and *E* provided the raw material for *Joshua* and *Judges*. Written tradition was at hand for *Samuel,* and the court and prophetic memoirs for *Kings*. The theme of the whole is the explanation of why Isarel was crushed by Assyria and Babylon, why the land was lost. It has been described as a great arch supported by two pillars: 1. Israel's commitment to Yahweh ratified in the building of Solomon's temple (*I Kings* chs. 5-8) involving a formal rejection of the gods of Canaan, and 2. Josiah's reform according to the commandments of the law book found in the temple. The Deuteronomic historiography, completed by 550 B.C., achieved a high standard of narrative description and of the explanation of significant detail within the framework of broad interpretation. The Deuteronomic historians were careful in chronology, and skillful in the use of sources. Their writing reveals a dramatic sense and humane sensitivity unparalleled in the ancient world. But *D* did not break through the limitations of its own perspective: the unresolved tension of Yahwist nationalism with its nomadic rejection of civilization, on the one hand, and monarchial secularism on the other. The *Book of the Kings* points up the tragic results of these two extreme party positions. On the one hand, Yahwist nationalism suffered the judgment of history: Josiah's glorious reign came to a bitter end in Egypt's victory over Judah and the meteoric rise of Babylon. On the other hand, the judgment of history fell with even greater force upon the monarchial secularism and inter-

nationalism of the reigns of Ahaz and Manasseh. Like Moses who
was allowed only to look but not to enter into the promised land, the
Deuteronomic historians lived by a vision which was not realized in
their time. They viewed the past from the perspective of the future,
i.e. in terms of a new, universal community under Yahweh, and of the
expansion of the old covenant toward the Isaianic 'city of God.'

Prophetic Historiography

The Deuteronomic history was entitled 'The Former Prophets.' It
was history related to the origins of the monarchy and the experience
of Israel as a monarchy under the covenant. In part its principles of
interpretation were drawn from the contemporary comment upon the
monarchy which was collected and edited under the title of 'The Latter
Prophets'. These titles—'Former' and 'Latter'—are significant for
several reasons: 1. the 'Latter Prophets' continue the interpretation of
Israel's historical existence under Yahweh far beyond the end of the
monarchy through the exile to the threshold of the Hellenistic world.
2. The prophetic interpretation of Israel's historical existence goes far
deeper than the simple covenant concept of the Deuteronomists. No
more than Samuel, were they ever sure that the monarchy was the
true basis of Israel's historical existence, or that it was essential to the
concept of 'the people of God.' 3. The 'Latter Prophets' stand between
the Deuteronomic historiography as a source of its principles of interpretation and a new notion of the Kingdom of Yahweh in which Israel
is still of crucial historical importance but under another historical form—
not as a monarchy but as a Church.

It is therefore essential that we consider the role of the prophet in
Israel and the development of the prophetic tradition in order to understand the great work of the final editing of Israelite historiography
that produced the *Old Testament* as we have it today. The last of
the great editorial schools is known as *P* and is characterized by a
priestly concern. Until quite recently, the prophetic character of that
priestly school has not received sufficient attention. *P* is a fitting
designation in so far as it stands for prophetic as well as priestly
perspectives.

The *Latter Prophets* in the Hebrew Bible comprises four collections
under the titles *Isaiah, Jeremiah, Ezekiel* and *The Book of the Twelve.*

These are commonly known as the literary prophets,—i.e., the prophets whose messages were recorded and preserved in books. We must keep in mind, however, that the prophets were not primarily literary men. They were speakers. They were men of speech and action who by their spoken words and their manner of life revealed the will of God to His people in concrete, historical situations.

Two types of prophetic tradition are distinguished in the *Old Testament*: 1. The ecstatic who sees the future through visions or trances—the dancing prophets. This is a type found in many primitive religions as the shaman, diviner, medicine man, dervish, wizard, Delphic priestess, etc. 2. The other prophetic tradition in the *Old Testament* is something unique in the history of religion. It begins with the figure of Samuel but has its classical proto-type in Elijah.

Behind the prophetic consciousness lies something of Israel's nomadic past: a memory of the life lived on the sand. Living close to the Palestinian wilderness and having cultural roots in the nomadic life of the desert, gave to the Israelite a sense both of the swift judgment and the sure grace of God. He was profoundly impressed by the power of his God both to bless and to curse. Such vivid impressions would have been encouraged by the sudden and terrifying storms of the desert and the unexpected discovery of the reviving waters of an oasis just at the moment when he despaired of survival. He was instinctively impressed by the frailty of man: the possibility of sudden doom and death and the impermanence of all things human. These impressions were the lessons of the desert: how quickly the shifting sands obliterate all traces of an encampment, how dependent man was upon the sources of food and water, how soon even a strong man could be reduced to a faint and pitiful creature when deprived of water, how powerless was man against the burning sun and the stinging, parching, desert wind, how wondrously the tiny plants and flowers spring up in the morning on the desert, but then how soon their fragile beauty is withered under the heat of the rising sun, how they appear to perish!

We of course do not have a tape recording of the messages of the prophets as they were delivered to the people of Israel and Judah. The prophetic books cannot be said even to be reconstructions of the speeches by the authors themselves. Prophetic literature, as we have it, consists of short poems connected with transitional prose additions to give the books a literary unity. It is probable that the books as we know them were constructed around very brief, sharp couplets. When these couplets were collected to be put into writing, explanatory settings and interpretative notes were added. Sometimes the editors inserted other notes dealing with the relevance for their own age of prophetic oracles of a past century.

Isaiah and *Habakkuk* furnish two clues to the origin of prophetic literature. Habakkuk is ordered to 'write the vision'—make it so plain, so clear, that even a runner could read it (*Hab.* 2:2-4). The vision is the theme of the book: 'Behold as for the unrighteous, his soul is not even within him; but the righteous man shall live by his faithfulness.' Isaiah was urged to prepare a written summary of his public declarations because those to whom he had spoken had rejected his message (30:8). Since Judah chose to ignore or forget his words, they are to be written down so that, at a later time, they might serve as a Judgment upon those who would not listen to what Yahweh was about to do. Jeremiah is told to 'take a scroll and write upon it all the words that I (Yahweh) have spoken to thee concerning Israel...from the days of Josiah (c. 600 B. C.) unto this day.' The prophet thereupon called in his secretary and dictated quite a lot!

The word of the prophet is itself historical reality. It continues long after his death as a witness to Yahweh, and as a witness against those who did not listen. It has the power to form the order of a new community whenever it is heard. And the word of the prophet lives on in the inner circle composed of those who hear and understand. It is their Scripture. The word, preserved in the lives of the remnant, is the true Israel.

The position of the prophet in Israel was unique in the history of historiography. He did not have a hereditary or constitutional office. He was not appointed by anyone, nor was he the spokesman of any organized faction in Israel. There were no established channels through which the prophet worked; nor was there any established pattern for his ministry. He stood over against the whole machinery of state and temple. The prophet appears when the office of king becomes regularized. Thus the prophet arises with the rise of the monarchy. But he stands over against the monarchy, over against the nation as the spokesman for Yahweh. He fulfilled in part the function of the judge who called Israel to remember the covenant. He is thus the spokesman of the divine law over against the positive law of the state or the arbitrary will of the king. He calls also upon the priest to fulfill his function, just as Moses had stood over the priestly office, and as Samuel had been summoned to witness what God was about to do to the House of Eli.

Elijah appears at the point when there is a real danger that the self-sufficiency of the house of Omri and its lack of enthusiasm for the covenant might destroy the uniqueness of the nation as the 'people of Yahweh.' The second great prophetic movement arises in response to the Assyrian thrust toward empire. With the Assyrian period, the first great literary prophets appear: Amos, Hosea and Micah.

In this prophetic literature Moses is the glorious figure of the past—the symbol of the mighty acts performed by Yahweh before the face, and through the lives of the fathers. He is the symbol of the covenant that *was* made and of the law that *was* given. The prophets are the voice of Yahweh in each moment of the insistent present. They speak of the covenant as a present reality, and in terms of the contemporary situation. It was their function 'to regain for Israel a presence under God' when Israel was in danger of losing its sense of historical existence under the covenant. The prophets therefore re-created Moses. For them he was not just a figure of the past who established once for all the order of Israelite history. Instead, he was 'the first in a line of prophets—who continued to bring Israel up from Egypt into existence under God.' Their remembrance of Moses was remembrance in the sense of a living tradition: membership in a community that remembered Moses and Joshua, the Judges, Samuel and Elijah. They saw that Israel's 'historical existence depended upon a continual response to Yahweh' as his present word was revealed through them to the people. In prophetic literature, 'the recall of the past was transformed into the call of the present.' The priests at Shechem rehearsed in solemnity on the day of the New Year the covenant made at Sinai and renewed by Joshua. Later they accepted into the liturgical elaboration, the prophetic commentary of the recent past (Elijah). The prophets were the expounders of the law in the immediate concrete situation. They were therefore fated to bear a heavy burden—the burden of serving Yahweh in the dangerous concreteness of an insistent political, economic, international and personal present. They spoke with the crispness of face-to-face confrontation: 'Thou art the man!' They put the covenant into fierce words of judgment upon what was happening at one concrete moment at the city gate or in the market stall or in the court of the king.

We shall examine one prophetic document as a classical type, both in the sense of literature and as having played a crucial role in Israelite history and historiography—the *Book of Isaiah*. *Isaiah* is a highly complex, literary masterpiece, and a profoundly significant theology of

Israel's history and of human culture. It is itself a history of prophecy from Amos through Ezekiel as the foundation for a new way for Israel wherein Israel itself becomes a visible covenant between Yahweh and all mankind.

My own theory of the Isaianic literature emphasizes the integrity of the book as a whole, and hence rejects the usual, sharp distinction made between chapters 1-39 and 40-55-66. The heart of the work is 40-55. From this perspective the author-editor prepared a history of prophecy, i.e. a history of Israelite theology as a drama of the process of revelation leading to an ultimate disclosure of Israel's historical role under Yahweh. *Isaiah*, thus interpreted, becomes the basis for the completion and canonization of the Law and the Prophets. It is the clue to the *P* document, the return of the exiles under Ezra, and the rehabilitation of Jerusalem as a holy city to be a light to the nations. This is admittedly a radical re-conception of the structure and meaning of *Isaiah*. It raises some important questions to which conclusive answers cannot easily be given, but it seems to me to deal with more of the facts in a realistic way than the generally accepted division of the book into the oracles of an Eighth Century prophet and those of one who wrote during the decade from 540 to 500 B.C. My own dating of the whole book would be at some time around 400 B.C., thereby connecting this history, anthology and theology of prophecy with the brilliant flowering of a renaissant Israel in Babylon just at the point of return under Ezra.

THE BOOK OF THE PROPHET ISAIAH

ANTECEDENTS: JEREMIAH

Jeremiah who witnessed the last days of Jerusalem was called the weeping prophet. Amos did not weep. What is new in Jeremiah is not so much the prophetic message as the prophetic man, the religious person. Amos is the stern deliverer of judgment, eager to pronounce sentence, fiercely excited, awaiting its execution. Hosea had understood that Yahweh's judgment of Israel would mean a wounding of God's own heart. Yahweh's suffering would involve something like the mixed emotions of a young husband towards an unfaithful wife whom he still loves. Jeremiah's weeping over Judah is similar to David's sorrow over the death of his rebellious son—'would that I could have died for thee, O Absalom, my son, my son.' Jeremiah bears Yahweh's sorrow in his own heart. The divine *ruach* (breath—spirit) is in the prophet. It is God's power, creative, vindicating, purging, redeeming. But the prophet has not God's glory nor wholeness. He suffers the agony of the brokenness between his several selves: prophet, poet, patriot and priest. The *charisma* of the prophet is the divine word spoken through man—Yahweh's truth through human personality. So suffering enters. Jeremiah was a suffering servant of Yahweh; for Jeremiah had his humanities, a humaneness not found in the nomadic piety of the Yahwist nationalists. Amos was God's wrath. Jeremiah bore both wrath and tenderness. He came from a priestly family bred to mediate between man and God. He carried the cry of man to God and the word of God to men.

Jeremiah loved the land and he loved the people, but he was called to see what the people could not know until it happened: that the nation would be destroyed, the people slain, the land bruised. He lived with this people as one who foresees that they must die; for he sees, through God's eyes, that they cannot reverse the momentum of their plunge toward self destruction. They have chosen to forsake the covenant, to choose death rather than life, to deny their own historical existence and clamber aboard the whirling joy wheel of the cyclical civilizations which will send them flying off into the dark night of meaningless death. They are like the unknowing passengers aboard an ill-fated plane, destined to plunge, with only the warning of a few moments of sheer terror, into flaming death. And the prophet, who alone knows what is coming, is a fellow passenger. In a real sense, he died many times for them on the long flight before the crash. They are gay, their eyes bright with excitement, with vine leaves in their hair, carelessly content with the free drinks, the insensate flirtations, the search for the soul in the pit of the senses, the business deal, pretentions and boastings, the blasphemous jest, the game of chance. With these obsessive joys and heartless cares, they deride the weeping prophet. Their moment of terror, when it comes, is quickly over. He has borne the tragic knowledge over the long flight, pondered its meaning of sin and judgment. He has asked of his soul what these doomed might have been, what cause they could have served, and he has considered the final moment, and thought of the one or two that might survive.

Jeremiah could have had no joy in telling them, even though they did not believe him, of what was coming; no taste for the wretched duty to caution them to prepare for death.

O Lord...thou art stronger than I
and thou hast prevailed.
I have become a laughingstock all the day:
everyone mocks me.
For whenever I speak, I cry out,
I shout 'Violence and destruction!'
For the word of the Lord has become for me
a reproach and derision all day long.
If I say, 'I will not mention him,
or speak any more in his name,'
there is in my heart as it were a burning fire
shut up in my bones,
and I am weary with holding it in,
and I cannot.

20:7-9

Jeremiah looked at the dangerously unsound misinterpretations of the Deuteronomic faith—the naive notion that the Jerusalem temple was a magic power in itself, that somehow Yahweh's power had been caught and sealed in it.

The word of the Lord came to Jeremiah: Stand in the gate of the Lord's house and proclaim there this word: Thus saith the Lord of hosts, the God of Israel, 'Amend your ways and your doings, and I will let you dwell is this place. Do not trust in these deceptive words: This is the temple of the Lord, the temple of the Lord, the temple of the Lord.'

You trust in deceptive words to no avail. Will you steal, murder, commit adultery, swear falsely, burn incense to Baal, and go after other gods that you have not known, and then come and stand before me in this house which is called by my name, and say 'We are delivered.' Go and look at my place that was in Shiloh where I made my name dwell at first, and see what I did to it for the wickedness of my people Israel. Now I will do to you what I did to Israel.

7:1-13

The real power of Yahweh to save is not in his temple but in the word of his prophet. Nor could Jeremiah be satisfied with the naive simplicity of the Deuteronomic notion that the good would prosper, that evil would be destroyed. He looked at Israel, broken by Assyria a century before. He looked at Judah as it was—ripe for destruction. He looked at the agents of destruction, at Assyria and at Babylon. What could be the final conclusion then of God's creation and of his redemptive purpose? Only this:

I looked on the earth, and lo, it was waste and void
and to the heavens, and they had no light.
I looked on the mountains, and lo, they were quaking,
and all the hills moved to and fro.
I looked, and lo, there was no man,
and all the birds of the air had fled.
I looked, and lo, the fruitful land was a desert,
and all its cities were laid in ruins
before the Lord, before his fierce anger.

4:23-26

This says two things: 1. That if total destruction comes, it too will be the work of God, the strange work of his wrath. 2. That if the people of Yahweh are wholly destroyed, creation will have lost its purpose. History will be erased. But this would be to defeat Yahweh's purpose. It would mean that Israel's defection had defeated her God, her infidelity had rendered him impotent to save, impotent except to destroy.

Somehow in his own suffering Jeremiah found a clue to Yahweh's way beyond his wrath, an alternative to the monarchy as Yahweh's means of fulfilling his promise to Abraham, and an alternative to the kingdom of David as the historical Israel under the covenant serving her Lord. There was something in the prophetic life, amidst its suffering, that bound him closer to Yahweh so that he participated in and shared Yahweh's sorrow over his people, so that he bore in himself as one man for all Israel the task of fulfilling the covenant. There was a strange power in Jeremiah after he had taken upon himself the response for all Israel. Even Zedekiah, the king, felt it, though he could not understand it, during the last confused days before the final fall. It was not just the word that was spoken, it was the person who was speaking. Jeremiah felt it within himself as a new sense of the prophetic mission: 'not only to pluck up and break down' but also 'to build and to plant.' In his own life, in his suffering, he came to the certainty that Yahweh had a purpose for Israel and for the land beyond the monarchy. Jeremiah came to believe that his own life was somehow to be used in this new venture. From the monarchy, Yahweh had already turned to a more responsive and effectual servant— the righteous remnant which should be the Abraham of a New Israel. Jeremiah suddenly knew that this had already happened centuries before in Elijah and then in Amos and Micah. He knew that the tumultuous days within the city, the spasms of its final agonies, as the

battering rams thundered on the gates, was not the mortal wounding
of Israel. Yahweh had raised up his new Israel long before. 'Behold
I formed you in the womb, I chose you ere ever you were born, I set
you apart: I have appointed you a prophet to the nations.' Jeremiah
endured by this faith in a new covenant, beyond the Mosaic which
had led to the monarchy that failed, a covenant with persons not with
kings, and a new law cut, not upon stone, but written into the heart,
not as a covenant code but as a way of life. By that faith Jeremiah
in the last days of the siege bought back his family land in Anathoth
and encouraged, in a bold letter, the exiles of 597 to face life and
survive. In Egypt the Jacob families had grown to clans and multiplied. In the new Egypt (Babylon) the exiles should 'build and plant.'
God's promise to them was as his promise to Abraham: that they
should create a new people.

EZEKIEL

Ezekiel saw how horribly wrong a vain religion could be among
the survivors in Jerusalem and in the ways of the nations. Rebellion
against God may find its greatest arrogance not in conduct but in
celebration, not in personal morality but in a grotesquely disguised
enmity with God—the witches' mass, the satanic sacrament.

He saw the holiness of God and the glory of the divine honour.
He could not believe that this honour could be profaned by the defeat
of God's purpose any more than it had been by the defection of Israel.
The ground of all existence was God's faithfulness to his own glory, to
the goodness of his creativity. As history began with his covenant
with Noah (not to destroy but to redeem) so Israel's historical existence
was now a deeper reality than before under the old covenant and
the monarchy; for it was grounded not upon Israel's response but
essentially in God's own purpose.

> Therefore say to the house of Israel, Thus says the Lord God: 'It is
> not for your sake, O house of Israel, that I am about to act, but for the
> sake of my holy name, which you have profaned among the nations to
> which you came. And I will vindicate the holiness of my great name, which
> has been profaned among the nations...and the nations will know that I
> am the Lord...When through you I vindicate my holiness before their eyes.
>
> 'For I will take you from the nations and gather you from all countries,
> and bring you into your own land. I will sprinkle clean water upon you

and you shall be clean from all your uncleanness, and from all your idols I will cleanse you. A new heart will I put within you; and I will take out of your flesh the heart of stone and give you a heart of flesh. And I will put my spirit within you and cause you to walk in my statutes and be careful to observe my ordinances....It is not for your sake I will act, says the Lord God; let that be known to you. . . .'

Ezek. 36:22-32

'Then I thought I would pour out my wrath upon them and spend my anger against them in the midst of the land of Egypt. But I acted for the sake of my name, that it should not be profaned in the sight of the nations among whom they dwelt, in whose sight I made myself known to them in bringing them out of the land of Egypt. So I led them out of the land of Egypt and brought them into the wilderness. I gave them my statutes and showed them my ordinances by whose observance man shall live.'

Ezek. 20:8b-11

A new kind of Israel was emerging. A community of priests clothed in righteousness replaces the monarchy, and a new kind of covenant is promised—instruction in righteousness. The charisma of the order of Israel has passed from the king to the priest.

ISAIAH 1-66

These were the new thoughts that the editor-author of *Isaiah* pondered as he reviewed the history of Eighth and Seventh Century prophecy and the process of revelation in the first part of his new theology of history. These centuries had been the essential preparation for the life of Jeremiah and the vision of Ezekiel. The 'former things,' *Former Prophets*, have now passed away. The monarchy is no more than the broken cradle of the new Israel. From Moses to Jeremiah was one dispensation, one historical movement based on the covenant. Now a new covenant, a new people, a new age is being ushered in. The old covenant is the sacred past of the portentious present (as the Old Testament became the Scripture of the earliest church). Everywhere in *Isaiah 1-66* we hear the new song, the song of the new. The call to sing the new song (*Is. 6:1-8*) is the vision of the New Year, a new child is born; a new son is given; a new word is to be proclaimed, a new commission given to the servant of Yahweh. Former things are now the testament of God's faithfulness. What Yahweh declared, that he fulfilled.

'The former things I declared of old,
　　they went forth from my mouth and I made them known;
　　then suddenly I did them and they came to pass.

From this time forth I make you hear new things,
　　hidden things which you have not known.
They are created now, not long ago;
　　before today you have never heard of them,
　　lest you should say, 'Behold, I knew them.'

For my name's sake I defer my anger,
　　for the sake of my praise I restrain it for you,
　　that I may not cut you off.
Behold, I have refined you, but not like silver;
　　I have tried you in the furnace of affliction.
For my own sake, for my own sake, I do it,
　　for how should my name be profaned?
My glory I will not give to another.'

                                        48 : 3, 6-7, 9-11

To have known the former things was the revelation given to Israel. Only Israel's God could instruct; for he alone is the God of creation and the Lord of history. Israel alone has up to this time been given the clue to history, enlightened to see its purpose and its plan. Greatest of all revelations was the message to the prophets: Samaria must be destroyed, Jerusalem must fall. Yahweh had made this known, known to his own people by his prophets. Now the survivors in Jerusalem and the exiles in Babylon are witnesses to it. Israel knows that Yahweh is the first and the last, that beside him there is no other.

But now the former things are made known to the nations and the new things revealed to them through the new Israel. The prophet challenges the gods, who are not gods, the idols of the nations, to show what they have had to do with history. (*Is. 41:21-29*) They have no such witness. They have known nothing of former things. They cannot speak to history because they look only to the world of space and the cycles of the natural order. (*Is. 41:7; 44:9-20*)

The God who is creator and judge and now redeemer is also revealer. Israel was told but did not know: Yahweh is King. Now it has seen Assyria destroyed, Lydia crushed, Babylon conquered, Egypt humbled —all these, proud for a day, risen up, and now fallen. The huge might of the great nations, seemingly irresistible, and then suddenly nothing —these mysteries, Israel in exile saw and pondered. But what impressed

Israel indelibly was the destruction of her own monarchy—Yahweh's judgment of his own nation. He had declared it and he did it. Yahweh indeed is King!

This is the new proclamation, the word of the New Year. 'In the year that King Uzziah died, I saw the Lord, sitting upon a throne, high and lifted up, and his train filled the temple. Holy, Holy, Holy is the Lord of hosts. The whole earth is full of his glory.' (*Is. 6:1-8*) New Year's day is the Day of Yahweh—the day of his judgment of the nations. Here is the echo of the Shechem covenant renewal, and of Ezekiel's vision of the holiness and glory of Yahweh, and of the Holiness Code of *Leviticus* which Ezekiel inspired.

> In the seventh month, in the first day of the month shall be a solemn rest unto you, a memorial proclaimed with the blast of horns, a holy convocation.
>
> *Lev.* 23-24f.

'Yahweh is King.' Rosh Hashanah (New Year's Day) is the reminder. The New Year's liturgy begins with the three blasts from the ram's horn: '*Tekiah*—blown in the desert to call the people to attention, the signal to break camp and prepare for departure or the signal to march in a new direction; *Shebarim*—the 'command to break with the past'—'Woe is me for I am a man of unclean lips and I dwell in the midst of a people of unclean lips!' Then again *Tekiah*. The New Year Liturgy has also three benedictions: 'God is affirmed as King of the universe; praised as supreme Judge; glorified as the world's Redeemer.'

'Whom shall I send and who will go for us'—the word of the Lord is the revelation of redemption. The whole past is now 'former things.' (I am interpreting this passage as the vision of the late Fifth Century author-editor of the whole book.)

> Remember not the former things
> nor consider the things of old.
> Behold I am doing a new thing.
> Now it springs forth, do you not perceive it?
> I will make a way in the wilderness
> and rivers in the desert.
>
> 43:18-19

The old, the former things were the deliverance from Egypt, the exodus. Now is the new thing: redemption and a new exodus—the exodus from Babylon.   The theme is creation.   Redemption is a new creation.

> 'Shower, O heavens, from above,
>   and let the skies rain down righteousness;
> let the earth open, that salvation may sprout forth,
>   and let it cause righteousness to spring up also;
>   I the Lord have created it.'
>
>   45:8

Creation is the theme as it is modulated from key to key: from the creation of the world (40:28) to the creation of Israel (43:15) to the creation of salvation (45:8; 43:14-15).

Here are the three moments of history under the three titles of God: creator, king-judge and redeemer.   The creation of the world continues in the creation of salvation history.   There is a new genealogy of heaven and earth.

Now it is the suffering servant after the classical type of Jeremiah who is the kingly agent.   Chapters 52:7-53-12 must, as Mowinckel urges, 'be read in the context of the whole eschatological drama' from creation to redemption, from Abraham to the Servant.   And the Servant is the classical type of the messenger (*malakh*), the prophet.   He is a new Jeremiah.

> Listen to me, O coastlands,
>   and hearken, you peoples from afar.
> The Lord called me from the womb,
>   from the body of my mother he named my name.
> He made my mouth like a sharp sword,
>   in the shadow of his hand he hid me;
> he made me a polished arrow,
>   in his quiver he hid me away.
> And he said to me, 'You are my servant,
>   Israel, in whom I will be glorified.'
> But I said, 'I have laboured in vain,
>   I have spent my strength for nothing and vanity;
> yet surely my right is with the Lord,
>   and my recompense with my God.'
> And now the Lord says,
>   who formed me from the womb to be his servant,
> to bring Jacob back to him,
>   and that Israel might be gathered to him;
> for I am honoured in the eyes of the Lord,
>   and my God has become my strength—

he says :
'It is too light a thing that you should be my servant
 to raise up the tribes of Jacob
 and to restore the preserved of Israel;
I will give you as a light to the nations,
 that my salvation may reach to the end of the earth.'
49:1-6

Now is revealed the true historical existence of Israel. Until now the true Israel has been hidden as an arrow in the quiver, as a sharp dagger in the hand. It seemed that the prophets had laboured in vain and spent their strength for nothing, but they have been the first born of the New Israel which is itself Yahweh's covenant with mankind—a light to the nations. The New Israel is itself the covenant given to the world; for the blows of history have awakened Israel to see and to care for a humanity not of the seed of Abraham or the community of Moses.

The New Israel is the *limmud* (disciple—student), the one who is taught in order that he may teach.

Bind up the testimony,
 send the teaching among my disciples.
I will wait for the Lord,
 who is hiding his face from the house of Jacob,
 and I will hope in him.
8:16f.

The Lord God has given me
 the tongue of those who are taught,
that I may know how to sustain with a word
 him that is weary.
Morning by morning he wakens,
 he wakens my ear
 to hear as those who are taught.
The Lord God has opened my ear,
 and I was not rebellious
 I turned not backward.
I gave my back to the smiters,
 and my cheeks to those who pulled out the beard;
I hid not my face
 from shame and spitting.
50:4-6

The New Israel speaks with the voice of the teacher. He instructs in the nature and attributes of God, the Everlasting One, the Creator.

He speaks quiet words, chastened words, gentle words, 'Faithfully he brings forth the right religion' (42:1-4). 'He does not cry or lift up his voice.' He does not declaim in the streets. With patience he leads the weary and the slow of heart, the fearful. 'He brings forth right religion as truth requires until he has established right religion in the earth; and for his instruction the far coasts wait.' (42:1-4) Patiently he teaches, delivers direction in the law until right religion is established, until every man has become a *limmud*—disciple. The prophet-judge was the interpreter of the first covenant. The priestly teacher, the man of godly learning, the patient, quiet man, is the interpreter of the new. He is the new Moses 'who undertakes to explain the law.'

And the new service is also worship—giving thanks to the creator: holy ritual. It is celebration as well as conduct, the sacrifice of thanksgiving as the expression of the sacramental life in which all things outward are visible signs of inward grace, a right religion in which all of life is itself a sacrament.

The way of Israel is to make straight a highway for her God, patiently to teach the law, in quiet confidence to sing the songs of Zion; for this is to 'walk by faith in the Living God and to pray without ceasing.' Isaiah's great prologue 40-41 (the announcements through the 'heavenly voices') was revised by an Isaianic disciple of the early second century A. D.

> In the beginning was the word and the word was with God and the word was God....He was the light that lighteth every man that cometh into the world....He came unto his own but his own received him not. But to as many as received him to them gave he power to become sons of God. *AND THE WORD WAS MADE FLESH AND DWELT AMONG US AND WE BEHELD HIS GLORY EVEN AS THE ONLY BEGOTTEN OF THE FATHER FULL OF GRACE AND TRUTH.*
>
>   *Jn.* 1:1ff.

The Final Shape Of *The Old Testament*.

I have suggested that *Isaiah* as a whole belongs to the great flowering of the Israelite Renaissance in Babylon in the last half of the Fifth Century before Christ. That renaissance began with a school of historical theology inspired by Jeremiah and Ezekiel. The overthrow of Babylon by Cyrus (539 B. C.) would have given the impetus to the great task of the reconstruction of tradition and of the religious community from the fragments that survived the monachy. During a century, that huge task of love and faith, slowly and by painstaking effort, came to fruition. Ezekiel had been the voice crying in the wilderness that called into a new unity the traditions of the Northern and Southern Kingdoms, the voice of resurrection that called up flesh and spirit upon the dry bones of a slain society, uniting priest and prophet in the common cause against the enemies of promise—those who had forgotten Zion, those who turned to the conqueror's gods, and the mysteries of brute force and sensualism, those who survived in Jerusalem or in Babylon to scoff or to weep over the pitiful end of the epic of Yahweh and his people. The Babylonian school of the faithful among the exiles would have had already at hand a rich literature. The *J* and *E* histories may well have been woven together during the Yahwist revival in the reign of Hezekiah. *E* and the Shechem document (which was the basis of the *D* code) probably came to Jerusalem after the fall of Samaria in 722. There is some reason to believe that the Shechem document went through an almost immediate revision upon arrival in line with the religious tradition of Judah and the Jerusalem temple worship, and was then the programme of Hezekiah's reform. During Manasseh's reign, Yahwist religion was almost eclipsed by foreign cultic influences in the court and even in the temple. But with Josiah in 621 the *D* code emerges again, and the reform is continued.

Josiah was able for a brief time to enlarge his kingdom to include almost the whole of the Davidic empire. It would not be unreasonable to assume that during the height of this national and religious revival the Deuteronomic histories of *Joshua*, with its new covenant theme, *Judges, Samuel* and a part of *Kings* received, at least, their first-draft form.

Following the Ezekiel mission (c. 550) the Holiness Code was compiled from temple records, traditions and contemporary interpretations. *H* is often described as the nucleus of *P*, the last important source of the *Pentateuch*, along with *J E* and *D*. *JEH* with *P* elements may have been completed around 500 B. C. It would have provided the history of Israel from creation through the exodus to the giving of the Law at Sinai with large parentheses in the narrative dealing with the wilderness tent shrine and the *H Code* of the cultic rules for ritual and conduct (*The Book of Leviticus*). During the writing of *Isaiah* the material of the P Code—the great creation story of *Genesis* 1:1-2:4a and the P tradition seen in the theological comment on the flood story, the covenant with Noah, and the patriarchal sages, would have received their final form (c. 500-450). All that now was wanting for the completion of the *Pentateuch* was the fitting of genealogies, which served both as a framework and as a connecting link, between the various sources. It would seem reasonable to suppose that the completion of the great *Torah*, the final editing of the Deuteronomic history, (The Former Prophets) the collection of the prophetic literature and its interpretation (The Latter Prophets), would have given an impetus to the return of the exiles to Jerusalem. This great work of historiography, as it came to completion, must have played its part in urging and securing the commission of Nehemiah (c. 450 B. C.). The following decades must have been a time of great excitement and religious fervour in the pious Israelite community in Babylon. It is in this setting—looking toward the great day of the institution of the Law of the King of Heaven (*H* in its Mosaic frame within the great corpus of tradition which was the *Pentateuch*)—that I would read the Gospel words of *Isaiah* 40ff. and see the highway (the sacred literature) for Yahweh over which his new people would return to Zion, and hear the great invitation: 'Whom shall I send and who will go for us?'

The Historical Form of Israel

Israelite historical writing began with the monarchy, but its central theme is not the monarchy. The first general history, *J*, though inspired by the monarchy, began with Abraham and reached its climax in the cutting of the Ten Commandments at Sinai. Though the structure of the Deuteronomic history is that of the reign of individual kings, yet the theme is the function of monarchy as an instrument of the covenant. We must look beneath and beyond the monarchy to discover the form of Israelite historical writing.

The ancient world exhibits two forms of culture: 1. The cosmological viewed as political order (Egypt and Mesopotamia), or as ethical order (China), or as natural law (Greece); and 2. the historical (Israel). Cosmological order moves from nature to human action. Israelite order moved from history to creation. Cosmological order leads to the concept of history as a sequence of predetermined phases reflecting a cosmic pattern. This is illustrated by the Han historiography which related previous reigns to the order of succession or the order of conquest of the five elements. When applied to universal history, the cosmological order suggests the sequence of civilizations after the pattern of nature—a tree sprouts from a seed, it matures, bears fruit and dies. Similarly, civilizations have a beginning, a flowering and then a decline (Spengler, Toynbee).

The form of the great ancient civilizations was cosmological or, more precisely, political with cosmic analogies. The two outstanding examples were Mesopotamia and China. Both fitted human action into cosmological categories, and hence regarded historiography as a branch of astrology. Both Ssu-ma Tan and Ssu-ma Chien were astrologers. Mesopotamia saw the cosmic order as essentially political—a hierarchy of deities structured as a state in terms of status and role. There were, however, revolutions or at least important cabinet shifts in heaven which were reflected according to Babylonian historiography in political reorganization in the human state. By and large both in Mesopotamia and in China, as well as in Greece, the pattern of the historical process was one of eternal recurrence, a cyclical movement of the rise and fall of dynasties.

Cosmological order contributed the concept of chronology, according to which either lunar or solar units of time provided the structure for the records of human action. Both Mesopotamia and China developed annalistic histories recording the action of the emperor within the span of the earth's annual circuit or within the 12-13 lunar units of the year. At best cosmological order produced dynastic histories of imperial action, reign by reign, during the course of one political structure. The great general history (*Tzu-chih t'ung-chien*) compiled summaries of the dynastic annals. Neither Mesopotamia nor China developed, to a determinative stage, the concept of cultural movements, of historical form with broader and more important categories than the dynastic schema.

Israel was unique in the ancient world in its development of a notion of historical form. Its origin as a nation was traced to historical events (exodus—Sinai—conquest) rather than to the divine ancestry of its first kings or to a cosmologically determined social order. Yahweh was not the national ancestor, and he was known through historical rather than natural phenomena. Israel's relation to Yahweh was in terms of a covenant—an historical encounter, involving a destiny based upon decision. Dr. Mendenhall, in his study of treaties between suzerains and vassals in the Ancient Near East of the second millennium B.C., has discovered a pattern that is similar to the covenant between Yahweh and Israel presented in *Exodus*. The sovereign announces, in the first person, the evidences of his good will toward the lesser nation. He tells how in the past the nation has been the recipient of his special favour. Then follows the conditions of the covenant: 1. This treaty cancels out all former treaties and prohibits the making of any new treaties in the future with another emperor. 2. This covenant shall be binding so long as the emperor lives. It is a sacred covenant to which the gods are witnesses. It is to be kept in a sacred place (temple) and read by the vassal king to his people on regularly appointed holy days. 3. The vassal state is held responsible for the keeping of internal peace and good order. 4. The benefits which shall come to the vassal state from its loyalty to the treaty and the curses that shall befall, if it defects, are enumerated. There is an obvious parallel between this treaty pattern and the Sinai covenant. The first three commandments bind Israel to an exclusive service to Yahweh. The Fourth Commandment is concerned with the observing of Yahweh's holy day, the Sabbath. Even from the time of Moses, the Sabbath may have been celebrated by the Israelites as a day of remembrance of the covenant. The second part of the Decalogue is concerned with establishing the structures of society. These include the family (honour due to parents), the limits of individual rights within the community (prohibition of murder) and in respect of property (prohibition of adultery and theft), and even of that state of mind that leads to these (coveting a neighbour's ox or wife). Finally there is the integrity of government and the courts (prohibition against false witness). All these commandments describe the conditions of the 'king's peace' which the vassal must keep.

This sense of an historical present, of encounter and covenant, gave an historical form to the past. Historical form involves a continuity of events regarded as the structure of the past that has its center of meaning in the present. This is something different from the cosmological or objective notion of time.

Each civilization has a center which is held to be its point of contact with the special source or ground of its being. Chinese civilization found this center in the concept of a *Chung Kuo* (中國)—the kingly or imperial center. Feudal states of lesser significance formed an outer circle which stretched out toward the darkness and disorder of the lands of the barbarians. With the subjection of the feudal states under the Ch'in the *Chung Kuo* was expanded to include the whole empire, i.e.

the whole of civilization, bounded by the rest of mankind—the barbarian outer circle.

For Israel the center was the ark of the covenant as the bearer of the power encountered at Sinai—the symbol of the power of historical event released from its concrete geographical and temporal setting to continue as a living tradition. Later the ark was enshrined in Jerusalem, and, with the division of the empire, Shechem became the *omphalos* (navel) of the Northern Kingdom. From the latter part of the Eighth Century, the center was not geographical. It was the prophetic word. Israel's point of contact with Yahweh was in the prophet. Finally it was the written revelation, the *Torah* (Law). In each instance the center was in the covenant, not in the monarchy or in the king.

In the historical form, to use Professor Voegelin's terms, the community seeks the true order of its being under God. Its true order is something to be discovered in history through the living out of the covenant, not something given. Israel was a people with a present seeking a nature—its true being. In cosmological form, civilizations are peoples with a nature that expresses itself in time.

Israel's historical form was expressed in symbols that grew out of and continued to participate in historical events. Egypt became the symbol of spiritual bondage, of spiritual death, of *sheol* (the grave). *The Exodus* was the symbol of deliverance from death, of being raised up from the grave. The desert was the void. *Wandering in the wilderness* became the symbol of the indecision, of the indecisive moment between the *no longer* and the *not yet*, between the meaninglessness of civilizations of brute force and sensualism and the purposelessness of nomadic existence. The *Conquest* became the symbol of a new alternative, the struggle toward a new kind of society beyond the cyclical civilizations and the nomadic rejection of culture. Through these symbols, events became historical. The past lives in the present because it has been released from the grave of time and space to be ingredient in the present. Israel's historical writing was an act of faith, and that faith was set within the forms of history.

Three historiographic symbols determined the structure of the *Old Testament*: 1. *Toroth* (law), 2. *toldoth* (genealogy) and 3. *berith* (covenant), according to recent studies from a 'form criticism' position (G. von Rad, I. Engnell, S. Mowinckel, Sheldon H. Bland and especially Eric Voegelin whose *Israel and Revelation* is the source of the general point of view of this section and of several of its specific interpretations).

Toroth was the divine instruction, the will of God, Israel's task as the servant of Yahweh, i.e. as the bearer of promise. It was subject always to interpretation as Israel lived its history in the present. *Deuteronomy* was not a second law but a new instruction in the law under the new conditions of the monarchy. Ezra's law of the king of Heaven was a second major instruction expanding the law from the conditions of the monarchy to a way of life in a non-political community. The law lived through instruction, for it was instruction; and instruction always means the living encounter of the past and the present.

Toldoth was the framework of history exposing the pedigree of the vital relationship of events as that of one generation to the next. 1. It gave to the movements of history, and to historiographic periodicy, the concreteness of the relationship of father to son, providing the concept of continuity and of the essential character of importance in the notion of the family line. Yet it safeguarded the concept of novelty and concreteness in the notion of the present generation, and of the individual person who is the bearer of the family line. 2. It expressed the essential unity of all mankind in the myth of the common ancestor (Adam). It also explained basic cultural differences according to the pattern of the branches of the one family tree (Adam to Noah). Most important of all, it provided a symbol for distinguishing the line of the bearers of promise (Noah to Abraham). 3. It gave to the concept of periodicy a corrective emphasis upon continuity. There is no genealogical break between Adam-Noah-Abraham-Moses. 4. It highlighted the principle of selection within the continuity of the family, the distinctiveness of societies, institutions, movements within history, the focusing toward particularity, and the expansion toward universalism —the narrowing from Noah to Abraham through Jacob to the twelve tribes, and finally, to the monarchy. Again the focusing toward the prophetic movement and the righteous remnant is the preparation for the expansion from the righteous remnant to a universal society. 5. The relating of periodicy to genealogy yielded the rich symbol of novelty in history, of the leap from one stage in the struggle to achieve a nature through history—the symbol of the orders of mankind. The first mankind is from Adam to Noah. A new humanity emerges with Abraham. Following this symbolism, the Christ is described in the New Testament as the first born of a new generation.

The third historiographic symbol was *berith* (covenant). Covenant symbolized the process of revelation by which the true order was made known at each crucial juncture of Israel's experience. It binds *torah* to history, to the specific event of the law. It is the symbol of the *I-Thou* relationship between men and God, of the immanence of God in the historical process, and of the transcendence of God to all human institutions, cultures, states and movements. It symbolizes both the nearness and the otherness of God. Above all, it symbolizes the character of mutuality in the relationship between God and man. Without this mutuality there could be no history, for then there would be no freedom. For his name's sake, God makes a new covenant with Israel; for the condition of history is that divine providence operates through historical agencies. The whole of Israel's history is a covenant history. Its periodicy is covenantal: 1. the covenant with Adam, 2. the covenant with Noah, 3 the covenant with Abraham, 4. the covenant with Moses, 5. the covenant with Ezra.

The *New Testament* means the New Covenant, and the Church was called the New Israel. Israelite historiography was true history because as Gregory of Nazianzus observed, 'it proceeds from beginnings through beginnings to new beginnings that have no end.' In Israelite historiography is the ground of world history, and historically it led for the first time to the writing of world history. The Israel of God is the people who have a history because they have a covenant, and, hence, a destiny beyond the rise and fall of civilizations. They owe their history to their destiny to be servants of God in his redemption of all creation. Preparation—mission—community—is history; for it is universal. Cosmological order is nature, but it is nature quite differently understood than from the viewpoint of modern science. It is nature after the pattern of the closed society under immutable law.

READINGS FROM THE OLD TESTAMENT

CREATION NARRATIVES: The *J* Account of Creation (*Genesis* 2:4b-9, 2:15-3:20, based on an ancient oral tradition).

In the day that the Lord God made the earth and the heavens, when no plant of the field was yet in the earth and no herb of the field had yet sprung up—for the Lord God had not caused it to rain upon the earth, and there was no man to till the ground; but a mist went up from the earth and watered the whole face of the ground— then the Lord God formed man of dust from the ground, and breathed into his nostrils the breath of life; and man became a living being.

And the Lord God planted a garden in Eden, in the east; and there he put the man whom he had formed. And out of the ground the Lord God made to grow every tree that is pleasant to the sight and good for food, the tree of life also in the midst of the garden, and the tree of the knowledge of good and evil.

The Lord God took the man and put him in the garden of Eden to till it and keep it. And the Lord God commanded the man, saying, 'You may freely eat of every tree of the garden; but of the tree of the knowledge of good and evil you shall not eat, for in the day that you eat of it you shall die.'

Then the Lord God said 'It is not good that the man should be alone; I will make him a helper fit for him.' So out of the ground the Lord God formed every beast of the field and every bird of the air, and brought them to the man to see what he would call them; and whatever the man called every living creature, that was its name. The man gave names to all cattle, and to the birds of the air, and to every beast of the field; but for the man there was not found a helper fit for him. So the Lord God caused a deep sleep to fall upon the man, and while he slept took one of his ribs and closed up its place with flesh; and the rib which the Lord God had taken from the man he made into a woman and brought her to the man. Then the man said,

'This at last is bone of my bones and flesh of my flesh;
She shall be called Woman,
    because she was taken out of Man.'

Therefore a man leaves his father and his mother and cleaves to his wife, and they become one flesh. And the man and his wife were both naked, and were not ashamed.

Now the serpent was more subtle than any other wild creature that the Lord God had made. He said to the woman, 'Did God say: You shall not eat of any tree of the garden?' And the woman said to the serpent, 'We may not eat of the fruit of the tree which is in the midst of the garden, neither shall you touch it, lest you die.' But the serpent said to the woman, 'You will not die. For God knows that when you eat of it your eyes will be opened, and you will be like God, knowing good and evil.' So when the woman saw that the tree was good for food, and that it was a delight to the eyes, and that the tree was to be desired to make one wise, she took of its fruit and ate; and she also gave some to her husband, and he ate. Then the eyes of both were opened, and they knew that they were naked; and they sewed fig leaves together and made themselves aprons.

And they heard the sound of the Lord God walking in the garden in the cool of the day, and the man and his wife hid themselves from the presence of the Lord God among the trees of the garden. But the Lord God called to the man, and said to him, 'Where are you?' And he said, 'I heard the sound of thee in the garden, and I was afraid, because I was naked; and I hid myself.' He said, 'Who told you that you were naked? Have you eaten of the tree of which I commanded you not to eat?' The man said, 'The woman whom thou gavest to be with me, she gave me fruit of the tree, and I ate.' Then the Lord God said to the woman, 'What is this that you have done?' The woman said, 'The serpent beguiled me, and I ate.' The Lord God said to the serpent,

'Because you have done this,
    cursed are you above all cattle,
    and above all wild animals;
Upon your belly you shall go,
    and dust you shall eat
    all the days of your life.
I will put enmity between you and the woman,
    and between your seed and her seed;
he shall bruise your head,
    and you shall bruise his heel.'
To the woman he said,
'I will greatly multiply your pain in childbearing;
    in pain you shall bring forth children,
yet your desire shall be for your husband,
    and he shall rule over you.'
And to Adam he said,
'Because you have listened to the voice of your wife,
    and have eaten of the tree
of which I commanded you,
    'You shall not eat of it,'
cursed is the ground because of you;
    in toil you shall eat of it all the days of your life;
thorns and thistles it shall bring forth to you;
    and you shall eat the plants of the field.
In the sweat of your face

you shall eat bread
till you return to the ground,
    for out of it you were taken;
you are dust,
    and to dust you shall return.'

The man called his wife's name Eve, because she was the mother of all living. And the Lord made for Adam and for his wife garments of skins, and clothed them.

The *P* Account of Creation (*Genesis* 1:1-24a, final edition c. 400 B.C.)

In the beginning God created the heavens and the earth. The earth was without form and void, and darkness was upon the face of the deep; and the Spirit of God was moving over the face of the waters.

And God said, 'Let there be light'; and there was light. And God saw that light was good; and God separated the light from the darkness. God called the light Day, and the darkness he called Night. And there was evening and there was morning, one day.

And God said, 'Let there be a firmament in the midst of the waters, and let it separate the waters from the waters.' And God made the firmament and separated the waters which were under the firmament from the waters which were above the firmament. And it was so. And God called the firmament Heaven. And there was evening and there was morning, a second day.

And God said, 'Let the waters under the heavens be gathered together into one place, and let the dry land appear.' And it was so. God called the dry land Earth, and the waters that were gathered together he called Seas. And God saw that it was good. And God said, 'Let the earth put forth vegetation, plants yielding seed, and fruit trees bearing fruit in which is their seed, each according to its kind, upon the earth.' And it was so. The earth brought forth vegetation, plants yielding seed according to their own kinds, and trees bearing fruit in which is their seed, each according to its kind. And God saw that it was good. And there was evening and there was morning, a third day.

And God said, 'Let there be lights in the firmament of the heavens to separate the day from the night; and let them be for signs and for seasons and for days and years, and let them be lights in the firmament of the heavens to give light upon the earth.' And it was so. And God made the two great lights, the greater light to rule the day, and the lesser light to rule the night; he made the stars also. And God set them in the firmament of the heavens to give light upon the earth, to rule over the day and over the night, and to separate the light from the darkness. And God saw that it was good. And there was evening and there was morning, a fourth day.

And God said, 'Let the waters bring forth swarms of living creatures, and let birds fly above the earth across the firmament of the heavens.' So God created the great sea monsters and every living creature that moves, with which the waters swarm, according to their kinds, and every winged bird according to its kind. And God saw that it was good. And God blessed them, saying, 'Be fruitful and multiply and fill the waters in the seas, and let birds multiply on the earth.' And there was evening and there was morning, a fifth day.

And God said, 'Let the earth bring forth living creatures according to their kinds: cattle and creeping things and beasts of the earth according to their kinds.' And it was so. And God made the beasts of the earth according to their kinds and the cattle according to their kinds, and everything that creeps upon the ground according to its kind. And God saw that it was good.

Then God said, 'Let us make man in our image, after our likeness; and let them have dominion over the fish of the sea, and over the birds of the air, and over the cattle, and over all the earth, and over every creeping thing that creeps upon the earth.' So God created man in his own image, in the image of God he created him; male and female he created them. And God blessed them, and God said to them. 'Be fruitful and multiply, and fill the earth and subdue it; and have dominion over the fish of the sea and over the birds of the air and over every living thing that moves upon the earth.' And God said, 'Behold, I have given you every plant yielding seed which is upon the face of all the earth, and every tree with seed in its fruit; you shall have them for food. And to every beast of the earth, and to every bird of the air, and to everything that creeps on the earth, everything that has the breath of life, I have given every green plant for food.' And it was so. And God saw everything that he had made, and behold, it was very good. And there was evening and there was morning, a sixth day.

Thus the heavens and the earth were finished, and all the host of them. And on the seventh day God finished his work which he had done, and he rested on the seventh day from all his work which he had done. So God blessed the seventh day and hallowed it, because on it God rested from all his work which he had done in creation.

These are the generations of the heavens and the earth when they were created.

CYCLICAL CIVILIZATION

(*Genesis* 11:1-9 *J*, based on an ancient oral tradition.)

Now the whole earth had one language and few words. And as men migrated in the east, they found a plain in the land of Shinar and settled there. And they said to one another, 'Come, let us make bricks, and burn them thoroughly.' And they had brick for stone, and bitumen for mortar. Then they said, 'Come, let us build ourselves a city, and a tower with its top in the heavens, and let us make a name for ourselves, lest we be scattered abroad upon the face of the whole earth.' And the Lord came down to see the city and the tower, which the sons of men had built. And the Lord said, 'Behold, they are one people, and they have all one language; and this is only the beginning of what they will do; and nothing that they propose to do will now be impossible for them. Come, let us go down, and there confuse their language, that they may not understand one another's speech.' So the Lord scattered them abroad from there over the face of all the earth, and they left off building the city. Therefore its name was called Babel, because there the Lord confused the language of all the earth; and from there the Lord scattered them abroad over the face of all the earth.

COVENANT HISTORY

1. Judgment and Promise (*Genesis* 6:11-22; 7:6-8:3; 9:1-17.)

Now the earth was corrupt in God's sight, and the earth was filled with violence. And God saw the earth, and behold, it was corrupt; for all flesh had corrupted their way upon the earth. And God said to Noah. 'I have determined to make an end of all flesh; for the earth is filled with violence through them; behold, I will destroy them with the earth. Make yourself an ark of gopher wood; make rooms in the ark, and cover it inside and out with pitch. This is how you are to make it: the length of the ark three hundred cubits, its breadth fifty cubits, and its height thirty cubits. Make a roof for the ark, and finish it to a cubit above; and set the door of the ark in its side; make it with lower, second, and third decks. For behold, I will bring a flood of waters upon the earth, to destroy all flesh in which is the breath of life from under heaven; everything that is on the earth shall die. But I will establish my covenant with you; and you shall come into the ark, you, your sons, your wife, and your sons' wives with you. And of every living thing of all flesh, you shall bring two of every sort into the ark, to keep them alive with you; they shall be male and female. Of the birds according to their kinds, and of the animals according to their kinds, of every creeping thing of the ground according to its kind, two of every sort shall come in to you, to keep them alive. Also take with you every sort of food that is eaten, and store it up; and it shall serve as food for you and for them.' Noah did this; he did all that God commanded him.

Noah was six hundred years old when the flood of waters came upon the earth. And Noah and his sons and his wife and his sons' wives with him went into the ark, to escape the waters of the flood. Of clean animals, and of animals that are not clean, and of birds, and of everything that creeps on the ground, two and two, male and female, went into the ark with Noah, as God had commanded Noah. And after seven days the waters of the flood came upon the earth.

In the six hundredth year of Noah's life, in the second month, on the seventeenth day of the month, on that day all the fountains of the great deep burst forth, and the windows of the heavens were opened. And rain fell upon the earth forty days and forty nights. On the very same day Noah and his sons, Shem and Ham and Japheth, and Noah's wife and the three wives of his sons with them entered the ark, they and every beast according to its kind, and all the cattle according to their kinds, and every creeping thing that creeps on the earth according to its kind, and every bird according to its kind, every bird of every sort. They went into the ark with Noah, two and two of all flesh in which there was the breath of life. And they that entered, male and female of all flesh, went in as God had commanded him; and the Lord shut him in.

The flood continued forty days upon the earth; and the waters increased, and bore up the ark, and it rose high above the earth. The waters prevailed and increased greatly upon the earth; and the ark floated on the face of the waters. And the waters prevailed so mightily upon the earth that all the high mountains under the whole heaven were covered; the waters prevailed above the mountains, covering them fifteen cubits deep. And all flesh died that moved upon the earth, birds, cattle, beasts, all swarming creatures that swarm upon the earth, and every man; everything on the dry land in whose nostrils was the breath of

life died. He blotted out every living thing that was upon the face of
the ground, man and animals and creeping things and birds of the air;
they were blotted out from the earth. Only Noah was left, and those
that were with him in the ark. And the waters prevailed upon the
earth a hundred and fifty days.

But God remembered Noah and all the beasts and all the cattle that
were with him in the ark. And God made a wind blow over the earth,
and the waters subsided; the fountains of the deep and the windows
of the heavens were closed, the rain from the heavens was restrained,
and the waters receded from the earth continually. At the end of a
hundred and fifty days the waters had abated.

And God blessed Noah and his sons, and said to them, 'Be fruitful and multiply, and fill the earth. The fear of you and the dread
of you shall be upon every beast of the earth, and upon every bird
of the air, upon everything that creeps on the ground and all fish of
the sea; into your hand they are delivered. Every moving thing that
lives shall be food for you; and as I gave you the green plants, I gave
you everything. Only you shall not eat flesh with its life, that is, its
blood. For your lifeblood I will surely require a reckoning; of every
beast I will require it and of man; of every man's brother I will require
the life of man. Whoever sheds the blood of man, by man shall his
blood be shed; for God made man in his own image. And you, be
fruitful and multiply, bring forth abundantly on the earth and multiply
in it.'

Then God said to Noah and to his sons with him, 'Behold, I establish my covenant with you and your descendants after you, and with
every living creature that is with you, the birds, the cattle, and every
beast of the earth with you, that never again shall all flesh be cut off
by the waters of a flood, and never again shall there be a flood to
destroy the earth.' And God said, 'This is the sign of the covenant
which I make between me and you and every living creature that is
with you, for all future generations: I set my bow in the cloud, and
it shall be a sign of the covenant between me and the earth. When
I bring clouds over the earth and the bow is seen in the clouds, I will
remember my covenant which is between me and you and every living
creature of all flesh; and the waters shall never again become a flood
to destroy all flesh. When the bow is in the clouds, I will look upon
it and remember the everlasting covenant between God and every
living creature of all flesh that is upon the earth.' God said to Noah,
'This is the sign of the covenant which I have established between me

and all flesh that is upon the earth.'

2. The Father of a New People

A. THE *J* ACCOUNT (*GENESIS* 12:1-4A, C. 950 B. C.)

Now the Lord said to Abram, 'Go from your country and your kindred and your father's house to the land that I will show you. And I will make of you a great nation, and I will bless you, and make your name great, so that you will be a blessing. I will bless those who bless you, and him who curses you I will curse; and by you all the families of the earth will bless themselves.'

B. THE *E* ACCOUNT (*GENESIS* 15:1-6 C. 850 B. C.)

After these things the word of the Lord came to Abram in a vision, 'Fear not, Abram, I am your shield; your reward shall be very great.' But Abram said, 'O Lord God, what wilt thou give me, for I continue childless, and the heir of my house is Eliezer of Damascus?' And Abram said, 'Behold, thou hast given me no offspring; and a slave born in my house will be my heir.' And behold, the word of the Lord came to him, 'This man shall not be your heir; your own son shall be your heir.' And he brought him outside and said, 'look toward heaven, and number the stars, if you are able to number them.' Then he said to him, 'So shall your descendants be.' And he believed the Lord; and he reckoned it to him as righteousness.

C. THE *P* ACCOUNT (*GENESIS* 17:1-8 C. 400 B. C.)

When Abram was ninety-nine years old the Lord appeared to Abram, and said to him, 'I am God Almighty; walk before me, and be blameless. And I will make my covenant between me and you, and will multiply you exceedingly.' Then Abram fell on his face; and God said to him, 'Behold my covenant is with you, and you shall be the father of a multitude of nations. I will make you exceedingly fruitful; and I will make nations of you, and kings shall come forth from you. And I will establish my covenant between me and you and your descendants after you throughout their generations for an everlasting covenant, to be God to you and to your descendants after you. And I will give to you, and to your descendants after you, the land of your sojournings, all the land of Canaan, for an everlasting possession; and I will be their God.'

3. Moses and the Covenant

A. *MYSTERIUM TREMENDUM* (*EXODUS* 19:14-19, *JE* c. 700 B.C.)

So Moses went down from the mountain to the people, and consecrated the people; and they washed their garments, And he said to the people, 'Be ready by the third day; do not go near a woman.'

On the morning of the third day there were thunders and lightnings, and a thick cloud upon the mountain, and a very loud trumpet blast, so that all the people who were in the camp trembled. Then Moses brought the people out of the camp to meet God; and they took their stand at the foot of the mountain. And Mount Sinai was wrapped in smoke, because the Lord descended upon it in fire; and the smoke of it went up like the smoke of a kiln, and the whole mountain quaked greatly. And as the sound of the trumpet grew louder and louder, Moses spoke, and God answered him in thunder.

B. THE TEN COMMANDMENTS (EXODUS 20:2-17, *E* c. 850 B.C.)

'I am the Lord your God, who brought you out of the land of Egypt, out of the house of bondage.

'You shall have no other gods before me.

'You shall not make yourself a graven image, or any likeness of anything that is in heaven above, or that is in the earth beneath, or that is in the water under the earth; you shall not bow down to them or serve them; for I the Lord your God am a jealous God, visiting the iniquity of the fathers upon the children to the third and the fourth generation of those who hate me, but showing steadfast love to thousands of those who love me and keep my commandments.

'You shall not take the name of the Lord your God in vain; for the Lord will not hold him guiltless who takes his name in vain.

'Remember the sabbath day, to keep it holy. Six days you shall labour, and do all your work; but the seventh day is a sabbath to the Lord your God; in it you shall not do any work, you, or your son, or your daughter, your manservant, or your maidservant, or your cattle, or the sojourner who is within your gates; for in six days the Lord made heaven and earth, the sea, and all that is in them, and rested the seventh day; therefore the Lord blessed the sabbath day and hallowed it.

'Honour your father and your mother, that your days may be long in the land which the Lord your God gives you.

'You shall not kill.

'You shall not commit adultery.

'You shall not steal.

'You shall not bear false witness against your neighbour.

'You shall not covet your neighbour's house; you shall not covet your neighbour's wife, or his manservant, or his maidservant, or his ox, or his ass, or anything that is your neighbour's.'

C. THE *D* INTERPRETATION OF THE COVENANT
(*DEUTERONOMY* 6:4-9, c. 550 B. C.)

'Here, O Israel: The Lord our God is one Lord; and you shall love the Lord your God with all your heart, and with all your soul, and with all your might. And those words which I command you this day shall be upon your heart; and you shall teach them diligently to your children, and shall talk of them when you sit in your house, and when you walk by the way, and when you lie down, and when you rise. And you shall bind them as a sign upon your hand, and they shall be as frontlets between your eyes. And you shall write them on the doorposts of your house and on your gates.'

D. THE *P* INTERPRETATION OF THE COVENANT BASED
ON THE HOLINESS CODE OF EZEKIEL. C. 550 B. C.
(*LEVITICUS* 19:14, 15-19 33-37; 23:4-11 c. 400 B. C.)

And the Lord said to Moses, 'Say to all congregations of the people of Israel, You shall be holy; for I the Lord your God am holy. Every one of you shall revere his mother and his father, and you shall keep my sabbaths: I am the Lord your God. Do not turn to idols or make for yourselves molten gods: I am the Lord your God.

'You shall do no injustice in judgment; you shall not be partial to the poor or defer to the great, but in righteousness shall you judge your neighbour. You shall not go up and down as a slanderer among your people, and you shall not stand forth against the life of your neighbour: I am the Lord.

'You shall not hate your brother in your heart, but you shall reason with your neighbour, lest you bear sin because of him. You shall not

take vengeance or bear any grudge against the sons of your own
people, but you shall love your neighbour as yourself: I am the Lord.

'You shall keep my statutes. You shall not let your cattle breed with
a different kind; you shall not sow your field with two kinds of seed nor
shall there come upon you a garment of cloth made of two kinds of stuff.

'When a stranger sojourns with you in your land, you shall not do
him wrong. The stranger who sojourns with you shall be to you as
the native among you, and you shall love him as yourself; for you
were strangers in the land of Egypt: I am the Lord your God.

'You shall do no wrong in judgment, in measures of length or
weight or quantity. You shall have just balances, just weights, a just
ephah, and a just hin: I am the Lord your God, who brought you out
of the land of Egypt. And you shall observe all my statutes and all
my ordinances, and do them: I am the Lord.'

These are the appointed feasts of the Lord, the holy convocations,
which you shall proclaim at the time appointed for them. In the first
month, on the fourteenth day of the month in the evening, is the Lord's
passover. And on the fifteenth day of the same month is the feast
of unleavened bread to the Lord; seven days you shall eat unleavened
bread. On the first day you shall have a holy convocation; you shall
do no laborious work. But you shall present an offering by fire to the
Lord seven days; on the seventh day is a holy convocation; you shall
do no laborious work.

4. Settlement and Tribal Federation in Palestine

> A. COVENANT RENEWAL AT SHECHEM (*JOSHUA* 24:1-28)
> (The Deuteronomic History, c. 550 B.C. based on a Northern
> tradition.)

Then Joshua gathered all the tribes of Israel to Shechem, and
summoned the elders, the judges, and the officers of Israel; and they
presented themselves before God. And Joshua said to all the people,
'Thus says the Lord, the God of Israel, 'Your fathers lived of old
beyond the Euphrates, Terah, the father of Abraham and of Nahor;
and they served other gods. Then I took your father Abraham from
beyond the River and led him through all the land of Canaan, and
made his offspring many. I gave him Isaac; and to Isaac I gave Jacob
and Esau. And I gave Esau the hill country of Seir to possess,
but Jacob and his children went down to Egypt. And I sent Moses

and Aaron, and I plagued Egypt with what I did in the midst of it; and afterwards I brought you out. Then I brought your fathers out of Egypt, and you came to the sea; and the Egyptians pursued your fathers with chariots and horsemen to the Red Sea. And when they cried to the Lord, he put darkness between you the Egyptians, and made the sea come upon them and cover them; and your eyes saw what I did to Egypt; and you lived in the wilderness a long time. Then I brought you to the land of the Amorites, who lived on the other side of the Jordan; they fought with you, and I gave them into your hand, and you took possession of their land, I destroyed them before you. Then Balak the son of Zippor, king of Moab, arose and fought against Israel; and he sent and invited Balaam the son of Beor to curse you, but I would not listen to Balaam; therefore he blessed you; so I delivered you out of his hand. And you went over the Jordan and came to Jericho, and you, and also the Amorites, the Perizzites, the Canaanites, the Hittites, the Girgashites, the Hivites, and the Jebusites; and I gave them into your hand. And I sent the hornet before you, which drove them out before you, the two kings of the Amorites; it was not by your sword or by your bow. I gave you a land on which you had not laboured, and cities which you had not built, and you dwell therein; you eat the fruit of vineyards and oliveyards which you did not plant.'

'Now therefore fear the Lord, and serve him in sincerity and in faithfulness; put away the gods which your fathers served beyond the River, and in Egypt, and serve the Lord. And if you be unwilling to serve the Lord, choose this day whom you will serve, whether the gods your fathers served in the region beyond the River, or gods of the Amorites in whose land you dwell; but as for me and my house, we will serve the Lord.'

Then the people answered, 'Far be it from us that we should forsake the Lord, to serve other gods; for it is the Lord our God who brought us and our fathers up from the land of Egypt, out of the house of bondage, and who did those great signs in our sight, and preserved us in all the way that we went, and among all the peoples through whom we passed; and the Lord drove out before us all the peoples, the Amorites who lived in the land; therefore we also will serve the Lord, for he is our God.'

But Joshua said to the people, 'You cannot serve the Lord; for he is a holy God; he is a jealous God; he will not forgive your transgression or your sins. If you forsake the Lord and serve foreign gods, then

he will turn and do you harm, and consume you, after having done
you good.' And the people said to Joshua, 'Nay; but we will serve
the Lord.' Then Joshua said to the people, 'You are witnesses against
yourselves that you have chosen the Lord, to serve him.' And they
said, 'We are witnesses.' He said, 'Then put away the foreign gods
which are among you, and incline your heart to the Lord, the God
of Israel.' And the people said to Joshua, 'The Lord our God we
will serve, and his voice we will obey.' So Joshua made a covenant
with the people that day, and made statutes and ordinances for them
at Shechem. And Joshua wrote those in the book of the law of God;
and he took a great stone, and set it up there under the oak in the
sanctuary of the Lord. And Joshua said to all the people, 'Behold,
this stone shall be a witness against us; for it has heard all the words
of the Lord which he spoke to us; therefore it shall be a witness
against you, lest you deal falsely with your God.' So Joshua sent the
people away, every man to his inheritance.

> B. YAHWEH DEFENDS HIS PEOPLE (*JUDGES* 5, from an
> ancient poem, c. 1200 B.C.)

Then sang Deborah and Barak
    the son of Abinoam on that day:

'That the leaders took the lead in Israel,
    that the people offered themselves willingly,
    bless the Lord!

'Here, O kings; give ear, O princes;
    to the Lord I will sing,
    I will make melody to the Lord, the God of Israel.

'Lord, when thou didst go forth from Seir,
    when thou didst march from the region of Edom,
the earth trembled,
    and the heavens dropped,
    yea, the clouds dropped water.
The mountains quaked before the Lord,
    yon Sinai before the Lord, the God of Israel.

'In the days of Shamgar, son of Anath,

in the days of Jael, caravans ceased
and travelers kept to the byways.
The peasantry ceased in Israel, they ceased
until you arose, Deborah,
arose as a mother in Israel.
When new gods were chosen,
then war was in the gates.
Was shield or spear to be seen
among forty thousand in Israel?
My heart goes out to the commanders of Israel
who offered themselves willingly among the people.
Bless the Lord.

'Tell of it, you who ride on tawny asses,
you who sit on rich carpets
and you who walk by the way.
To the sound of musicians at the watering places,
there they repeat the triumphs of the Lord,
the triumphs of his peasantry in Israel.

'Then down to the gates marched the people of the Lord.

'Awake, awake, Deborah!
Awake, awake, utter a song!
Arise, Barak, lead away your captives,
O son of Abinoam.
Then down marched the remnant of the noble;
the people of the Lord marched down for him against the
mighty.
From Ephraim they set out thither into the valley,
following you, Benjamin, with your kinsmen;
from Machir marched down the commanders,
and from Zebulun those who bear the marshal's staff;
the princes of Issachar came with Deborah,
and Issachar faithful to Barak;
into the valley they rushed forth at his heels.
Among the clans of Reuben
there were great searchings of heart.
Why did you tarry among the sheepfolds,
to hear the piping for the flocks?

Among the clans of Reuben
    there were great searchings of heart.
Gilead stayed beyond the Jordan;
    and Dan, why did he abide with the ships?
Asher sat still at the coast of the sea,
    settling down by his landings.
Zebulun is a people that jeopardized their lives to the death;
    Naphtali too, on the heights of the field.

'The kings came, they fought;
    then fought the kings of Canaan,
at Taanach, by the waters of Megiddo;
    they got no spoils of silver.
From heaven fought the stars,
    from their courses they fought against Sisera.
The torrent Kishon swept them away,
    the onrushing torrent, the torrent Kishon.
    March on, my soul, with might!

'Then loud beat the horses' hoofs
    with the galloping, galloping of his steeds.

'Curse Meroz, says the angel of the Lord,
    curse bitterly its inhabitants,
because they came not to the help of the Lord,
    to the help of the Lord against the mighty.

'Most blessed of women be Jael,
    the wife of Heber the Kenite,
    of tent-dwelling women most blessed.
He asked water and she gave him milk,
    she brought him curds in a lordly bowl.
She put her hand to the tent peg
    and her right hand to the workmen's mallet;
she struck Sisera a blow,
    she crushed his head,
    she shattered and pierced his temple.
He sank, he fell,
    he lay still at her feet;
    at her feet he sank, he fell;

where he sank, there he fell dead.

'Out of the window she peered,
    the mother of Sisera gazed through the lattice:
'Why is his chariot so long in coming?
    Why tarry the hoofbeats of his chariots?'
Her wisest ladies make answer,
    nay, she gives answer to herself,
'Are they not finding and dividing spoil?—
    A maiden or two for every man;
spoil of dyed stuffs for Sisera,
    spoil of dyed stuffs embroidered,
    two pieces of dyed work embroidered for my neck as spoil?'

'So perish all thine enemies, O Lord!
    But thy friends be like the sun as he rises in his might.'

5. The Monarchy under Yahweh (*I Chronicles* 29:10-18, Priestly interpretation, c. 350 B.C. *I Kings* 8:12-9:9, the Deuteronomic History, c. 550 B.C.)

Therefore David blessed the Lord in the presence of all the assembly; and David said: 'Blessed art thou, O Lord, the God of Israel our father, for ever and ever. Thine, O Lord, is the greatness, and the power, and the glory, and the victory, and the majesty; for all that is in the heavens and in the earth is thine; thine is the kingdom, O Lord, and thou art exalted as head above all. Both riches and honour come from thee, and thou rulest over all. In thy hand are power and might; and in thy hand it is to make great and to give strength to all. And now we thank thee, our God, and praise thy glorious name.

'But who am I, and what is my people, that we should be able thus to offer willingly? For all things come from thee, and of thy own have we given thee. For we are strangers before thee, and sojourners, as all our fathers were; our days on the earth are like a shadow and there is no abiding. O Lord our God, all this abundance that we have provided for building thee a house for thy holy name comes from thy hand and is all thy own. I know, my God, that thou triest the heart, and hast pleasure in uprightness; in the uprightness of my heart I have freely offered all these things, and now I have seen thy people, who are present here, offering freely and joyously to thee. O Lord, the God of Abraham,

Isaac, and Israel, our fathers, keep for ever such purposes and thoughts
in the hearts of thy people and direct their hearts toward thee.'

Then Solomon said,

'The Lord has set the sun in the heavens,
  but has said that he would dwell in thick darkness.
I have built thee an exalted house,
  a place for thee to dwell in for ever.'

Then the king faced about, and blessed all the assembly of Israel,
while all the assembly of Israel stood. And he said, 'Blessed be the
Lord, the God of Israel, who with his hand has fulfilled what he promised
with his mouth to David my father, saying, 'Since the day that I brought
my people Israel out of Egypt, I chose no city in all the tribes of Israel
in which to build a house, that my name might be there; but I chose
David to be over my people Israel.' Now it was in the heart of David
my father to build a house for the name of the Lord, the God of Israel.
But the Lord said to David my father, 'Whereas it was in your heart
to build a house for my name, you did well that it was in your heart;
nevertheless you shall not build the house, but your son who shall be
born to you shall build the house for my name.' Now the Lord has
fulfilled his promise which he made; for I have risen in the place of
David my father, and sit on the throne of Israel, as the Lord promised,
and I have built the house for the name of the Lord, the God of Israel.
And there I have provided a place for the ark, in which is the covenant
of the Lord which he made with our fathers, when he brought them
out of the land of Egypt.'

Then Solomon stood before the altar of the Lord in the presence
of all the assembly of Israel, and spread forth his hands toward heaven;
and said, 'O Lord, God of Israel, there is no God like thee, in heaven
above or on earth beneath, keeping covenant and showing steadfast
love to thy servants who walk before thee with all their heart; who hast
kept with thy servant David my father what thou didst declare to
him; yea, thou didst speak with thy mouth, and with thy hand hast
fulfilled it this day. Now therefore, O Lord, God of Israel, keep with
thy servant David my father what thou hast promised him, saying,
'There shall never fail you a man before me to sit upon the throne of
Israel, if only your sons take heed to their way, to walk before me as
you have walked before me.' Now therefore, O God of Israel, let thy
word be confirmed, which thou hast spoken to thy servant David my
father.

'But will God indeed dwell on the earth? Behold, heaven and the highest heaven cannot contain thee; how much less this house which I have built! Yet have regard to the prayer of thy servant and to his supplication, O Lord my God, hearkening to the cry and to the prayer which thy servant prays before thee this day; that thy eyes may be open night and day toward this house, the place of which thou hast said, 'My name shall be there,' that thou mayest hearken to the prayer which thy servant offers toward this place. And hearken thou to the supplication of thy servant and of thy people Israel, when they pray toward this place; yea, hear thou in heaven thy dwelling place; and when thou hearest, forgive.

'If a man sins against his neighbour and is made to take an oath, and comes and swears his oath before thine altar in this house, then hear thou in heaven, and act, and judge thy servants, condemning the guilty by bringing his conduct upon his own head, and vindicating the righteous by rewarding him according to his righteousness.

'When thy people Israel are defeated before the enemy because they have sinned against thee, if they turn again to thee, and acknowledge thy name, and pray and make supplication to thee in this house; then hear thou in heaven, and forgive the sin of thy people Israel, and bring them again to the land which thou gavest to their fathers.

'When heaven is shut up and there is no rain because they have sinned against thee, if they pray toward this place, and acknowledge thy name, and turn from their sin, when thou dost afflict them, then hear thou in heaven, and forgive the sin of thy servants, thy people Israel, when thou dost teach them the good way in which they should walk; and grant rain upon the land, which thou hast given to thy people as an inheritance.

'If there is famine in the land, if there is pestilence or blight or mildew or locust or caterpillar; if their enemy besieges them in any of their cities; whatever plague, whatever sickness there is; whatever prayer, whatever supplication is made by any man or by all thy people Israel, each knowing the affliction of his own heart and stretching out his hands toward this house; then hear thou in heaven thy dwelling place, and forgive, and act, and render to each whose heart thou knowest, according to all his ways (for thou, only, knowest the hearts of all the children of men); that they may fear thee all the days that they live in the land which thou gavest to our fathers.

'Likewise when a foreigner, who is not of thy people Israel, comes from a far country for thy name's sake, (for they shall hear of the great name, and thy mighty hand, and of thy outstretched arm), when he comes and prays toward this house, hear thou in heaven thy dwelling place, and do accordingly to all for which the foreigner calls to thee, in order that all the peoples of the earth may know thy name and fear thee, as do thy people Israel, and that they may know that this house which I have built is called by thy name.

'If thy people go out to battle against their enemy, by whatever way thou shalt send them, and they pray to the Lord toward the city which thou hast chosen and the house which I have built for thy name, then hear thou in heaven their prayer and their supplication, and maintain their cause.

'If they sin against thee—for there is no man who does not sin— and thou art angry with them, and dost give them to an enemy, so that they are carried away captive to the land of the enemy, far off or near; yet if they lay it to heart in the land to which they have been carried captive, and repent, and make supplication to thee in the land of their captors, saying, 'We have sinned, and have acted perversely and wickedly'; if they repent with all their enemies, who carried them captive, and pray to thee toward their land, which thou hast chosen, and the house which I have built for thy name; then hear thou in heaven thy dwelling place their prayer and their supplication, and maintain their cause and forgive thy people who have sinned against thee, and all their transgressions which they have committed against thee, and grant them compassion in the sight of those who carried them captive, that they may have compassion on them (for they are the people, and thy heritage, which thou didst bring out of Egypt, from the midst of the iron furnace). Let thy eyes be open to the supplication of the servant, and to the supplication of thy people Israel, giving ear to them whenever they call to thee. For thou didst separate them from among all the peoples of the earth, to be the heritage, as thou didst declare through Moses, thy servant, when thou didst bring our fathers out of Egypt, O Lord God.'

Now as Solomon finished offering all this prayer and supplication to the Lord, he arose from before the altar of the Lord, where he had knelt with hands outstretched toward heaven; and he stood and blessed all the assembly of Israel with a loud voice, saying, 'Blessed be the Lord who has given rest to his people Israel, according to all that he promised; not one word has failed of all his good promise, which he uttered by Moses his servant. The Lord our God be with us, as he was with our fathers; may he not leave us or forsake us; that he may incline our hearts to him, to walk in all his ways, and to keep his commandments, his statutes, and his ordinances, which he commanded our fathers. Let these words of mine, wherewith I have made supplication before the Lord, be near to the Lord our God day and night, and may he maintain the cause of his servant, and the cause of his people Israel, as each day requires; that all the peoples of the earth may know that the Lord is God; there is no other. Let your heart therefore be wholly true to the Lord our God, walking in his statutes and keeping his commandments, as at this day.'

Then the king, and all Israel with him, offered sacrifice before the Lord. Solomon offered as peace offerings to the Lord twenty-two thousand oxen and a hundred and twenty thousand sheep. So the king and all the people of Israel dedicated the house of the Lord. The same day the king consecrated the middle of the court that was before the house of the Lord; for there he offered the burnt offering and the cereal offering and the fat pieces of the peace offerings, because the bronze altar that was before the Lord was too small to receive the burnt offering and the cereal offering and the fat pieces of the peace offering.

So Solomon held the feast at that time, and all Israel with him a great assembly, from the entrance of Hamath to the Brook of Egypt, before the Lord our God, seven days. On the eighth day he sent the people away, and they blessed the king, and went to their homes joyful and glad of heart for all the goodness that the Lord had shown to David his servant and to Israel his people.

When Solomon had finished building the house of the Lord and the king's house and all that Solomon desired to build, the Lord appeared to Solomon a second time, as he had appeared to him at Gibeon. And the Lord said to him, 'I have heard your prayer and your supplication, which you have made before me; I have consecrated this house which you have built, and put my name there for ever; my eyes and my heart will be there for all time. And as for you, if you will walk before me, as David your father walked with integrity of heart and uprightness, doing according to all that I have commanded you, and keeping my statutes and my ordinances, then I will establish your royal throne over Israel for ever, as I promised David your father, saying, 'There shall not fail you a man upon the throne of Israel.' But if you turn aside from following me, you or your children, and do not keep my commandments and my statutes which I have set before you, but go and serve other gods and worship them, then I will cut off Israel from the land which I have given them; and the house which I have consecrated for my name I will cast out of my sight; and Israel will become a proverb and a byword among all peoples. And this house will become a heap of ruins; everyone passing by it will be astonished, and will hiss, and they will say, 'Why has the Lord done thus to this land and to this house?' Then they will say, 'Because they forsook the Lord their God who brought their fathers out of the land of Egypt, and laid hold on other gods, and worshiped them; and served them; therefore the Lord has brought all this evil upon them.'

6. The Monarchy under Judgment (*Hosea* 11:1-9; 12:1-9,13,14; 13:1, 4-11, c. 745 B.C.)

When Israel was a child, I loved him,
   and out of Egypt I called my son.
The more I called them,
   the more they went from me;
they kept sacrificing to the Baals,
   and burning incense to idols.

Yet it was I who taught Ephraim to walk,
   I took them up in my arms;
   but they did not know that I healed them.
I led them with cords of compassion,
   with the bands of love,
and I became to them as one
   who ceases the yoke on their jaws,
   and I bent down to them and fed them.

They shall return to the land of Egypt,
   and Assyria shall be their king,
   because they have refused to return to me.
The sword shall rage against their cities,
   consume the bars of their gates,
   and devour them in their fortresses.
My people are bent on turning away from me;
   so they are appointed to the yoke,
   and none shall remove it.

How can I give you up, O Ephraim!
   How can I hand you over, O Israel!

How can I make you like Admah!
    How can I treat you like Zeboiim!
My heart recoils within me,
    my compassion grows warm and tender.
I will not execute my fierce anger,
    I will not again destroy Ephraim;
    for I am God and not man,
    the Holy One in your midst,
    and I will not come to destroy.

Ephraim herds the wind,
    and pursues the east wind all day long;
they multiply falsehood and violence;
    they make a bargain with Assyria,
    and oil is carried to Egypt.

The Lord has an indictment against Judah,
    and will punish Jacob according to his ways,
    and requite him according to his deeds.
In the womb he took his brother by the heel,
    and in his manhood he strove with God.
He strove with the angel and prevailed,
    he wept and sought his favour.
He met God at Bethel,
    and there God spoke with him—
the Lord the God of hosts,
    the Lord is his name:
'So you, by the help of your God, return,
    hold fast to love and justice,
    and wait continually for your God.'

A trader, in whose hands are false balances,
    he loves to oppress.
Ephraim has said, 'Ah, but I am rich,
    I have gained wealth for myself';
but all his riches can never offset
    the guilt he has incurred.
I am the Lord your God
    from the land of Egypt:
I will again make you dwell in tents,

as in the days of the appointed feast.

By a prophet the Lord brought Israel up from Egypt,
    and by a prophet he was preserved.
Ephraim has given bitter provocation;
        so his Lord will leave his blood-guilt upon him,
        and will turn back upon him his reproaches.

When Ephraim spoke, men trembled;
        he was exalted in Israel;
        but he incurred guilt through Baal and died.

I am the Lord your God
        from the land of Egypt;
you know no God but me,
        and besides me there is no saviour.
It was I who knew you in the wilderness,
    in the land of drought;
but when they had fed to the full,
        they were filled, and their heart was lifted up;
        therefore they forgot me.
So I will be to them like a lion,
        like a leopard I will lurk beside the way.
I will fall upon them like a bear robbed of her cubs,
        I will tear open their breast,
and there I will devour them like a lion,
        as a wild beast would rend them.

I will destroy you, O Israel;
        who can help you?
Where now is your king, to save you;
where are all your princes, to defend you—
those of whom you said,
        'Give me king and princes'?
I have given you kings in my anger,
        and I have taken them away in my wrath.

7. Beyond Monarchy

        A. A NEW COVENANT (*JEREMIAH* 31:27-33, c, 590 B.C.)

'Behold, the days are coming, says the Lord, when I will sow the house of Israel and the house of Judah with the seed of man and the seed of beast. And it shall come to pass that as I have watched over them to pluck up and break down, to overthrow, destroy, and bring evil, so I will watch over them to build and to plant, says the Lord. In those days they shall no longer say:

'The fathers have eaten sour grapes, and the children's teeth are set on edge.'

But every one shall die for his own sin; each man who eats sour grapes, his teeth shall be set on edge.

'Behold, the days are coming, says the Lord, when I will make a new covenant with the house of Israel and the house of Judah, not like the covenant which I made with their fathers when I took them by the hand to bring them out of the land of Egypt, my covenant which they broke, though I was their husband, says the Lord. But this is the covenant which I will make with the house of Israel after those days, says the Lord: I will put my law within them, and I will write it upon their hearts; and I will be their God, and they shall be my people. And no longer shall each man teach his neighbour and each his brother, saying, 'Know the Lord,' for they shall all know me, from the least of them to the greatest, says the Lord; for I will forgive their iniquity, and I will remember their sin no more.'

(EZEKIEL 36:22-32, c. 550 B.C.)

'Therefore say to the house of Israel, Thus says the Lord God: It is not for your sake, O house of Israel, that I am about to act, but for the sake of my holy name, which you have profaned among the nations to which you came. And I will vindicate the holiness of my great name, which has been profaned among the nations, and which you have profaned among them; and the nations will know that I am the Lord, says the Lord God, when through you I vindicate my holiness before their eyes. For I will take you from the nations, and gather you from all the countries, and bring you into your own land. I will sprinkle clean water upon you, and you shall be clean from all your uncleannesses, and from all your idols I will cleanse you. A new heart I will give you, and a new spirit I will put within you; and I will take out of your flesh the heart of stone and give you a heart of flesh. And I will put my spirit within you, and cause you to walk in my statutes and be careful to observe my ordinances. You shall dwell in the land which I give to your fathers; and you shall be my people, and I will be your God. I will deliver you from all your uncleannesses, and I will summon the grain and make it abundant and lay no famine upon you. I will make the fruit of the tree and the increase of the field abundant, that you may never again suffer the disgrace of famine among the nations. Then you will remember your evil ways, and your deeds that were not good; and you will loathe yourselves for your iniquities and your abominable deeds. It is not for your sake that I will act, says the Lord God; let that be known to you. Be ashamed and confounded for your ways, O house of Israel.'

   B.   NEW ISRAEL (*ISAIAH* 6:1-8; 40:1-44:8; 45:1-6; 48:1-7; 52:7-53:12; 56:1-8 c. 400 B.C.)

In the year that King Uzziah died I saw the Lord sitting upon a throne, high and lifted up; and his train filled the temple. Above him stood the seraphim; each had six wings: with two he covered his face, and with two he covered his feet, and with two he flew. And one called to another and said:
   'Holy, holy, holy is the Lord of hosts;
   the whole earth is full of his glory.'
And the foundations of the thresholds shook at the voice of him who called, and the house was filled with smoke. And I said: 'woe is me! For I am lost; for I am a man of unclean lips, and I dwell in the midst of a people of unclean lips; for my eyes have seen the King, the Lord of hosts!'
   Then flew one of the seraphim to me, having in his hand a burning coal which he had taken with tongs from the altar. And he touched my mouth, and said: 'Behold, this has touched your lips; your guilt is taken away, and your sin forgiven.' And I heard the voice of the Lord saying, 'Whom shall I send, and who will go for us?' Then I said, 'Here I am! Send me.'

   Comfort, comfort my people,
      says your God.
   Speak tenderly to Jerusalem
      and cry to her
   that her warfare is ended,
      that her iniquity is pardoned,
   that she has received from the Lord's hand
      double for all her sins.

A voice cries:
'In the wilderness prepare the way of the Lord,
    make straight in the desert a highway for our God.
Every valley shall be lifted up,
    and every mountain and hill be made low;
the uneven ground shall become level,
    and the rough places a plain.
And the glory of the Lord shall be revealed,
    and all flesh shall see it together,
    for the mouth of the Lord has spoken.'

A voice says, 'Cry!'
    And I said, 'What shall I cry?'
All flesh is grass,
    and all its beauty is like the flower of the field.
The grass withers, the flower fades,
    when the breath of the Lord blows upon it;
    surely the people is grass.
The grass withers, the flower fades;
    but the word of our God will stand for ever.
Get you up to a high mountain,
    O Zion, herald of good tidings;
lift up your voice with strength,
    O Jerusalem, herald of good tidings,
    lift it up, fear not;
say to the cities of Judah,
    'Behold your God!'
Behold, the Lord God comes with might,
    and his arm rules for him;
behold, his reward is with him,
    and his recompense before him.
He will feed his flock like a shepherd,
    he will gather the lambs in his arms,
he will carry them in his bosom,
    and gently lead those that are with young.

Who has measured the waters in the hollow of his hand
    and marked off the heavens with a span,
enclosed the dust of the earth in a measure
    and weighed the mountains in scales

and the hills in a balance?
Who has directed the Spirit of the Lord,
    or as his counselor has instructed him?
Whom did he consult for his enlightenment,
    and who taught him the path of justice,
and taught him knowledge,
    and showed him the way of understanding?
Behold, the nations are like a drop from a bucket,
    and are accounted as the dust on the scales;
    behold, he takes up the isles like fine dust.
Lebanon would not suffice for fuel,
    nor are its beasts enough for a burnt offering.
All the nations are as nothing before him,
    they are accounted by him as less than nothing and emptiness.

To whom then will you liken God,
    or what likeness compare with him?
The idol! a workman casts it,
    and a goldsmith overlays it with gold,
    and casts for it silver chains.
He who is impoverished chooses for an offering
    wood that will not rot;
he seeks out a skilful craftsman
    to set up an image that will not move.

Have you not known? Have you not heard?
    Has it not been told you from the beginning?
    Have you not understood from the foundations of the earth?
It is he who sits above the circle of the earth,
    and its inhabitants are like grasshoppers;
who stretches out the heavens like a curtain,
    and spreads them like a tent to dwell in;
who brings princes to nought,
    and makes the rulers of the earth as nothing.

Scarcely are they planted, scarcely sown,
    scarcely has their stem taken root in the earth,
when he blows upon them, and they wither,
    and the tempest carries them off like stubble.

To whom then will you compare me,
    that I should be like him?
      says the Holy One.
Lift up your eyes on high and see:
    who created these?
He who brings out their host by number,
    calling them all by name;
by the greatness of his might,
    and because he is st.ong in power
    not one is missing.

Why do you say, O Jacob,
    and speak, O Israel,
'My way is hid from the Lord,
    and my right is disregarded by my God?'
Have you not known? Have you not heard?
The Lord is the everlasting God,
    the Creator of the ends of the earth.
He does not faint or grow weary.
    his understanding is unsearchable.
He gives power to the faint,
    and to him who has no might he increases strength.
Even youths shall faint and be weary,
    and young men shall fall exhausted;
but they who wait for the Lord shall renew their strength,
    they shall mount up with wings like eagles,
they shall run and not be weary,
    they shall walk and not faint.

Listen to me in silence, O coastlands;
    let the peoples renew their strength;
let them approach, then let them speak;
    let us together draw near for judgment.

Who stirred up one from the east
    whom victory meets at every step?
He gives up nations before him,
    so that he tramples kings under foot;
he makes them like dust with his sword,
    like driven stubble with his bow.

He pursues them and passes on safely,
 by paths his feet have not trod.
Who has performed and done this,
 calling the generations from the beginning?
I, the Lord, the first,
 and with the last; I am He.

The coastlands have seen and are afraid,
 the ends of the earth tremble;
 they have drawn near and come.
Every one helps his neighbour,
 and says to his brother, 'Take courage!'
The craftsman encourages the goldsmith,
 and he who smooths with the hammer him who strikes the anvil,
saying of the soldering, 'It is good';
 and they fasten it with nails so that it cannot be moved.

But you, Israel, my servant,
 Jacob, whom I have chosen,
 the offspring of Abraham, my friend;
you whom I took from the ends of the earth,
 and called from its farthest corners,
saying to you, 'You are my servant,
 I have chosen you and not cast you off;'
fear not, for I am with you,
 be not dismayed, for I am your God;
I will strengthen you, I will help you,
 I will uphold you with my victorious right hand.

Behold, all who are increased against you,
 shall be put to shame and confounded;
those who strive against you
 shall be as nothing and shall perish.
You shall seek those who contend with you,
 but you shall not find them;
those who war against you
 shall be as nothing at all.
For I, the Lord your God,
 hold your right hand;

it is I who say to you, 'Fear not,
 I will help you.'

Fear not, you worm Jacob,
 you men of Israel!
I will help you, says the Lord;
 Your redeemer is the Holy One of Israel.
Behold, I will make of you a threshing sledge,
 new, sharp, and having teeth;
you shall thresh the mountains and crush them,
 and you shall make the hills like chaff;
You shall winnow them and the wind shall carry them away,
 and the tempest shall scatter them.
And you shall rejoice in the Lord;
 in the Holy One of Israel you shall glory.

When the poor and needy seek water,
 and there is none,
 and their tongue is parched with thirst,
I the Lord will answer them,
 I the God of Israel will not forsake them.
I will open rivers on the bare heights,
 and fountains in the midst of the valleys;
I will make the wilderness a pool of water,
 and the dry land springs of water.
I will put in the wilderness the cedar,
 the acacia, the myrtle, and the olive;
I will set in the desert the cypress,
 the plane and the pine together;
that men may see and know,
 may consider and understand together,
that the hand of the Lord has done this,
 the Holy One of Israel has created it.

Set forth your case, says the Lord;
 bring your proofs, says the King of Jacob.
Let them bring them, and tell us what is to happen.
Tell us the former things, what they are,
 that we may consider them,
that we may know their outcome;

or declare to us the things to come.
Tell us what is to come hereafter,
 that we may know that you are gods;
do good, or do harm,
 that we may be dismayed and terrified.
Behold, you are nothing.
 and your work is nought;
 an abomination is he who chooses you.

I stirred up one from the north, and he has come.
 from the rising of the sun, and he shall call on my name;
he shall trample on rulers as on mortar,
 as the potter treads clay.
Who declared it from the beginning, that we might know,
 and beforetime, that we might say, 'He is right'?
There was none who declared it, none who proclaimed
 none who heard your words.
I first have declared it to Zion,
 and I give to Jerusalem a herald of good tidings.
But when I look there is no one;
 among these there is no counselor
 who, when I ask, gives an answer.
Behold, they are all a delusion;
 their works are nothing;
 their molten images are empty wind.

Behold my servant, whom I uphold,
 my chosen, in whom my soul delights;
I have put my spirit upon him,
 he will bring forth justice to the nations.
He will not fail or be discouraged
 till he has established justice in the earth;
 and the coastlands wait for his law.

Thus says God, the Lord,
 who created the heavens and stretched them out,
 who spread forth the earth and what came from it,
who gives breath to the people upon it
 and spirit to those who walk in it:
'I am the Lord, I have called you in righteousness,

I have taken you by the hand and kept you;
I have given you as a covenant to the people;
    a light to the nations,
    to open the eyes that are blind,
to bring out the prisoners from the dungeon,
    from the prison those who sit in darkness.
I am the Lord, that is my name;
    my glory I give to no other,
    nor my praise to graven images.
Behold, the former things have come to pass,
    and new things I now declare;
before they spring forth
    I tell you of them.'

Sing to the Lord a new song,
    his praise from the end of the earth!
Let the sea roar and all that fills it,
    the coastlands and their inhabitants.
Let the desert and its cities lift up their voice,
    the villages that Kedar inhabits;
Let the inhabitants of Sela sing for joy,
    let them shout from the top of the mountains.
Let them give glory to the Lord,
    and declare his praise in the coastlands.
The Lord goes forth like a mighty man,
    like a man of war he stirs up his fury;
he cries out, he shouts aloud,
    he shows himself mighty against his foes.

For a long time I have held my peace,
    I have kept still and restrained myself;
now I will cry out like a woman in travail,
    I will gasp and pant.
I will lay waste mountains and hills,
    and dry up all their herbage;
I will turn the rivers into islands,
    and dry up the pools.
And I will lead the blind
    in a way that they know not,
in paths that they have not known

I will guide them.
I will turn the darkness before them into light,
    the rough places into level ground.
There are things I will do,
    and I will not forsake them.
They shall be turned back and utterly put to shame,
    who trust in graven images,
who say to molten images,
    'You are our gods.'

Hear, you deaf;
    and look, you blind, that you may see!
Who is blind but my servant,
    or deaf as my messenger whom I send?
Who is blind as my dedicated one,
    or blind as the servant of the Lord?
He sees many things, but does not observe them;
    his ears are open, but he does not hear.
The Lord was pleased, for his righteousness' sake,
    to magnify his law and make it glorious.
But this is a people robbed and plundered,
    they are all of them trapped in holes
    and hidden in prisons;
they have become a prey with none to rescue,
    a spoil with none to say, 'Restore!'
Who among you will give ear to this,
    will attend and listen for the time to come?
Who gave up Jacob to the spoiler,
    and Israel to the robbers?
Was it not the Lord, against whom we have sinned,
    in whose ways they would not walk,
    and whose law they would not obey?
So he poured upon him the heat of his anger
    and the might of battle;
it set him on fire round about, but he did not understand;
    it burned him, but he did not take it to heart.

But now thus says the Lord,
    he who created you, O Jacob,
    he who formed you, O Israel:

'Fear not, for I have redeemed you;
   I have called you by name, you are mine.
When you pass through the waters I will be with you;
   and through the rivers, they shall not overwhelm you;
when you walk through fire you shall not be burned,
   and the flame shall not consume you.
For I am the Lord your God,
   the Holy One of Israel, your Saviour.
I give Egypt as your ransom,
   Ethiopia and Seba in exchange for you.
Because you are precious in my eyes,
   and honoured, and I love you,
I give men in return for you,
   peoples in exchange for your life.
Fear not, for I am with you;
   I will bring your offspring from the east,
   and from the west I will gather you;
I will say to the north, Give up,
   and to the south, Do not withhold;
bring my sons from afar
   and my daughters from the end of the earth,
every one who is called by my name,
   whom I created for my glory,
   whom I formed and made.'

Bring forth the people who are blind, yet have eyes,
   who are deaf, yet have ears!
Let all the nations gather together,
   and let the peoples assemble.
Who among them can declare this,
   and show us the former things?
Let them bring their witnesses to justify them,
   and let them hear and say, It is true.
'You are my witnesses,' says the Lord,
   'and my servant whom I have chosen,
that you may know and believe me and understand that I am He.
Before me no god was formed,
   nor shall there be any after me.
I, I am the Lord,
   and besides me there is no saviour.

I declared and saved and proclaimed,
    when there was no strange god among you;
    and you are my witnesses,' says the Lord.
'I am God, and also henceforth I am He;
    there is none who can deliver from my hand;
    I work and who can hinder it?'

Thus says the Lord,
    your Redeemer, the Holy One of Israel:
'For your sake I will send to Babylon
    and break down all the bars,
    and the shouting of the Chaldeans will be turned to lamentations.
I am the Lord, your Holy One,
    the Creator of Israel, your King.'
Thus says the Lord,
    who makes a way in the sea,
    a path in the mighty waters,
who brings forth chariot and horse,
    army and warrior;
they lie down, they cannot rise,
    they are extinguished, quenched like a wick:
'Remember not the former things,
    nor consider the things of old.
Behold, I am doing a new thing;
    now it springs forth, do you not perceive it?
I will make a way in the wilderness
    and rivers in the desert.
The wild beasts will honour me,
    the jackals and the ostriches;
for I give water in the wilderness,
    rivers in the desert,
to give drink to my chosen people,
    the people whom I formed for myself
that they might declare my praise.

'Yet you did not call upon me, O Jacob;
    but you have been weary of me, O Israel!
You have not brought me your sheep for burnt offerings,
    or honoured me with your sacrifices.
I have not burdened you with offerings,

or wearied you with frankincense.
You have not bought me sweet cane with money,
    or satisfied me with the fat of your sacrifices.
But you have burdened me with your sins,
    you have wearied me with your iniquities.

'I, I am He
    who blots out your transgressions for my own sake,
    and I will not remember your sins.
Put me in remembrance, let us argue together;
    set forth your case, that you may be proved right.
Your first father sinned,
    and your mediators transgressed against me.
Therefore I profaned the princes of the sanctuary,
    I delivered Jacob to utter destruction
    and Israel to reviling.

'But now hear, O Jacob my servant,
    Israel whom I have chosen!
Thus says the Lord who made you,
    who formed you from the womb and will help you:
Fear not, O Jacob my servant,
    Jeshurun whom I have chosen.
For I will pour water on thirsty land,
    and streams on the dry ground;
I will pour my Spirit upon your descendants,
    and my blessing on your offspring.
They shall spring up like grass amid waters,
    like willows by flowing streams.
This one will say, 'I am the Lord's,'
    another will call himself by the name of Jacob,
and another will write on his hand, 'The Lord's,'
    and surname himself by the name Israel.'

Thus says the Lord, the King of Israel
    and his Redeemer, the Lord of hosts:
'I am the first and I am the last;
    besides me there is no god.
Who is like me? Let him proclaim it,
    let him declare and set it forth before me.

Who has announced from of old the things to come?
    Let them tell us what is yet to be.
Fear not, nor be afraid;
    have I not told you from of old and declared it?
    And you are my witnesses!
Is there a God besides me?
    There is no Rock; I know not any.'

Thus says the Lord to his anointed, to Cyrus,
    whose right hand I have grasped,
to subdue nations before him
    and ungird the loins of kings,
to open doors before him
    that gates may not be closed:
'I will go before
    and level the mountains,
I will break in pieces the doors of bronze
    and cut asunder the bars of iron,
I will give you the treasures of darkness
    and the hoards in secret places,
that you may know that it is I, the Lord,
    the God of Israel, who call you by your name.
For the sake of my servant Jacob,
    and Israel my chosen,
I call you by your name,
    I surname you, though you do not know me,
I am the Lord, and there is no other,
    besides me there is no God;
    I gird you, though you do not know me,
that men may know, from the rising of the sun
    and from the west, that there is none besides me;
    I am the Lord, and there is no other.'

Hear this, O house of Jacob,
    who are called by the name of Israel,
    and who came forth from the loins of Judah;
who swear by the Lord,
    and confess the God of Israel,
    but not in truth or right.
For they call themselves after the holy city,

and stay themselves on the God of Israel;
the Lord of hosts is his name.

"The former things I declared of old,
    they went forth from my mouth and I made them known;
    then suddenly I did them and they came to pass.
Because I know that you are obstinate,
    and your neck is an iron sinew
    and your forehead brass,
I declared them to you from of old,
    before they came to pass I announced them to you,
lest you should say, 'My idol did them,
    my graven image and my molten image command them.'

"You have heard; now see all this;
    and will you not declare it?
From this time forth I make you hear new things,
    hidden things which you have not known.
They are created now, not long ago;
    before today you have never heard of them,
    lest you should say, 'Behold, I knew them.'

How beautiful upon the mountains
    are the feet of him who brings good tidings,
who publishes peace, who brings good tidings of good,
    who publishes salvation,
    who says to Zion, 'Your God reigns.'
Hark, your watchmen lift up their voice,
    together they sing for joy;
for eye to eye they see
    the return of the Lord to Zion.
Break forth together into singing,
    you waste places of Jerusalem;
for the Lord has comforted his people,
    he has redeemed Jerusalem.
The Lord has bared his holy arm
    before the eyes of all the nations;
and all the ends of the earth shall see
    the salvation of our God.

Depart, depart, go out thence,
    touch no unclean thing;
go out from the midst of her, purify yourselves,
    you who bear the vessels of the Lord.
For you shall not go out in haste,
    and you shall not go in flight,
for the Lord will go before you,
    and the God of Israel will be your rear guard.

Behold, my servant shall prosper,
    he shall be exalted and lifted up,
    and shall be very high.
As many were astonished at him—
    his appearance was so marred, beyond human semblance,
    and his form beyond that of the sons of men—
So shall he startle many nations;
    kings shall shut their mouths because of him;
for that which has not been told them they shall see,
    and that which they have not heard they shall understand.

Who has believed what we have heard?
    And to whom has the arm of the Lord been revealed?
For he grew up before him like a young plant,
    and like a root out of dry ground;
he had no form or comeliness that we should look at him,
    and no beauty that we should desire him.
He was despised and rejected by men;
    a man of sorrows, and acquainted with grief;
and as one from whom men hide their faces
    he was despised, and we esteemed him not.

Surely he has borne our griefs
    and carried our sorrows;
yet we esteemed him stricken,
    smitten by God, and afflicted.
But he was wounded for our transgressions,
    he was bruised for our iniquities;
upon him was the chastisement that made us whole,
    and with his stripes we are healed.
All we like sheep have gone astray;

we have turned every one to his own way;
and the Lord has laid on him
    the iniquity of us all.
He was oppressed, and he was afflicted,
    yet he opened not his mouth;
like a lamb that is led to the slaughter,
    and like a sheep that before its shearers is dumb,
    so he opened not his mouth.

By oppression and judgment he was taken away;
    and as for his generation, who considered
that he was cut off out of the land of the living,
    stricken for the transgression of my people?
And they made his grave with the wicked
    and with a rich man in his death,
although he had done no violence,
    and there was no deceit in his mouth.
Yet it was the will of the Lord to bruise him;
    he has put him to grief;
when he makes himself an offering for sin,
    he shall see his offspring, he shall prolong his days;
the will of the Lord shall prosper in his hand;
    he shall see the fruit of the travail of his soul and be satisfied;
by his knowledge shall the righteous one, my servant,
    make many to be accounted righteous;
    and he shall bear iniquities.
Therefore I will divide him a portion with the great,
    and he shall divide the spoil with the strong;
because he poured out his soul to death,
    and was numbered with the transgressors;
yet he bore the sin of many,
    and made intercession for the transgressors.

Thus says the Lord:
    'Keep justice, and do righteousness,
for soon my salvation will come,
    and my deliverance be revealed.
Blessed is the man who does this,
    and the son of man who holds it fast,
who keeps the sabbath, not profaning it,

and keeps his hand from doing any evil.'
Let not the foreigner who has joined himself to the Lord say,
　　'The Lord will surely separate me from his people';
and let not the eunuch say,
　　'Behold, I am a dry tree.'
For thus says the Lord:
　　To the eunuchs who keep my sabbaths,
　　who choose the things that please me
　　and hold fast my covenant,
I will give in my house and within my walls
　　a monument and a name
　　better than sons and daughters;
I will give them an everlasting name
　　which shall not be cut off.

'And the foreigners who join themselves to the Lord,
　　to minister to him, to love the name of the Lord,
　　and to be his servants,
every one who keeps the sabbath, and does not profane it,
　　and hold fast my covenant—
these I will bring to my holy mountain,
　　and make them joyful in my house of prayer;
their burnt offerings and their sacrifices
　　will be accepted on my altar;
for my house shall be called a house of prayer
　　for all peoples.
Thus says the Lord God,
　　who gathers the outcasts of Israel,
'I will gather yet others to him
　　besides those already gathered.'

4

GREEK

HISTORICAL WRITING

Classical Studies in Western Culture

THE ASIAN STUDENT OF WESTERN civilization may quite early in his survey reading ask the question: Why is so much emphasis placed upon the Greeks—why does the history of Western thought always begin with a long introduction that examines in detail Greek literature and history, Greek science and art? The Asian student who has gone beyond survey courses to special studies and research might put the question in a sharper way: Why has the West, even the modern West, been so interested in Greek civilization? Why has this always been true of the West? Whether the Asian student concentrates upon the Roman Empire or upon the Twelfth Century or the Nineteenth Century, he is soon aware that one of the major and perennial interests of Western historians has been the study of Greek civilization.

Yet neither Medieval Europe nor the Modern West could be described as truly Greek. Indeed, both Medieval and Modern Europe rejected more than they received from Greek culture. The most vehement of the rebels of the modern West were rebels against Greek thought—Martin Luther, Galileo, Immanuel Kant, Kierkegaard and Nietzsche, and the pioneers in all the new sciences in the Nineteenth Century. But even more significant than these protests and rejections, is the fundamental disparity of mood and emotion, of response and value judgment, between the Greek mind and the Western mind, whether the latter be Medieval, Renaissance or Modern. Arnold Toynbee in his *Greek Civilization and Character* has observed that the Western outlook was not anticipated by the Greek perspective. There was much in Greek culture which must always remain foreign to the West because so much of Greek life has never been experienced by the West nor has the West any

real capacity to respond to it. Western music, the mathematics of
movement and of infinity, the structure and dynamic of our industrial
society, our sociological image, our political ideology are deviations from
Greek civilization.

What answers then can be given to the question of the place of
Greek culture in Western thought? Perhaps the first is that there is
a demand upon a great people to explore its pedigree. A civilization
that is important either in terms of endurance or achievement seeks to
understand the sources of its strength. The search for roots is itself
a symbol of achievement and a recognition of destiny. The great ages
of all civilizations have been ages of renaissance, of the renewal of the
past or the re-interpretation and re-conception of the past. Yet great
ages do not rise when men face backwards. They are not the times
of the dogmatic worship of antiquity. Indeed the study of the past
may be a form of exploration of the frontiers of the present and a thrust
through such frontiers toward new notions of the character of importance.
Each culture has an idealized past, indeed each culture creates a past
for itself. The times of decision within a culture invite reflection and
vision, and these reflections establish the foundation upon which the
past is re-created. It has often been said that the West finds in the
Greeks what it looks for. 'Greek civilization' is the magic mirror in
which the West can glimpse its own image at the important moments
of its significant discoveries and decisive choices.

Whenever the West has come to such thresholds of discovery and
decision it has undertaken a new portrait of Greek civilization. This
was true of the great leap forward in the Twelfth Century (new
political ideas, new structures of society and commerce, the revival of
theological and scientific thought). All these were associated with,
though not necessarily dependent upon, the revival of Greek studies.
The relation was one of interdependence. It is largely true that a
revealing glimpse of Western self-interpretation (the self image of
European civilization) at any crucial point in history may best be had
from the contemporary studies of Greek civilization.

A second answer is that, despite the major differences between
ancient Greece and the Modern West there is still an important element
of continuity. One parent of the graphic and plastic arts as well as
the national and scientific thought of the West was Greek. In other
words the Greeks asked the questions to which the West has always
responded and continues to respond. The Greek answer is not the
answer of the West today nor the answer of the West at any time

since the passing away of Greek civilization. The Western answer to these questions is a function of its own experience, its own response, not only to its Greek but also to its Hebrew heritage. It is also of course a response to the character of its own experience. The important point remains—the Greeks asked the questions which the West could not ignore, the questions for which it had a capacity to respond.

The West has sought to understand itself also in contrast to Greek civilization. However different from each other have been the ages of Western civilization (the Patristic, the later Medieval, the Renaissance), the decisive line still comes at the passing away of Hellenism. European civilization is a new beginning. The Church Fathers (even those who prized very highly their classical past) describe the new society and its values in contrast to Hellenism. The study of classical thought in the Twelfth Century (related to the rise of the university and flowering in the great synthesis of Thomas Aquinas) was closer to the Fathers than to Hellenism. It saw itself in contrast to paganism quite as sharply as did the Patristic age. Despite the secularization of the West since the Seventeenth Century, the contrast between the modern mind and Greek civilization is even greater than between the Medieval mind and that of Athens during her golden age. What the West is in itself— what of itself it has become—is thus seen in sharpest outline against the background of its Greek heritage. What it is since its beginnings, what it is in contrast to its beginnings—this too is an insight to be gained by the West from its Hellenistic studies.

One aspect of this contrast is the relation of thought and action in classical Greece, in the Christian Synthesis of the great Church Fathers, in the Scientific Revolution of the Seventeenth Century and in the life of our own time. Toynbee in one place defines the genius of Greek culture as its capacity to have been diverted from action to the study of action. Before Hellenism died that diversion had gone further. It had moved on from the concrete viewed then as the distorted to the universal and the eternal viewed as perfection. Christian philosophy with its strong strain of Hebrew realism was able at least in part to overcome this polarity of the Greek mind with the Gospel of the Eternal Word that had indeed *become flesh* — a Gospel which seized upon the concrete richness of the unique event which could bear eternal significance.

What we have chosen as selected readings from Greek historical thought are passages from the great names among Greek historians— Herodotus, Thucydides, the schools of Xenophon and Polybius; and the themes we have chosen are in accord with the subject matter of the greater bulk of Greek historical writing. But you will find very little in them of importance to your knowledge of history— perhaps a few facts you did not know before. Of a few events you may learn a little more. Were you to read the whole of this literature—and you could do this quite easily in a few months as an extra curricular project— you would have the reward of being introduced to a fairly long list of names of people and places, of gods and shrines, of hints at customs and ways of thought. Yet of important knowledge you would have so little more than you will gain from these few passages.

The first thing you must ask of them is that they provide some answers to another kind of questions than that of the events themselves. The more important questions are: Why were these events remembered? Why were they of interest to these historians? Why were these events described in a certain way by Herodotus and in a certain way by Thucydides? You will know after your reading very little about the Persian War and the Pelopponesian War, very little about the early history of the Greek people. But you should know something of importance about the interest and the insights of Herodotus and Thucydides, and, therefore, something about the importance of their past as the Greeks remembered it. You should have a sense of what history meant to the Greeks—why they wrote it and what they learned from their writing in the attempt better to understand themselves. And you should also learn something of the Western mind: Why these passages seem important to the Western student and why it is that he believes that they help him better to understand himself.

It has been estimated that four-fifths of all Greek historical writing deals with war. We could extend this beyond the historians and say that the larger part of all Greek literature deals with war or has its setting against the background of war. Homer's *Iliad* and *Odyssey* have their setting in the Trojan War and its aftermath. Aeschylus' *House of Atreus* is set in the same frame. The successful resistance to the Persian invasion was the inspiration of Pindar and of much Greek poetry. Plato's *Republic* reflects the deeper level of Athenian response to the experiences of the Pelopponesian campaigns. Yet Greek historical writing is not essentially, nor even superficially, military history. It was not for the most part the campaigns themselves—logistics, strategy or tactics—that interested the writers or their audiences, but rather the human response and its meaning. They tell us very little of the actual events. They write rather of men, the inner motivations of the human spirit and the soul of the city, the human significance of encounter and conflict, of victory and defeat.

So a first insight into Greek historical writing would be that it is contemplative, a second look at action in which the whole city was involved and not only in a strictly physical or economic way, but also in a humane way. History is thought about action. First of all it is the clearer picture, possible only in thought, of the what and who and why of action. History is a refinement of action from the chaos that is perceived by the senses to the essential drama discovered by thought.

It is significant that most Greek historians—certainly the best of them—were men once active on the forefront of Greek politics and military affairs who had been broken in their careers as rising men of action. They were men diverted by circumstances that were in most instances irrational, and in all instances unjust, from public careers to the life of private reflection, from action to thought. This was true of Thucydides, Xenophon and Polybius; and it was true at least in the plan of Plato. Herodotus was the bold adventurer who sought in the perils and excitement of travel what was denied him of the thrills of the political arena. But he came to write his histories in the quiet hours when by disposition he too was diverted from action to thought.

History is thought, the structuring of the multitudinous sounds and sights of life into a story told, not by an idiot, but by an artist and a prophet. The historian reduces chaos to plot—the wildly gushing brute and blind torrent of action into the unities of creativity, purposive conquest and intentional response under the rational categories of pride and envy, fate and doom, and the humane categories of sin, judgment and grace.

The Themes of Greek History

The Poetry of History

To the selections from Aeschylus' *Agamemnon* and Herodotus' *Histories* we have given the title: 'The Poetry of History'. They are an elaboration upon a theme at least as old as Homer and as pervasive in Greek thought as the motto *know thyself*, or the caution *nothing in excess*. We have called it the Poetry of History in the sense of the rhythm of history—the pattern of history: The Greek pattern traces the fall not only of men but of nations along the points on the downward curve from wealth to luxury and reckless living to arrogance, madness and doom. Again it is the poetry of history because Aeschylus' poem catches the Greek theme of life of which Aristotle spoke when he suggested that poetry was more precise and less ambiguous than history. More than any other vice the Greeks feared arrogance both because it seemed to them the worst enemy of what they cherished most—politically and aesthetically as well as morally—and because it was their own besetting sin. What they most admired was the spirited man of considerate pride, zealous for victory and jealous of honour. Such a man could so easily become the arrogant man, who in losing his self control, must lose all: nobility, balance, humanity. Arrogance was at times regarded as the dread disease—the curse which the gods in envy put upon a man. Most often it is described as a madness which men and nations bring upon themselves when they allow themselves to be deceived by fortune—the fortune of wealth or of power, of special talent or of wondrous love—into believing that they could count themselves different from other men, exempt from the law of heaven and the dictates of fellow feeling. Here in Aeschylus' poem, arrogance is described as the grandfather of all vice. Untruth and recklessness are born of this arrogance. They defeat all efforts (either in one's own life or in the state) to achieve harmony, balance and peaceful justice. Herodotus, at about the time Aeschylus' poem was written, and Thucydides sometime later, were able to explain by this 'philosophy' how the mighty empire of Persia was defeated at Marathon, Thermopylae and Salamis: it was because its strength betrayed it into an arrogance which blinded it to the strength of others; and its strength betrayed it into a recklessness that led to folly and defeat. Aeschylus was the Greek prophet of grim, inexorable justice, and here he traces the pedigree of doom: wealth (*plutos*), luxury (*koros*), pride (*hybris*), blindness (*ate*), madness (*atasthalia*), retribution (*tisis*) and doom (*nemesis*).

'THE POETRY OF HISTORY'

FROM AESCHYLUS' *AGAMEMNON*

From the beginning of time men have known this hard truth:
  Great Wealth is never childless and its children are Misfortune;
  For no man can be sure to keep what he possesses, and his possessions,
    while he has them, teach him only pride, false hope and evil ways.
  And as from Father comes the son, so also Great Fortune begets as child
    Tears that cannot be dried, a Broken Heart past mending.

The wise man alone is not deceived either by folly or by foolish men.
He knows that every evil deed is parent to its punishment
    And from it issues child after child——children of wrath, children of
       sorrow
From one wrong comes forth another, each sin begets a worse.
Only to the man who walks the straight path of righteousness, whose life
    is simple and whose ways are humble,
Comes a fair return from life and honour from his fellows.

But Ancient Wrong brings forth each whelping season once again its evil
    offspring.
And this New Wrong as a lusty brat will shout and laugh amid the tears
    of a man,
And have Untruth who knows no fear nor any holy thing as comrade and
    protector;
For against the monstrous Lie men cannot win, nor even plead their cause.
Two powers of darkness thus consume that house wherein the Ancient
    Wrong as guest once entered.

But Justice brightens the humble cottage of the poor
And honours him, who with his own lot, is content.
But from the unclean hand upon the golden stair
She turns away to seek and save her own;
For neither by wealth nor rank is she deceived,
And in due course will come, by her decree, to all, the hour of destiny.

'THE ENVY OF THE GODS'

FROM HERODOTUS' *HISTORIES* VII 10

In the following excerpt from the Seventh Book of the *Histories*,
Herodotus has put into the speech of the elder and wiser man, Artabanus,
the uncle of the Persian Emperor Xerxes, the clearest expression in
classical literature of the Greek concept of the 'envy of the gods' and
the nature of human piety.

    In my experience, good judgment is more valuable than any other
accomplishment. Even if something goes amiss, the soundness of the original
judgment remains unaffected and its frustration is due to Fortune. Conversely,
bad judgment may reap a windfall if Fortune elects to favour the result but
it remains bad judgment none the less. You observe how God blasts with
his thunderbolt the animals that overtop their fellows, and how he cannot
bear them to show off, while the little animals never irritate him; and you
also observe how he invariably directs these shafts of his upon the highest
houses and the tallest trees. God loves to cut short everything that overtops

its kind. In this way a great army is destroyed by a small army in certain circumstances——as, for instance, when God in his envy sends down panic upon them, or thunder. Then they perish, and their last state is unworthy of their first. God suffers no one to be proud except himself.

The Chances and Changes of Fortune

In this passage from Herodotus on the chances and changes of fortune, we have a typical expression of Greek pessimism, and a summary of the wisdom of the poet sages. 'Surely,' the poet had written, 'there is nothing more pitiable than man among all things that breathe and creep upon the earth.'

> Mark ye the leaves, for men are like thereto.
> 　　When leaves by winds into the dust are whirled
> Soon the green forest buddeth millions new,
> 　　And lo, the beauty of spring is on the world.
> So come, so pass, all that are born of man.
> <div align="right"><i>Iliad</i> VI</div>

The setting of Herodotus' sober reflection upon the brevity of life has many parallels in world literature. The *Bhagavadgita* begins with the meditations of Arjuna, surveying the battle field before the clash of armies. Wolfe was reminded of *Grey's Elegy*, written in a parish grave-yard, before the battle of Quebec. In Chinese history and literature (e.g. *Tang Shu* and *The Three Kingdoms*) it would appear to be the tradition of generals to indulge in reflection only after the battle, as in the case of Wen Tien Hsiang (文天祥) who wrote his famous poem (正氣歌) while in prison.

The Homeric hero—the ideal knight of highest honour and excellence (*arete*)—addresses his troops just before the deadly encounter: 'Ah, friend, if once escaped from this battle we were for ever to be ageless and immortal, neither would I fight myself in the foremost ranks, nor would I send thee into the war that giveth men renown, but now, for assuredly ten thousand fates of death do every way beset us, and these no mortal may escape nor avoid, now let us go forward, whether we shall give glory to other men, or others to us.'

Like Homer, Herodotus describes a strangely noble pessimism not unmixed with piety. It is just this all-too-narrow bond encircling human life that urges upon men a regard for their fellow mortals. It is the ethic of a brief and toil-laden life wherein the fellowship of suffering ought to lead men to respect one another, to be kind, honest, courageous and generous. In such a life 'it is foolish to cherish resentment.' So the wisdom of *sophrosyne* (the mellow wisdom) teaches, in this Sophoclean homily:

> Life is mostly froth aud bubble
> Two things stand like stone:
> Kindness in another's trouble
> Courage in your own.

HERODOTUS' *HISTORIES* VII 44-46

When they arrived at Abydos, Xerxes wished to review his army. An observation platform of white marble had been constructed beforehand upon some high ground in the neighbourhood, and from this station, which commanded a view of the shore, Xerxes surveyed the land forces and the fleet. As he surveyed them, he was overcome by the desire to see his fleet engage in tactical manoeuvers, and when these were carried out and the Phoenicians of Sidon were victorious, he was delighted with the manoeuvers and with the whole expedition. When he saw the surface of the Dardanelles covered by the fleet and the headlands and the lowlands in the territory of Abydos swarming with troops, Xerxes proceeded to congratulate himself, but after that he wept. His tears were noticed by his uncle Artabanus, who had originally expressed his opinion so frankly in a sense unfavourable to the campaign against Greece. Perceiving that Xerxes had begun to weep, Artabanus taxed him with it. 'Your Majesty,' he said, 'there is an extraordinary inconsistency in your behaviour now and a moment ago. First you congratulate yourself and then you weep.'—— 'I was struck with pity,' Xerxes answered, 'at the thought of the brevity of all human life, when I realized that, out of all these multitudes, not a single individual will still be alive a hundred years from now.'——'In life,' replied Artabanus, 'we have other experiences more pitiable than that. Our lifetime is indeed as brief as you say; and yet there is not a single individual, either in this army or in the world, so happy that in this span, brief as it is, he will not find himself wishing, not once but many times over, that he were dead and not alive. The blows of misfortune and the ravages of disease make even the shortest life feel long; and so death comes as a blessed release for man from an evil existence, while God is proved an envious God in his dealings with man by the taste of sweetness in life with which he tantalizes him.'

THE SECOND SICILIAN EXPEDITION

Thucydides' (470-400 B.C.) description of the disastrous second

Athenian expedition against Syracuse in 413 B.C. has won the highest honours for vivid detail. The following is one of the finest passages in the whole of his history. We are made to feel the several crosscurrents in the mood of the Athenians before the final decision to launch the expedition.

The mixed feelings of over-confidence and a vague sense of tempting fate are suggested in a simple style of straightforward reporting. Athens was at the moment of this fatal decision already pressed by Sparta with the support, at least in sympathies, of the whole of the Peloponnesus in a dreary war of attrition. Athens had, by an ugly ambition that involved her in greed and cruelty unworthy of her finer spirit, brought upon herself the hatred of all Greece. In part supported by a false belief that she was invulnerable, in part by an arrogance that deluded her into believing that she could do no wrong, and in part by the continuously multiplying demands upon her resources and an increasing lust for greater wealth and luxury, she was now tempted to defy all prudence. Carried on the crest of these waves of folly and passion the decision is taken to open up a second front at the very moment when her resources are failing in the contest already at hand.

The chances and changes of mortal fortune are here vividly described in several ways. Nicias, a good man — a man of judgment—proved to be the worst choice; for what was needed, once the unfortunate decision had been taken, was a man of action—the kind of man Thrasymachus insisted was best qualified to rule—the strong man with singleness of purpose. Nicias, the good man, proved indecisive, and, because of his conscience, led the expeditionary forces to their ruin. The reversal of fortune is seen in the pitiful rout and slaughter, the pathetic shambles at the end of the campaign early in the autumn in contrast to the proud and mighty fleet that set sail in late summer—the mightiest and best provisioned fleet Athens had ever put to sea. Arrogant Athens is reduced to a suppliant pleading for her sons, now captives, of whom 'few returned to see their homes out of the many who had left them.'

THUCYDIDES VI 24-26, 30-52, VII 43, 44, 84-87
THE DECISION

Nicias, throughout his speech, had estimated the requirements of the campaign at a high figure, with the idea that he would either deter the Athenians from it altogether or would at any rate have succeeded in reducing the risk to a minimum if he were still compelled to sail. The Athenians, however, were not cured of their eagerness for the expedition by the burdensomeness of the armaments entailed, but felt the impulse more strongly than ever, and the result of Nicias' speech was the exact opposite of his intention. His advice was approved as offering an ample margin of insurance for the safety of the expedition.

A veritable passion for the adventure took possession of all alike. The older men imagined that they would either conquer their objectives or that, at the worst, a force of this strength would be immune from disaster; the men of military age were inspired by a longing to see and study strange lands and by a confidence that they would return in safety; while the oarsmen in the boats and the private soldiers looked forward to earning money in the immediate future and to acquiring new dominions from which a continuing source of income would be assured. The intense eagerness of the majority constrained those individuals who had doubts or fears to bear them in silence, for fear of being considered unpatriotic if they recorded a negative vote. Eventually, a private member rose to remonstrate with Nicias for his senseless caution and delays, and called upon him to declare once and for all, in this assembly of his countrymen, what armaments the country was to vote him. Much against his will, Nicias replied that, subject to further consultation with his colleagues at greater leisure, his provisional estimate of the forces required was not less than a hundred warships (the number of actual Athenian ships, suitable for use as transports, to be determined later, and the remainder to be demanded from the Allies), and a minimum combined total of five thousand Athenian and Allied infantry, which should, if possible, be exceeded. The rest of the armaments which they were to provide for the expedition, and which were to include native and Cretan archers and slingers and any other special battalions which might be considered essential, were to be of proportionate strength. He had no sooner finished speaking than the Assembly voted the generals full powers, with authority to settle the strength of the forces and all the details of the expedition at their own discretion. Preparations were begun forthwith, contingents were demanded from the Allies, and troops were conscripted in Athens. The country had just recovered from the plague and from the continuous war; the Armistice had enabled Athens to recruit her manpower from a new generation and to accumulate a reserve in the treasury; and therefore little difficulty was experienced in regard to ways and means.

THE START

It was midsummer when the expedition to Sicily set sail. The majority of the Allies, the grain ships, the merchantmen and the rest of the fleet had been given their rendezvous, for an earlier date, at Corfu, with the intention that the whole fleet should cross the Adriatic from that point to the heel of Italy in a single convoy. The Athenians themselves and any Allied nations who happened to find themselves at Athens, went down to Piraeus on the day appointed, and proceeded to man their ships for the voyage. They were accompanied to the port by practically the entire population of the city, both citizens and aliens. The natives, who were seeing off their respective friends, relatives or sons, as the case might be, went with mingled sensations of hope and sorrow——hope of the conquests which they might make and sorrow at the thought that they might never see their friends again, considering the distance from home of their objectives. At this point, when they were on the verge of parting from one another in perilous circumstances, they realized the risks more vividly than at the time when they had voted for the expedition. They were encouraged, however, by the evidence of their eyes, when they saw the strength of the expeditionary force collectively and in detail. As for the aliens and the remainder of the crowd, they came as spectators of what was universally regarded as an imposing and extraordinary enterprise; for this was the most extravagant and magnificent armada of Hellenic forces that had ever, up to that time, set sail from the shores of a single country. In actual numbers of vessels and troops, the expedition which sailed with Pericles to Epidaurus and subsequently with Hagnon to Potidaea (430 B.C.) was not inferior. But the sensation which this armada created was due to its great boldness and its brilliant display no less than to its crushing superiority of force over the prospective enemy, but chiefly to the fact that it was the greatest and most ambitious overseas expedition that had ever been attempted.

When the ships had been manned and all the equipment which they intended to take with them was at last on board, the call for silence was sounded on the bugle and prayers customary before weighing anchor were offered up——not in each ship separately, but by all in unison, conducted by a herald. Cups were filled from end to end of the armada, and libations were poured from golden and silver goblets by the soldiers and officers. The prayer was taken up by the crowd on shore, in which the citizens were joined by sympathetic foreign spectators. Then the military cheer was given, the religious service was concluded, and anchors were weighed. The ships started in line ahead and raced as far as the island of Aegina, whence they made their best speed to Corfu, which was the rendezvous for the rest of the fleet.

THE LAST ATTACK

Demosthenes who was second-in-command decided that it was impossible to approach and scale the heights by daylight without being observed. He therefore gave orders that rations for five days should be served out to the troops; took over all the engineers, with supplies of weapons and of materials required for fortifying a new position in the event of success; paraded the entire army in the early hours of the night under his own command, with Eurymedon and Menander as his colleagues; and advanced against the heights, Nicias remaining in reserve within the Athenian lines. They struck the heights at Euryelus, where the first expeditionary force had originally climbed them, took the Syracusan pickets by surprise, attacked and captured the Syracusan post established at this point and inflicted casualties upon the garrison. The majority of the garrison, however, immediately scattered in the direction of the three cantonments which had been established on the heights in outworks of the main line, and which were held respectively by the Syracusans, the other Sicilian Hellenes and their non-Sicilian allies.

The fugitives brought information of the attack and reported it to the six hundred Syracusan troops who were in the front line on this sector of the heights. These troops immediately moved forward in support, but were met by Demosthenes and the Athenians and were forced to retire after offering strong resistance. The Athenians immediately continued their advance, in order to push on to their objectives before their momentum was expended; while other detachments, detailed for this purpose when the attack was first launched, proceed to capture and disorganize the defenses previously constructed by the Syracusans, the garrison of which failed to hold its ground. The Syracusans, their allies and the force commanded by Gylippus (the Spartan military attache at Syracuse, who saved the situation) now began to move forward in support from their cantonments, but the boldness of the night attack had taken them by surprise; they were in a state of panic when they came into collision with the Athenians, and at first they were overpowered and compelled to retreat. In the course of their advance, however, the Athenians were abandoning their formation, partly on the assumption that the battle was already won, and partly in an effort to dispose as quickly as possible of all enemy forces which had not yet been engaged and which might find an opportunity to re-form if there were any slackening in the Athenian attack.

At this critical moment the Boetians first arrested the Athenians' advance, delivered a counterattack, forced them to retreat, and turned the retreat into a rout. When this occurred, the Athenians so completely lost their discipline and their presence of mind that it has not been easy to obtain any consecutive account of what followed from either side. Even in operations by day-light, which are less confusing, the individual combatants find it difficult to follow the general development of the action beyond their own immediate sector, and precise information is therefore hardly to be expected from participants in the only night operations of the late war in which considerable forces were engaged. Although there was a bright moon, there was only the low visibility characteristic of moon-light, which enables the eye to discern a human form in its field of vision without enabling it to identify it with any confidence as a friend's. Masses of infantry belonging to both armies were manoeuvering in a confined space, and on the Athenian side some troops was already giving way, while others were still advancing victoriously in the first impetus of their attack. A considerable portion of the Athenian reserves had also either just climbed or were in the act of climbing the heights, so that they did not know what points to take as their objective.

From the moment that the rout had begun, the troops in front had completely lost their formation, and the noise made it difficult to distinguish friend and foe. The Syracusans and their allies were cheering vociferously to one another to follow up their victory, while engaging all who came into contact with their lines. The Athenians were attempting to establish contact with one another, and were treating all troops approaching from the opposite direction as enemy forces, although actually they might be friends already in retreat towards the rear. They were also constantly challenging one another for the password, which was their only means of mutual identification, but which threw their own ranks into confusion when everyone was challenging at once. Incidentally this betrayed the Athenian password to the enemy, while it was not so easy for the Athenians to discover theirs, since as victors they had kept their formation and were therefore able to identify one another more easily. In consequence, whenever the Athenians encountered a weaker body of the enemy, the latter escaped through their knowledge of the Athenian password, while whenever the Athenians failed to answer the enemy's challenge, they were annihilated.

They suffered most of all, however, from the cheering, which created confusion owing to its similarity on the two sides. Whenever a cheer was given by the Argives, Corcyraeans and other Dorian contingents serving with the Athenians, the Athenians fell into a panic, and the same thing happened among the enemy. When once their formation had been lost, friends and fellow-countrymen came into conflict with one another at a number of points in the line, until eventually they not only lost their nerve, but actually came to blows and could only be parted with difficulty. In their flight from the pursuing forces, many met their death by throwing themselves over the cliffs, owing to the narrowness of the way down from the heights; and although the majority of the survivors who reached the plain succeeded in escaping to the camp, a certain number of the new replacements lost their way and wandered over the country until they were overtaken by daylight, when the Syracusan cavalry cut them off and annihilated them.

THE LAST STAND

With the return of daylight, Nicias set his force in motion, and the Syracusans and their allies attacked his, as before, with converging volleys of missiles. The Athenians pushed forward towards the River Assinarus, partly under the pressure of converging attacks from a powerful cavalry supported by other arms, from which they expected some relief if they succeeded in crossing the stream, and partly under stress of exhaustion and the stimulus of thirst. When they reached the bank, they threw themselves in, and all discipline was at an end. Each individual soldier was determined to be the first to cross, and the attacks of the enemy were already making it difficult to cross at all. Forced, as they were, to proceed in a huddled mass, they stumbled over and trampled upon one another, and some of them were tangled in the baggage and carried away by the stream. The opposite bank of the river, which was steep, was lined by the Syracusans, who showered stones from above upon the Athenians, most of whom were drinking greedily and jostling one another in the hollow bottom of the river. The Peloponnesians came down to close quarters and began a butchery, especially of those in the river. In an instant the water had been fouled, but nevertheless the majority continued to drink it, muddied and blood-stained as it was, and even fought to reach it.

Eventually, when the corpses were piled in heaps in the river and the force had been cut to pieces——Nicias surrendered personally to Gylippus, whom he trusted more than he did the Syracusans, and begged him and the Spartans to do what they liked with his own person, if only they would stop their butchery of his men. After this, Gylippus ordered that quarter should be given; all survivors not hidden by their captors (as a large number were) were rounded up as prisoners; and the three hundred men who had broken through the line of pickets during the night were captured by troops dispatched in pursuit. The percentage of the Athenian force officially collected as prisoners was not large, while the number of those spirited away was so great that all Sicily was filled with them, the reason being that, unlike Demosthenes' force, they had not become prisoners by a formal surrender. A large number was actually killed outright. Considerable numbers had also been killed previously in the frequent engagements that had accompanied the march. Nevertheless, many succeeded in saving themselves——some immediately, and others by escaping at a later date, after having been reduced to slavery. These found an asylum at Catana.

The Syracusans and their allies now concentrated their forces, provided for the transport of the captured material and of as many of the prisoners as possible, and marched back to the city. All Athenian and Allied citizens who had been captured were deposited in the quarries as being the safest method of internment, with the exception of Nicias and Demosthenes, who were put to death——against the will of Gylippus. Of all Greeks in my generation Nicias least deserved such a fate, considering the strictness with which his life was regulated on the highest principles.

The Prisoners in the quarries were barbarously treated at the beginning by Syracusans. At the end of that period they were all sold into slavery, except the Athenians and those Sicilians and Italians who had joined the expedition on the Athenian side. An accurate figure for the total number of prisoners would be difficult to give, but it was certainly not less than seven thousand.

This tragedy, which was the greatest that occurred in the late war, and, in my opinion, in all recorded Hellenic history, conferred unparalleled glory upon the conquerors and inflicted unparalleled disaster upon the victims. They were utterly defeated in every way; there was nothing on the small scale in any of their sufferings; fleet, army and everything else was annihilated in the literal sense of the word, and few returned to see their homes out of the many who had left them.

On the Cycles of Civilization

This passage from Plato's *Timaeus* has been chosen for two reasons. It deals with an old and favourite theme of Greek historians: the cyclical pattern of history based upon recurrent world aeons and it deals with the Greek interest in cultural origins, pointing up the Greek's curiosity about other peoples and the Greek's willingness to compare, with an open mind, his own traditions and those of other nations.

Hecataeus of Miletus, perhaps the first Greek historian, is said to have travelled to Egypt and to have discussed with the priests there the question of which nation had the longer history. He was convinced that the Greeks owed much to the Egyptians, and that Egyptian records and traditions had a more solid foundation in fact than those of the Greeks. He returned home determined to review the traditions of his own people with a critical mind, and to sift out the true from the false, the reasonable from the fanciful.

Herodotus was probably influenced by Hecataeus' high regard for Egypt as the earliest center of civilization in this world age. He was led to examine Greek traditions in a critical light. The Greek notion of world ages tended to make thoughtful men humble. Their own civilization with its victories and achievements could not be held up as something unique or unusual. Many such civilizations had been the precise parallel of one's own in many former world aeons; and in the aeons to come there would be other civilizations fulfilling the lot ordained for them which would be no better and no worse than now was Greece in the fulfilling of her destiny.

Since we do not have any genuine fragments from Hecataeus' writings the following passage from Plato may serve as a type of the theme of the origins and cycles of civilization. The passage indicates three qualities which enabled the Greeks to write history: curiosity, humility and an open mind.

PLATO'S *TIMAEUS* 21E-23C

In the Egyptian Delta, round the head of which the channel of the Nile divides, there is a department called Sais, with a departmental capital of the same name. The people of this town have a patron goddess whose name in Egyptian is Neith——corresponding, as they aver, to the Greek Athena. The Saites claim to be great admirers of Athens and to be in some sense specially related to the Athenian nation. Solon, according to his own account, had travelled to Sais and had been received there with distinguished honours. During his stay he had taken opportunities of consulting the leading experts among the priests upon ancient history, and had made the discovery that he himself and all his fellow Greeks were in a state of almost total ignorance on the subject.

On one occasion he sought to lead them into a discussion upon antiquity by entering upon an exposition of the most ancient traditions of Greece relating to the so-called primeval Phoroneus and Niobe, whence he descended to the period after the Deluge, narrated the legendary history of Deucalion and Pyrrha, recited the genealogies of their descendants and attempted to supply a chronological basis for dating the events in his story. This drew from an extremely aged priest among Solon's hearers the words: 'Solon, Solon! You Greeks are perpetual children. Such a thing as an old Greek does not exist.'——'What do you mean?' rejoined Solon. 'All of you,' continued the aged priest, 'are young in mind. Your minds contain no thoughts handed down from antiquity by ancient tradition and no knowledge from ancient times. There is a reason for this, which I will explain. A series of catastrophes in a variety of forms has befallen, and will continue to befall, the human race, the greatest being those effected through the agency of fire or water, while the others, which are of less violence, are produced by an infinity of different causes.'

In Hellas you have a tradition that Phaethon, the child of the Sun, once harnessed his father's chariot but proved incompetent to drive it along his father's course, with the result that he burnt up everything on the face of the Earth before his own career was cut short forever by the thunderbolt. Although this tradition has been dressed in a legendary form, it preserves the scientific fact that, at immense intervals of time, there is a chance in the orbit of the heavenly bodies revolving round the Earth and a catastrophe which overtakes life on this planet in the shape of a vast conflagration. At this juncture the inhabitants of regions with a mountainous relief, a high altitude or an arid climate pay a heavier toll than those of riverain or maritime zones; and on these occasions we in Egypt are rescued by the Nile, our unfailing saviour, from a problem from which he is immune himself.

There are other occasions on which the Gods cleanse the Earth with a deluge of water, and in these circumstances the shepherds and herdsmen on the mountains survive, while the inhabitants of your towns in Hellas are swept away to sea by the rivers. In Egypt, however, water never descends upon the fields from above——not even in these deluvial epochs—— but rises from below by a Law of Nature which never varies. Thus, for

the above reasons, the traditions preserved in Egypt are the most ancient
in the world, the scientific truth being that in every locality where there
are not prohibitive extremes of heat or cold, the human population is
subject to periodic increases and decreases. Glorious or important or in
any way remarkable events in the history of Hellas or of Egypt itself or of
any other region within our field of knowledge are consequently recorded
and preserved in our shrines here in Egypt since a remote antiquity.

On the other hand, human society in Hellas or elsewhere has always
just arrived at the point of equipping itself with written records and the
other requisites of civilization, when, after the regular interval, the waters
that are above the firmament descend upon you like a recurrent malady
and only permit the illiterate and uncultivated members of your society
to survive, with the result that you become as little children and start
again from the beginning with no knowledge whatever of ancient history
either in Egypt or in your own world. Let me tell you, Sir, that the
genealogies which you have recited in your account of your Hellenic past
are scarcely above the level of children's fairy tales. In the first place,
you have only preserved the memory of one deluge out of a long previous
series, and in the second place, you are ignorant of the fact that your
own country was the home of the noblest and the highest race by which
mankind has ever been represented. You yourself and your whole nation
can claim this race as your ancestors through a fraction of the stock that
survived a former catastrophe, but you are ignorant of this, owing to the
fact that, for many successive generations, the survivors lived and died
illiterate.

The Canons of Historiography

The Problem of the Historicity of Heracles

The questioning of traditions was the beginning of Greek historical
wisdom. In the following passage, Herodotus considers the story of
Heracles as it had been preserved from one generation to the next
without being subjected to either rational or historical examination. It
is interesting to note his method: first he came to recognize the
problem of the historicity of Heracles when he was introduced to a
different tradition than that held by the Greeks. The problem, as he
saw it then, was whether the Heracles tradition was Greek or Egyptian
in origin. He sought to find a clue in language (the source of the
name itself). Then he explored the supposed genealogy of Heracles
and the broad parallel between Greek and Egyptian theogonies. Next
he considered the possibilities of direct cultural contact between the
two peoples in antiquity and the bearing of this evidence upon the

source of the Heracles legend.

A second major stage in his research comes with his journey to Tyre to gather material on Heracles from a third source: the Phoenician tradition. He was able to ascertain that one Heracles shrine in Tyre was more ancient than his shrines in Greece. He was also able to prove that the Heracles known to the Greeks as the son of Amphitryon was not the same Heracles honoured at a second shrine which he visited in Tyre. In the light of his discoveries made both in Egypt and Tyre he reviewed the several Greek traditions and sought a reconstruction of the history of the Heracles saga that would take account of all the facts. Herodotus' method was comparative.

HISTORIES II 43-45

In regard to Heracles, I heard it stated in Egypt that he was one of the twelve Gods; but I never succeeded in finding a trace in Egypt of the other Heracles with whom Greeks are familiar. Certainly the name was not borrowed from the Greeks by the Egyptians but (if at all) from the Egyptians by the Greeks, and this by the particular Greeks who gave the name of Heracles to the son of Amphitryon. One of the many pieces of evidence that I find convincing on this point is the fact that the parents of Heracles, Amphitryon and Alcmena, were of Egyptian extraction, and the further fact that the Egyptians deny all knowledge of the names of Poseidon and the Dioscuri. These latter Gods have not been admitted into the Egyptian Pantheon, while, if they had borrowed the name of any divinity at all from Greece, these three would have made a particularly strong and not a particularly faint impression upon their memories. It is my personal belief and considered judgment that the Egyptians had at that epoch already taken to the sea and that there was also by then a seafaring element in Greece——conditions which would have made the names of these gods more familiar to the Egyptians than the name of Heracles. (Poseidon and the Dioscuri were the Greek patron saints of navigation). The Egyptians have, however, an ancient God of their own called Heracles, whom they include among their Twelve Gods; and the date at which they place the procreation of these Twelve Gods by the Eight is seventeen thousand years before the reign of Amasis (569-525 B.C.).

Wishing to obtain precise information on these points from those qualified to give it, I sailed to Tyre in Phoenicia, where I heard that there was a shrine consecrated to Heracles. I found it richly furnished with a large number of gifts, including two columns, one of refined gold and the other of emerald (the latter shone brightly even in the dark). I entered into conversation with the priests of this god and asked them the date at which the shrine had been founded, whereupon I learned that they, no less than the Egyptians, were in disagreement with the Greeks. They told me that the founding of the shrine was coeval with the foundation of Tyre itself, the date of which event was 2300 years ago.

At Tyre I saw a second shrine of a Heracles entitled 'Heracles of Thasos,' and in Thasos itself (which I have also visited) I discovered a shrine of Heracles originally founded by Phoenicians who had colonized the island in the course of a voyage in search of Europa (a Phoenician princess who was kidnapped by the God Zeus in the form of a bull and carried away by him to Crete)——an event anterior by five generations to the birth in Greece of the Heracles whose father was Amphitryon.   The results of my researches demonstrate clearly that Heracles was an ancient God; and in my opinion, the most correct procedure is that followed by those Greeks who have founded and maintained duplicate shrines of Heracles, in which they honour the respective bearers of the name with two distinct rituals——one as an immortal included among the Olympians, and the other as a saint (in Greek, 'Hero').   The Greeks, who commit themselves to a number of ill-considered statements, recite a particularly childish legend relating to Heracles.   Once upon a time Heracles visited Egypt, when the Egyptians decorated him like a sacrificial victim and led him forth in solemn procession to be sacrificed to Zeus.   Up to this point the hero made no resistance, but when they were proceeding to sacrifice him at the altar, he fought for his life and slew them to the last man. In my opinion this story betrays the utter ignorance of the Greeks regarding Egyptian character and institutions.   Among the Egyptians, even animal sacrifices are tabu, with the sole exception of sheep, bulls and bull-calves. That they should make human sacrifices is therefore inconceivable.   Again, on the Greek assumption that there was only one Heracles, and that this single individual was a human being, the idea that he should have slain his tens of thousands is irreconcilable with the course of Nature.   That concludes my observations on the subject——for which I devoutly trust that neither gods nor priests will bear me ill will.

ON THE RECONSTRUCTION OF HISTORY

Polybius, the last of the great Greek historians (200-120 B.C.) was deeply interested in historiography, and he is our chief source on the subject of the historian's task from a classical viewpoint.   In the following excerpt he rejects the notion that it is the art of the historian to reconstruct history rather than to report what actually happened and to account for the significance of actual events.   He accuses the Sicilian historian, Timaeus, of reconstructing history on the lines of what could or should have happened, and of what could or should have been said.   He was, Polybius claims, a kind of ghost writer, not an historian—an odd kind of ghost writer who prepared the speeches of famous men *after* these speeches had been delivered.   The historian should not be a novelist.   A sharp distinction is to be made between history and historical fiction. History is not just the collecting of facts—certainly it is not the making up of facts. It is giving a reasonable account of *why* certain words that were actually used and certain deeds that were actually done ended either in success or failure. History is a reasonable account of human action in respect of its consequences. Polybius here accuses Timaeus. He could have accused Thucydides of ghost writing the speeches of Pericles—after they were delivered. But Thucydides would have answered: I did not distort, I sharpened the image of the past. I took great pains to sift the testimony of conflicting witnesses. I struggled through the ambiguities, confusion and the misleading evidence which make up the raw stuff of history and then brought what was important and relevant into sharper focus. Of the two men, Thucydides and Polybius, there are the questions: which was the greater historian and which was the greater realist?

POLYBIUS, *HISTORIES* XXXVI 1 and XII 25

Possibly some of my readers may be curious to know how it is that I have not attempted to shine by reproducing the speeches delivered by the various parties, when I had such grand themes and so great opportunities to dramatize them. Why have I not followed the example of the majority of historians, who marshal the speeches proper to the occasion on either side? The fact that I personally do not reject this branch of historical writing has been made sufficiently clear in several passages of my work, in which I have frequently reported the speeches and compositions of public men; but it will now become evident that I am not willing to follow this practice in season and out of season, considering that it would not be easy to find a more magnificent theme than the present (Third Punic War 150/149 B.C.) or more abundant material to serve up to my readers. I may add that nothing would be simpler for me than to produce a literary effort of the kind, were I not convinced that the same rule applies to the historian as to the politician. The politician's duty is not to make speeches or to enlarge upon every detail of any subject that comes up for discussion, but to adapt his words to the given occasion; and similarly the historian's duty is not to practise upon his readers or to show off his literary ability at their expense, but to do his best to investigate and elucidate the words actually spoken, confining himself throughout to the most vital and effective passages....

It is proverbial that one drop from the largest jar is enough to identify the whole of the liquid which it contains, and the moral of this is applicable to the subject in hand. When once one or two misstatements have been made deliberately, it is evident that no further reliance or confidence can

be placed in any of the assertions of such a writer. In the hope of
convincing even the ardent champions of Timaeus, I propose to say
something concerning his policy and practice in regard to speeches and
pleadings, diplomatic notes and, in short, all the kinds of rhetoric, which
may almost be regarded as summaries of events and as the unifying element
of historical writing. The fact that Timaeus has falsified, and intentionally
falsified, the speeches included in his works, can hardly have escaped his
readers. Instead of reproducing the words spoken in their actual form,
he decides what ought to have been said and then proceeds to reconstruct
the speeches and to create what he considers to be the more appropriate
framework of events for their settings, precisely as though he were a
student who had been set a theme as an exercise and was endeavouring to
make it an occasion for the display of his abilities, instead of reporting
the words actually spoken.

It is the function of History in the first place to ascertain the exact
words actually spoken, whatever they may be, and in the second place to
inquire into the cause which crowned the action taken or the words spoken
with success or failure. The bare statement of the facts themselves is
merely entertaining without being in the least instructive, whereas the
additional explanation of the cause makes the study of history a fruitful
employment. The analogies that can be drawn from similar situations to
our own offer materials and presumptions for forecasting the future, in
regard to which they sometimes act as a warning, while at other times
they encourage us to strike out boldly into the oncoming tide of events
in virtue of a historical parallel. A historian, however, who suppresses
both the words spoken and their cause and replaces them by imaginary
narratives and empty rhetoric destroys, in so doing, the characteristic
quality of history; and this is precisely the offense of which Timaeus is
guilty. The fact that every volume of his works is full of such spurious
matter is common knowledge.

THE PLACE OF GEOGRAPHY IN HISTORY

Arnold Toynbee has given the following paragraphs from Polybius
the title 'The Place of Geography in History.' To what extent should
special topics such as geography be included in the reconstruction of
the past? We should remember that the first Greek historians (Hecataeus
and Herodotus) were as much interested in geography as in history.
Hecataeus is said to have chosen this ambitious title for his work: *The
Geography of Hecataeus*, i.e. *Hecataeus' Description of the World*.
Herodotus would today be described as the writer of a travelogue.

Polybius is one of the first to question the nature of the relation
of geography to history, and he is one of the first historians to discuss
the value of monographic or special studies. What would be the

value of his proposed monograph on geography to the historian? Does Polybius regard geography as a subject for a special study, helpful to the historian, or does he regard geography as a branch of history—a discipline alongside others which together make up the field of history?

POLYBIUS, *HISTORIES* III 57-59

Now that I have brought my own narrative and the commanders of the opposing forces and the war itself ('Second Punic' war——between Rome and Carthage) to the threshold of Italy, I wish, before discussing military operations, to mention briefly certain points which are related to my work. Possibly some readers may be curious to know how it is that, after enlarging upon the geography of Northwest Africa and Spain, I have not given special attention to the Straits of Gibraltar, the Atlantic Ocean and its peculiar phenomena, the British Isles and the tin industry, or the silver mines and gold mines in Spain itself——subjects to which previous historians have devoted many pages of controversy.

My reason for leaving aside this branch of history has not been any idea that it is irrelevant, but an unwillingness, in the first place, to interrupt the narrative and divert the attention of the serious reader from my special study. In the second place, I have decided not to deal with this material in a disjointed or incidental manner, but to assign to this branch a special place and time of its own and then to give as accurate an account of it as may lie in my power. My readers must therefore not be astonished if in the following chapters, when I come to other regions of special geographical interest, I leave aside this branch of inquiry ——my reasons for doing so having now been explained.

If any reader insists upon receiving this information a little at a time, region by region, he may possibly be unaware that he is behaving very like the glutton at the dinner table. The glutton who tastes every dish does not genuinely enjoy any of the dishes at the moment of eating and does not obtain any permanent benefit from them in the way of digestion and nourishment, but precisely the contrary. Similarly, the gluttonous reader defeats himself, whether his aim be momentary amusement or permanent instruction.

The actual need of close thinking and of reform in the direction of greater accuracy under which this branch of history at present labours more than any other, is made manifest by many considerations, of which I will mention the most important. Almost all writers of history, or at any rate the vast majority, have attempted to describe the situation and the peculiarities of countries on the borderline of our known habitable world, and in doing so the majority have fallen into many errors. There is therefore no excuse for leaving this subject aside, but, at the same time, whatever has to be said in answer to earlier historians must be said with the full attention of the mind and not in a casual and disjointed manner. Nor, again, must it be said in a spirit of censure or in a tone of disapproval.

It is fairer to praise their efforts while correcting their ignorance, in recognition of the fact that, had these writers been able to avail themselves of the opportunities of the present day, they should have made corrections and rearrangements in much of their own published work.

In the past, it would be impossible to point to more than an insignificant number of Greeks who have attempted to investigate the borderlands—the deterrent being the difficulties of the enterprise. At that time the dangers of sea travel were almost literally innumerable, though they were only a fraction of the dangers by land. Even, moreover, if a traveler succeeded, by choice or necessity, in reaching the ends of the Earth, he was still likely to be defeated in the accomplishment of his object. Any extensive firsthand observation was rendered difficult by the fact that some regions had declined or were devastated and others were uninhabited, while the differences of human speech made it still more difficult to obtain information by asking about the objects that could be seen.

Even, however, when the information was obtained, the most difficult achievement of all, from the observer's point of view, was to resist the temptations of sensationalism and marvel-mongering, to give his own first allegiance to the truth and to report to us the whole truth and nothing but the truth. In consequence, accurate historical research into the subjects aforementioned was not so much difficult as impossible in times past; and, so far from deserving censure for their errors and omissions, the writers of the day may justly claim our approval and admiration for such facts as they ascertained and for the degree to which they advanced the knowledge of the subject under difficult conditions.

In modern times, however, the Empire of Alexander in Asia and the supremacy of Rome elsewhere have opened up almost the entire world to sea or land travel, while men of action could turn from military and political careers and find in the new conditions many important advantages for investigation and research into the subject of geography, so that it is now our duty to acquire better and more accurate knowledge in this new science. I shall attempt to make my own contribution to this branch of inquiry, and I shall hope to guide serious students into the subject in a comprehensive way. Indeed, my principal object in exposing myself to the dangers which I have encountered in my travels in Africa and Spain, and also in Gaul and on the Ocean which washes the further shores of these countries, has been to correct the ignorance of our earlier writers in this branch of knowledge and to make this part of the world as familiar to the Greek public as the lands of our nearer neighbours.

Self Interpretation in History

The Athenian Image of Athens

Each winter there was held in Athens a memorial service in

remembrance of those who had been the first to fall in the heroic defence of Greece against the Persian Invasion. Thucydides reports without comment the solemn details of the burial of these dead and of the annual arrangement of the memorial service. Now in the winter of 431 B.C. Athens was again involved in a life and death struggle. The previous summer the uneasy unity of Greece under Athenian supremacy had come to an end with the outbreak of the Peloponnesian War. Now Athens was pitted, not against a foreign invader, but against her own sister states. It was, in a sense, a civil war. As Lincoln, in the Nineteenth Century of our era recalled in the honouring of those who fell at Gettysburg the fundamental ideals of the American democracy which had been born eighty-seven years before in the heroic days of the Revolution, so Pericles, on this winter day in 431 B.C., chose to remind the people of Athens not only of the heroes of years before at Marathon, but also to recall, in this second great crisis of her life, the creed of Athens—the grounds of a just war—the preservation of those ideals by which this small city state could lay just claim to a right to rule. Thucydides makes of this event the occasion to set down the classic apology for Athenian civilization.

You will note at the end of this selection a brief excerpt from the Thucydidean speech of Pericles which was delivered just one year later. You will note the realism of this report on the war, now that the city has felt the losses and sacrifices of a year at war. The last word on that wretched war belongs also to Thucydides.

THUCYDIDES, *HISTORIES*, BOOK II 34-36

The same winter, the Athenians observed an ancestral custom by giving a public funeral to those who had fallen in the first campaign of the war. The procedure is that the remains of the dead should lie in state before the ceremony for three days, during which the relatives have an opportunity to pay their tribute. The procession itself consists of hearses bearing cypresswood coffins, one of each battalion, in which the remains of that battalion's dead are assembled, while a single coffin draped but empty, commemorates the missing. Anyone, Athenian or alien, is at liberty to follow, and the female relatives of the dead attend to wait at the tomb. They are buried in the national tomb, in the most beautiful suburb of the town, which is the regular burial place for those who die on the field of honour, except the dead of Marathon, whose gallantry was felt to be so conspicuous that they were buried where they fell. When the grave has been filled, a speaker chosen by the state for his distinction of intellect and character delivers a fitting oration and then the mourners disperse. That is the ceremonial, and, throughout the war, the custom was observed when occasion arose. On this first occasion the choice fell upon Pericles, son of Xanthippus; and, when the moment arrived, he came forward from the monument, mounted the high platform that had been constructed for the occasion in order that his voice might carry to the greatest distance, and delivered himself as follows:

'It has been the practice of my predecessors to commend the statesman who added this address to the customary procedure. It is right, they tell us, that such an address should be delivered at the burial of those who have fallen on the field of honour. For my own part, I am inclined to think that those who have proved their worth by their deeds would be sufficiently honoured by receiving tribute in the same kind——such a tribute, in fact, as meets your eyes in this public ceremonial——that it would be wiser not to entrust the reputations of so many brave men to the uncertain talents of a single speaker. It is by no means easy for a speaker to do justice to a theme when it is difficult to convince the audience that he is speaking the truth. The friends of the dead who know their story will probably feel his words inadequate both in style and content, while strangers, out of jealousy, will suspect a certain exaggeration, if the qualities attributed to the dead surpass their own. The truth is that the praise of others is only tolerable so long as the hearers feel that they would each have risen to the occasion had the part fallen to them. They begrudge and therefore refuse to believe whatever is beyond their range. Tradition demands that such a speech should be given; and so I must defer to the custom in my turn and must do my best to satisfy the different views and feelings of my audience.

'I shall begin with our ancestors, for this is an occasion on which a tribute to their memory is both due and proper. This country has ever been inhabited by the same race, whose valour has bequeathed it as a home of freedom from one generation to another down to this day. All honour to our forefathers and, above all, to our own fathers, who by their labours added to their heritage and handed on to ourselves the great empire which we now possess. The boundaries of that empire have been extended in almost every quarter by many of those present who are not yet past the prime of life, and the resources of the commonwealth have been developed by our efforts to the maximum of self-sufficiency, for peace or for war. The military achievements by which our possessions were successively acquired, and the vigour displayed by our fathers and ourselves in repelling the aggressions of our enemies, Persian or Greek, are too familiar for me to weary you with their recital; but I shall attempt to describe the institutions which have won us our position and the qualities inherent in our public and private life to which it owes its greatness, before proceeding to perform my duty toward those who lie here, because I believe that this theme is proper to the occasion and edifying to my audience, including the strangers in our midst.

'The constitution under which we live seeks no inspiration from abroad, and so far from being borrowed it has been taken as an example. The possession of the franchise by a majority instead of a minority has earned for it the title of Democracy. Before the law, equality is assured to every citizen in his dealings with his neighbour; the recognition of personal distinction in any field and political advancement which is its reward are determined by merit and not by social standing; and no stigma attaches to poverty which can bar the career of any man capable of serving the state. We lead a life of freedom not only in our politics but in our mutual tolerance of private conduct. We do not resent our neighbour doing what he pleases, nor subject him to those marks of disapproval which poison pleasure though they may inflict no formal injury; and while our private intercourse is thus free from constraint, this does not react to the detriment of law and order, which are preserved by a wholesome respect for the constituted authorities and for the laws of the land, especially those which protect the victims of injustice and those whose moral sanction is so strong that there is no need for them to be written.

'We have understood how to vary work with recreation by an annual succession of civic and religious festivals and by the refinement of our homes, the daily delight of which assists us to banish care. The size of our city attracts imports from every part of the world, and the products of our own country are not more thoroughly ours to enjoy than those of other climes.

'We also differ in our military institutions from our opponents. We throw our country open to all mankind, and never resort to aliens' acts in order to conceal information which might possibly assist the enemy if it fell into his hands. We prefer to rely upon our valour in the field and not upon secret military preparations. In education, again, we leave it to our opponents to cultivate manliness by a labourious training from their tender years upward, while we, with our undisciplined life, are as ready as they to face every reasonable danger. This is proved by the facts. The Spartans never invade our country alone, but with the combined forces of their confederacy, whereas, when we attack our neighbours, we seldom find difficulty in defeating them, though we are the invaders and they are defending their homes. Again, our united forces have never yet been faced by any opponent, because we are continually dispersing them on expeditions by land, in addition to the requirements of our fleet. Yet whenever they encounter a fraction of our forces and defeat them, they then boast that they have been victorious against our total strength, while, if they are worsted, they maintain that it has taken our total strength to secure the victory. However that may be, the fact that we preserve a military spirit by a life of ease instead of deliberate hardship and by a natural rather than an artificial courage gives us a double advantage. We are not compelled to anticipate the rigours of war, yet we face them, when they come, as courageously as those who are in perpetual training.

'But these are not our country's only claims to admiration. Besides all this, we cultivate the arts without extravagance and the intellect without effeminacy. We care more for the uses of wealth than for its show, and see the real disgrace of poverty not in admission of the fact but in neglect to seek a remedy. Our politicians do not neglect their private affairs, and the rest of us devote ourselves to business without losing touch with politics. We are unique in regarding men who take no part in politics as not merely unambitious but unprofitable; and we are all sound judges, if not creative statesmen, in public affairs. In our belief, action suffers not from discussion but from lack of discussion to enlighten before it is taken; and we combine to an exceptional degree the qualities of daring and deliberation, whereas in most natures courage is the fruit of stupidity and hesitation, the penalty of reflection. Yet the finest characters are surely those which realize the most clearly where pleasure and pain await them, yet are not deterred by their knowledge from facing the worst. We are equally exceptional in our moral standards, for we make our friends by performing and not by receiving services; and the party which confers the obligation is of course the firmer friend of the two, in his efforts to keep the recipient in his debt by continued kindness, while the debtor's feelings are blunted by the knowledge that any return he makes will be not a favour but an obligation. We alone are inspired by the spirit of freedom to put self-interest aside and to do good regardless of the consequences.

'In short, I maintain that the Commonwealth of Athens is the School of Hellas and that the individual Athenian will never meet his equal for self-reliance, versatility, and gallantry in whatever situation he may find himself. The proof that this is not empty boast but sober reality is afforded by the power of our country, which is the fruit of our national character. Athens alone of her contemporaries more than justifies her promise by her performance; she alone is a power by whom it is no dishonour to her enemies to be worsted and no grievance to her subjects to be ruled. Nor will our power pass without a memorial. The proofs by which we have signalized it insure us the admiration of our contemporaries and of all posterity. We need no Homer to praise us nor other poet to clothe our achievements with the ephemeral glamour that wilts under the light of truth. Our daring has forced an entrance into every sea and every land, and everywhere we have raised imperishable monuments of our presence for good or for evil.

'Such is the country in whose cause these dead have made their noble choice. Rather than be bereft of her, they died on the field of honour, and the least that we who survive them can do is to spend ourselves, one and all, in her service. If I have enlarged upon her genius, my purpose has been to show you that we possess a greater treasure to fight for than those who can boast of no similar inheritance, and to place my eulogy of the heroes whom I am privileged to commemorate upon an uncontrovertible foundation. The substance of that foundation has been laid already, for the Athens which I have praised is what the heroism of these and others like them has made her——men whose fame, almost alone in all Hellas, is only commensurate with their deserts. They have all died a soldier's death, whether that death gave the first glimpse of the spirit that was in them or set the seal upon it. Valour in the field in defense of home and country covers a multitude of sins. Such public service out-weighs many disservices in private life and enables those who render it to redeem their characters. Among these dead there were both rich and poor; yet the rich were not unnerved by the temptation to prolong the enjoyment of their wealth, nor the poor induced to postpone the risk of death by the prospect of even yet exchanging poverty for ease. In their eagerness to strike a blow at their enemies they rose superior to such motives; they held this risk to be the noblest that a man can take; and they took it deliberately, in order to strike their blow, though without abandoning their other aspirations. Committing the uncertain chances of success into the keeping of Hope, they trusted in nothing but their own right hands to accomplish the work that lay before them. They felt that to lose their lives in action was to save them in a truer sense than to save them by giving way, and so they turned their backs on moral disgrace and stood their ground in physical combat, until the swift stroke of Fate released them from this mortal life in an ecstasy not of fear but of glory.

'Thus these dead acquitted themselves as became Athenians, and it is for us who survive them to see that we face the foe with a resolution as unfaltering as theirs, though we may legitimately pray to be spared their fate. You know what are the rewards of valour as well as the most long-winded speaker could expound them to you; but, instead of reviewing them in generalizations, you are privileged to contemplate day by day the manifestations of our country's power. Be her lovers, and when her greatness fills your understanding, realize that it is the achievement of men——men who dared for her and planned for her and faced death for her, and who never felt that failure in an enterprise was a reason for depriving their country of their valour, the noblest offering that they could lay at her feet. They gave their lives to their country and won immortal praise for themselves——immortal praise and the noblest of all tombs, not merely the tomb in which their bodies lie, but that in which their glory is enshrined at all times, for word or deed to recall it, world without end. The tomb of heroes is the whole earth, and epitaphs inscribed in the land of their birth are not the only monuments that mark it. In lands which they never knew they possess monuments not graven on stone but implanted in the hearts of all men.

'Take them as your examples; learn from them that happiness consists in freedom and freedom in valour; and never stand aside from the perils of wars. The unfortunate, with no prospect of success before them, who are generally expected to be reckless of their lives, have less call to be so than those whose career is still exposed to the risk of a change for the worse and who have therefore most to lose by a catastrophe. To men with souls the degradation of cowardice is something more painful than an instantaneous death in the glory of their strength and patriotism.

'There is a lesson in this for the parents, here present, of the dead, to whom I now address myself with a message of consolation rather than condolence. They realize the changes and chances of this mortal life—a life in which true success is to be found in some end as glorious as that achieved by their children (whatever sorrow it may bring upon themselves) and in an existence in which happiness of others—— such happiness as once rejoiced your own hearts——will often remind you of your loss; and that what wounds is not the absence of blessings outside our experience but the withdrawal of blessings grown familiar to us by use. But your duty is endurance——tempered by the hope of other children, in the case of those who are still of an age to have them. These babes yet unborn, with whom some of you will be blessed, will efface from the hearts of their parents the memory of those that are not, and will banish the specters of depopulation and insecurity from the country. Citizens who have not children to give as hostages to Fortune can never play so fair or just a part in politics as their fellows. As for those of you who are too old to replace their loss, they must console themselves with the happiness that has attended the longer portion of their lives and with the comparative brevity of the remainder, and must find relief for their own pain in their children's glory. Nothing is immortal but the spirit of honour, and the true alleviation of the lean years is not to have made a fortune, as some would have it, but to have earned the esteem of others. Turning to the sons and brothers, here present, of the dead, I foresee that they have a formidable task before them. No one has anything but praise for the departed; and even if you do wonders, you will be fortunate if you are regarded not as their equals but as barely their inferiors. The living have always jealousy to contend with others, while those no longer in our path are honoured with an affection unqualified by rivalry. There are also new-made widows among you, on whose account I must not pass over the duties of women; but one sentence will convey the sum of the matter. Your highest ambition should be not to fall below the level on which you have been placed by nature, and to be as little heard of as possible, for good or evil, among the other sex.

'The task imposed upon me by custom is now accomplished to the best of my ability. My words are said, and these dead have received the martial honours due to their mortal remains. The country has still to honour them by educating their children at the public expense until they come of age. This honour, which commences from today, is the prize which Athens offers to these heroes and to their survivors in the race which they have run; and what prize could be better. For where the rewards of valour are, there will valiant men be gathered together....

'And now, bewail your dead and go your ways.'

This was the address with which the funeral of the fallen was celebrated that winter, which concluded the first year of the war.

ONE YEAR LATER

Pericles: 'Do not think you are fighting for the simple issue of letting this or that state become free or remain subject to you. You have an empire to lose. You must realize that Athens has a mighty name in the world because she has never yielded to misfortunes and has today the greatest power that exists. To be hated has always been the lot of those who have aspired to rule over others. In the face of that hatred you cannot give up your power——even if some sluggards and cowards are all for being noble at this crisis. Your empire is a tyranny by now, perhaps as many think wrongfully acquired, but certainly dangerous to let go.'

5

THE HISTORIOGRAPHY
OF THE
NEW TESTAMENT

THE FIRST IMPRESSION one gets from reading the Synoptic Gospels is that they tell a simple story in a straightforward way. There is vivid detail in the descriptions of people and action—the vividness of a story told by an excited and observant child. There is an almost naive reporting of what the disciples said, how they were so often surprised, so often mistaken, so often very much like children. And, as in a child's story, quite incredible things are told in the same matter of fact way as the most ordinary events of everyday.

A closer reading of these Gospels, however, raises a good many questions about this first impression of a straightforward story told in a simple way. Certain signs of artistry are detected, and hints of a deeper symbolism begin to appear behind both the historical details and the miracle stories. The simple words themselves gradually reveal symbolic character. They are used in a certain way and they are found to have profound literary and historical and theological implications. At a little deeper level of analysis a mass of scholarship is uncovered involving an intimate knowledge of the Old Testament and of its interpretative traditions. The narrative sequences are not simple reporting: a subtle artistry and symbolism lies beneath the surface. A literary unity is glimpsed which has much to do with historical form, but very little to do with straightforward history. We are soon aware that the Gospels are not primarily history at all: the detail points away from plot to theme, from event to symbol, from fact to faith. Even the order of the narratives is discovered to have been determined by the appropriate order of interpretation rather than the actual order of events.

What we have then in these documents is not primarily history but an interpretation in historical form of history, or, more precisely, of one complex event—the Christ. The Gospels furnish the historiographic canons for the interpretation of the Christ event. They are not historical biographies of the Jesus of history. Historical detail is important in the Gospels only in so far as it was considered important by the apostles for their testimony given to convince Jews and Gentiles that Jesus was the Christ. As in a court, this was the basic issue which men, like a judge and a jury, had to decide: was the man Jesus of Nazareth truly the Christ. The apostles are witnesses on the affirmative side. They bring into their testimony the words and deeds of Jesus which they believed would help to establish their case. Any other details about his life would be irrelevant, not to the point. This is one reason why the Gospels are not historical biographies. It was not their purpose to present a full, orderly, chronological record of the life of Jesus. Their purpose was to choose incidents from his life, selections from his speeches, to document their testimony.

The pictures that we have of Jesus in the Gospels are, therefore, not photographs. They are not precise, historical accounts. They are portraits. A portrait differs from a photograph because it is the main purpose of the artist to show the inner character, the spirit of his subject. To do this he may alter or even distort the physical features. 'It is not every man,' said an old Scotsman, 'who can look like his portrait.' But the portrait must be recognizable. You must be able to say: 'That is Mr. Chen. Yes, that is really the man himself, the man as I know him not only by his hair and eyes and nose, not only by what I can see, but as I know him as a whole person.' The portrait must be a picture of the man as he is known by those who have lived with him, walked with him, worked with him, shared his inner thoughts and dreams and sorrows. Gospels are recognizable portraits of the Christ as he was known by the inner circle of his disciples, the apostles, and through them, by the early Christian Church.

The New Testament is quite clear about this distinction between photograph and portrait. It speaks about this under the terms of 'Christ known after the flesh' and 'Christ known after the spirit.' St. Paul wrote: 'Now we know him (Jesus) no longer after the flesh but after the spirit.' He is saying that now Jesus, the man, is no longer with us. We cannot see him, listen to him, ask him questions, go with him from place to place and observe his deeds. Now we can know him only through our own experience of him as he confronts us when we hear or read the apostolic witness, and as we commit ourselves to him as the Christ who is our Saviour and Lord. It is this last way of coming to know the Christ which Albert Schweitzer emphasized in a famous passage from his great book, *The Quest of the Historical Jesus*. The image of Jesus that we would get from the Gospels if we took them as simple historical biographies 'has fallen to pieces, cleft and disintegrated by the concrete historical problems which came to the surface one after another. The study of the life of Jesus has had a curious history. It set out in quest of the historical Jesus, believing that when it had found Him it could bring Him straight into our time as a Teacher and Saviour. It loosed the bonds by which He had been riveted for centuries to the stony rocks of ecclesiastical doctrine, and rejoiced to see life and movement coming to the figure once more, and the historical Jesus advancing, as it seemed, to meet it. But He does not stay; He passes by our time and returns to His own. . . .He comes to us as One unknown, without a name, as of old by the lakeside. He comes to those men who knew Him not. He speaks to us the same word: 'Follow thou me!' and sets us to the tasks which He has to fulfill for our time. He commands. And to those who obey Him, whether they be wise or simple, He will reveal Himself in the toils, the conflicts, the sufferings which they shall pass through in His fellowship and, as an ineffable mystery, they shall learn in their own experience who He is.'

What little we know of Jesus after the flesh (as an historical figure), what little we can know of the actual words that he spoke, of the actual deeds he performed, is not enough to write a biography or a precise and significant treatise on his political, social or even religious ideas. He wrote nothing either of his thought or of his life. Yet he continues through all the centuries since his time to be one of the most commanding figures of history. He is a figure of history, but what we know of him and what is his historical significance has very little to do with the historical details about him. It has to do with the impact that he made upon the first small group of disciples and through their lives and their witness upon the ongoing life of the Church as a force within human culture.

What is important about him is not what he was as the Jesus of history—even the earliest Christians knew very few details of his life. What is important about him is what was remembered of him as the Christ of Faith, what was proclaimed in witness to him as the Christ by those whose lives were transformed by his spirit and thus empowered to do great deeds in his service.

Yet all that we have just said does not mean that the Christ event

is not historical. Its basis in history is exactly the heart of the Gospel
narrative. 'God once entered so fully into history in the Christ event
that this unique entrance can be designated by dates just like every
other historical event: under the Emperor Augustus (*Luke* 2:1); under
the Emperor Tiberius (*Luke* 3:1).' The blast of the Gospel is that 'the
word became flesh and dwelt in our midst.' And not only was the
Christ event determinative because it was historical. It was the event
which made the past meaningful, the crucial event in the long course
of the perfecting of salvation history that began with creation itself; for
it was the creative word that was made flesh. Hence the incarnation
also revealed as its ultimate fulfillment the whole redemption history
that was Israel and the whole redemption history that was mankind.
Through the incarnation it was seen that God had 'nowhere (in no
culture) left himself without a witness.' The whole of the past was
seen to belong to 'the fullness of time' for the coming of the Christ.

The Christ event thus became the mid-point of all history. It was
both fulfillment and crisis. The Gospels thereby contribute a new
concept of historical time: the concept of *kairos*—the moment of
revelation which is also the moment of crisis. Paul wrote (*Romans*
13:11) 'We know concerning the *kairos* how it is full time now for
you to wake out of sleep. For salvation is now nearer than when we
first believed.' The Gospel is just this: salvation is not something to
be looked for in some other world, in the heavens. It has already
drawn nigh, here in this world, in time. Therefore, *now* the New
Age has already begun—the Kairos of the Reign of God. The decisive
battle that will prove to have decided the victory over sin and death
has already been won on the cross and on Easter morning. Easter
Day was the greatest Day of Yahweh.

The Gospel concept of the Christ event as the mid-point of history
has these crucial implications for Christian historiography. The whole
past has a unity. It all belongs to the preparation for the Gospel. The
whole of culture has a unity. Whatever of enduring value there is in
all human culture is from that 'light that lighteth every man.' It is
the work of the redemptive creativity of God that was made flesh in
the man Christ Jesus. This is the basis of universal history. Also
there is a perspective in the mid-point for understanding the past.
Paul observes in *II Corinthians* 3:14 that 'a veil lay over the books of
Moses until in Christ the veil was lifted.' Cullmann remarks that in
the Gospel view an understanding of the past 'which combines creation,
primitive sagas and history, has only now become possible, because

only now in Christ have we gained the criterion for interpreting and orienting the entire process in a concrete way.'

Now the message of the prophets is fully understood for its fulfillment in Christ is the concrete embodiment of its inner meaning. But the Christ event is the fulfillment of an historical process as well, i.e. 'fulfillment according to the Scriptures' (The Old Testament history of Israel).

1. History before the mid-point, seen as fulfillment, the working out in the historical process of the preparation for the Gospel, is history seen in the light of 'myth' in the same sense as the myth of 'cyclical time' (Spengler or Toynbee) based upon cosmological order or the myth of evolutionary progress (18th and 19th century romantic histories).

2. Christ as the mid-point gives to the present a quality of crisis. Even though the decisive battle has been won, the war is not yet over. The present is a crucial time. It is an insistent present. The old age, which is still present even though the new age has begun, is the *kairos* of an indecisive struggle for domination by many powers. Among them is the demonic power which appears still to control the world. The important words are not 'this world' and some 'other world (heaven)' that is above this world in a two-storied universe. The important terms are not spatial but temporal symbols: the 'no longer' and 'the already' and the 'not yet'. Now that the mid-point of history has been reached there is evoked the sense of urgency and crisis: the urgency of decision and the demand for radical devotion. The whole of the New Testament *kairos* belongs to the 'already' which looks with excitement toward the 'not yet'. In Jesus' preaching, this note of urgency is strong. 'Repent and believe!' 'Let the dead bury their dead!' The time is short. Action must be taken. Men must throw themselves into the service of the powers of the new age without reserve, with unqualified commitment. Nothing must stand in the way, no impediments must be tolerated. 'If your hand offends you, cut it off, if your eye offends you, pluck it out....It is better to go into the new age as a partial casualty than to perish in the judgment.'

3. The mid-point provides the impetus for a significant history—the history of the new age. It was already in the First Century seen to be important to set down this history prefaced by the Gospel of the Christ event. This is the history of the triumphant spread of the Gospel 'from Jerusalem to Judea and Samaria and unto the uttermost parts of the world.' And it is the history of the new people, the new Israel of God, the Christian Church. *The Gospel of Luke* and *The*

Book of the Acts of the Apostles are two parts of one history. *Luke* is the prologue (the Christ event) and *Acts* is the history of the new age under the power of the Holy Spirit in the Christian Church. *Acts* tells the story of the expansion of Christianity in the Roman world of the First Century, the story of the apostolic ministry as a light to the Gentiles. It could be entitled 'The Glorious History of the Holy Spirit and the Apostolic Mission.'

The mission of two apostles forms the simple structure of *The Book of the Acts:* 1. Peter and the apostolic mission to the Jews, 2. Paul and the apostolic mission to the Gentiles. The inner structure points to a further historiographic canon: the work of the Holy Spirit in relation to history. The Spirit as experienced in the Church is a new power within the life of the community and of its individuals. Its working, which is experienced and therefore known at first hand in the community, is the key to the structure of event, to the structure of the historical process itself. Thus the experience of the Holy Spirit is also an insight into the past, lighting up the whole course of 'redemption history' from creation to the Christ.

After the *Book of the Acts of the Apostles* had been written (c. A.D. 96), the interest of the early Church centered upon the re-interpretation of the Scriptures, i.e. the Old Testament history from Creation to the restoration of Jerusalem under Ezra; but it did so in the broadest context of the chronologies of other peoples (Justin Martyr, Clement of Alexandria, Julius Africanus, Augustin, and Orosius).

It is interesting to note that the first full history of the Church came only after the triumph of Christianity in the Roman Empire, when under Constantine, Christianity became the religion of the state. We have previously noted that the first history of Israel came with the monarchy established by David and that the first Chinese history came with the first unified empire under the Ch'in.

Part Three

Modern Historiography

HISTORY AS
SCIENCE AND PHILOSOPHY

Modern Historiography

FROM NEW TESTAMENT times (A.D. 60-150) to Vico (1668-1744) is a leap of fifteen hundred years. The intervening centuries are important. Two factors, both of which belong to that interval, are the basic ingredients of modern historiography: 1. the Christian concepts of universal history, periodicy and providence, 2. the scientific revolution of the Seventeenth Century which had its roots in the new physics. The first modern physicist was Philoponus who lived in the Sixth Century of our era, and the foundations of Newtonian physics were laid by William of Occam and the fellows of Merton College, Oxford, and Jean Buridan and Bishop Oresme, who taught at the University of Paris in the Fourteenth Century.

At the beginning of the Seventeenth Century these new elements had produced a revolution in the notion of knowledge. Galileo, Bacon, Descartes, Hobbes, to mention only the most famous, openly revolted against their university training. All of these considered the curriculum antiquated, and the syllabus of required knowledge useless. Both Bacon and Descartes advocated a new structure of studies. Bacon suggested three faculties: poetry (literature), history, and philosophy. His new philosophy was a science faculty with the departments of mathematics, physics and metaphysics. Descartes was content with two: poetry and mathematics. Both allowed for the superior faculty of theology in which neither was much interested.

History for Bacon was a background study, an intermediate stage between poetry (imagination) and science (experimental research and practical application). The most useful of all histories, he believed, would be a history of trades, i.e. a systematic treatment of origins and developments in the field of technology—alchemy, the refining of metals, and mechanics, the invention of machines. Descartes could not see any real value in history. He believed that all real knowledge was either mathematical or theological, quantitative or authoritatively qualitative. That fundamental distinction may be traced back at least as far as William of Occam. It was popularized in Galileo's famous essay, *Il Saggiatore* (*The Assayer*), on the primary and secondary qualities of matter. Here primary qualities are defined as those inherent in matter itself—weight, size, shape, etc. All these are quantitative and hence best described by mathematics. Secondary qualities are those which man attributes to matter on the basis of his mental perception. Colour, smell, taste, sound—all these have their source in man's senses not in matter itself. They are qualitative and subjective. Galileo in another essay describes the new science of physics in terms of measurement—quantitative analysis of motion in terms of mass (weight), space (distance) and time (measurable intervals). Descartes' ‚new science' was strictly limited to quantitative analysis based upon ‚clear and distinct ideas' and expressed in 'the perfect universal language' of mathematics. Even the Cartesian rationalists who found in quantitative analysis the only certain source of knowledge recognized that important areas of human concern lay beyond the purely quantitative. Hobbes (1588-1679), a friend and disciple of Descartes, attempted a rationalistic analysis of the origins and structure of government. He was determined to pursue his study on the basis of clear and distinct ideas set forth in a rigorously rationalistic treatise. Society, like nature, he regarded as a machine. Hobbes' *Leviathan* was a rationalistic rather than an empirical study. It made little use of history, and excluded as irrational all cultural traditions of the origins and development of historic communities (e.g. the Greeks, Romans, Medieval peoples).

Modern historiography began in the Eighteenth Century with Giambattista Vico who saw the need for a new science, distinct from the rationalistic and purely quantitative approach of the physical sciences. The modern university is built upon these two major disciplines and basic methods—the scientific and the historical. From Vico to the Twentieth Century they were regarded as distinct and mutually exclusive fields and methods. Science studied nature and history was concerned with man. Science dealt with the inexorable and determined laws of nature conceived as a machine. History explored the realm of freedom and qualitative human experience. From Vico onward, history was the science of society, the rise and development of social structures (tribal and national groups), institutions (government, law and religion), and cultural expressions (language, literature and art). Classics, political science, and biblical literature were among the first historical studies to be accepted as university subjects. History as a separate academic discipline was not found in most universities before the early years of the Nineteenth Century. Even a century ago most universities in Europe and America did not have chairs in history.

Departmental programmes were adopted in the Nineteenth Century when it was believed that history could answer important questions in an objective way only if it were studied as an independent discipline with its own aims and methods. The historian who had no prior interest in sociological, economic, religious, or political theory was considered the more objective student of nations, religions, and institutions. Further, the late Eighteenth and the Nineteenth Centuries were keenly conscious of a new tension between the past and the present. The historian stood as the mediator between traditional society and the new rationalistic criticism of tradition. Such criticism was felt to be a duty of a self-determining free society on the threshold of a new age. The American and French Revolutions, the increasing impact of the scientific revolution upon culture, the industrial revolution in England, and the rise of modern empires involving a new kind of internationalism—all these created a demand for history as a new scientific discipline that could aid in the reshaping of society.

The selected readings in this section have been chosen not only for their content but also because they have become historic markers of the paths historiography has taken from the Eighteenth Century to the present. They illustrate the development of modern historiography as method and as theory. Certain recurrent questions in both areas characterize modern notions of history. One set of questions is asked by historians in their attempt to clarify the nature of their task: Is history a science or an art? What kind of knowledge is the subject matter of history? Is it the historian's task merely to investigate and record past events or should his research be justified only in terms of its bearing on the present? Should the historian go beyond explanation to interpretation and judgment? Does it make sense to speak of causes in history?

Another set of questions is asked in an attempt to clarify our understanding of the historical process: Are there general laws or significant patterns in history? Is there one dominant factor that determines the course of events or does the historical process evolve from the interplay of many factors? One further recurrent issue raises the question of a correlation of some kind between the way the historian thinks of his task and the way he answers questions about history.

Giovanni Battista Vico: History as a New Science

Vico was born in the latter half of the Seventeenth Century (1668) in Naples, Italy. His own university study in arts was thus against the background of the scientific revolution with its emphasis upon mathematical knowledge which left little place for human experience or qualitative values.

Vico's life illustrates the brute pressures of science and rationalistic philosophy upon education in the Eighteenth Century. He was the son of a poor bookseller, and throughout his career he eked out a meager living from the small salary which the university paid for a professor of rhetoric. For some years he hoped that he might be given a chair in the law faculty which would have provided a comfortable living. But that post was denied him, and he was forced to spend much of his time on menial clerical jobs. It must have been a bitter misfortune to Vico to have spent his life in a faculty which had little status and less privilege in his university. But the new science and its rationalistic philosophy imposed an even greater burden upon him. He had to live in a university and in a world that was incapable of understanding or appreciating his thought. He was denied even the encouragement of a small circle of friends with whom he could share something of his active intellectual life.

To read Vico today makes us sure that he should have been given a chair in the law faculty. If his lectures in rhetoric were like his style in writing, his transfer to the faculty of law would have been no loss to his former students. No book published in the Eighteenth Century could have been less faithful to the ideals of clear and distinct ideas and rigorous lean logic than Vico's *New Science* (1725). But the title itself for a book on history is of fundamental significance. Most books published during Vico's lifetime (1688-1744) used the word *new* in their titles. Their authors had been influenced by the great pioneers of the Seventeenth Century Scientific Revolution—Kepler's *New Astronomy*, Galileo's *Two New Sciences*, Bacon's *Novum Organum*. These titles suggest a new and different kind of knowledge and a new method of learning and research. Vico, against the main current of thought in his age, boldly insists that history is a new science—a new and different kind of learning more realistic and empirical and hence more valuable than mathematics and the physical sciences.

What man can learn of nature is limited. Man did not create the world and he can never hope fully to understand it. If it is, as the scientists (Eighteenth Century) say a vast machine, no one who neither designed nor constructed that machine can have more than a partial knowledge of either its structure or function. Physical science is simply nature as interpreted by a creature. It cannot tell us what nature is in itself. It can speak only of nature as man sees it.

In Vico's time, Leibniz, who was one of the foremost mathematicians and rationalists, had urged this more modest claim for physical science. The mathematical sciences should, he felt, be regarded as a road to explore rather than a goal of perfect knowledge which man could reach. With Leibniz, Vico declared that only God could have perfect knowledge of nature. He saw the value of mathematics for physical science within the limits of a road to be explored. But he reminded his generation that mathematics was man-made. It was exact because it was the perfect description of quantities within the arbitrary sphere of nature as conceived by man. Mathematics was simply a description of that conceptual universe. It was not distilled from nature itself. It was not empirical—it was purely rational, i.e. according to human reason.

For history, Vico claimed the kind of knowledge that is derived from a real and objective world—the world of events. Here alone ascertainable facts were the basis of a true science. Man can have an accurate and adequate knowledge of events because he is himself a maker of history. God alone made the world (nature) but man is a collaborator with God in the making of history. Our knowledge of social institutions and of human experience can, therefore, be far more profound than our knowledge of the physical universe. Man is closer to culture than he is to matter. History is the story of the beginnings and development of the human spirit based upon the demonstrable data of objective events. Therefore in this science there is the closest relation between knowing and doing. It is active. Historical knowledge involves participation in the events themselves. Physical science is a merely passive contemplation. This is a half truth that has persisted, in fact from the Seventeenth Century, into our own time. Thomas Huxley's definition of science as 'sitting down before the facts like a little child' states precisely what was the target of Vico's criticism. The real point of Vico's argument was best stated by Professor C.C.J. Webb two hundred years after the *New Science:* the higher the reality that is known the deeper becomes the relation between the knowing subject and the reality apprehended. Here the subject that knows is not simply a passive observer, an onlooker. And the object that is known is not only an object, but is itself a subject—a thou who confronts the knower. History is the story of what happened to us. Thus, Vico's *New Science* makes a clear distinction between history and natural science.

There is a living continuity between the past and the historian—the human spirit. The essentially human continues throughout all ages and in all peoples. Yet history in contrast to physical science is not the description of a machine which is, apart from wear, the same as when it was manufactured. There has been a significant development of the human spirit, and there are new and different elements involved in man's making of history in the various ages and among the several great cultures. Nevertheless, a general pattern within all great cultures can be discerned. Each of the early cultures in its own way passed through three stages of social organization: the Divine, the Heroic and the Civil. In each of these there was a distinctive spirit expressed throughout the life and work of the age. Yet different cultures will exhibit significant contrasts when compared on any one given level (e.g. the heroic or the civil).

But philosophy is not speculation. It is not an imposing of a rationalistic and arbitrary scheme upon the past. Philosophy must accommodate itself to the evidences of what actually happened as derived from the documents themselves. It cannot, as did Hobbes, theorize on the basis of what might have happened or what should have occurred. Only when philosophy deals fairly with its task of reconstruction from the documents themselves can it discern the pattern of their relations. The laws of history must first be found in events and then be so widely illustrated by similar events that they can be applied fruitfully to the understanding of the present. So much of Vico's contribution is to be found in his *Axioms* (patterned after Bacon's *Aphorisms*), brief notes on his insights, which were never organized into a precise and systematic treatise. Yet the seeds of most modern historiography are found in Vico: 1. the emphasis upon both 'universal history' and upon a faithful use of documents (Neibuhr and von Ranke and Acton), 2. the concept of history as the development of the human spirit (Hegel and Dilthey), the three stage theory of man's spiritual development expressed in social structures (Hegel, Comte and Marx), 3. the relation of the past to the present (Acton, Oakshott and Collingwood), 4. the relation of history to science and to art (Dilthey and Croce) and 5. the role of providence in the historical process (Butterfield).

SELECTED READINGS FROM VICO

TYPES OF GOVERNMENT, LANGUAGE, AND JURISPRUDENCE

So this New Science or metaphysic, (i.e. as distinct from physics) considers the common nature of nations in the light of divine providence, on the basis of a study of origins involving the acts of God and the ventures of men in society. It thus establishes a system of the natural law of nations, which proceeds with the greatest equality and constancy through ages...as the three periods through which the world had passed. These are: 1. The age of the gods, in which societies believed they lived under divine governments, and everything was commanded them by signs and oracles, which are the oldest thing in history. 2. The age of the heroes, in which superior men ruled everywhere in aristocratic commonwealths, on account of certain special natural gifts by which they were regarded to be superior to the common people. 3. The age of men, in which all men recognized themselves as equal in human nature. Therefore there were established first the popular commonwealths and then the monarchies, both of which are forms of human government.

Three kinds of language correspond to the three ages or governments. They are the mute languaage of signs and physical objects; heroic emblems, comparisons, images, metaphors, and the like; and the human or civic language which gives rise to law. Along with these are also three corresponding types of jurisprudence or rule, namely the rule of the gods by the mystic theology of the poets; the rule of the heroes by reason of state; and the free commonwealth by universal laws..

PHILOSOPHY AND PHILOLOGY (HISTORY)

Philosophy (logic and physical science) contemplates reason; philology (i.e., historical research into the roots and development of language) observes the authority of human choice. The philologians are all grammarians, historians, critics who study the language and deeds of peoples. The certainty of what they find the philosophers need in order to be certain, although the philologians also need the reasoning of the philosophers in order to know the truth.

Human choice, by its nature most uncertain, is made certain and determined by the common sense of men with respect to human needs or utilities, which are the two origins of the natural law of nations.

Common sense is judgment without reflection, shared by an entire class, an entire people, an entire nation, or the whole human race....

Uniform ideas originating among entire peoples unknown to each other must have a common ground of truth. (It is not true that they originated in one nation and passed on to others only later. Natural law is a case in point) The natural law of nations began in human customs springing from the common nature of all nations which is the proper subject of our Science.

The nature of peoples is first crude, then severe, then benign, then delicate, finally dissolute.

THE NEW SCIENCE: HUMAN CUSTOMS AND DIVINE PROVIDENCE.

But in the night of thick darkness enveloping the earliest antiquity, so remote from ourselves, there shines the eternal and never-failing light of a truth beyond all question: that the world of civil society has certainly been made by men, and that its principles are therefore to be found within the modifications of our own human mind. Whoever reflects on this cannot but marvel that the philosophers should have bent all their energies to the study of the world of nature, which, since God made it He alone knows; and that they should have neglected the study of the world of nations or civil world, which, since men had made it, men could hope to know.

We observe that all nations, barbarous as well as civilized, though of independent origins in different countries and ages, keep these three customs: all have some religion, all contract solemn marriages, all bury their dead. And in no nation, however savage and crude, are any human activities celebrated with more elaborate ceremonies and more sacred solemnity than religion, marriage and burial. For, by the axiom that *uniform ideas, born among peoples unknown to each other must have a common ground of truth*, it must have been revealed to all nations that from these three institutions civilizations everywhere arose, and therefore they must be most devoutly observed by them all, so that the world should not again become a bestial wilderness.

The first men had strong impulses like beasts. Fear of some divine power imposed form and measure on these bestial passions and transformed them into human passions. From this thought must have sprung the impulse proper to the human will, to hold in check the physical passions, so as either to quiet them altogether as becomes the sage, or at least to direct them to better use, as becomes the civil man. This control over the motion of their bodies is certainly an effect of the freedom of the human will, and thus of free will, which is the home and seat of all the virtues, including justice. When informed by justice, the will is the source of all that is just and of all the laws demanded by justice.

But men because of their corrupted nature are under the tyranny of self-love, which compels them to make private utility their chief guide. Seeking everything useful for themselves and nothing for their companions, they cannot bring their passions under control to direct them toward justice. We thereby establish the fact that man in the bestial state desires only his own welfare; having taken wife and begotten children, he desires his own welfare along with that of his family; having entered upon civil life, he desires his own welfare along with that of his city; when its rule is extended over several peoples, he desires his own welfare along with that of the nation; when the nations are united for defence, treaties of peace, alliances and commerce, he desires his own welfare along with that of the entire human race. In all these conditions man desires principally his own advantage. Therefore it is only by divine providence that he can be held within these orders to practice justice as a member of the society of the family, the state, and finally of mankind. Unable to attain all the utilities he wishes, he is constrained by these orders to seek those which are his due; and this is called just. That which regulates all human justice is therefore divine justice, which is administered by divine providece to preserve human society.

The New Science, in this respect, must be a 'rational civil theology of divine providence.' Divine providence is to be observed not so much in things of nature but in the economy of civil things, in keeping with the full meaning of applying to providence the term divinity, from *divinari*, to divine; that is, to understand what is hidden in them, their consciousness. It is this that makes up the first and principal part of the subject matter of jurisprudence, namely the divine things on which depend the human things which make up its other and complementary part. Our new science must therefore be a demonstration, so to speak, of the historical fact of providence, for it must be a history of the forms of order which, without human discernment or intent, and often against the designs of man, providence has given to this great city of the human race. For though this world has been created in time, the orders established therein by providence are universal and eternal.

(Divine providence) develops its orders by means as easy as the natural customs of men. Since it has infinite wisdom as counselor, whatever it establishes is order. Since it has for its end its own immeasurable goodness, whatever it ordains must be directed by a good always superior to that which men have proposed to themselves. Reflect with what ease social customs and institutions are brought into being, sometimes quite contrary to human intentions, yet fitting together by themselves. Compare these institutions with one another and observe the order by which they appear at the proper times in the various nations according to the needs of each culture as a particular stage of its development.

In reasoning of the origins of things divine and human in the world, we reach those first beginnings beyond which it is vain curiosity to demand others earlier: and this is the defining character of (first) principles. We explain the particular ways in which they come into being, that is to say, their nature, the explanation of which is the distinguishing mark of science. And finally (these proofs) are confirmed by the eternal properties (the things) preserve, which could not be what they are if the things had not come into being just as they did, in those particular times, places and fashions, which is to say with those particular natures.

In search of these natures of human things our science proceeds by a severe analysis of human thoughts about the human necessities or utilities of social life, which are the two perennial springs of the natural law of nations, as we have remarked in the *Axioms*. In its second principal aspect, our Science is therefore a history of human ideas, on which it seems the metaphysics of the human mind must proceed....

(The criterion of our search for origins is) that taught by divine providence and common to all nations, namely the common sense of the human race, determined by the necessary harmony of human things, in which all the beauty of the civil world consists. The decisive sort of proof in our Science is therefore this: that, once these orders were established by divine providence, the course of the affairs of the nations had to be, must now be, and will have to be such as our Science demonstrates.

Our Science therefore comes to describe at the same time an ideal universal history traversed in time by the history of every nation in its rise, progress, maturity, decline and fall. Indeed we go so far as to assert that whoever reflects upon this Science is convinced that this ideal history is based upon the facts and, has, and will have to be. For the first certain principle above stated we can deduce from our argument that this world of nations has certainly been made by man, and its structure must therefore be found within the historical developments of the human mind. And history cannot be more certain than when he who creates the things also describes them. Thus our Science proceeds exactly as does geometry, which, while it constructs out of its elements or contemplates the world of quantity, but with a reality greater in proportion to that of the orders having to do with human affairs, in which there are neither points, lines, surfaces, nor figures. And this very fact is an argument, O reader, that these proofs are of a kind divine, and should give thee a divine pleasure; since in God, knowledge and creation are one and the same thing.

From Vico to Hegel

Vico's *New Science* raised history to the level of a new philosophy just as Bacon had a century before made physical science, based upon observation and experiment, the content of his new philosophy. Both Bacon and Vico had scattered through their writings a number of insights that became seminal ideas of scientific and historical thought in the latter part of the Eighteenth Century. Both Bacon and Vico believed that experience (experiment in physical science, philology in historical science) provided a more solid foundation than Cartesian rationalism based on mathematics. The issue between the rationalists and the empiricists now became a fundamental problem for science, history and philosophy. Hobbes in his study of government had on principle ignored historical research. We have no need, of experience, he argued, to deduce geometric propositions from axioms. Similarly in social science, if we start from clear and distinct ideas we need only the discipline of logical thought to reach valid conclusions. Certain effects must of necessity follow from certain causes. The notion of cause and effect was the foundation of physical science. Hobbes insisted that it was equally fundamental to social science. A given cause must produce a certain effect or a given effect presupposes a certain cause. The premise of early Eighteenth Century science (physical and social) was the belief that the world can be known by man because it is rational. Since it was the creation of a mathematical Mind it will reveal itself to human reason. This simple faith was attacked by a Scotsman, David Hume. He argued that there can be no rational demonstration of the notion that effects necessarily follow from causes. It is only because we expect that when one event occurs another must occur. But this expectation is based upon our experience rather than on our reason.

> We are determined by Custom alone to suppose the future conformable to the past. When I see a billiard-ball moving towards another, my mind is immediately carry'd by habit to the usual effect, and anticipates my sight by conceiving the second ball in motion. There is nothing in these objects, abstractly considered, and independent of experience, which leads me to form any such conclusion: and even after I have had experience of many repeated effects of this kind, there is no argument, which determines me to suppose, that the effect will be conformable to past experience. The powers, by which bodies operate, are entirely unknown. We perceive only their sensible qualities: and what *reason* have we to think, that the

same powers will always be conjoined with the same sensible qualities.

'Tis not, therefore, reason, which is the guide of life, but custom. That alone determines the mind, in all instances, to suppose the future conformable to the past. However easy this step may seem, reason would never, to all eternity, be able to make it.

This is a very curious discovery!

This is quite like Vico's criticism of Descartes' clear and distinct ideas. 'The fact that I think my ideas clear and distinct only proves that they are so to me, and that I believe them, not that they are true.' The implications of this critique of rationalism point up the problem of the relation between the human mind and the external world. They involve also the notion of human nature. Both these issues came to be equally important to physical science and to history.

It was to the latter issue that that the Romantic scholar, Johann Gottfried Herder (1734-1803) contributed a number of significant, insights. Herder was a Lutheran pastor trained in the Graeco-Roman classics and in biblical literature. He had as a theological student attended Kant's lectures on philosophy at Konigsberg and was both inspired and negated. Later he was a bitter critic of those aspects of Kant's thought which he did not understand. Kant in turn was both influenced and irritated by Herder. At forty he read the first of the twenty volumes of Herder's great work entitled *Contributions (Ideen) Toward a Philosophy of the History of Man*. His review, published a year later, was unsympathetic. Yet Herder from that time on did influence Kant's evaluation of rationalism and his notion of the character and importance of history. Vico had been the lonely prophet who saw the distortions inherent in the rationalism of the physical sciences. Herder began to write at the beginning of the Romantic reaction against rationalism. He speaks for man, for the liveliness and warmth of the human spirit which neither Descartes nor Hobbes could appreciate. He saw in the cultures of the past a greater individuality and concrete richness than could be pressed into the rigid patterns of uniform stages of the rationalistic schemes. He urges his contemporaries to seek beneath the surface of offical records to find the spirit of the culture. The historian should listen to the 'voices of the people.' His material must include poetry, songs, legends, and art.

Herder's most fruitful insight was his notion of the unique quality of each culture. Each great people presents the historian with a special type of humanity. Each people has a characteristic nature that expresses itself in its own way in history. Like a particular species of flower that is transplanted from one soil to another, a people will be what it is despite the extremes of geography or climate because its history is primarily a function of its nature.

What is the principal law, that we have observed in all the great occurrences of history? In my opinion it is this: *that every where on our Earth whatever could be has been, according to the situation and wants of the place, the circumstances and occasions of the times, and the native or generated character of the people.* Admit active human powers, in a determinate relation to the age, and to their place on the Earth, and all the vicissitudes in the history of man will ensue. Here kingdoms and states crystallize into shape: there they dissolve, and assume other forms. Here from a wandering horde rises a Babylon: there from the straitened inhabitants of a coast springs up a Tyre: here, in Africa, an Egypt is formed: there, in the deserts of Arabia, a Jewish state: and all these in one part of the World, all in the neighbourhood of each other. Time, place, and national character alone, in short the general cooperation of active powers in their most determinate individuality, govern all the events that happen among mankind, as well as all the occurrences in nature. Let us place this predominant law of the creation in a suitable light.

As man originates from and in one race, his figure, education, and mode of thinking, are thus genetic. Hence that striking national character, which, deeply imprinted on the most ancient people, is unequivocally displayed in all their operations on the Earth. As a mineral water derives its component parts, its operative powers, and its flavour, from the soil through which it flows; so the ancient character of nations arose from the family features, the climate, the way of life and education, the early actions and employments, that were peculiar to them. The manners of the fathers took deep root, and became the internal prototype of the race. The mode of thinking of the Jews, which is best known to us from their writings and actions, may serve as an example: in the land of their fathers, and in the midst of other nations, they remain as they were; and even when mixed with people they may be distinguished for some generations downward. It was and it is the same with all the nations of antiquity, Egyptians, Chinese, Arabs, Hindus, etc. The more secluded they lived, nay frequently the more they were oppressed, the more their character was confirmed.

Herder appears to have thought of man as having a nature which was expressed in history. The character of a people was not determined by its historical experience. Its experience was an expression of its character. He did, however, distinguish between two levels of civilization. On one level (the majority of cultures) men had lived without any real consciousness of an historic existence. On this level there was very little development. Such societies were static. He saw European civilization in contrast to such societies as genuinely historical—articulately conscious of its past and aware of its role in a dynamic process involving significant transformations in government, economy, art, philosophy and religion. Herder did not himself pursue the implications of this new kind of society as a 'historical' rather than a 'natural organism'. He did, however, point up the issue of the relation of nature to history and of nature to man. Historical existence, he concluded, is a consciousness of history and a responsible relationship to its laws involving a spiritual life.

To achieve a truly historical existence is to experience and actually to participate in a spiritual life involving understanding and freedom. Such a life is something more than the experience of a given nature. It is a fulfilment of that nature—a perfecting of nature in history.

Herder did not deal with the problem of the relation of experience to reason or of the relation of mind or spirit to the physical universe. He did not examine the structure of events in the cause-effect sequence.

It may by said that neither physical science nor history reached the level of 'philosophy' before Immanuel Kant (1724-1804). Kant tells us that the scepticism of Hume was for him a rude awakening from the 'dogmatic slumbers' of rationalism. Hume had undermined the whole rationale of the new science. He had raised the serious questions: Is science at all rational? Are its basic assumptions (concepts of substance, cause and effect, natural law) grounded in reason or are they merely illustrations of the habits of man's mental life? Do they have any real relation to nature at all?

The thrust of these questions was directed at the new science of history as well as at Newtonian physics. Hume had not merely destroyed reason to make room for experience. The historian as well as the scientist had been called to give a reasoned answer to the question: what is the nature and the validity of man's knowledge of the external world either as nature or as the past.

Kant attacked this fundamental problem by an analysis of reason— the kinds of judgments that are made in science, history, and theology. He concluded that there are some basic categories that are necessary to any knowledge man can have of the physical world. Euclidean space and Newtonian time, subtance and the notion of cause and effect are essential to an understanding of the physical universe. But these categories were not derived from experience. They are not products of inductive reason on the basis of empirical evidence. They are simply the way and the only way that we can know the external world. We can know nature only in terms of these categories. Physical science is a knowledge of the universe *as man apprehends it.* The human mind makes a picture of nature just as a camera makes a picture. What the camera sees depends upon its equipment—lenses, shutter, etc. as well as upon the object. The picture taken by the camera is the object as seen by the camera. Similarly science is nature *as seen by man.* Hence science cannot be the basis of philosophy. Physics can give us no certain knowledge of the world as it is in itself. It is valid knowledge only to the extent that it turns out to be useful. If science enables us to live in the world by making a better adjustment to our external environment and by controlling aspects of its powers, it is a worthy endeavour.

Understanding and wisdom, however, have their source in the moral imperative that is laid upon man by his inner nature as a spiritual being. It is by faith not by mathematical reason that we come to affirm the meaning of human existence in terms of freedom and purpose. History rather than the physical world is the sphere of faith and freedom—the realm of the will and the arena of moral action. Man as he is in his inmost being knows history as determined by an absolute moral imperative. History as viewed by the historian—from the standpoint of a spectator—is determined by natural law (cause and effect). In 1783 Kant wrote an essay entitled, *A Plan (Ideen) for a Universal History* in which he discussed the kind of law or control that operates in history. With the rationalists he regarded the past as the ages of ignorance. History gave no evidence that its courses were guided by man's rational decision or foresight. To the contrary, history appeared to the spectator (historian) as the record of man's folly, vanity, passion and selfishness. Not even the greatest among the leaders of men, nor indeed even the philosophers, had been able to live their own lives according to reason. Yet history did evidence certain lines of development particularly in the emergence of new and better social structures (government). There did appear to be, despite man's evil purposes, an increasing capacity in society to encourage rationality and moral freedom. Within history, therefore, some plan of nature must be operative. History, despite man's selfish motives, has proved a training or education of the human race. The development of human reason required a long course of training. Nature gave to man the capacity to be a rational, free and moral being. But it was through history that this capacity has been and must be realized. Kant illustrates this by a reference to the development of mathematics. Euclid could not have written his *Elements of Geometry* without the foundation that had been laid by Thales and Pythagoras. Kepler, Descartes, Newton and Leibniz built upon Euclid. One significant aspect of man's rational faculty is his capacity to profit from past experience, and to appropriate and build upon the work of others. Through history, nature's purpose for man is realized. Indeed it is of the very nature of reason that it can mature only through the historical process.

Herder's distinction between static societies in contrast to the dynamic and rational character of Europe in the Scientific Revolution and the Enlightenment appears again in Kant. He asks why some societies continued over long periods with little more change than is found in a colony of bees or in an ant heap. Other societies have exhibited a dynamic development over the course of a single century (e.g. Athens during the period from 500-400 B.C.). The 'spring' of historical development Kant finds in the thrust of selfish and anti-social motives, on the one hand, and in man's inherent desire for peace, on the other. There is here an echo of Hobbes. A century later, Comte, Durkheim, and then Bergson contrasted the individualistic and selfish thrust of intelligence with the cooperative and social determination of instinct in ants and bees. In the push of sentient self-assertion and in the pull of the desire for peace, man, quite against his will and in spite of his follies, is led to break through the bonds of the static society, and then to devise a new society with greater freedom, but demanding greater responsibility. It is in this way that man is led through the dialectic of conflicting purposes to develop his reason and to accept responsible spiritual freedom. History is, thus by Nature's plan, the education of the human race. Human reason (spirit) is the product of the historical process.

Kant's decisive contribution to historiography was his sense of its essential role in the modern world. He was himself a mathematician, geographer, and astronomer, although, like Herder, his university study had been theology. He saw, even more clearly than Hume, that Newtonian science was purely descriptive and that its description of the universe was from a necessarily limited viewpoint. He foresaw that its genius was practical. It could invent gadgets but it could not create a philosophy. To put it quite simply, nearly two hundred years ago, Kant knew that Newtonian science had very little to say to man, and that the implications of its practical thought would, if applied to the meaning of human life, prove to be a tragic distortion of man's self understanding. He therefore urged his contemporaries to look to history as the realm of meaning and the foundation of philosophy.

Georg W. F. Hegel: History as Understanding

Georg Wilhelm Friedrich Hegel (1770-1831) took up the challenge of Kant's proposed plan for a universal history. He did not have Kant's training in mathematics and Newtonian physics, and perhaps, for this reason, was more optimistic about the common ground of nature and history.

Hegel was convinced that there could be no science or history unless there was an inherent correspondence between the human mind as Knower and the external world as the Known. He begins with the question: Is there a unity that includes the subject (man) and the object (the external world both as nature and history). If there is, then there is also a real correspondence between the world as it appears to man and as it is in itself. Similarly there is a real correspondence between the phenomena of history, the meaning of history, and the mind of man as historian. Hegel's conclusion was based on a judgment of history—that is to say, he was convinced that the answer to his fundamental question was to be found in history. If there were such a unity it would be known to man only in and through the historical process. The relation of subject and object (the Knower and the Known) would have to be dialectical—i.e. the interaction of opposing forces. The whole of Hegel's philosophy is a philosophy of history—and his history is a new kind of philosophy. His famous lectures on the *Philosophy of History*, delivered at the University of Berlin (1822-1823), began with a careful distinction between history as merely descriptive and history as a normative discipline fulfilling the high purpose of philosophy. The chief end of history as a discipline is man's understanding of himself as a spiritual being. There history is the history of thought. Action has meaning only as the outward expression of thought. We cannot answer the simple question of *what* happened until we can give some reasoned account of *how* it happened and *why* it happened.

But *what* happened is no less rooted in bare, actual occurrence than
it is in explanation and interpretation. The philosopher is an
historian. His first task is an empirical study of historical phenomena.
His ultimate task is explanation.

The most general definition that can be given, is that the philosophy
of History means nothing but the thoughtful consideration of it. Thought
is, indeed, essential to humanity. It is this that distinguishes us from the
brutes. In sensation, cognition, and intellection; in our instincts and
volitions, as far as they are truly human, Thought is an invariable element.
To insist upon Thought in this connection with history may, however,
appear unsatisfactory. In this science it would seem as if Thought must
be subordinate to what is given, to the realities of fact; that this is its
basis and guide: while philosophy dwells in the region of self-produced
ideas, without reference to actuality. Approaching history thus prepossessed,
Speculation might be expected to treat it as a mere passive material; and,
so far from leaving it in its native truth, to force it into conformity with
a tyrannous idea, and to construe it, as the phrase is, *a priori*. But as it
is the business of history simply to adopt into its records what is and has
been, actual occurrences and transactions; and since it remains true to its
character in proportion as it strictly adheres to its data, we seem to have
in philosophy, a process diametrically opposed to that of the historiographer.

The only Thought which philosophy brings with it to the contemplation
of History, is the simple conception of *Reason*; that Reason is the Sovereign
of the World; that the history of the world, therefore, presents us with a
rational process.

It is, in fact, the wish for rational insight not the ambition to amass a
mere heap of acquirements, that should be presupposed in every case as
posssessing the mind of the learner in the study of science.

It is only an inference from the history of the World, that its development
has been a rational process; that the history in question has constituted
the rational necessary course of the Word-Spirit——that Spirit whose nature
is always one and the same, but which unfolds this its one nature in the
phenomena of the World's existence. This must, as before stated, present
itself as the ultimate *result* of History. But we have to take the latter as it
is. We must proceed historically — empirically. Among other precautions
we must take care not to be misled by professed historians who (especially
among the Germans, and enjoying a considerable authority), are chargeable
with the very procedure of which they accuse the philosopher—introducing
a priori inventions of their own into the records of the past. It is, for
example, a widely current fiction, that there was an original primeval
people, taught immediately by God, endowed with perfect insight and
wisdom, possessing a thorough knowledge of all natural laws and spiritual

truth.

Even the ordinary, the 'impartial' historiographer, who believes and professes that he maintains a simply receptive attitude; surrendering himself only to the data supplied him—is by no means passive as regards the exercise of his thinking powers. He brings his categories with him, and sees the phenomena presented to his mental vision, exclusively through these media.

To him who looks upon the world rationally, the world in its turn presents a rational aspect. The relation is mutual.

There could be no historical knowledge apart from a real correspondence between the logic of event and the logic of thought. History and thought do indeed, even on the surface, exhibit a significant likeness. Action involves subject and object and the conflict of wills. Thought involves an idea and its criticism. It is dialectical. In its most elementary form the dialectic, either of thought or of history, begins with a thesis or a subject (man as a person who seeks to know). To this thesis nature presents an antithesis (the impersonal world which resists the Knower). There is then the conflict of thesis and antithesis. Both in thought and in action this conflict is resolved by a synthesis —a more adequate perspective that unites in a new idea the essential and valid elements of both partial views. Synthesis is something more than a resolution of contradiction. It is a new thesis in thought and a new level of self-realization of spirit in history. The whole of existence is involved in this process of thesis, antithesis and synthesis. It is the structure of processes of both thought and event. Historical events—all the concrete realities of life—are involved in the process. History is not a meaningless cycle of birth and death. It moves through conflict and contradiction toward fulfillment—from mere logical possibility through the concrete richness of events toward the full self-consciousness of Spirit which is perfect freedom. Even the perpetually perishing makes its eternal contribution to the development of spirit.

A new principle does in fact enter into the Spirit of a people that has arrived at full development and self-realization; it dies not a simply natural death—for it is not a mere single individual, but a spiritual, generic life; in its case natural death appears to imply destruction through its own agency....The Spirit of a people exists as a *genus*, and consequently carries within it its own negation. A people can only die a violent death when it has become naturally dead.

The bud disappears when the blossom breaks through, and we might say that the former is refuted by the latter; in the same way when the fruit comes, the blossom may be explained to be a false form of the plant's existence, for the fruit appears as its true nature in place of the blossom. These stages are not merely differentiated; they supplant one another as being incompatible with one another. But the ceaseless activity of their own inherent nature makes them at the same time moments of an organic unity, where they do not merely contradict one another, but where one is as necessary as the other; and this equal necessity of all moments constitutes from the outset the life of the world.

We can now define the nature, field, aims, and value of the normative discipline of history philosophically considered. It is a universal history of mankind because it deals with the universal categories of being in historical existence (Passion and Reason, Spirit and Freedom). Vico, Herder and Kant had seen that only through the whole course of civilization and only by comparison and contrast of the many varieties of culture could the 'new science' be either trustworthy or significant. Hegel, however, by his definitions of the subject matter of history and the nature of the historical process, makes universality a necessary aspect of understanding in history. The development of the Spirit must include the whole of history; for the Spirit has 'not anywhere left itself without a witness.'

It must be observed at the outset, that the phenomenon we investigate— Universal History——belongs to the realm of *Spirit*. The term '*world*,' includes both physical and psychical Nature. Physical Nature also plays its part in the World's History, and attention will have to be paid to the fundamental natural relations thus involved. But Spirit, and the course of its development, is our substantial object.

On the stage on which we are observing it——Universal History——Spirit displays itself in its most concrete reality.

The nature of Spirit may be understood by a glance at its direct opposite——*Matter*. As the essence of Matter is Gravity, so, on the other hand, we may affirm that the substance, the essence of Spirit is Freedom. All will readily assent to the doctrine that Spirit, among other properties, is also endowed with Freedom; but philosophy teaches that all the qualities of Spirit exist only through Freedom; that all are but means for attaining Freedom; that all seek and produce this and this alone.

It may be said of Universal History, that it is the exhibition of Spirit in the process of working out the knowledge of that which it is potentially. And as the germ bears in itself the whole nature of the tree, and the taste and form of its fruits, so do the first traces of Spirit virtually contain the whole of that History.

The German nations, under the influence of Christianity, were the first to attain the consciousness that man as man is free: that it is the *freedom* man as man is free of Spirit which constitutes its essence. This consciousness arose first in religion, the inmost region of Spirit; but to introduce the principle into the various relations of the actual world, involves a more extensive problem than its simple implantation; a problem whose solution and application require a severe and lengthened process of cultural development.

2. The plot of history is the development of freedom as the living expression of the Spirit in its gradual achievement of self-consciousness.

The History of the world is none other than the progress of the consciousness of Freedom; a progress whose development according to the necessity of its nature, it is our business to investigate.

The general statement given above, of the various grades in the consciousness of Freedom——and which we applied in the first instance to the fact that the Eastern nations knew only that *one* is free; the Greek and Roman world only that *some* are free; while we know that all men absolutely (man *as man*) are free——supplies us with the mode of its discussion.

What appears to the historian is the passage from thesis and antithesis to synthesis as a new thesis—what appears is a realization of man's capacity to become a rational being. The historian cannot ignore this fact of development involving the 'judgment' of the enemies of freedom whether they be individuals, social structures or whole cultures. Yet the immediate action that constitutes such judgment is itself mixed in motive, seemingly passionate and irrational. Kant had observed the paradox of evil pressing men toward good, but Hegel discovered in this paradox a clue to the logic of the process itself. Passion is reason's power in the concrete historical situation. Individual action is passionate and selfish. But that action is the agent of reason. Men make history but history develops man's capacity to be rational. The spirit of a people reaches out toward articulate self-consciousness in the great individuals, the heroes of the society. Hegel called them 'world historical individuals.' Their goals may have been purely selfish but their drives were the force that broke through the bounds of the old order and created the need of new social structures. Through them, all that is potential in the spirit of a people comes to realization. Their passion was the tool of reason. In terms of the concrete situation and the stage of the Spirit's self consciousness, their actions were rational.

Historical men——*World-Historical Individuals*——are those in whose aims such a general principle [Freedom] lies. Caesar, in danger of losing a position, belongs essentially to this category. Caesar was contending for the maintenance of his position, honour, and safety; and since the power of his opponents included the sovereignty over the provinces of the Roman Empire, his victory secured for him the conquest of that entire Empire; and he thus became the Autocrat of the State. That which secured for him the execution of a design....was, however, at the same time an independently necessary feature in the history of Rome and of the world. It was not, then, his private gain merely, but an unconscious impulse that occasioned the accomplishment of that for which the time was ripe. Such are all great historical men——whose own particular aims involve those large issues which are the will of the World-Spirit. They may be called Heroes, inasmuch as they have derived their purposes and their vocation, not from the calm, regular course of things, sanctioned by the existing order; but from a concealed fount....They are men, therefore, who appear to draw the impulse of their life from themselves; and whose deeds have produced a condition of things and a complex of historical relations which appear to be *their* interest, and *their* work. Such individuals had no consciousness of the general Idea they were unfolding, while prosecuting those aims of theirs; on the contrary, they were practical, political men. But at the same time they were thinking men, who had an insight into the requirements of the time——*what was ripe for development.* This was the very Truth for their age, for their world....If we go on to cast a look at the fate of these World-Historical persons, whose vocation it was to be the agents of the World-Spirit——we shall find it to have been no happy one. They attained no calm enjoyment; their whole life was labour and trouble; their whole nature was nought else but their master-passion. When their object is attained they fell off like empty hulls from the kernel. They die early, like Alexander; they are murdered, like Caesar; transported to St. Helena, like Napoleon. This fearful consolation——that historical men have not enjoyed what is called happiness——this consolation those may draw from history, who stand in need of it; and it is craved by Envy——vexed at what is great and transcendant——striving, therefore, to depreciate it, and to find some flaw in in it ...Alexander of Macedon partly subdued Greece, and then Asia; therefore he was possessed by a *morbid craving* for conquest He is alleged to have acted from a craving for fame, for conquest; and the proof that these were the impelling motives is that he did that which resulted in fame. What pedagogue has not demonstrated of Alexander the Great and of Julius Caesar that they were instigated by such passions, and were consequently immoral men?——whence the conclusion immediately follows that he, the pedagogue, is a better man than they,

because he has not such passions; a proof of whsich lies in the fact that he
does not conquer Asia.... 'No man is a hero to his *valet-de-chambre*,'
is a well-known proverb; I have added——and Goethe repeated it ten years
later——'but not because the former is no hero, but because the latter is a
valet.' He takes off the hero's boots, assists him to bed, knows that he
prefers champagne, etc. Historical personages waited upon in historical
literature by such psychological valets, come poorly off; they are brought
down by these their attendants to a level with——or rather a few degrees
below the level of——the morality of such exquisite discerners of spirits.

Behind these agents (the world-historical individuals) is the principle
of action—the means which Freedom uses for its realization.

What means does this principle of Freedom use for its realization?

The question of the *means* by which Freedom develops itself to a World,
conducts us to the phenomenon of History itself. Although Freedom is,
primarily, an undeveloped idea, the means it uses are external and
phenomenal; presenting themselves in History to our sensuous vision. The
first glance at History convinces us that the actions of men proceed from
their needs, their passions, their characters and talents; and impresses us
with the belief that such needs, passions and interests are the sole springs
of action——the efficient agents in this scene of activity. Among these
may, perhaps, be found aims of a liberal or universal kind——benevolence
it may be, or noble patriotism; but such virtues and general views are but
insignificant as compared with the World and its doings. Passions, private
aims, and the satisfaction of selfish desires, are on the other hand, most
effective springs of action. Their power lies in the fact that they respect
none of the limitations which justice and morality would impose on
them; and that these natural impulses have a more direct influence over
man than the artificial and tedious discipline that tends to order and
self-restraint, law and morality. When we look at this display of passions,
and the consequences of their violence; the Unreason which is associated
not only with them, but even (rather we might say *especially*) with *good*
designs and righteous aims; when we see the evil, the vice, the ruin that
has befallen the most flourishing kingdoms which the mind of man ever
created, we can scarce avoid being filled with sorrow at this universal taint
of corruption....But even regarding History as the slaughter-bench at which
the happiness of peoples, the wisdom of States, and the virtue of individuals
have been victimized —— the question involuntarily arises —— to what
principle, to what final aim these enormous sacrifices have been offered.

The *first* remark we have to make, and which is what we call
principle, aim, destiny, or the nature and idea of Spirit, is something merely
general and abstract. Principle——plan of Existence——Law-——is a hidden,
undeveloped essence, which *as such*——however true in itself——is not
completely real. Aims, principles, etc., have a place in our thoughts, in

our subjective design only; but not yet in the sphere of reality. That which exists for itself only, is a possibility, a potentiality; but has not yet emerged into Existence. A *second* element must be introduced in order to produce actuality——viz., actuation, realization; and whose motive power is the Will ——the activity of man in the widest sense. It is only by this activity that that Idea as well as abstract characteristics generally, are realized, actualized; for of themselves they are powerless. The motive power that puts them in operation, and gives them determinate existence, is the need, instinct, inclination, and passion of man.

Passion, it is true, is not quite the suitable word for what I wish to express. I mean here nothing more than the human activity as resulting from private interests——special, or if you will, self-seeking designs——with this qualification, that the whole energy of will and character is devoted to their attainment.

But the history of mankind does not begin with a *conscious* aim of any kind, as it is the case with the the particular circles into which men form themselves of set purpose. The mere social instinct implies a conscious purpose of security for life and property; and when society has been constituted, this purpose becomes more comprehensive. The History of the World begins with its general aim——the realization of the Idea of Spirit ——only in an *implicit* form that is, as Nature; a hidden, most profoundly hidden, unconscious instinct; and the whole process of History (as already observed), is directed to rendering this unconscious impulse a conscious one. Thus appearing in the form of merely natural existence, natural will——that which has been called the subjective side——physical craving, instinct, passion, private interest, as also opinion and subjective conception—— spontaneously present themselves at the very commencement. This vast complex of volitions, interests and activities, constitute the instruments and means of the World-Spirit for attaining its object; bringing it to consciousness, and realizing it. And this aim is none other than finding itself——coming to itself——and contemplating itself in concrete actuality. But that those manifestations of vitality on the part of individuals and peoples, in which they seek and satisfy their own purposes, are, at the same time, the means and instruments of a higher and broader purpose of which they know nothing——which they realize unconsciously——might be made a matter of question; rather has been questioned, and in every variety of form denied and rejected as mere dreaming and 'philosophy.' But on this point I announced my view at the very outset, and asserted our hypothesis and our belief, that Reason governs the world, and has consequently governed its history.

The question also assumes the form of the union of *Freedom* and *Necessity*; the latent abstract process of Spirit being regarded as *Necessity*, while that which exhibits itself in the conscious will of men, as their interest, belongs to the domain of *freedom*.

He is happy who finds his condition suited to his special character, will, and fancy, and so enjoys himself in that condition. The History of the World is not the theatre of happiness. Periods of happiness are blank pages in it, for they are periods of harmony——periods when the antithesis is in abeyance.

I will endeavour to make what has been said more vivid and clear by examples.

The building of a house is, in the first instance, a subjective aim and design. On the other hand we have, as means, the several substances required for the work——Iron, Wood, Stones. The elements are made use of in working up this material: fire to melt the iron, wind to blow the fire, water to set wheels in motion, in order to cut wood, etc. The result is, that the wind, which has helped to build the house, is shut out by the house; so also are the violence of rains and floods, and the destructive powers of fire, so far as the house is made fire-proof. The stones and beams obey the law of gravity——press downward——and so high walls are carried up. Thus the elements are made use of in accordance with their nature, and yet to co-operate for a product, by which their operation is limited. Thus the passions of men are gratified; they develop themselves and their aims in accordance with their natural tendencies, and build up the edifice of human society; thus fortifying a position for Right and Order *against themselves.*

3. The Principal of Freedom finds its concrete embodiment in the state. Subjective mind (the self-consciousness of the individual) and even the seminal ideas of a pre-national culture (myths, sagas and cultic forms) belong to the discipline of psychology in its broadest sense. Only in the state does a civilization attain to objective mind. Here again Hegel follows Kant's view that history as phenomena (as events appear to the spectator or historian) is political history, the rise and development of the state. Men make history but history makes the state and hence the state is the prime object of historical study.

St. Augustin had seen the secular state (the Roman Empire) as at best neutral and for the most part in conflict with purpose in history. In contrast to the Church as the bearer of the City of God was the state as the bearer of the City of Man in revolt against God. Augustin here had followed the biblical and Alexandrian Jewish historians who distinguished between the meaningful course of events in the experience of Israel as the people of God and the meaningless cycles of brute force and sensualism that characterized the nations of the Gentiles.

Both Joachim di Fiore and Thomas Aquinas gave a larger place to social institutions as the agencies of divine providence. Hegel goes further to find in secular institutions, particularly in the state, the locus of historical significance: 'That harmony which has resulted from the painful struggles of History, involves the recognition of the Secular as capable of being an embodiment of Truth, whereas it had been formerly regarded as evil only, as incapable of good—the latter being considered essentially other worldly.' Indeed it is in the state that religious experience comes to its most effective and concrete expression. Law (the Constitution of the State), he wrote, 'is the work of centuries, the idea and the consciousness of what is rational, in so far as it is developed in a people.' Therefore, 'It is nothing but a modern folly to try to alter a corrupt moral organization by altering its political constitution and code of laws without changing the religion—to make a revolution without having made a reformation, to suppose that a political constitution opposed to the old religion could live in peace and harmony with it and its sanctities, and that stability could be procured for the law by external guarantees....' The object of the historical process, for man, is the state. Here freedom is achieved through law. Man's capacity to be rational is realized in his free acceptance of law. Through law the spirit knows and enjoys freedom. Bertrand Russell illustrated this concept of freedom by the story of a man 'who habitually runs his head into brick walls, from an unwillingness to allow that bricks are harder than skulls.' Such a man is persistent but he is not as free as the man who accepts the ‚authority' of the wall and the 'laws of physics.'

> We have spoken of *means*; but in the carrying out of a subjective, limited aim, we have also to take into consideration the element of a *material*, either already present or which has to be procured. Thus the question would arise: What is the material in which the Ideal of Reason is wrought out? The primary answer would be——personality itself——human desires—Subjectivity generally. In human knowledge and volition, as its material element, Reason attains positive existence....As a subjective will, occupied with limited passions, it is dependent, and can gratify its desires only within the limits of this dependence. But the subjective will has also a substantial life——a reality——in which it moves in the region of *essential* being, and has the essential itself as the object of its existence. This essential being is the union of *subjective* with the *rational* Will: it is the moral Whole, the *State*, which is that form of reality in which the individual has and enjoys his freedom; but on the condition of his recognizing, believing in, and willing that which is common to the Whole.

Subjective volition——passion——is that which sets men in activity, that which effects 'practical' realization. The Idea is the inner spring of action; the State is the actually existing, realized moral life. For it is the Unity of the universal, essential Will, with that of the individual; and this is 'Morality.' The Individual living in this unity has a moral life....In the history of the World, only those peoples can come under our notice which form a state. For it must be understood that this latter is the realization of Freedom, i.e. of the absolute final aim, and that it exists for its own sake. It must further be understood that all the worth which the human being possesses——all spiritual reality, he possesses only through the State. For his spiritual reality consists in this, that his own essence——Reason——is objectively present to him, that it possesses objective immediate existence for him. Thus only is he fully conscious; thus only is he a partaker of morality——of a just and moral social and political life. For Truth is the Unity of the universal and subjective Will; and the Universal is to be found in the State, in its laws, its universal and rational arrangements....For Law is the objectivity of Spirit; volition is its true form. Only that will which obeys law, is free; (or it obeys itself——it is independent and so free). When the State or our country constitutes a community of existence; when the subjective will of men submits to laws——the contradiction between Liberty and Necessity vanishes. The Rational has necessary existence, as being the reality and substance of things, and we are free in recognizing it as law, and following it as the substance of our own being.

The state of Nature is, therefore, predominantly that of injustice and violence, of untamed natural impulses, of inhuman deeds and feelings. Limitation is certainly produced by Society and the State, but it is a limitation of the mere brute emotions and rude instincts; as also, in a more advanced stage of culture, of the premeditated self-will of caprice and passion. This kind of constraint is part of the instrumentality by which only, the consciousness of Freedom and the desire for its attainment, in its true——that is Rational and Ideal form——can be obtained.

The State is the Idea of Spirit in the external manifestation of human Will and its Freedom. It is to the State, therefore, that change in the aspect of History indissolubly attaches itself; and the successive phases of the Idea manifest themselves in it as distinct *principles*.
Summing up what has been said of the State, we find that we have been led to call its vital principle, as actuating the individuals who compose it——Morality. The State, its laws, its arrangements, constitute the right of its members; its natural features, its mountains, air, and waters, are *their* country, their fatherland, their outward material property; the history of this State, *their* deeds; what their ancestors have produced, belongs to them and lives in their memory. All is their possession, just as they are possessed by it; for it constitutes their existence, their being.

This Spirit of a people is a *determinate* and particular Spirit, and as, just stated, further modified by the degree of its historical development.

> The remark next in order is, that each particular National genius is to
> be treated as only One Individual in the process of Universal History. For
> that history is the exhibition of the divine, absolute development of Spirit
> in its highest forms——that gradation by which it attains its truth and
> consciousness ot itself. The forms which these grades of progress assume
> are the characterstic 'National Spirits' of history; the peculiar tenor of their
> moral life, of their Government, their Art, Religion, and Science.

4. History, philosophically considered, must be distinguished from
descriptive physical science because the course of world history points
to a final purpose. History deals not only with what has happened in
the past. It reveals to us the process of action and its goal. It is
therefore truly philosophical—normative rather than merely scientific
—descriptive. The distinction is fundamental: 'History in general is
the development of Spirit in Time, as nature is the development of
the Idea in Space.'

> The mutations which history presents have been long characterized in
> general, as an advance to something better, more perfect. The changes
> that take place in Nature exhibit only a perpetually self-repeating cycle; in
> Nature there happens 'nothing new under the sun,' and the multiform play
> of its phenomena so far induces a feeling of *ennui*; only in those changes
> which take place in the region of Spirit does anything new arise.

Further the course of history, in contrast to nature, exhibits a
graduated development through the spiral progression of the dialectical
process.

> Universal History exhibits the *gradation* in the development of that
> principle whose substantial *purport* is the consciousness of Freedom. The
> first step in the process presents that immersion of spirit in Nature which
> has been already referred to; the second shows it as advancing to the
> consciousness of its freedom. But this initial separation from Nature is
> imperfect and partial, since it is derived immediately from the merely
> natural state, is consequently related to it, and is still encumbered with it
> as an essentially connected element. The third step is the elevation of the
> soul from this still limited and special form of freedom to its pure universal
> form; that state in which the spiritual essence attains the consciousness and
> feeling of itself. These grades are the ground-principles of the general
> process; but each of them on the other hand involves within *itself* a
> process of formation——constituting the links in a dialectic of transition.

Finally Hegel is explicit in his judgment of the place of history in the modern world. Man *is* his history. He cannot know himself except through history; for what he is now in the 'insistent present' is a function of history. 'History is always of great importance for a people; since by means of that it becomes conscious of the path of development taken by its own spirit, which expresses itself in laws, manners, customs, and deeds. History presents a people with their own image in a condition which thereby becomes objective to them.' Morever his knowledge is essentially historical knowledge. A subject must therefore be studied from the perspective of its history. Science *is* the history of science. Art is the history of art. Social science is the history of ideas and institutions. We cannot over-estimate the profound influence which Hegel has exercised in this respect upon the course of university education in the West during the past century. In the whole range of academic pursuits it has become a commonplace that history is the key to understanding.

Throughout the Nineteenth Century (in Marx as well as in Acton) history was normative and philosophical in the Hegelian sense. There **is** even in the least Hegelian of contemporary historians a feeling for Hegel's epigramatic conclusion: 'The history of the world is the world's court of justice.'

7

Mits der

Kommunistischen Partei.

Karl Marx & J.Engels

London
1848

TYPES OF MODERN THEORY:
POSITIVIST AND MARXIST

History as the Science of Society

HISTORIOGRAPHY IN THE Nineteenth Century may be described as variations upon selected themes from Vico and Hegel. Two of these themes are dominant: 1. the notion that history is rational in pattern, process and purpose, and 2. that its general course reveals a development both of human reason and of social institutions. Universal history is thus still the aim of the historian but there is after Hegel a recognition of the need of special studies. The rise and development of specific institutions or even aspects of institutions becomes the ideal of historiography. Research in specific topics in history parallels the speculative laboratory experiments of the physical scientist.

Hegel had held up before his students the challenge of the great task of the future—the filling out with detailed studies of the universal history of mankind. F. C. Bauer applied Hegelian perspectives to the study of doctrine in the development of the Christian Church. He traced the dialectical movement from the thesis of the Jerusalem Church (James) and the antithesis of Gentile Churches (Paul) to the first synthesis of apostolic Christianity (Peter). D. F. Strauss and L. A. Feuerbach also made special studies, as Hegelians, of religion in relation to universal history. Feuerbach's famous study of the *Essence of Christianity* which rejected all forces and purposes in history except those of nature and man himself had a decisive influence upon Nietzsche and Karl Marx. Both Strauss and Feuerbach traced the source of theological doctrines to myth which they identified with subjective mind rather than, as in Hegel, with Absolute mind. In these early Left Wing Hegelians a new school of history had its rise—positivist historiography. Vico's assumption of Divine Providence and Hegel's ultimate explanation in terms of Absolute Mind realizing itself through the development of the Spirit were rejected by the new 'scientific' historians.   Further the sharp distinction which Vico and Hegel had made between nature and man and hence between natural science and history was now regarded as a tearing apart of the seamless robe of true knowledge.   Early Nineteenth Century historiography was deeply impressed by the success of the physical sciences and by their method.   Historians turned again to the discovery of cause and effect sequences as the structure of the historical process.   Scientific history in accord with the physical sciences now attempted to proceed from effects (historical phenomena) to causes and then to general laws.   Some historians were content to ascertain the effects (the facts of history) and leave the search for causes and the framing of laws to their successors.   These early 'positivists' regarded history as a purely academic discipline.   They were convinced that their first duty was to devise rules of evidence.   Several new terms now appeared *methodics* as the discipline of historical method which began with *heuristics* (canons of acceptable evidence in relation to the use of documents).   *Hermeneutics* (interpretation) in the sense of both general explanation and value judgment could be undertaken only in the distant future, if at all.   This kind of 'positivist' history rendered a valuable if limited service.   It produced a vast body of historical detail based upon painstaking philological scholarship and specialized research.   Among its many adherents one of the more outstanding was Theodor Mommsen (1817-1903) who devoted a long career to the editing of the *Corpus inscriptionum Latinorum*—an emmended text of all known Roman inscriptions—including tablets, coins, and monuments as well as documents.   Yet his *History of Rome* and his later *History* (for which he won the Nobel prize of 1902) was, apart from a fine-tooth comb raking in the learned dust of obscure details, a failure.   What was left after the dust had been disturbed and sifted was only the skeleton of the past—inert and lifeless bones.   Much of this kind of positivist history merited the criticism of sheer 'historicism' which we met in Albert Schweitzer's *Quest of the Historical Jesus.*

History as Social Physics—Auguste Comte

Another line of positivist historiography begins with Auguste Comte and his ideal of a *social physics*.   Comte was born in the university town of Montpellier in southern France.   His limited formal education was in natural science as a mathematical discipline. Comte was a rebel spirit even as a student. His rebellion against his home involved both religion and politics since his father was both a devout Catholic and a loyal supporter of tradition in politics. His historical vision comes from Vico, and there is much in his writings that was at least at second hand from Hegel. Comte was, nonetheless, a bold deviationist from that classical historiography. He coined the word *Positivist* as descriptive of the truly scientific in fact and method. *Positive knowledge* is the only certain knowledge because it is based exclusively upon demonstrable or empirical facts. The interpretation of these facts cannot go further than a cause-effect explanation. Neither theological nor philosophical notions of first principles are positive (scientific), and hence must be formally rejected. The end of historical study is, like that of physical science, prediction and material transformation. Social physics rather than philosophy should be the arbiter of the meaning and use of historical data.

Comte's social physics had its roots, however, in the theology of Joachim di Fiore and the philosophies of Vico and Hegel. It had 'emerged' in the course of world history as a necessary fulfillment of the development of human reason as applied to the science of man. It is indeed the crown of the sciences; for it deals with the more complex phenomena of human nature and history. It had, therefore, not only like all positive science to wait until the dawn of the Age of Science (Comte's own time), but also until the lower sciences had been developed. That development was not only historical but according to a pattern of logical necessity. Mathematics had perforce to be the first of the sciences. Astronomy was based upon it. Next in the rational hierarchy comes physics, then chemistry and physiology. Only then could social physics appear. All positive science is knowledge of nature as observed. Such knowledge man possesses now for the first time in the new positivist age of human culture that began with the Scientific Revolution of the Seventeenth Century. But the new age had its necessary antecedents. Primitive man could conceive the world only in fantasy by myth and ritual (religion). The intermediate age (the metaphysical) marked the passage of the human race from subjective to critical and speculative thought.

FROM *POSITIVE PHILOSOPHY*

From the study of the development of human intelligence, in all directions, and through all times, the discovery arises of a great fundamental law, to which the mind of man is necessarily subject. This law rests on a solid foundation of proof, both in the facts of our organization of our knowledge and in our histoiical experience. The law is this: that each of our leading conceptions——each branch of our knowledge——passes successively through three different theoretical conditions: the Theological, or imaginative and fanciful; the Metaphysical or abstract; and the Scientific, or positive. In other words the human mind, by its nature, employs in its progress three methods of conceiving the world. The character of these is essentially different, and even radically opposed. Hence arise three philosophies, or general conceptions of phenomena. Each excludes the others. The first is the only possible way by which man could first approach an understanding of the world; and the third is the inevitable and final state of human development. The second is merely a transitional stage.

In the theological state, the direct action of supernatural beings is supposed to be the cause of all things. The metaphysical state begins when belief in deities is displaced by a notion of abstract forces. In the final, positive state man gives up the vain search for ultimate principles, the origin and notions of the destiny of the universe and the causes of phenomena. He now turns instead to the study of the laws of nature as it is observed——the invariable relations of succession and resemblance. Reasoning and observation, duly combined, are the means of this knowledge. What is now understood when we speak of an explanation of facts is simply the establishment of a connection between single phenomena and some general facts, the number of which continually diminishes with the progress of science.

Each of the two previous systems arrives at its ultimate perfection by positing one First Principle as the cause of all phenomena. In theology it is a personal God; in metaphysics it is impersonal Nature. Similarly, the ultimate perfection of the positive system will be achieved when all social phenomena can be known as particular aspects of a single general fact—such as gravitation in Newtonian astronomy. Our positive philosophy thus regards all phenomena as subject to invariable natural laws and it aims to reduce these laws to the smallest possible number, and explain all phenomena by them, as in the case of the law of gravity, which explains a wide variety of physical phenomena.

Human knowledge progresses from the theological through the metaphysical to the positive stage. Our most advanced sciences still bear many vestiges of the two earlier periods through which they have passed. And we note also that different kinds of knowledge pass through the three stages at different rates and so have not arrived at the stage of a positivist science at the same time. The rate of advance depends on the nature of the knowledge in question. Any kind of knowledge advances toward the positive stage in proportion to its generality, simplicity, and independence of other pursuits. Astronomical science, which is above all made up of facts that are general, simple, and independent of other sciences, arrived first; then terrestrial physics; then chemistry; and at length, physiology....

Though related to physiology, social phenomena demand a distinct classification, both on account of their importance and of their complexity. They are the most individual, the most complicated, the most dependent on all others; and, therefore, they must be the latest——positive sociology could not have appeared before the physical sciences. This branch of science has not yet entered into the domain of positive philosophy. Theological and metaphysical methods, exploded in other departments, are still exclusively applied, both in the way of inquiry and discussion, in all treatment of social subjects, though the best minds are heartily weary of the eternal disputes about divine right and the sovereignty of the people. This is the great gap and the only gap which has to be filled in order to constitute, solid and entire, the positive philosophy. Now that the human mind has grasped celestial and terrestrial physics—— mechanical and chemical; organic physics, both vegetable and animal——there remains one science, to fill up the series of sciences of observation——*Social Physics*. This is now man's greatest need. It is the principle aim of the present work to establish this science.

History is therefore of prime importance; for man's social existence *is* the historical process. History as a discipline is the basic method of social physics. It seeks out from the past what really appeared in the process (phenomena) and exhibits the causal connections between events. Social physics builds upon these the laws of human nature and behaviour. Here then, as also in physical science, 'understanding' proceeds from individual events to movements, and thence to universal laws, i.e. from the acts of individuals to the universal motions of humanity.

FROM *PLAN OF THE SCIENTIFIC OPERATIONS NECESSARY FOR REORGANIZING SOCIETY*

All men who have exercised a real and lasting influence upon the human race...have, at every epoch, perceived what were the changes which the state of Civilization tended to bring about. When they had clearly grasped the nature of these changes, they proposed to their contemporaries doctrines and institutions in harmony with them. Whenever their conceptions were in accord with the real state of affairs, the changes so foreseen presented no problem of painful adjustment. The new social forces, which had long been silently growing, suddenly appeared by the proclamation of these leaders on the political scene with all the vigour of youth.

History having been, up to the present time, written and studied in a superficial spirit, such coincidences and striking results, have not been properly understood, but, as might be naturally supposed, have created only astonishment. These facts, when misapprehended, even help to keep alive the Theological and Metaphysical belief in the infinite power of legislators over Civilization. They would maintain this superstitious idea in minds otherwise disposed to reject it, were it not apparently supported by observation. This untoward result arises from the circumstance that in these great events we see only men, never the forces which irresistibly compel them. Instead of recognizing the dominant influence of Civilization, the efforts of these far-seeing men are regarded as the true causes of the improvements effected. But actually these changes would have occurred, though somewhat more slowly, without their intervention. No one troubles himself with considering the huge disparity between the alleged cause and the results. Yet this disparity makes the explanation much more difficult to understand than the fact itself. People look at the appearance and neglect the reality which is behind. In a word...we mistake the actors for the drama. Such an error is exactly of the same nature as that of the American Indians who attributed to Christopher Columbus the eclipse which he had foreseen.

Generally speaking, when the individual appears to exert a great influence, it is not due to his own abilities, since these are extremely small. Forces external to him act in his favour, according to laws over which he has no control. His whole power lies in the intelligent apprehension of these laws through observation, his forecast of their effects, and the power which he thus obtains of subordinating them to the desired end, provided he employs them in accordance with their nature. The effect once produced, ignorance of natural laws leads the spectator, and sometimes the actor himself, to attribute to the power of man what is really only due to his foresight....

In ascertaining what is to be the New System of Society it is necessary to ignore the question of its advantages or disadvantages. The principal, indeed, the only question, should be: What is that Social System indicated by observation of the past, which the progress of Civilization *must* establish.

Comte's programme of Positivist Science in some respects recalls Plato's education of the philosopher-king. It proceeds from physical to social science, and it has as its end the cultivation of scientist rulers of the state. Comte was the founder of social science as an independent discipline, and he established an 'apostolic succession' of secular clergy —men and women who carried the zeal of an evangelical ministry into the cause of social science dedicated to the curing of social ills and the salvation of mankind from the errors of religion and philosophy! It has been said, however, that Comte's rigid scheme of the three stages was more dogmatic and far less profound than the doctrine of the Trinity. Among those who were his most faithful followers, 'positivism converted even natural science into a new system of dogma and superstition.' It is significant that Comte devoted the last years of his life to the foundation of a 'positivist religion' with a creed, a ritual and a calendar of holy days for the saints of science.

Marxist Historiography: *The Roots of Dialectical Materialism*

In the founding of a secular religion Karl Marx (1813-1883) proved more successful than Comte. Marx was born in Trier, the native town of St. Ambrose (the teacher of St. Augustin). His family was Jewish, but his father became a Protestant in 1824. With the rest of the family, young Karl, aged eleven, was baptized. Something of his prophetic vigour may be traced back to his heritage in the ancient Israelite prophets of social justice.

Karl Marx's early university education was at Bonn in the faculty of law. After one year he left that pleasant and quiet town for the more lively university of Berlin where he studied history and philosophy. It is said that he read Hegel day and night for three weeks. Then he announced his conversion to dialectical philosophy and was received into the fellowship of the young Hegelians who exercised the first lasting influence on his life. (Ludvig Feuerbach had already left Berlin and had forsaken theology to study natural science at Erlangen.) The year Marx took his doctorate at Berlin, Feuerbach published his famous book on *The Essence of Christianity*. Its thesis was that theology was simply the outward projection of man's inward nature, and that the basis of human nature was to be found in physiology. 'Man is what he eats.' Here Marx found his first clue to a new historiography in the suggestion that cultural ideas could be explained in terms of the material condition of the society that produced them. Feuerbach had taught him how 'to stand Hegel on his head.' Marx meant by this boast that Hegel's historiography made logic prior to nature, and, therefore, that logic was the key to the historical process. Nature could determine only the environmental setting of history. For Marx, as for Feuerbach, history was the expression of nature. Hence its causes were to be sought in natural facts. Marx' materialist basis of history was thus quite close to the positivist science (social physics) of Comte. Both Positivism and Marxism rejected out of hand Hegel's 'metaphysical' notions of spirit and freedom. In place of spirit as the ultimate principle of history Marx dealt with production as the basic 'natural' fact. In place of the Absolute he put the classless society— man's realization in history of his own nature (Feuerbach) or the full achievement of man in a scientific society (Comte).

But Marx was closer to Hegel in his notion of the one dominant factor in the historical process. For Hegel that was the state as the embodiment of the spirit in history. Marx, of course, denied the reality of spirit, but found another dominant factor—production. Here again Marx is 'Hegel on his head' or without his head. The state for Hegel was the realization of objective mind as the fullest human achievement of the spirit of a people. For Marx, production was the basis upon which society or the state was built. All else in history, including art and religion, was simply the reflection of the one dominant factor of economics.

Marx' materialism was, however, different from Eighteenth Century naturalism. The whole course of materialist philosophy from the Greeks through the Eighteenth Century, Marx insisted, had failed to understand and explain human action. Former materialists, including Feuerbach, had regarded man as passive, or at best as a part (the same as all others) of the great machine of nature. Man, however, as Vico and Hegel had seen, was actively related to his material environment. His perception and understanding of nature constituted an act of the will, not just a passive looking on as a spectator. Man did react against his environment, and he could transform his environment. The older materialism was a philosophy of resignation and acceptance. If man was determined by material conditions including those of his own physiology, he could not initiate or even hasten social reform. All that man could do would be to know what was happening to him— to understand the theory and accept the necessity of the historical process. There is a strong apocalyptic strain in Marx' notion of the inevitable march of history toward the classless society; but there is also an equally strong strain of pragmatic activism, demanding of man an active revolt against the powers of the present age. The older materialism had yet another weakness in that each individual was considered as a private person with his own feelings and motivations based only on his own self interest. Materialism had in the past been anti-historical. It had been blind to the role of cultural and historical experience in the moulding of the individual consciousness.

Marx' own dialectical materialism first emerges as the result of his struggle through the contradictory elements of Hegel's philosophy of the spirit with its dynamic notion of history and the positivism and materialism of Feuerbach. In his criticism of the eleven 'theses' which he found in Feuerbach, Marx indicates not only his great indebtedness to that older deviationist from Hegel but also his own 'synthesis' of science and history.

THESES ON FEUERBACH

1. The chief defect of all hitherto existing materialism, that of Feuerbach included, is that [the material basis of human life and of man's physical environment] is conceived only as a first principle of philosophy but not [in terms of the concrete and realistic facts of man's actual life and social experience]. Man's active and actual relation to nature was developed not by materialism but by idealism (Hegel). [But Hegel did not see the real force of action in history in the real and concrete facts of [economic struggle]. Feuerbach in his *Essence of Christianity* is concerned only with theory. He explains Christianity in terms of doctrine and regards practice as Judaic legalism [in contrast to grace and faith.] Hence he does not grasp the significance of revolutionary or practical dialectical activity.

2. The question whether objective truth can be attributed to human thought is not a matter of theory, but is a practical question. In practice man must prove (test) the truth. Only in doing is there a real knowing of the reality and the power of ideas. (Note the use here of Vico's notion of the doer as knower.)

3. The Materialist doctrine that men are products of circumstance and social traditions and therefore that all change in men is the effect of changes in circumstance and training misses the obvious point that behind changed circumstances are the actions of men. The educator himself has had to be educated by some one. The real principle of change is revolution. Change occurs when men revolt.

4. Feuerbach considered that he had liberated men from the training of false religion when he explained that theology was the projection of man's sense of need and of his own sentiments in the concept of a transcendent God. He overlooked the fact that after this explanation has been accepted, the chief work of liberation has still to be accomplished. The needs and sentiments of men produce theology because they are self contradictory and inadequate. (Religion is the opiate of people.) Only by reforming these contradictory sentiments will the real need of man be met. Thus, for example, once the earthly family is discovered to be the secret

of the holy family, the former must then itself be criticized in theory and revolutionized in practice.

5. Feuerbach was right in his rejection of metaphysical speculation and his appeal to sense perception and inductive logic based upon empirical facts, but he failed to recognize the natural facts of man's real life and concrete social experience as the source of really positive knowledge.

6. Feuerbach did see that the essence of religion was actually in man's own feelings, but he failed to see that his abstract notion of the individual is not man at all. He failed to see man as he is, i.e. as the function not only of his own physiology but also of the totality of his social relations.

7. Feuerbach saw that religious belief had no real object but he failed to grasp the chief point, namely, that religious delusions are themselves the products of society, and that the abstract individual to whom he attributes religious sentiment is himself a member of a particular form of society.

8. Social life is essentially practical. All the so called enigmas of history that have led to the errors of mystical theories could have been explained in a rational way if their explanation had been sought in the concrete facts of the material conditions of social life.

9. Feuerbach failed with his contemplative materialism (because he did not understand sense experience as a practical activity) to see man as a 'social actor' in the economic community. He could only, as a spectator, see men as single individuals in a 'civil society.'

10. The standpoint of the old materialism is civil society; the standpoint of the new materialism is human society——i.e. socialized humanity.

11. The philosophers have only interpreted the world, each in his own way; the point, however, is to change the world.

Hegel had described history as dynamic and progressive. He had discovered the logic of necessity in the emergence of its successive stages. Further the historical process revealed a parallel development both of human reason and of the rationality of the world. Man's progress toward freedom was a correlation of his developing reason which enabled him to accept the rationality of the world. The real was the rational, and hence freedom was the acceptance of *what is by necessity*. Marx' dialectical materialism had also the notion of a necessary or inevitable development from one stage to the next.

But men should themselves take an active part in the process. They feel the wrongs and the pressures of the present and should organize to rebel against them. Further, the conditions of life in the new age could be foreseen, and hence it was the duty of man to press toward that 'kingdom of righteousness' — the classless society. There is a religious zeal in Marx' notion of the duty of man toward the coming age. That age to come had for him, and for his followers up almost to the mid-point of our century, the form of the Kingdom of God. All must be sacrificed to prepare for its coming. Men must take sides in the conflicts of the present age of class struggle. Only such as witness to the future will be worthy of it. The biblical notion of *Kairos*, the crisis of the present, gave a sense of urgency, commitment and of destiny to Marx' doctrine of history.

Two other influences upon Karl Marx have a bearing on the revolutionary and religious thrust of Marx's historiography. One of these was his own serious academic study of the new economy of Nineteenth Century Europe. For several generations before his time political theorists had recognized the dynamic role of capitalism in many areas of European culture and society. The industrial revolution in England by the Nineteenth Century had changed the life of the cities, and the exploitation of natural resources (coal) had changed the face of the land. Capitalism was seen to have a vitality greater than any previous economy, but its explosive drives toward ever increasing rates of production had their harsh aspects in the forcing of social change. Labour, as well as natural resources, was a raw material to the new 'captains of industry'. In 1776 Adam Smith published the first modern classic in economics, *The Wealth of Nations*. It contained the first analysis of the role of labour in modern industry. A keen awareness of the changing structure of society—of new classes, of the growth of populations, of the problems of the industrial city, of rents and interest, of trade, banking and international relations prompted new studies of law, ethics and education, particularly in England. The utilitarian movement which sought 'the greatest good for the greatest number' reflected an awakened social consciousness. Jeremy Bentham, its founder, James Stuart Mill (who befriended Auguste Comte), Malthus (the Anglican clergyman who warned against population growth) and the socialist factory owner, Robert Owen, form a part of the background of Marx's social concern. A more direct and immediate influence was Ricardo's *Principles of Political Economy and Taxation* (1817) which defined exchange value in terms of the quantity of labour necessary to the production of any given article.

A second and similar influence was the French Socialist Movement. English liberalism sought the betterment of the working class within the existing economy.   French socialism was more radical.   Saint-Simon introduced Marx to the theory of class conflict as the catalytic agent of social change.   After failing to win a university post at Bonn (1842), Marx had briefly been one of the editors of a liberal journal which brought him into contact with continental socialists.   He was at that time still the academic economist interested in legal and political theory. But when the journal was banned by the Prussian Government in 1843 he went to Paris to learn something of the growth of French socialism at first hand, and to study the effects and continuing force of the French Revolution.

Marx now became convinced that the dialectic in history of necessity involved revolution, and that the cradle of revolution must be the mass of workers employed in industrial production.   In 1848, with Engels, Marx published his *Communist Manifesto* which gave definite content to his final thesis on Feuerbach: 'The philosophers have interpreted the world in various ways; the point however is to change it.'

FROM *THE COMMUNIST MANIFESTO: The Inevitable Victory of the Proletariat.*

Modern bourgeois society with its relations of production, of exchange and of property is a society that has conjured up gigantic means of production and of exchange. It is like the magician who is no longer able to control the powers of the under world whom he has called up by his spells. For many years past the history of industry and commerce is but the history of the revolt of modern productive forces against modern conditions of production, against the property relations that are the conditions for the existence of the bourgeoisie and of its rule. It is enough to mention the commercial crises that by their periodical return put the existence of the entire bourgeois society on trial, each time more threateningly. In these crises a great part not only of the existing products, but also of the previously created productive forces, are periodically destroyed. In these crises there breaks out an epidemic of over-production which would have seemed absurd in all earlier periods. Society suddenly finds itself put back into a state of momentary barbarism. It appears as if a famine or a universal war of devastation had cut off the supply of every means of subsistence. Industry and commerce seem to be destroyed. And why? Because there is too much civilization, too much means of subsistence, too much industry, too much commerce. The productive forces at the disposal of society no longer tend to further the development of the conditions of bourgeois property. On the contrary, they have become too powerful for these conditions and they are fettered. As soon as they break out of these chains, they bring disorder into the whole of bourgeois society and endanger the existence of bourgeois property. The conditions of bourgeois society are too narrow to comprise the wealth created by them. And how does the bourgeoisie get over these crises? On the one hand, by enforced destruction of a mass of productive forces; on the other, by the conquest of new markets, and by the more thorough exploitation of the old ones. That is to say, by paving the way for more extensive and more destructive crises, and by diminishing the means whereby crises, are prevented.

The weapons with which the bourgeoisie felled feudalism to the ground are now turned against the bourgeoisie itself.

But not only has the bourgeoisie made the weapons that bring death to itself; it has also called into existence the men who are to use those weapons——the modern working class——the proletarians.

In proportion as the bourgeoisie, i.e., the capitalist class, is developed, in the same proportion is the proletariat, the modern working class, developed. This is a class of labourers, who live only so long as they find work, and who find work only so long as their labour increases capital. These labourers must sell themselves in small amounts. They are a commodity, like every other article of commerce, and they are consequently exposed to all the uncertainties of competition, to all the fluctuations of the market.

But with the development of industry the proletariat not only increases in number; it becomes concentrated in greater masses, its strength grows, and it feels that strength more. The various interests and conditions of life within the ranks of the proletariat are more and more equalized. This happens in proportion as machinery destroys all distinctions of labour, and nearly everywhere reduces wages to the same low level. The growing competition among the bourgeois, and the resulting commercial crises, make the wages of the workers ever more fluctuating. The unceasing and ever more rapidly developing improvement of machinery makes their life more and more insecure. The conflicts between individual workmen and individual bourgeois take on more and more the character of conflicts between two classes. Thereupon the workers begin to form combinations (trade unions) against the bourgeois. They join together in order to keep up the rate of wages. They found permanent associations in order to prepare beforehand for these occasional revolts. Here and there the contest breaks out into riots.

The rio and victories of the workers, if any, are short-lived at first.

But they serve to unite on a broader and broader basis the workers into
a class, and consequently into a party. This is due in part to the improved
means of communication created by modern industry itself. Meanwhile,
internal divisions of interest develop among the ruling classes and the
bourgeoisie is often forced to give concessions to the workers and even
appeal to them for help in its political struggle. This is how reformed
measures may come about, and how the proletariat is supplied further
with its own elements of political and general education. These are the
weapons it uses to fight the bourgeoisie. Not only that but entire sections
of the ruling classes are pushed into the proletariat because of the advance
of industry, or they are at least threatened in their conditions of existence.
These also supply the proletariat with fresh elements of enlightenment and
progress.

Finally, in times when the class struggle nears the decisive hour, the
process of dissolution going on within the ruling class, in fact within the
whole range of the old society, assumes such a violent, glaring character,
that a small section of the ruling class cuts itself off, and joins the
revolutionary class, the class that holds the future in its hands. Therefore,
just as at an earlier period, a section of the nobility went over to the
bourgeoisie, so now a portion of the bourgeoisie goes over to the
proletariat. This portion of the bourgeoisie is composed of those who
have raised themselves to the level of comprehending theoretically the
historical movement as a whole.

Of all the classes that stand face to face with the bourgeoisie today,
the proletariat alone is a really revolutionary class. The other classes
decay and finally disappear in the face of modern industry. The proletariat
is the special and essential product.

The lower middle class is not revolutionary but conservative because its
members fight the bourgeoisie only in order to save themselves and their
interests that belong to the past. They become revolutionary only when
they identify themselves with the proletariat and thus defend, not their
past or present, but future interests. Others may also be swept into the
struggle, identifying themselves with either side of the impending battle.
Meanwhile, the living conditions of the worker worsen. Modern industrial
labour, modern subjection to capital, the same in England as in France,
in America as in Germany, has stripped him of every trace of national
character. Law, morality, religion, are to him so many bourgeois
prejudices, behind which lie just as many bourgeois interests.

All the preceding classes that got the upper hand tried to strengthen
their already acquired status by subjecting society at large to their conditions
of appropriation. The proletarians cannot become masters of the productive
forces of society, except by destroying their own previous mode of
appropriation, and thereby also every other previous mode of appropriation.

They have nothing of their own to secure and to fortify. Their mission is to destroy all previous securities for, and insurances of, individual property.

All previous historical movements were movements of minorities, or in the interest of minorities. The proletarian movement is the self-conscious, independent movement of the immense majority, in the interest of the immense majority. The proletariat, the lowest layer of our present society, cannot stir, cannot raise itself up, without all the upper layer of official society being sprung into the air.

Though not in substance, yet in form, the struggle of the proletariat with the bourgeoisie is at first a national struggle. The proletariat of each country must, of course, first of all settle matters with its own bourgeoisie.

Previously, every form of society has been based, as we have already seen, on the the antagonism of oppressing and oppressed classes. But in order to oppress a class, certain conditions must be assured to it under which it can, at least, continue its slavish existence. The serf, in the period of serfdom, raised himself to membership in the commune, just as the petty bourgeois, under the yoke of feudal absolutism, managed to develop into a bourgeois. The modern labourer, on the contrary, instead of rising with the progress of industry, sinks deeper and deeper below the conditions of existence of his own class. He becomes very poor, and poverty develops more rapidly than population and wealth. And here it becomes evident, that the bourgeoisie is unfit any longer to be the ruling class in society, and to impose its conditions of existence upon society as an overriding law. It is unfit to rule because it cannot assure an existence to its slave within his slavery, because it cannot help letting him sink into such a state that it has to feed him, instead of being fed by him. Society can no longer live under this bourgeoisie, in other words, its existence is no longer compatible with society.

The essential condition for the existence and for the sway of the bourgeois class, is the formation and increase of capital;t he condition for capital is wage labour. Wage labour rests exclusively on competition between the labourers. The advance of industry, whose involuntary promoter is the bourgeoisie, replaces the isolation of the labourers which is due to competition with their revolutionary combination, which is due to association. The development of modern industry, therefore, cuts from under its feet the very foundation on which the bourgeoisie produces and appropriates products. What the bourgeoisie therefore produces, above all, are its own gravediggers. Its fall and the victory of the proletariat are equally inevitable. In place of the old bourgeois society, with its classes and class antagonisms, we shall have an association, in which the free development of each is the condition for the free development of all.

In the *Manifesto* Marx and Engels identified the classes that had emerged in capitalist society—the bourgeois and the proletariat. The action of history in the present age is the struggle between them. All the mystery and the idealistic facade of the Hegelian dialectic have been stripped away to reveal the concrete realities of that struggle in real life. Behind the classes is the structure of capitalism. Bourgeois and proletariat are themselves products of the capitalist system of production. And they are only parts of one social system—the society which was organized by the demands of a new method of production. At first there was a temporary harmony of the parts. But conflict was inevitable. The working of the system itself leads inevitably to class struggle. That struggle must also inevitably become more intense and ruthless until the ultimate victory of the proletariat.

The historical process is thus both the development and the conflict of economic classes. There is one basic force within this process— production. The push of progress, the growth of science, through the invention of new tools and more efficient methods changes the mode of production. Tools and methods are productive forces. Whoever controls these has power. But he is opposed by the social structure based upon the older mode of production. The vested property interests of the former generation also have power. Total conflict between the two powers leads inevitably to revolution. In the capitalist society, labour potentially controls the powers of production, but the bourgeois has the political and social power of vested interest. The bourgeois are the property owners. They acquired their wealth by their revolution against the feudal lords. Now the proletariat has the power of production but it will win control of wealth only by revolution against the bourgeois. The dynamic of history is the power of production. It creates social organization. It is also the basis of conflict between those who held the power in the past and now control wealth and those who now hold the power of production but must win its material benefits by revolution.

FROM THE CRITIQUE OF POLITICAL ECONOMY: Forces of the Historical Process

In the social production which men carry on they enter into definite relations that are indispensable and independent of their will. These relations of production correspond to a definite stage of development of their material powers of production. The totality of these relations of production constitutes the economic structure of society. This structure is the real foundation upon which legal and political superstructures arise and to which definite forms of social consciousness correspond. The mode of production of material life conditions the general character of the social, political and spiritual processes of life. It is not the consciousness of men that determines their being, but, on the contrary, their social being determines their consciousness. At a certain stage of their development, the material forces of production in society come in conflict with the existing relations of production (the property relations) within which they had been at work before. From the forms of development of the forces of production these relations turn into their hindrances. Then a period of social revolution occurs. When the economic foundation changes, the entire immense superstructure is more or less rapidly transformed. In considering such transformations the distinction should always be made between the material transformation of the economic conditions of production which can be determined with the precision of natural science, and the legal, political, religious, aesthetic or philosophical——in short ideological, forms in which men become conscious of this conflict and fight it out. Just as our opinion of an individual is not based on what he thinks of himself, so can we not judge of such a period of transformation by its own consciousness. On the contrary, this consciousness must rather be explained from the contradictions of material life, from the existing conflict between the social forces of production and the relations of production. No social order ever disappears before all the productive forces for which there is room in it have been developed; and new, higher relations of production never appear before the material conditions of their existence have matured in the womb of the old society. Therefore, mankind always sets itself only such problems as it can solve; since, on closer examination, it will always be found that the problem itself arises only when the material conditions necessary for its solution already exist or are at least in the process of formation. In broad outline we can designate the Asiatic, the ancient, the feudal, and the modern bourgeois modes of production as progressive epochs in the economic formation of society. The bourgeois relations of production are the last antagonistic form of the social process of production; not in the sense of individual antagonisms, but of conflict arising from conditions surrounding the life of individuals in society. At the same time the productive forces developing in bourgeois society create the material conditions for the solution of that antagonism. With this social formation, therefore, the prehistory of human society comes to an end.

Although this 'critique' was written in 1859, three years after *The German Ideology* it provides the background for the famous passage in which Marx discusses the materialist basis of history and ideology. Marx belongs within the classical tradition of modern historiography. We cannot understand him as a historian apart from Vico's *New Science* and Hegel's *Philosophy of History* as well as the positivist and socialist movements of his own time. Yet, as these few excerpts from his discussion of historical theory have shown, he stood Hegel on his head. Up side down Hegelianism is an altogether different kind of history than either that of Vico or of Hegel. It is not only a revision of the three stages. Hegel had already given to Vico's scheme a dialectical, and hence a more internally dynamic, form. Marx's scheme of Primitive Communism, the Age of Class Struggle and the Classless society merely points to what is more significant in Marxist historiography. The phenomena of history are economic and social organizations not the state (civil society) as in Hegel. But behind the phenomena is the more crucial issue of materialistic naturalism. Vico and Hegel had sought to free history from nature. They made a clear distinction between physical sciences and the new science of history. Marx goes back to the naturalism they rejected. His history too is a quantitative science— the measurement of production, of wealth and of force. There is no significant uniqueness in national cultures. The voices of the people are actually saying only the same thing whether they speak in Greek or Chinese, in Bantu, German, French or English. In the *Manifesto* Marx wrote: 'The working men have no country.'

FROM *THE GERMAN IDEOLOGY*

The premises from which we begin are not arbitrary ones, not dogmas, but real premises from which abstraction can be made only in imagination. They are the real individuals, their activity and their material conditions of life. These conditions include those which they find already in existence and those produced by their activity. These premises can thus be established in a purely empirical way.

The first premise of all human history is, of course, the existence of living human individuals. The first fact to be established, therefore, is the physical constitution of these individuals and their consequent relation to the rest of Nature. Of course we cannot here investigate the actual physical nature of man or the natural conditions in which man finds himself——geological, climatic and so on. All historiography must begin from these natural bases and their modification in the course of history by men's activity.

Men can be distinguished from animals by consciousness, by religion, or by anything one likes. They themselves begin to distinguish themselves from animals as soon as they begin to produce their means of subsistence. This step is determined by their physical constitution. In producing their means of subsistence men indirectly produce their actual material life.

The way in which men produce their means of subsistence depends in the first place on the nature of the existing means which they have to reproduce. This mode of production should not be regarded simply as the reproduction of the physical existence of individuals. It is already a definite form of activity of these individuals, a definite way of expressing their life, a definite mode of life. As individuals express their life, so they are. Therefore, what they are, coincides with their production, with what they produce and with how they produce it. What individuals are, therefore, depends on the material conditions of their production....

The production of ideas, conceptions and consciousness is at first directly interwoven with the material activity and the material intercourse of men, the language of real life. Representation and thought, the mental intercourse of men, at this stage still seem to come directly from their material behaviour. The same applies to mental production as it is expressed in the political, legal, moral, religious and metaphysical language of a people. Men are the producers of their conceptions, ideas, etc. They are real, active men, as they are conditioned by a determinate development of their productive forces, and of the system of social relationships which corresponds to these, up to its most extensive forms. Consciousness can never be anything else than conscious existence, and the existence of men is their actual life process. If in all ideology men and their circumstances appear upside down as in a camera obscura, this phenomenon arises from their historical life process just as the inversion of objects on the retina does from their physical life-process.

In direct contrast to German philosophy, which descends from heaven to earth, here we ascend from earth to heaven. That is to say, we do not set out from what men say, imagine, or conceive, nor from what has been said, thought, imagined, or conceived of men, in order to arrive at man in the flesh. We begin with real, active men, and from their real life process show the development of the ideological reflexes and echoes of this life-process. The images of the human brain also are necessary expressions of men's material life-process, which can be empirically established and which is bound to material preconditions. Morality, religion, metaphysics, and other ideologies, and their corresponding forms of consciousness, no longer retain therefore their appearance of independent existence. They have no history, no development. It is men, who, in developing their material production and their material intercourse, change their real existence, their thinking and the products of their thinking. Life is not determined by consciousness, but consciousness by life. Those who adopt the first method of approach (i.e., the German philosophers) begin with consciousness, regarded as the living individual. Those who adopt the second approach, which corresponds with real life, begin with the real living individuals themselves, and consider consciousness only as their consciousness.

This second approach begins with men in their actual process of development under definite conditions. As soon as this active life-process is presented, history ceases to be a collection of dead facts, as it is even with the empiricists who still deal in abstractions. Nor is history the imaginary activity of imaginary creatures, as with the idealists.

Speculation ceases at real life, where positive science begins. This science is a presentation of the practical activity which is also the actual progress of development of men. Abstract notions of consciousness are replaced by real knowledge. Hence philosophy as an independent discipline is no longer justified.

(Thus) history does not end by being resolved into 'self-consciousness,' as 'spirit of the spirit,' rather at each stage of history there is found a material result, a sum of productive forces, a historically created relation of individuals to Nature and to one another. This is handed down from generation to generation. It is a mass of productive forces, capital and circumstances, which is indeed modified by the new generation but which also determines the conditions of its life and gives it a definite development, a particular character. Hence circumstances make men just as much as men make circumstances....

The whole previous conception of history has either completely neglected this real basis of history or else has considered it a secondary matter without any connection with the course of history. Consequently, history is always written in accordance with an external standard. The real production of life is not treated historically, while what is historical appears as separated from ordinary life. Thus the relation of man to Nature is excluded from history and in this way the opposition between Nature and history is established....History is nothing but the succession of the separate generations, each of which exploits the materials, the forms of capital, the productive forces handed down to it by all preceding ones. Thus a generation, on the one hand, continues the rational activity in completely changed circumstances and on the other, modifies the old circumstances with a completely changed activity.

The ideas of the ruling class are, in every age, the ruling ideas: i.e., the class which is the dominant material force in society is at the same time its dominant intellectual force. The class which has the means of material production at its disposal has control at the same time over the realm of thought and ideas. Consequently, the ideas of those who lack the means of creating an ideology are, in general, subject to thought control. The dominant ideas are nothing more than the ideal expression of the dominant economic pattern.... and thus of the relationships which make one class the ruler. The ideas of the ruling class are the ruling ideas of the age, and are proclaimed as 'eternal laws,' for the purpose of maintaining the existing mode of material relationships.

The thinkers of the dominant class, its active ideologists, earn their living by developing and perfecting the self delusion of the class. The attitude (of others) to these ideas and illusions is more passive and receptive, because they are in reality the active members of this class and have less time to make up illusions and ideas about themselves....

The existence of revolutionary ideas in a particular age presupposes the existence of a revolutionary class. The revolutionary class appears from the beginning not as a class but as the representative of the whole society, confronting the single ruling class. This is so because at the beginning its interest is really more closely connected with the common interest of the other non-ruling classes. It has not yet developed into the particular interest of a particular class. The victory of the revolutionary class benefits many individuals of the other classes, but only in so far as it puts these individuals in a position to raise themselves into the ruling class. Every new class....achieves its domination only on a broader basis than that of the previous ruling class. (This explains why increasingly abstract or universal ideas come to hold sway in the development of history.) On the other hand, the opposition of the non-ruling class to the new ruling class later develops all the more sharply and profoundly. These two characteristics entail that the struggle to be waged against this new class has as its object a more decisive and radical negation of the previous conditions of society than could have been accomplished by all previous classes which desired to rule.... This whole appearance that the rule of a certain class is only the rule of certain ideas, comes to a natural end, of course, as soon as society ceases at last to be organized in the form of class-rule, that is to say as soon as it is no longer necessary to represent a particular interest as general or 'the general interest' as ruling.

Mao Tse-tung

Marxism became the faith of a young Chinese from Hunan in 1920. Mao Tse-tung later became the chairman of the Communist party of China and then in 1949 the leader of the Six Hundred Million citizens of the People's Republic. Mao applied Marxist theory to the history of his own nation. Neither Marx nor Lenin had ever given particular attention to Asian society. Mao's principles of interpretation are however easily traceable through Stalin back to Marx.

FROM *THE CHINESE REVOLUTION AND THE CHINESE COMMUNIST PARTY, DECEMBER 1939.*

Developing the same lines as many other nations of the world, the Chinese nation (chiefly the Hans) first went through some tens of thousands of years of life in classless primitive communes. Up to now approximately, 4,000 years have passed since the collapse of the primitive communes and the transition to class society, first slave society and then feudalism. In the history of Chinese civilization, agriculture and handicraft have always been known as highly developed; many great thinkers, scientists, inventors, statesmen, military experts, men of letters, and artists have flourished, and there is a rich store of classical works. The compass was invented in China very long ago. The art of paper-making was discovered as early as 1,800 years ago. Block-printing was invented 1,300 years ago. In addition, movable types were invented 800 years ago. Gun-powder was used in China earlier than in Europe. China, with a recorded history of almost 4,000 years, is therefore one of the oldest civilized countries in the world.

The Chinese nation is not only famous throughout the world for its stamina and industriousness, but also as a freedom-loving people with a rich revolutionary tradition. The history of the Hans, for instance, shows that the Chinese people would never submit to rule by the dark forces and that in every case they succeeded in overthrowing or changing such a rule by revolutionary means. In thousands of years of the history of the Hans, there have been hundreds of peasant insurrections, great or small, against the regime of darkness imposed by the landlords and nobility. And it was the peasant uprisings that brought about most dynastic changes. All the nationalities of China have always rebelled against the foreign yoke and striven to shake it off by means of resistance. They accept a union on the basis of equality, not the oppression of one nationality by another. In thousands of years of history of the Chinese nation many national heroes and revolutionary leaders have emerged. So the Chinese nation is also a nation with a glorious revolutionary tradition and a splendid historical heritage....

Although China is a great nation with a vast territory, an immense population, a long history, a rich revolutionary tradition, and a splendid historical heritage, yet she remained sluggish in her economic, political, and cultural development after her transition from the slave system into the feudal system. This feudal system, begining from the Chou and Ch'in dynasties, lasted about 3,000 years....

It was under this feudal system of economic exploitation and political oppression that the Chinese peasants throughout the ages led a slave-like life in dire poverty and suffering. Under the yoke of feudalism they had no freedom of person. The landlords had the right to beat and insult them and even to put them to death at will, while the peasants had no political rights whatever. The extreme poverty and backwardness of the peasants resulting from such ruthless exploitation and oppression by the landlord class is the basic reason why China's economy and social life has remained stagnant for thousands of years....

The ruthless economic exploitation and political oppression of the peasantry by the landlord class forced the peasants to rise repeatedly in revolt against its rule....However, since neither new productive forces, nor new relations of production, nor a new class force, nor an advanced political party existed in those days, and consequently peasant uprisings and wars lacked correct leadership as is given by the proletariat and the Communist party today, the peasant revolutions invariably failed, and the peasants were utilized during or after each revolution by the landlords and the nobility as a tool for bringing about a dynastic change. Thus, although some social progress was made after each great peasant revolutionary struggle, the feudal economic relations and feudal political system remained basically unchanged.

Only in the last hundred years did fresh changes take place....It was not until the middle of the nineteenth century that great internal changes took place in China as a result of the penetration of foreign capitalism.

As China's feudal society developed its commodity economy and so carried within itself the embryo of capitalism, China would of herself have developed slowly into a capitalist society even if there had been no influence of foreign capitalism. The penetration of foreign capitalism accelerated this development.

Yet this fresh change represented by the emergence and development of capitalism constitutes only one aspect of the change that has taken place since imperialistic penetration into China. There is another aspect which co-exists with it as well as hampers it, namely, the collusion of foreign imperialism with China's feudal forces to arrest the development of Chinese capitalism....

The contradiction between imperialism and the Chinese nation, and the contradiction between feudalism and the great masses of the people, are principal contradictions in modern Chinese society....The struggles arising from these contradictions and their intensification inevitably result in the daily-developing revolutionary movements. The great revolutions of modern and contemporary China have emerged and developed on the basis of these fundamental contradictions....The national revolutionary struggle of the Chinese people has a history of exactly one hundred years dating from the Opium War of 1840, and of thirty years dating from the revolution of 1911. As this revolution has not yet run its full course and there has not yet been any signal achievement with regard to the revolutionary tasks, it is still necessary for all the Chinese people, and above all the Chinese Communist Party, to assume the responsibility for a resolute fight....

FROM *ON NEW DEMOCRACY, JANUARY, 1940*

The first stage of the Chinese revolution (itself subdivided into many minor stages) belongs so far as its social character is concerned, to a new type of bourgeois-democratic revolution, and is not yet a proletarian-socialist revolution; but it has long become part of the proletarian-socialist world revolution and is now even an important part of such a world revolution and its great ally. The first step in, or the first stage of, this revolution is certainly not, and cannot be, the establishment of a capitalist society under the dictatorship of the Chinese bourgeoisie; on the contrary, the first stage is to end with the establishment of a new-democratic society under the joint dictatorship of all Chinese revolutionary classes headed by the Chinese proletariat. Then, the revolution will develop into the second stage so that a socialist society can be established in China.

FROM *LET A HUNDRED FLOWERS BLOOM, FEBRUARY, 1957*

Never has our country been as united as it is today. The victories of the bourgeois-democratic revolution and the socialist revolution, coupled with our achievements in socialist construction, have rapidly changed the face of old China. Now we see before us an even brighter future. The days of national disunity and turmoil which the people detested have gone forever. Led by the working class and the Communist Party, and united as one, our 600 million people are engaged in the great work of building socialism....

A Critique of Marxist Historiography

There have been many thoughtful criticisms of the views of Marx and his followers. Those made by Bertrand Russell, the contemporary British philosopher and social reformer, are fairly representative. He interprets Marx's 'materialism' as a kind of 'pragmatic activism.' This activist element is most evident today in Chinese communism. In his critique, Russell carefully distinguishes Marx's metaphysical notions from his historical studies in order to do justice to the latter.

Bertrand Russell, Freedom and Organization, 1814-1914. (Excerpts and abstracts from Chap. XVIII)

First, let us be clear what 'dialectical materialism' is. Metaphysically it is materialistic, but in method it adopts a Hegelian dialectic. Marx took over from Hegel an evolutionary outlook, according to which the stages of evolution can be characterized in clear logical terms. That is, the historical process follows a plan which a man could foretell, if he is intelligent enough. Marx claimed to have done just that. The materialism enters into the picture in the doctrine that the prime cause of all social phenomena is the method of production and exchange prevailing at any given period.

Thus, Engels wrote in 1877: 'It was seen that all past history, with the exception of its primitive stages, was the history of class struggles: that these warring classes of society are always the products of the modes of production and of exchange—in a word, of the economic conditions of their time; that the economic structure of society always furnishes the real basis, starting from which we can alone work out the ultimate explanation of the whole superstructure of juridical and political institutions as well as of the religious, philosophical, and other ideas of a given historical period.'

The discovery of this principle, according to Marx and Engels, showed that the coming of Socialism was inevitable.

'From that time forward,' Engels wrote, 'Socialism was no longer an accidental discovery of this or this ingenious brain, but the necessary outcome of the struggle between two historically developed classes—the proletariat and the bourgeoisie. Its task was no longer to manufacture a system of society as perfect as possible, but to examine the historico-economic succession of events from which these classes and their antagonism had of necessity sprung, and to discover in the economic conditions thus created the means of ending the conflict. But the Socialism of earlier days was as incompatible with this materialistic conception as the conception of the French materialists was with dialectics and modern natural science. The Socialism of earlier days certainly criticized the existing capitalistic mode of production and its consequences. But it could not explain them, and, therefore, could not get the mastery of them. It could only simply reject them as bad.

The materialist conception of history starts from the proposition that the production of the means to support human life, and, next to production, the exchange of things produced, is the basis of all social structure; that in every society that has appeared in history, the manner in which wealth is distributed and society divided into classes or orders, is dependent upon what is produced, how it is produced, and how the products are exchanged. From this point of view the final causes of all social changes and political revolutions are to be sought, not in men's brains, not in man's better insight into eternal truth and justice, but in changes in the modes of production and exchange. They are to be sought, not in the *philosophy*, but in the *economics* of each particular epoch. The growing perception that existing social institutions are unreasonable and unjust, that reason has become unreason, and right wrong, is only proof that in the modes of production and exchange changes have silently taken place, with which the social order, adapted to earlier economic conditions, is no longer in keeping. From this it also follows that the means of getting rid of the incongruities that have been brought to light, must also be present, in a more or less developed condition, within the changed modes of production themselves. These means are not to be invented by deduction from fundamental principles, but are to be discovered in the stubborn facts of the existing system of production.

The conflicts which lead to political revolutions are not primarily mental conflicts as people have believed. 'This conflict between productive forces and modes of production,' Engels continued, 'is not a conflict engendered in the mind of man, like that between original sin and divine justice. It exists, in fact, objectively outside us, independently of the will and actions even of the men that have brought it on. Modern Socialism is nothing but the reflex, in thought, of this conflict in fact; its ideal reflection in the minds, first, of the class directly suffering under it, the working-class.'

My criticisms of dialectical materialism may be summarized in four propositions: 1. that materialism, in some sense, may be true, though it cannot be known to be so; 2. that the elements of dialectic which Marx took over from Hegel made him regard history as a more rational process than it has in fact been, convincing him that all changes must be in some sense progressive, and giving him a feeling of certainty in regard to the future, for which there is no scientific warrant; 3. that the whole of his theory of economic development may perfectly well be true if his metaphysic is false, and false if his metaphysic is true, and that but for the influence of Hegel it would never have occurred to him that a matter so purely empirical could depend upon abstract metaphysics; 4. with regard to the economic interpretation of history, it seems to me very largely true, and a most important contribution to sociology; I cannot, however, regard it as *wholly* true, or feel any confidence that all great historical changes can be viewed as developments. Let us take these points one by one.

1. *Materialism.* Marx's materialism is not the same as that of the 18th century. In his 'materialist conception of history' he never emphasizes philosophical materialism, but only the *economic causation* of social phenomena. An examination of his *Eleven Theses on Feuerbach* will show that the philosophy there is very similar to what is now

known under the name of pragmatism or instrumentalism, associated with Dr. John Dewey.

Old fashioned materialism regarded matter to be the cause of sensation and sensation to be something false, an unreal abstraction. Watch a cat receiving impressions from a mouse: its nostrils dilate, its ears twitch, its eyes are directed to the right point, its muscles become taut. All this is action, mainly of a sort to improve the informative quality of impressions, partly such as to lead to fresh action in relation to the object. And as a cat with a mouse, so is a textile manufacturer with a bale of cotton. The bale of cotton is an opportunity for action, it is something to be transformed, by the machinery which is itself a product of human activity.

Now Marx maintains that we are always active: we are never merely passive in relation to matter, even in our purest 'sensation.' We are never merely apprehending our environment, but always at the same time altering it. 'Philosophers have only *interpreted* the world in various ways,' Marx declared, 'but the real task is to *alter* it.' The older conception of knowledge is incorrect. We do not know an object by passively receiving an impression of it but rather by being able to act upon it successfully. That is why the test of truth is practical. Truth is not static but becomes something which is continually changing and developing. That is why Marx called his materialism 'dialectical', because it contains within itself, like Hegel's dialectic, an essential principle of progressive change.

It seems to me that Engels did not quite understand this point, but this pragmatism of Marx might have been occasional. For he certainly held that some propositions were 'true' in a more than pragmatic sense. Engels came closer to the older form of materialism. So did Lenin. For my part, I do not think materialism in the older form can be proved. I think Lenin is right in saying that it is not disproved by modern physics. Since his time and largely as a reaction against his success, respectable physicists have moved further and further from materialism, and it is naturally supposed, by themselves and by the general public, that it is physics which has caused this movement. I agree with Lenin that no substantially new argument has emerged since the time of Berkeley, with one exception. This one exception, oddly enough, is the argument set forth by Marx in his theses on Feuerbach, and completely ignored by Lenin. If there is no such thing as sensation, if matter, as something we passively apprehend, is a delusion, and if 'truth' is a practical rather than a theoretical conception, then old-fashioned materialism, such as Lenin's, becomes untenable. And Berkeley's view becomes equally untenable, since it removes the object in relation to which we are active. Marx's instrumentalist theory, though he calls it materialistic is really not so. As against materialism, its arguments have indubitably much force. Whether it is ultimately valid is a difficult question, on which I have deliberately refrained from expressing an opinion, since I could not do so without writing a complete philosophical treatise.

2. *Dialectic in History.* The Hegelian dialectic was a full-blooded affair. If you started with any partial concept and meditated on it, it would presently turn into its opposite; it and its opposite would combine into a synthesis, which would, in turn, become the starting point of a similar movement, and so on until you reached the Absolute Idea, on which you could reflect as long you liked without discovering any new contradictions. The historical development of the world in time was merely an objectification of this process of thought. This view appeared possible to Hegel, because for him mind was the ultimate reality; for Marx, on the contrary, matter is the ultimate reality. Nevertheless he continues to think that the world develops according to a logical formula. To Hegel, the development of history is as logical as a game of chess. Marx and Engels keep the rules of chess, while supposing that the chessmen move themselves in accordance with the laws of physics, without the intervention of a player.

In speaking of the 'stubborn facts' of economic system, Engels said, as quoted above, 'the means of getting rid of the incongruities that have been brought to light, *must* also be present, in a more or less developed condition, within the changed modes of production themselves.' This 'must' betrays a relic of the Hegelian belief that logic rules the world. Why should the outcome of a conflict in politics always be the establishment of some developed system? This has not, in fact, been the case in innumerable instances. The barbarian invasion of Rome did not give rise to more developed economic forms, nor did the expulsion of the Moors from Spain, or the destruction of the Albigenses in the South of France. Before the time of Homer the Mycenaen civilization had been destroyed, and it was many centuries before a developed civilization again emerged in Greece. The examples of decay and retrogression are at least as numerous and as important in history as the examples of development. The opposite view, which appears in the works of Marx and Engels, is nothing but nineteenth-century optimism.

This matter has a practical as well as a theoretical importance. Communists always assume that conflicts between Communism and Capitalism 'must' in the end lead to the establishment of Communism. They do not realize that it might also lead to barbarism. We all know that modern war is a somewhat serious matter, and that in the next world war it is likely that large populations will be virtually exterminated by poison gases and bacteria. Can it be seriously supposed that after a war in which the great centres of population and most important industrial plants had been wiped out, the remaining population would be in a mood to establish scientific Communism?—I am afraid the dogmatic optimism of the Communist doctrine must be regarded as a relic of Victorianism.

There is a further point about the Marxist dialectic. Hegel believed that history leads up to the Prussian State, the perfect embodiment of the Absolute Idea working through history. Marx had no love for this State. To him, history leads up instead to the Communist Soceity. We heard nothing about the further revolutions after the establishment of Communism. Marx said in the last paragraph of *La Misere de la Philosophie:* 'It is only in an order of things in which there will no longer be classes or class-antagonism that *social evolutions* will cease to be *political revolutions.*' What these social evolutions are to be, or how they are to be brought without the motive power of class conflict, Marx does not say. Indeeed, it is hard to see how, on his theory, any further evolution would be possible. Except from the point of view of present-day politics, Marx's dialectic is no more revolutionary than that of Hegel. Moreover, since all human development has, according to Marx, been governed by conflicts of classes, and since under Communism there is to be only one class, it follows that there can be no further development, and that mankind must go on for ever and ever in a state of Byzantine immobility. This does not seem plausible, and it suggests that there must be other possible causes of political events besides those of which Marx has taken account.

3. *Irrelevance of Metaphysics.* The belief that metaphysics has any bearing upon practical affairs is, to my mind, a proof of logical incapacity. Different physicists have different metaphysical views and that makes no difference whatever to their physics. That is because, in physics, there is some genuine knowledge, and whatever metaphysical beliefs a physicist may hold must adapt themselves to this knowledge. In so far as there is any genuine knowledge in the social sciences, the same thing is true. Whenever metaphysics is really useful in reaching

a conclusion, that is because the conclusion cannot be reached by scientific means, i.e. because there is no good reason to suppose it true. What can be known, can be known without metaphysics, and whatever needs metaphysics for its proof cannot be proved.

Marx advances in his books much detailed historical argument, in the main perfectly sound, but none of this in any way depends upon materialism. For example, free competition tends to end in monopoly. This is an empirical fact whose evidence has nothing to do with materialism or any metaphysic. Marx's metaphysic makes things more cut and dried and precise than they are in real life. It also gives him a certainty about the future which goes beyond the warrant of a scientific attitude. But in so far as his doctrines of historical development can be shown to be true, his metaphysic is true, his metaphysic is irrelevant. The question whether Communism is going to become universal, is quite independent of metaphysics. It may be that a metaphysic is helpful in the fight: early Mohammedan conquests were much facilitated by the belief that the faithful who died in battle went straight to Paradise, and similarly the efforts of Communists may be stimulated by the belief that there is a God called Dialectical Materialism Who is fighting on their side, and will, in His own good time, give them the victory. On the other hand, there are many people to whom it is repugnant to have to profess belief in propositions for which they see no evidence, and the loss of such people must be reckoned as a disadvantage resulting from the Communist metaphysic.

4. *Economic Causation in History.* Marx is right in judging that economic causes are basic to the great movements in history. This is true not only in politics, but also in religion, art, and morals. There are, however, important qualifications Marx failed to make. a. Marx did not allow nearly enough for the time lag. Christianity, for example, rose in the Roman Empire and was a product of the social system of that time. But it survived through many centuries and had enough life to resist Marx's own ideas. In the Western world its political influence is still enormous. Yet Marx treated it as moribund, in accordance with his logic of historical development. I think it may be conceded that *new* doctrines that have any success must bear some relation to the economic circumstances of their age, but old doctrines can persist for many centuries without any such relation of any vital kind.

b. Marx did not allow for the fact that a small force may be decisive in affecting historical development where great forces are in the

balance.   History is not simply made by great movements or causes
in a grand style.   Without Lenin, for example, it is difficult to believe
that the Russian Revolution would have achieved what it did.   And the
career of Lenin before that could have terminated or been irrevocably
altered by a number of accidents, such as being refused by a German
minister to leave Germany for Russia.   Another example is that if the
Prussians had happened to put a better general at the battle of
Valmy, they might have wiped out the French Revolution.   Again, it
seems plausible that if Henry VIII had not fallen in love with Anne
Boleyn, the United States of America would not now exist.   The place
would have been part of Spanish America to this day.

c.   In Marx's rigid view, economic conflicts are always between
classes, whereas most of them have been between races or nations.   In
early 19th century, English industrialism was internationalistic in outlook
because it expected to retain its monopoly of industry.   This determined
Marx's own outlook about industrialism.   Bismark, however, soon gave
a different turn to events and industrialism ever since has grown more
and more nationalistic, contrary to Marx's prophecy.   Even the conflict
between capitalism and Communism takes increasingly the form of a
conflict between nations.   Of course, national conflicts are very largely
economic, but the lines dividing nations are determined by causes not
mainly economic.   What in history have important economic components
or effects are certainly not for that necessarily economic in nature.
Medical cause, like the Black Death, or malaria and yellow fever in
tropics, are clear examples.

d.   Marx traced social development primarily to changes in the
methods of production and he did not explain why the latter come
about.   In fact, changes in the methods of production largely came
about because of scientific discoveries and inventions.   These are made,
according to Marx, when the economic situation calls for them.   Is that
the case at all? Why was there practically no experimental science from
the time of Archimedes to the time of Leonardo? During the six
hundred years after Archimedes economic conditions were favourable to
scientific work.   But it was the growth of science after the Renaissance
that led to modern industry, rather than the other way around.   This
intellectual causation of economic processes was not adequately recognized
by Marx.

FROM *WISDOM OF THE WEST* 1950

Marx was likely correct in holding that the general scientific interests of a society reflect in some measure the social interests of its dominating group. For example, one might see a relation between the revival of astronomy during the Renaissance and the expansion of trade and the power of the rising middle class. But it is not easy to explain either one by the other alone. Marx, however, failed to see that solutions of particular scientific problems have no necessary connection with social pressures of any kind whatsoever, although there are times when a problem is studied in response to some urgent need of the moment. Marx's failure was in not recognizing the scientific movement as an independent force in society. The pursuit of science in history has its own momentum which gives it a measure of autonomy, despite its important links with other fields of development. This is true of all forms of disinterested inquiry. Dialectic materialism over-simplifies what happens in history between economic and intellectual activities.

Marx was not entirely correct in his forecasts on what would happen in the field of economics. He assumed, for example, that the rich would become richer and the poor poorer, until the dialectic tension of this 'contradiction' became so strong that revolution was inevitable. This is not what did happen in the industrial nations of the world. They have, since Marx's time, devised methods of regulation which modified the forms of economic struggle in ways that Marx never dreamed of. Economic freedom became limited and social welfare schemes were introduced. When the revolution did come, it was not, as Marx predicted, in the industrialized Western part of Europe, but in agrarian Russia.

Marxist philosophy is the last great system of the 19th century. Its great appeal and widespread influence is due in the main to the religious character of its utopian prophecies, as well as to the revolutionary element in its programme for action. The economic interpretation of history is one of a number of general theories of history that are ultimately derivative from Hegel. The same is true about Croce's theory of history as the story of liberty.

History can be viewed in many ways, and many general formulae can be invented which cover enough of the ground to seem adequate if the facts are carefully selected. I suggest, without undue solemnity, the following alternative theory of the causation of the Industrial Revolution: industrialism is due to modern sicence, modern science is due to Galileo, Galileo is due to Copernicus, Copernicus is due to the Renaissance, the Renaissance is due to the fall of Constantinople, the fall of Constantinople is due to the migration of the Turks, the migration of the Turks is due to the desiccation of Central Asia. Therefore the fundamental study in searching for historical causes is phydrography.

8

TYPES OF THEORY:

HUMANIST

The Rise of Academic History

PARALLEL IN TIME with the Positivist and Marxist historians but
divergent in spirit and method were the academic historians of the
Nineteenth Century. We have called them humanists because this is
a broad description that includes men of various backgrounds and with
different interests who shared a common heritage in the scholarship
and spirit of Erasmus. We could describe them also as the fathers of
academic history. Von Ranke, Acton, and Ku Chieh-kang (顧頡剛)
were university men of sound reputation, respected by their colleagues
in other fields for their broad understanding, their active interest
in the common tasks of the university community, and above all,
for their industry and patient open-minded scholarship.

They belonged to a tradition which can be traced through Vico to
the greatest of the humanists. In their immediate background were
the classics masters who had patiently laid the foundation of modern
philology. Many of these had also pioneered in Biblical studies, where
so much of the best work in textual criticism and historical interpretation
was developed in the early Nineteenth Century. After the tumult and
the shouting of the Positivists and the left wing Hegelians (Feuerbach,
Strauss and the Bauers) these still small voices of the sober and patient
scholars had an even stronger appeal.

In part the later humanist historiography was a reaction against
the excesses of Positivism and Marxism. Sound scholarship has always
demanded for its basic tasks a mood of sober and dispassionate enquiry.
Few of the humanists lived in an ivory tower. Indeed for the most
part they pursued their tasks in fulfillment of a high calling to serve
humanity. But they were convinced that more than other men, the

historian should be hesitant to give judgment before he had looked at all *ascertainable* facts with an equal eye. They looked upon the French sociologist historians and upon the Marxists as advocates who were defending a client or prosecuting a defendant. The proper functions of the academic historian, they were convinced, should be that of a judge. He should be objective, open-minded—yet critical. He should be trained to sift the sound arguments of the advocate from his special pleading. Above all, he must insist that all the facts should come out. Only after all the evidence had been heard could the judge begin his work of assessment and evaluation. Some humanist historians felt quite strongly that the final decision should not be taken by the judge but by the jury—that it should be indeed the verdict of history. The historian should advise on the kind of evidence presented in the relevant documents and on its bearing in the case. He should warn the jury against false witness and unsupported claims. He should present a carefully organized summing up — but no more. If the historian goes further he has qualified his own function. To take final decisions is to prejudice his own judgment for further studies.

Though not all academic historians accepted so narrow a function, they all rejected in principle the *using* of history in the service of other disciplines (sociology or political science) or of party causes by socialist or royalist.

Humanist historiography was also critical of the Positivist and Marxist confusion of historical with physical science. In this view Comte and Marx had taken a backward step toward the subjection of history to physical science. They were not impressed by the pseudo science of natural law theories applied to history—or to cycles of civilization analogous to the fixed orbits of the planets. Nor did they see any good reason to believe that the key to history was to be found in biology. While the French sociologists and other Positivists (e.g. J.B. Bury, Durkheim, Levy Bruhl, Hurbert and Mauss) saw profound implications for history in Darwin's *Origin of Species* (1859), the academic historians were more cautious. Because they regarded scientific hypothesis as sacred law 'profitable for reproof, correction and instruction in righteousness,' the positivists seized upon natural selection as a new law of history. Collingwood observed that 'the victory of evolution in scientific circles meant that the positivist reduction of history to nature was qualified by a partial reduction of nature to history.' Academic historians, however, remained unconvinced that organic evolution was proof positive of inevitable progress. The whole notion of natural law whether it was employed to prove a cyclical pattern or to argue the case for a glorious third age had little appeal to the more careful historians. Humanist historiography rejected any philosophy which claimed that physical science was the only kind of knowledge and the only objective approach. They had seen very little objectivity in the positivist or materialist historians. The doctrinaire schemes of Comte and Marx raised grave doubts concerning the validity of any whole-of-history-in-three-stages theory. The academic historians preferred to concentrate on the development of a particular idea or a specific movement as studies important in their own right rather than as parts or pieces to be fitted or forced into the framework of predetermined stages. Such studies, they felt, allowed the facts to speak to the historian rather than providing a platform upon which the historian could talk back to the past. Marxist history looked and sounded like a ventriloquist's dummy. Whenever it spoke you could see Marx's lips moving.

Academic history emerged not only as a reaction against the excess of doctrinaire social science. For the most part it was a positive response to new sources of knowledge. The latter part of the Nineteenth Century witnessed the rise of several quite technical disciplines that provided the historian as the judge with expert witnesses. Some of these were quite specialized such as numismatics (the study of coins) and sphragistics (the study of seals). Archeological finds, whether they were turned up by enthusiastic amateurs like Heinrich Schliemann who spent a shrewd trader's fortune in pursuit of a youthful dream of the romance of Troy or by specialists like Sir Arthur Evans, Seiss, and Noeldeke, furnished more solid facts than even ancient documents. Fragments of Minoan jars made more trustworthy witnesses than fragments from Greek historians quoted by Church Fathers concerning the early civilization of Crete. Philology had developed by the third quarter of the century into a comparative study that gave the historian a knowledge of the growth of language. It revealed significant relations within the Indo-Germanic family. The historian trained in philology could find in language clues to the source and development of the spirit of an ancient culture (Humbolt and Usener). Before the Nineteenth Century, European scholars had some knowledge of Chinese from the Jesuit and Franciscan missionaries. Sanskrit, Pali, and Pehlevi came later to open up a whole new world of Hindu and Persian studies. Hieroglyphics were deciphered by Champollion who had travelled with Napoleon to Egypt. The knowledge that poured into Europe of the languages and vast literatures of China, India, Burma, and elsewhere in the Far East gave a new dimension to the concept of world history. The earliest studies made by Bopp and Bournoff and Max Müeller expanded the world of the historians as dramatically as Galileo's *Star Messenger* had enlarged the world of the astronomers. The new frontiers of history humbled the academic historian. He dared not even consider a world history until, as he was convinced, generations of scholarship had explored and mapped out these vast areas of human culture hitherto almost unknown. Academic historiography concentrated therefore upon the more nearly manageable studies of ancient Greece and Rome and of Biblical literature.

The mass of materials ferreted out and discovered by chance remains perhaps the most impressive achievement of historians throughout history. That immense store of knowledge of itself demanded attention. Its proper use in turn demanded a more rigorous and systematic method. The second great achievement of Academic history was its conscientious dealing with documents. For facts on the level of certainty, corroborative witnesses from a variety of sources became the accepted rule. An ancient description of a palace or temple was received as substantial evidence only after the stones themselves had been excavated, weighed and measured. Academic integrity demanded the most careful and critical examination of documents. In the case of an important document the first task was the tracing of its sources. Niebuhr spent years searching for Livy's sources by a line by line and even word by word study of the Latin text. The sources themselves had to be reconstructed as in the Graff-Wellhausen reconstruction of *J*, *E*, and *P*. Sources were significant not only for the dating of documents but also for the bearing of the evidence they afforded. It was not only a question of what was written but why it was written—i.e. the point of view of the author-editor in terms of the life situation in which he wrote. The historian can exegete the Pentateuch only after he has discovered why its various sources were collected into a single document, what were the views of the compilers and editors, and what were the pressures of the Jewish community both negative and positive upon its scholars.

Classical and Semitic studies had enjoyed a gradual and fruitful development since the Renaissance. Two years after Erasmus published his magnificent Greek text of the New Testament, Jacob ben Cheyyim's *Biblia Hebraica* (1517) appeared. Jean Astruc and Herder in the latter part of the Eighteenth Century opened up new frontiers in Old Testament scholarship. Semler's famous *Introduction to the Old*

Testament anticipated by a hundred years the watch word of the academic historians — presuppositionless history. The controversial study made by K. H. Graff (d. 1886) and J. Wellhausen (d. 1875) of the sources of the Pentateuch was a model for documental study well into our own century. The master philologist was the ideal historian who could identify the vocabulary and style of a narrow period, a school and even an individual.

Some of the academic historians were quite adventuresome men engaged throughout their lives in an active search for documents as for buried treasure. Constantin Tischendorf (1815-1874) who was professor of theology at Leipzig searched through the libraries and monastic centers of Europe and the Near East from 1840-1860, with the zeal of a CID inspector, for manuscript evidence for the text of the Bible. His discovery in 1859 of the *Codex Sinaiticus* (Fourth Century A.D.) in the monastery of St. Catherine on Mt. Sinai was one of the great finds of the century. Von Ranke, all through his active years, considered that research involved searching for his materials. Lord Acton by his importunate demands rediscovered neglected documents in the Vatican Library and did much to make that important archive more readily open to historians.

We can trace to the academic historians also the contemporary interest in 'form history', i.e. the analysis of the nature and function of the forms of expression—myth, saga, poetry, drama, liturgy, polemic, apology, etc. The evidence of a document can best be understood and evaluated when we know how it was used by its first readers—how they were expected to respond—1. whether as to fact, to instruction, to law, to persuasion, to criticism, to consolation; and 2. whether as an appeal to reason, to conscience, or to aesthetic feeling.

Humanist history was content to observe the varieties of human experience. It desired first of all to know what had happened, to ascertain how actually it happened and why it happened, not in terms of some general scheme of reason or of fate but within the relevant context of its own temporal and physical environment. Academic history was often reluctant to judge as to whether the event was a 'good thing' or a 'bad thing' in terms of present views of the cause of the angels. It was even less eager to judge the event from the standpoint of a philosophical or sociological absolute. Its strength was also its weakness—pure academic history is pure historicism—a naive faith, based on no evidence that objective fact is important. History for history's sake makes no more sense than art for art's sake.

Neither has a sake. Only people have a sake—we—now—here who must accept life's demand that we fulfill in the duties and decisions of our little hour the meaning of our existence. Further, it is our nature, whether we be chemists or historians to conduct our lives according to some value judgment—a judgment at least concerning the character of importance. Only by self deception can we deny the self in us that directs our interests and frames our judgments. In the last resort presuppositionless history can mean only two things—that which has no intrinsic interest or value for us or self-deception either unconscious or highly developed. It is probably true that the only valid basis, both psychologically and rationally, of a concern objectively to ascertain facts of any sort derives from a faith in a significance that is beyond the facts themselves. That living, restless faith is no less evident in von Ranke, Acton, and Ku Chieh-kang then it was in Comte and Marx. *Academic* in its concrete meaning connotes an affirmation of a way of life, of the kind of privilege and responsibility that the university man has come to cherish.

Leopold Von Ranke

Leopold von Ranke (1785-1886) is the classical type of the humanist and academic historian. He had the proper training of a philologist. While Hegel,the professor of philosophy, lectured on the vast sweep of reason's way in history, von Ranke, almost unnoticed, trained a small group of students at the same university in the critical use of historical evidence. That little seminar was significant: it was a beginning in the study of history as an independent discipline. While Hegel pressed backward to find the foundations of philosophy in history, von Ranke moved with deliberate confidence across the frontier from philology into history. He taught several generations of students to judge the evidence before they judged the event. He was, in the best sense of the word, the historian's historian. By his teaching and by his own scholarship historiography did become a new science quite distinct from physical science and from philosophy. Von Ranke's notions about history grew out of his work in history. He was not a theologian as was Hegel or, as in his own way, was Karl Marx. Yet in contrast to both he was in spirit a religious man. Religious experience rather than a doctrinal perspective (either theological or philosophical) led him to a reverence for events in and of themselves. He believed that the events of life could bear in themselves the meaning of life. He believed in the significance beyond itself of unique event and so he defended the possibility of novelty. Against his contemporaries (both Hegel and Marx) he regarded the historical process as essentially open. History was not either all freedom or all necessity but an interplay of free choice and necessity and hence it offered the possibility of the emergence of significant novelty. The humanism of von Ranke is seen both in the joy he found in conscientious study and in his humility.

His two great works were *The History of Popes* and *History of the Germanic Peoples from 1495-1514.* Such manageable yet significant studies he believed must be the substance of academic historiography. His insistence upon the analysis of documents and the weighing of evidence as demonstrated by his own industry over the course of a long professional career sometimes impressed his students and his colleagues more than the fairly dull studies which he published. His own career appeared to point to enquiry for its own sake. Most of his studies were, however, on important themes. In an age of spectacular theories his own conclusions seemed pale and pedantic. His most persuasive writing—the passages that are alive today—express his concern for method and his belief in the worthwhileness of history as an academic discipline. He never lost faith in that venture. At the age of eighty-six he began the task which he firmly believed was the goal of all research and the ultimate responsibility of the historian—the writing of a world history.

FROM *HISTORY OF THE GERMANIC PEOPLES 1495-1514*

To history has been assigned the office of judging the past, of instructing the present for the benefit of future ages. To such high offices this work does not aspire: It wants only to show what actually happened *as it actually happened.*

But whence the sources for such a new investigation? The basis of the present work, the sources of its material, are memoirs, diaries, letters, diplomatic reports, and original narratives of eyewitnesses; other writings were used only if they were immediately derived from the above mentioned or seemed to equal them because of some original information. These sources will be identified on every page; a second volume, to be published concurrently, will present the method of investigation and the critical conclusions.

Aim and subject mould the form of a book. The writing of history cannot be expected to possess the same free development of its subject which, in theory at least, is expected in a work of literature; I am not sure it was correct to ascribe this quality to the works of the great Greek and Roman masters.

The strict presentation of the facts, contingent and unattractive though they may be, is undoubtedly the supreme law. After this, it seems to me, comes the exposition of the unity and progress of events. Therefore, instead of starting as might have been expected with a general description of the political institutions of Europe——this would certainly have distracted, if not disrupted, our attention——I have preferred to discuss in detail each nation, each power, and each individual only when they assumed a pre-eminently active or dominant role. I have not been troubled by the fact that here and there they had to be mentioned beforehand, when their existence could not be ignored. In this way, we are better able to grasp the general line of their development, the direction they took, and the ideas by which they were motivated.

Finally what will be said of my treatment of particulars, which is such an essential part of the writing of history? Will it not often seem harsh, disconnected, colourless, and tiring? There are, of course, noble models both ancient and——be it remembered——modern. I have not dared to evaluate them: theirs was a different world. A sublime ideal does exist: the event in its human intelligibility, its unity, and its diversity, this should be within one's reach. I know to what extent I have fallen short of my aim. One tries, one strives, but in the end it is not attained. Let none be disheartened by this! The most important thing is always that we deal with, as Jakobi says, humanity as it is, explicable or inexplicable: the life of the individual, of generations, and of the nations, and at times the hand of God above them.

FROM *WORLD HISTORY IX* 2

It has often been noted that a certain kind of antagonism exists between an immature philosophy and history. From *a priori* ideas one used to infer what must be. Without realizing that these ideas are exposed to many doubts, men set out to find them reflected in the history of the world. From the infinitude of facts, one then selected those which seemed to confirm these ideas. And this has been called the philosophy of history. One of these ideas which the philosophy of history presses time and again, as an irrefutable claim, is that the human race moves along a course of uninterrupted progress, in a steady development towards perfection.... If this were to some extent true, than general history would have to investigate the progress which mankind makes in the indicated direction from century to century; in that case the scope of history would consist in tracing the development of these concepts in their appearance, their manifestation in the world. But this is by no means true. First of all, the philosophers themselves entertain entirely diverse opinions about the nature and selection of these, supposedly dominant, ideas. Furthermore they very wisely restrict their views to only a few nations in the history of the world, while regarding the life of all the others as naught, as a mere supplement. Otherwise, it could not be overlooked for a moment that from the beginning to the present day the nations of the world have developed in the most diverse manner.

There are really only two ways of acquiring knowledge about human affairs: through the perception of the particular, or through abstraction; the latter is the method of philosophy, the former of history. There is no other way, and even revelation comprehends both abstract doctrines and history. One must distinguish clearly between these two sources of knowledge. Nevertheless those historians are also mistaken who consider history simply an immense aggregate of particular facts, which it behooves one to commit to memory. Whence follows the practice of heaping particulars upon particulars, held together only by some general moral principle. I believe rather that the discipline of history——at its highest——is itself called upon, and is able, to lift itself in its own fashion from the investigation and observation of particulars to a universal view of events, to a knowledge of the objectively existing relatedness.

Two qualities, I think, are required for the making of the true historian: first he must feel a participation and pleasure in the particular for itself. If he has a real affection for this human race in all its manifold variety to which we ourselves belong, an affection for this creature that is always the same yet forever different, so good and so evil, so noble and so bestial, so cultured and so brutal, striving for eternity yet enslaved by the moment, so happy and so wretched, content with so little and yet craving so much! If he feels this affection for the living being as such, then he will——without considering the progress of events——enjoy seeing how man has perennially contrived to live. He will readily follow the virtues which man sought, the faults which could be detected in him, his fortune and misfortune, the development of his nature under such diverse conditions, his intuition and his morals, and——so as to encompass everything——also the kings under whom men have lived, the sequence of events, and the development of major enterprises——and all this he will try to follow without any purpose beyond the pleasure in individual life itself. Just as one takes delight in flowers without thinking to what genus of Linnaeus or to what order and family of Oken they belong; in short, without thinking how the whole manifests itself in the particular.

Still, this does not suffice; the historian must keep his eye on the universal aspect of things. He will have no preconceived ideas as does the philosopher; rather, while he reflects on the particular, the development of the world in general will become apparent to him. This development, however, is not related to universal concepts which might have prevailed

at one time or another, but to completely different factors. There is no
nation on earth that has not had some contact with other nations. It is
through this external relationship, which in turn depends on a nation's
peculiar character, that the nation enters on the stage of world history, and
universal history must therefore focus on it. Some nations on earth were
armed with this power before others and these came to exert a pre-eminent
influence on the rest. The transformations which, for better or for worse,
the world has experienced, will be seen to have originated chiefly in these
nations. Hence we ought not to focus our attention on those general
concepts which to some men appear as the dominant forces, but on those
nations themselves that have played a pre-eminent, active role in history.
We should concern ourselves with the influence which these nations have
had on one another, with the struggles they have waged with one another,
with their development in peace and war.

Lord Acton

Few great scholars at Berlin were also great teachers. Von Ranke
was one of those few. Long after new facts had left his work
outdated, his influence continued upon those whom he taught largely
by the example of his humane and conscientious scholarship. Lord
Acton, the devout Roman Catholic professor of history at Cambridge,
was among the greatest of his disciples. We may, indeed, regard his
life work as a fulfilling of tasks which von Ranke's approach had
created. For the most part his students had become specialists either
in the development of a single thesis or in the interplay of events
within a brief span of years. Toward the end of the Nineteenth
Century the number of monographic studies in specialized areas of
historical research had become so great that the major task was the
collecting into manageable volumes of the best articles on related themes.
Academic historians were proud of the fact that their writing belonged
to the class of critical notes that could appear only in learned journals.
In 1859 Heinrich von Sybel, one of von Ranke's earlier students
founded the German journal, *Historische Zeitschrift*. The leading
French journal under the editorship of Gabriel Monod was first published
in 1876. Mandel Creighton, later Bishop of London, produced the
first issue of the *English Historical Review* in 1886, and J. F. Jameson
brought out the *American Historical Review* in 1895.

Acton could speak for a whole generation of senior academic
historians when he referred to von Ranke as 'my master' in his inaugural
address at Cambridge. 'We meet him (von Ranke) at every step.'
Acton had not prior to his appointment to the Cambridge chair spoken

so favourably of von Ranke. He had in fact as a younger scholar sided with that generation of the master's students who preferred an even more objective and specialized approach. Now, however, he saw the need to organize the growing field of historical knowledge. Acton reaffirmed Ranke's ideal of universal history and he urged his colleagues and students to accept the moral responsibility of their high calling.

He was closer to Ranke than to his own generation when he spoke with some feeling in the Inaugural Lecture against the prevailing attitude of the Academic historians: 'But the weight of opinion is against me when I exhort you never to debase the moral currency or to lower the standard of rectitude, but to try others by the final maximum that governs your own lives, and to suffer no man and no cause to escape the undying penalty which history has the power to inflict on wrong.' Acton had British thoroughness and he had the humaneness of the British mind. He did not however have a systematic mind, nor did he have the courage to go beyond the collecting and organizing of special studies. Acton himself wrote very little. But he was, like Ranke, a conscientious teacher, and he was a man who thought and worked and lived with a sense of history. He regarded religion and liberty as major concerns of man and hence also of history. Throughout his career he worked toward the goal of a history of man's search for freedom. The chief result of this effort was a huge file of hand written notes on small slips of paper which he left at his death.

Acton's one substantial monument is the *Cambridge Modern History* which he edited. The subject itself reflects von Ranke's shift of emphasis in historical study from classics to European civilization. Very little of Acton, except his conception of the project, is to be found in these volumes. The *Cambridge Modern History* is a collection of the published notes of others. It has been said that Acton was capable of writing every one of these essays himself. By his editorial labours he did fulfill his urge to survey a whole range of monographic studies in a large area. And yet his own personal notes will probably survive, or at least surpass in value, his editorial labours.

FROM *LETTER TO CONTRIBUTORS TO THE CAMBRIDGE MODERN HISTORY*

1. Our purpose is to obtain the best history of modern times that the published or unpublished sources of information admit.

The production of material has so far exceeded the use of it in literature that very much more is known to students than can be found in historians, and no compilation at second hand from the best works would meet the scientific demand for completeness and certainty.

In our own time, within the last few years, most of the official collections in Europe have been made public, and nearly all the evidence that will ever appear is accessible now.

As archives are meant to be explored, and are not meant to be printed, we approach the final stage in the conditions of historical learning.

The long conspiracy against the knowledge of truth has been practically abandoned, and competing scholars all over the civilized world are taking advantage of the change.

By dividing our matter among more than one hundred writers we hope to make the enlarged opportunities of research available for the main range of modern history.

Froude spoke of 100,000 papers consulted by him in manuscript, abroad and at home; and that is still the price to be paid for mastery, beyond the narrow area of effective occupation.

We will endeavour to procure transcripts of any specified documents which contributors require from places out of reach.

2. It is intended that the narrative shall be such as will serve all readers, that it shall be without notes, and without quotations in foreign languages.

In order to authenticate the text and to assist further research, it is proposed that a selected list of original and auxiliary authorities shall be supplied in each volume, for every chapter or group of chapters dealing with one subject.

Such a bibliography of modern history might be of the utmost utility to students, and would serve as a substitute for the excluded references.

We shall be glad if each contributor will send us, as early as he finds it convenient, a preliminary catalogue of the works on which he would reply; and we enclose a specimen, to explain our plan, and to show how we conceive that books and documents might be classified.

3. Our scheme requires that nothing shall reveal the country, the religion, or the party to which the writers belong.

It is essential not only on the ground that impartiality is the character of legitimate history, but because the work is carried on by men acting together for no other object than the increase of accurate knowledge.

The disclosure of personal views would lead to such confusion that all unity of design would disappear.

4. Some extracts from the editor's Report to the Syndics will show the principles on which the Cambridge History has been undertaken.

'The entire bulk of new matter which the last forty years have supplied amounts to many thousands of volumes. The honest student finds himself continually deserted, retarded, misled by the classics of historical literature, and has to hew his own way through multitudinous transactions, periodicals, and official publications, where it is difficult to sweep the horizon or to keep abreast. By the judicious division of labour we should be able to do it, and to bring home to every man the last document, and the ripest conclusions of international research.

'All this does not apply to our own time, and the last volumes will be concerned with secrets that cannot be learned from books, but from men.

'The recent Past contains the key to the present time. All forms of thought that influence it come before us in their turn, and we have to describe the ruling currents, to interpret the sovereign forces, that still govern and divide the world.

'By Universal History I understand that which is distinct from the combined history of all countries, which is not a rope of sand, but a continuous development, and is not a burden on the memory, but an illumination of the soul. It moves in a succession to which the nations are subsidiary. Their story will be told, not for their own sake, but in reference and subordination to a higher series, according to the time and the degree in which they contribute to the common fortunes of mankind.

'If we treat History as a progressive science, and lean especially on that side of it, the question will arise, how we justify our departure from ancient ways, and how we satisfy the world that there is reason and method in our innovations.

'To meet this difficulty we must provide a copious, accurate, and well-digested catalogue of authorities.'

'Our principle would be to supply help to students, not material to historians. But in critical places we must indicate minutely the sources we follow, and must refer not only to the important books, but to articles in

periodical works, and even to original documents, and to transcripts in
libraries. The result would amount to an ordinary volume, presenting a
conspectus of historical literature, and enumerating all the better books, the
newly acquired sources, and the last discoveries. It would exhibit in the
clearest light the vast difference between history, original and authentic, and
history, antiquated and lower than the high-water mark of present learning.

'We shall avoid the needless utterance of opinion, and the service of a
cause.

'Contributors will understand that we are established, not under the
Meridian of Greenwich, but in Long. 30° W.; that our Waterloo must be
one that satisfies French and English, Germans and Dutch alike; that
nobody can tell, without examining the list of authors, where the Bishop
of Oxford laid down the pen, and whether Fairbairn or Gasquet, Liebermann
or Harrison took it up.'

Ku Chieh-kang—A Pioneer in Critical Chinese Historiography

In our very general survey of the story of man as historian it seems
most fitting to include Ku Chieh-kang within the circle of academic
humanist historians. There is of course no exact parallel between him
and the European school of von Ranke. Yet in our broad outline there
is a comparable sense of the importance of history in the modern
world and of the need to approach the great documents of the past
with the devotion of careful and critical scholarship. In our typological
survey of ancient Chinese historiography we did not attempt more than
a characterizing sketch of traditional Chinese views of history. Nor
can we do greater justice to later developments. We are however
privileged to have the following contribution from Dr. Robert Kramers,
recently appointed to the Chair of Sinology at the University of Zurich.
Professor Kramers develops the broader theme of modern Chinese
historical thought around his study of Ku Chieh-kang.

Toward Modern Times by Robert Kramers

The preceding pages did not attempt to give a comprehensive survey
of Chinese historiography. They rather attempted to characterize the
traditional Chinese views of history. We shall try to do the same
especially for the modern period, and we shall limit ourselves even
more: we will look through the eyes of only one modern Chinese

historian.

In the past there was change and development in historical writing and in the conception of history; the different stages can be said to be parallel with the development of Chinese society as a whole. Yet the dominant ideas remained substantially the same. History was a lesson in morality. It reminded—and especially the men at the centre of the world: the Emperor and his ministers—of the principles of correct behaviour in harmony with a well-ordered universe. Nothing can better express this sense of moral historical judgment than the saying by Mencius: 'Confucius completed the *Spring and Autumn* (*Annals*), and rebellious minsters and villainous sons were struck with terror.' (Mencius 3B.9)

But, as this quotation also shows, it is not enough to characterize the traditional view of history as a lesson in morality and correct behaviour. The criteria for this morality had been given by China's greatest sage, Confucius. These criteria had been worked out anew by the great Sung philosophers, who in a new way reaffirmed Confucian orthodoxy. To them, Confucius was at the center of history. From him and his teachings, man could learn to see the working of the *Tao*, the orderly movement of the universe. For the writing of history, this insight was laid down by the great philosopher Chu Hsi (朱熹), who remodelled Ssu-ma Kuang's *Tzu-chih t'ung chien* into the *T'ung-chien-kang-mu* (通鑑綱目). In this work, the principles of historical writing were made to conform closely to the model of the *Ch'un ch'iu*, especially the method of 'praise and blame', believed to have been created by Confucius. This method was clearly outlined by Chu Hsi in his Preface to the *T'ung-chien-kang-mu*.

FROM CHU HSI: *GENERAL RULES FOR THE WRITING OF THE OUTLINE AND DIGEST OF THE GENERAL MIRROR (T'UNG-CHIEN-KANG-MU)*

The legitimate dynasties are Chou, Ch'in, Han, Chin, Sui, and T'ang. Feudal states are those which have been enfeoffed by legitimate dynasties. Usurpers are those who usurp the throne, interfere with the legitimate line of succession, and do not transmit their rule to their heirs. The periods in which there is no legitimate line appear between Chou and Ch'in, Ch'in and Han, Han and Chin, Chin and Sui, Sui and T'ang and the Five Dynasties period.

Rulers of legitimate dynasties: those of Chou are called 'kings,' those of Ch'in, Han, and after are called 'emperors.' Rulers of feudal states:

those of Chou are referred to by state, feudal rank, and name. Those
who unlawfully usurped the title of king are referred to as 'so-and-so, the
ruler of such-and-such a state'; from the Han on they are referred to as
'so-and-so, the king of such-and-such.' Those who usurped the title of
emperor are referred to as 'so-and-so, the lord of such-and-such.' Those
who revolted and usurped the throne of a legitimate dynasty are referred
to by name only.

Ascending the throne, legitimate dynasties: when the Chou kings passed
their rule on to their heirs, write: 'his son so-and-so was set up' and note
that this person then became king so.and-so. When the succession is by
natural heir, write: 'so-and-so succeeded to the throne.' When someone
establishes a state and sets himself up as ruler, write: 'so-and-so set
himself up as king of such-and-such a title.' When up, write: 'so-and-so
honoured so-and-so with such-and-such a title.' Someone usurps a state
and begins to style himself emperor, write: 'so-and-so (title, family and
personal name) styled himself emperor.' When the rule of a state is
transferred to a brother of the ruler, this is called 'transmission'; when to
someone else, it is called 'cession.'

Deaths: In cases of rulers of legitimate dynasties, write: 'deceased;'
and if the death occurred outside the palace, note the place. If the ruler
died before his first year of rule was out, write: 'departed.' If the person
was stripped of his honours, write: 'died.' In cases of grand empress
dowagers, empress dowagers, and empresses, write: 'Empress so-and-so of
such-and-such a family, deceased.' In case of suicide, write: 'suicide;'
where guilty of a crime, add the word 'crime.' Where the person was
innocent but put in prison and died, write: 'imprisoned and killed.' Deaths
of ex-empresses who had been demoted from their position need not be
recorded, but if in the course of the narrative they are mentioned, write:
'died.' In cases where a state perished and the empress lost her rank but
continued to maintain virtuous conduct and strive for the restoration of
the state, use her former title and write: 'deceased.' From Ch'in and Han
on when a king or peer dies, in all cases write: 'died,' but if the person
was particularly worthy, note his posthumous name. In cases of rulers
who usurped states and took the title of emperor, write: 'The lord of
such-and-such a state, so-and-so, died.' For all rulers and chieftains of
barbarian tribes, write: 'dead,' as well as for leaders of rebel bands.

When rulers of legitimate dynasties make progresses through the
provinces, write: 'the emperor went to such-and-such a place.' When
visiting offices or private houses, write: 'honoured with a visit,' for
schools use 'inspected' or 'observed.' If the ruler fled, this must be
truthfully recorded.

Diplomatic conferences should all be recorded. If there is a leader,
write: 'so-and-so met so-and-so at such-and-such a place.' If there is no

leader, write: 'so-and-so and so-and-so met at such-and-such a place.'

In the case of legitimate dynasties, when inferiors turn against superiors, it is called 'revolt.' If it is planned but not carried out, write: 'planned revolt.' If troops are turned against the palace, write: 'raised troops and attacked the palace.'

If there is a ruler in China at the time when barbarians invade, write: 'invaded and plundered' or 'plundered such-and-such a district.' If the affair is minor, write: 'pillaged such-and-such a place.' If there is no ruler in China at the time, simply say: 'entered within the borders' or 'entered the passes,' etc.

When a legitimate dynasty uses troops against its subjects who have usurped or revolted, it is called 'subjugating' or putting down,' against barbarian tribes who are not subjects, it is called 'attacking,' etc. When recording wars against enemy states, write: 'destroyed them,' against rebels and bandits, write: 'pacified them.'

It is impossible to record the district, native town, and genealogy of all men; only in the case of worthy men should these be briefly noted. In the case of deaths of ministers, it is only necessary to record those of all prime ministers. For worthy men note their office, honorary title, family and personal names, 'died,' and add their posthumous name, but for ordinary men omit honorary title, family name, and posthumous name.

All natural disasters and prodigies should be recorded. In cases of lucky omens some may be recorded to show that they are doubtful, others to show that they are frauds.

In the traditional Chinese society it was hard to rebel against the orthodox views of history. Yet the seeds of rebellion were there; and especially during the Ch'ing dynasty the orthodoxy of the Neo-Confucian school of learning was attacked by scholars. But there was no all-out attack. Rather did it seem that such an attack, which would overthrow the orthodoxy, was prepared by the leading trend in scholarship towards textual criticism. All ancient texts, including the sacred canonical writings of Confucianism, were subjected to painstaking scrutiny. It has been suggested that this scholarly development of textual criticism was mainly due to the fact that open criticism and judgment of the Manchu court was, to say the least, very unhealthy. Textual research was a safer way to undermine the orthodox views by means of establishing solid factual knowledge.

It was not until the Republican period that the all-out attack on tradition and Confucian orthodoxy reached its full fury. This cultural revolution is known under several names: May Fourth Movement, Literary Renaissance, New Culture Movement. We cannot give a description here of the tremendous intellectual ferment to which the invasion of Western ideas has contributed so much. Western ideas were not only prominent for their own sake; they also helped to formulate alternatives to the old orthodoxy. To the negative slogan of the time: 'Down with the Confucian shop', belonged the positive slogan of 'science and democracy'. The names of Hu Shih (胡適), Ch'en Tu-hsiu (陳獨秀), Ts'ai Yüan-p'ei (蔡元培) and of many others are so familiar that we do not need to elaborate on them.

As far as traditional way of life was concerned, and the highest values on which it rested, it was a time of 'debunking,' a time in which the hollowness of the old social pattern was exposed. Naturally there were others who went against this revolutionary trend, and who attempted to salvage the eternal values of the old culture. China had to adjust to the modern world, but China was also the product of its long and glorious history. Could all this past be cut off with one stroke, as the revolutionaries wished?

So it became a vital necessity to reinterpret Chinese history. But this was and is no easy task. It certainly was not easy in those early days of the Republic, which was a time of action, not of reflection. Hence the debate on Chinese history and its interpretation was, as all debates in those days, passionate and not always detached from ulterior motives.

Decidedly the best example of this search for truth in the realm of Chinese historical study is the monumental series entitled *Ku shih pien* (古史辨), 'A symposium on Ancient History', of which the first volume appeared in 1926. The editor of the first five volumes is the historian whom we wish to introduce here: Ku Chieh-kang (顧頡剛), who himself contributed several articles and letters to the series. A number of eminent scholars contributed also to the debate, and the resulting collection is still of the greatest importance for the study of Chinese views of history. Something of an open-minded enquiry broke through in them, something of a spirit which seems hard to find today. And this open-mindedness is particularly evident in Ku Chieh-kang, for whom the passionate search for truth is all-important. We can see it in the *motto* which he had chosen for the *Ku shih pien* series. It was taken from the *Testament of Art* by the French sculptor Rodin:

Be thoroughly and passionately truthful. Never hesitate to express what you feel, even if you find yourself to be in opposition to accepted ideas. Perhaps you will at first not be understood. But your isolation will not last long. Friends will join you soon: for what is profoundly true for one man is true for all.

It is fortunate for us that Ku Chieh-kang has written a Preface to the *Ku shih pien* which is far more meaningful than an ordinary preface. He has chosen to expand it into an autobiographical account of his growth as a historian, and we thus learn not only of his personal struggles and problems, but also of the mood of unrest and change to which his contemporaries too were subjected.

Born in 1893 in a scholar's family, Ku received a classical education at the hands of a tutor who, because he was a good friend of Ku's grandfather, was extra severe with the boy. Education in those days followed the classical pattern, and included much corporal punishment. Ku believes that this traditional method succeeded in making him a confirmed stammerer for life. But it also gave him much of the material on which he was to work later. And we sense the true scholar's disdain, when he tells us what he thinks about the new type of 'Western' education which he had to suffer later:

When I entered the University and was engaged in my own studies, time became more precious to me, but I cannot say that my teachers were interested in conserving that time to the best advantage. As I look over my diary covering the first years of the Republic, I find the pages filled with many complaints on this score. I was of the opinion that the only good reason for learning was to give men an opportunity to investigate the facts in accordance with the dictates of their natures. But all I got was vague and inconsequential chattering by teachers, who neither disclosed their innermost feelings nor described impartially things as they are. And so the weary months and years dragged on, with instructors interested only in drawing their salaries, and students in winning their diplomas——both mutually deceiving and taking unfair advantage of each other. Having merely their own aims in view, they were perfectly willing to let me, who was looking for a genuine education, waste my precious hours in the stupidities of the class-room. To be sure, I did obtain a few immature scientific concepts, but I might have obtained these by reading several books on science or performing a few experiments, instead of spending more than ten years of valuable time. On the whole, it is painful to contemplate how Chinese youth is slaughtered in those institutions, and even more regrettable to think that our youth willingly submits to such treatment.

This quotation may still serve as a reminder to teachers (and future teachers) today, even though modern types of education in China have progressed beyond the stages of infancy.

Ku Chieh-kang soon had a tremendous range of interests, stretching beyond classical literature to local folklore and opera. Even before Dr. Hu Shih came to be his teacher at the Peking National University, he had already directed his interest to history, and was already very critical of traditional viewpoints. Around 1915 Ku had planned to edit a kind of Encyclopedia of Learning; the plan was too ambitious to materialize, but he had preserved the Preface which he had prepared for it. At the time he was very much under the influence of his teacher Chang T'ai-yen (章太炎 1868-1936), a thinker of great originality, not as conservative as some believe. In this Preface, Ku says:

> Mr. Chang (possibly Chang T'ai-yen) says,
> 'The function of history is to reflect both the good and the bad, like a mirror which reproduces faithfully, without attempt to embellish or conceal, both the beautiful and the ugly.' I compile this work on the plan here suggested, bringing together both the true and the false, the controversial and the well - established. Lao-tzu says, 'The good man is the bad man's teacher; the bad man is the material upon which the good man works.' That is to say, the very impediments in the search for truth may be the materials that promote a knowledge of truth; this makes it all the more difficult to leap to conclusions about what is true and what is false. Traditional scholarship commonly emphasized the classics at the expense of the minor philosophers; it emphasized Confucian learning at the expense of the 'eight schools' hence the controversy between 'modern text' and 'ancient text' between the Han and Sung schools, each claiming that the other is mistaken. He who attempts to arbitrate between them is likely, in the end, to be partial to one or the other. Not conversant with the background of the issues involved, the contender has no foundation on which to base his argument and the arbitrator finds himself unable to reach a settlement. One might say, in clarification of these issues, that the classics represent merely the history of antiquity; that Confucianism was just one of the nine contending currents of thought; that the supremacy of either the 'ancient text' or the 'modern text' factions was based largely upon whether or not one or the other had official recognition; and that the distinction between the Han and Sung schools is primarily a question of viewpoint, each motivated by different purposes and emphasizing different aspects of truth. It is not necessary to admit only one's own scholarship to the exclusion of others——to bestow honour on one as if he were a divinity, or to blame the other as if he were a demon.

We see that Ku agrees with his master that much former scholarship was false and biased. Yet he sees the value of this scholarship as historical material itself. He again quotes Chang, who pronounces the verdict that 'though their writings (of biased scholars) are voluminous enough to fill heaven and earth, and they should be discarded if they do not make the search for truth their primary aim.' But Ku himself adds that these works should still be preserved: 'They should be discarded because they are false, but should be retained in order that one may find why they are false.' He continues:

Some time ago, a friend of mine, seeing on my desk some works on the ceremonials of state-worship, exclaimed, 'That is all nonsense! It has no relation to the everyday facts of life. Why scholars of former times should have regarded those books as marvellous treasures is quite inexplicable to me.' I replied that such a conclusion is not necessarily true; the work of former scholars was, that they seized upon doctrinaire theories from which to deduce their principles, holding that new truth is not to be discovered, and that the old is unalterable. They praised the sages and were influenced by them, but not in the right direction; they attributed their own ideas to the men of antiquity, but lacked the power of selection. Little wonder, then, that there arose in time a general distaste for their writings. If, perchance, there were some who did not hold such subservient views but placed themselves in the position of unbiased observers, then, although they were mistaken, they still might have left something worth looking at. All the more would this be true of those emblems of state-worship from which one can ascertain the kind of social patterns that dominated men's minds. In my previous treatment of learning, I said that the student must first observe and then assimilate. Observation means that I accept whatever object comes to my mind and recognize it to be such,——a process known as induction. Assimilation means that I have a definite principle in mind and select what corresponds with it——that is to say, deduction. If we take these principles to guide us in our investigations, not even the commonest tales that are told on the streets, however vulgar and degraded they may otherwise seem to be, can be cast aside as meaningless.

Scholarship of the old type was concerned almost exclusively with the classics, the histories, rhythmic prose, and essays. What the learned called systematization was classical, and not scientific systematization. Unacquainted with the scientific method, they looked down upon all comparative study as an indication of inferior scholarship. Each investigator held fast to the particular school in which he was brought up, and was unwilling to penetrate the unity that connects all things, ignoring the fact that learning is common to the whole world, and therefore cannot be restricted to any one country or to any particular school. Learning, that labels itself as belonging to one country or to a special school, is a factor in the history of learning but cannot itself be called learning. To look upon the history of learning as learning itself is to place the mind in bondage to ancient literature; and since such literature ceases to change, scholarship itself ceases to progress.

Those who adhere to a particular school of thought always assert that the aim of their teaching is to discover some all-pervading unity, holding that learning, without underlying principles, breeds disorder and confusion. Yet such underlying, connecting principles of life can never be found in the teachings of any particular school; they must be sought in the facts of life itself. If we continue to exalt special schools of thought so as to emphasize assimilation of knowledge at the expense of observation, the students of our time will remain in a quandary as to what sort of learning they ought to pursue; they will look upon the words of their teachers as law and gospel, with the result that they would rather violate the principles of truth than contradict the words of their teachers. That our scholarship to-day is beclouded, and our writings unintelligible, is due to the dominance of these special schools. Now that we have scientific methods which encourage scholars to draw their materials directly from ascertainable data, the barriers which schools interpose to scholarship can more readily be removed. I venture to remind all adherents of particular schools that the purpose of learning is to discriminate between fact and falsehood. He who knows that a theory is unfounded and still adheres to it for factional reasons, can only be regarded as a thoroughly irresponsible person. If what his school advocates is really true, he can disconnect himself from that school and yet hold to the principle as something irrevocable. Why should he want to be bound to a faction and refuse to contemplate the larger implications of his studies?

In order to show more clearly how Ku works with the materials of ancient history, we give below a number of quotations from his *Ku shih pien* Preface. The study of ancient history was so important because many of the principal values of the Chinese tradition were bound up with antiquity, and it is precisely in these materials that history and myth are inextricably interwoven. Thus, it is important first of all to evaluate the historical sources. In one place Ku tells us how he compiled two chronological tables of ancient written materials, one according to tradition, and one according to their probable age:

These two tables seem at first sight to be quite commonplace, but when they are compared, they reveal instantly the most striking contradictions and stratifications. I discovered from them that people of former times looked upon the materials of ancient history as all on the same plain, that is to say, horizontally. They made no attempt to differentiate episodes of different periods, which accounts in part for their rapid multiplication. Now, however, we view history vertically; beginning with a single thread, we see how it rapidly divided into many strands of various lengths, that hang down in confusion like the pendants of pearls from the official headdress of former emperors, which can be unravelled only by a clear differentiation of the various layers. Only by making this phenomenon clear to myself, was I able to obtain a measurably intelligible conception of ancient history.

A more concrete example is the way in which Ku tries to unravel the traditions about Emperors, such as Yao, Shun and Yu:

> Neither the *Odes* nor the *Classic of History* (with the exception of the first few chapters of the latter) make any mention of Yao or Shun, precisely as if the people of those times knew nothing of them. The *Analects* refer to them, but in no clear and factual manner. It is only in the *Canon of Yao* that their virtues and administrative exploits are splendidly portrayed. These facts seem, in my opinion, to show that Yu had already made his appearance in the Western Chou period (1122-770 B. C.), but that Yao and Shun first emerged in the later years of the Spring and Autumn era (722-481 B.C.). That is to say, the earlier these figures appear in the accepted chronology, the later they actually emerged in history. As a matter of fact, Yu was known before Yao and Shun; and Yao and Shun were known long before Fu-hsi and Shen-nung, but in the traditional chronology the order was entirely reversed. With these facts in mind, I venture to set up the following hypothesis: *that our traditional knowledge of Chinese antiquity was built up in successive strata, but in an order exactly the reverse of the actual occurrence.*

We may not entirely agree with Ku's hypothesis, but we can recognize that his approach to the historical materials is of great significance for the development of scholarly methods. As Ku himself states further on:

> One can obtain a much clearer conception of ancient Chinese history if one looks at it from the standpoint of the evolutionary manner, in which the data were actually put together in different stages. Looked at from that viewpoint only, one conceives that the emperors of antiquity were so superbly good, because the histories, in which they are pictured, were crystallized at a time when the concept of assimilation by virtue was uppermost in the minds of scholars. One needs only to strip away the various layers of traditions, in the order in which they were crystallized, to discover that actual conditions were quite different from what they portrayed.

In handling old and venerable classical materials in this way Ku did not fail to get criticized. But the criticisms did not always do him justice, as the following quotation, on the problem whether Emperor Yu was a historical figure, shows:

'An Analytical Study of Great Men' made the following statement:

'When great men reach the zenith of their greatness, it frequently happens that many deeds are attributed to them with which they had in reality no direct connection. When this happens they become mysterious figures, symbols around whom there gathers a whole chain of events. Examples of this are the exploits of the Great Yu in controlling the floods, and the stories that gathered about Shakyamuni, and Mr. Ku Chieh-kang doubts the actual existence of the Great Yu. I hold that men of this type have become symbols for attaching a chain of other circumstances, but we cannot on that account say that they never existed. In recent times Sun Yat-sen has become a symbol of the Chinese revolution, but I know with certainty that Sun Yat-sen lived.'

I have heard many criticism of this nature——all of which run to the effect that we have no right to overthrow the place of Yu in history, simply because he took on supernatural characteristics. Since I feel that such criticism seriously misapprehends my point of view, I take this opportunity to make my position clear. Whether there really was such a man as Yu, we have now no way of knowing. Taking into consideration the earliest, extant records, Yu is depicted as a personage rich in supernatural characteristics; and because he was reverenced in various localities, the stories that relate to him enjoyed wide circulation. The reason why we now know him to be an historical figure, is only because of many kinds of records which are the result of a processing of Yu's mythical stories through historical arrangement. We need only to place in one category what is said in the *Odes*, in the *Classic of History*, and on the inscribed bronzes, and in another category the philosophical and historical writings of the pre-Ch'in period (before 255 B.C.), and a comparison of the two will show that the stories, which are historical in nature, arose at a later time. For this reason, I say that Yu, being originally a divinity, was transformed into a man; and in maintaining this position, I merely follow the chronological order of the various traditions. I hold that when Messrs. Liu Ch'u-hsien and Fung Yu-lan declare that Yu was originally a man and later was deified, they really over-emphasize these later traditions; and what is more, interpret earlier traditions in the light of later ones. Even laying aside, for the time being, the question whether Yu was in reality a man or a divinity, he was certainly regarded by the people of remote antiquity as one who partook of the nature of divinity. For instance, the common people to-day make sacrifices both to the God of War (*Kuan-ti* 關帝) and to the Kitchen God (*Tsao-shen* 灶神), nevertheless, it is well known that the latter is a divinity pure and simple, while the former was once a man who was subsequently deified. Yet in the eyes of the people who perform these sacrifices this distinction is certainly not made. They merely believe that a divinity is almighty and omniscient, and that he possesses a personality (does not the Jade Emperor have [the common] family name *Chang*?) that makes it possible for him to come down to earth and be a man, if he so desires. Since the distinction between divinity and humanity did not exist, the two forms are really interchangeable. We know that Kuan Yu, (關羽), Han Tou (華佗), Pao Ch'eng (包拯), Chang San-feng (張三丰), and General

Pu (卜將軍) were originally human beings who became divine. On the other hand, we know, that the God of Literature (Wen Ch'ang 文昌) was originally a constellation in the region of the North Star, but that later he was said to be a Szechuan general of the Posterior Chin dynasty (936-948 A.D.) named Chang E-tzu (張惡子). Similarly, Hsiang Chun (湘君) and Hsiang Fu-jen (湘夫人) were originally divinities presiding over the River Hsiang (湘河), but afterwards were looked upon as daughters of the Emperor Yao.

From this we see that the change from a man to a divinity and vice versa was a common phenomenon; we have no right to emphasize one element at the expense of the other, all we can do is to ascertain the place that a personality held in the imagination of the people at a given time. It is possible, of course, that Yu was a historical figure, but if we reason from those literary materials of the Spring and Autumn period, which have come to our notice, we may definitely conclude that *prior* to that time, Yu was given the characteristics of a divinity. Since the most ancient records are now inaccessible to us, we have no way of ascertaining what he was in the last analysis, but judging from writings *after* the Spring and Autumn period, I can definitely state that he had the characteristics of a man.

We can see from this quotation something of the tremendous consequences of Ku's methods for Chinese historiography. In another passage he describes how to him this change towards new scholarship came as a liberation:

In the second place, it is plain that scholars of former generations were, on the whole, lacking in far-sightedness and in breadth of viewpoint; they believed that genuine scholarship confines itself solely to the investigation of orthodox classical works. We know now, however, that facts are the only true basis of learning; that scholarship does not consist in blind acceptance, but in genuine research. As a result, our eyes have been opened to a new world of hitherto uninvestigated and unorganized materials; questions which once were believed to have no significance have now taken on an entirely new meaning. Our position to-day is like that of a prisoner, who has long been confined within walls beyond which his eyes could not penetrate; while he was there he felt reasonably satisfied, but the walls have hardly opened and the shackles fallen from him before a thousand new sights meet his vision——an unending succession of strange-looking houses, exotic flowers and queer animals. In a world so new, he hardly knows how to organize his existence; the excitement and perplexity of his environment bring grief and joy in equal proportions.

But elsewhere Ku reveals that he did not easily come to adopt this critical attitude towards past scholarship. It took him some time to stop feeling an heretic:

> Whenever in my youth I perused works that caused me to make mental reservations, I was invariably haunted by the feeling that those works, having already been investigated by famous scholars, could not in the nature of the case reveal any glaring errors. I was reminded that textual cricitism had reached its zenith in the Ch'ing dynasty, that everything had already been clearly investigated, and all one needed to do was to contemplate with satisfaction what those scholars had done. Since our own task was to investigate the ultimate principle in things, it was quite unnecessary to travel over again the road, which had been traversed so successfully before us. When I first assayed to doubt ancient writings, I laboured under the illusion that only works of antiquity abound in errors, but now, after making a few minor studies (like those noted above), I find that modern historical writings, and biographies of more recent personalities, are filled with the same stupidities. My investigation of the labours of the Ch'ing scholars convinced me that theirs also was only pioneer work in the field of textual criticism. After this experience, I concluded that even the most celebrated and seemingly incontrovertible works are often founded upon sand, that they frequently rest upon dangerous cavities or upon pillars that have long been decayed. Every reinvestigation brings up new problems which make old theories untenable. thus proving how boundless is the sea of knowledge, the vastness of which one cannot even contemplate without a sigh.

Much of Ku's approach can be explained by this hard-won critical spirit with which he evaluated previous scholarship. But he is honest enough to realize that a new basis for true scholarship should be soundly thought out. In the following account of what he believes to be the scientific method, Ku at least takes the trouble to define his views. Too many people at that time (and many today!) shouted the slogan of scientific method without knowing what it meant.

> I am constantly in the habit of saying that we should apply the scientific method to the re-evaluation of our national culture, and my friends often laud me for doing so. But if I were asked what the scientific method really is, I fear that my analysis of it would not square with the zeal with which I proclaim the slogan. Hence I repeatedly ask myself, 'What are the fundamental concepts that underlie the scientific approach?' In attempting to answer in terms of my development during the past twenty years, the following immutable and enduring impressions come to my mind. When I was twelve or thirteen years of age, I purchased several zoological and botanical charts, which impressed me with their clear and detailed classification of living organisms. When later I entered elementary school and began reading an introductory work on science, I was distressed by its unsystematic treatment of the subject. Meanwhile I observed at the home

of a friend a text-book on mineralogy, which classified minerals very clearly according to their degrees of hardness, and while I did not know how the computations were made, I admired the systematic arrangement so much that I borrowed the book in order to copy it. After entering middle school I learned that the only method that chemistry has to ascertain what elements compose a given substance, is to study its reactions under different conditions and draw conclusions in the light of the observed phenomena. Moreover, through my study of logic, I learned that only by the application of the inductive method can one add to one's knowledge. Modern science begins with the building of hypotheses——basing itself on these working postulates, it proceeds to gather more evidence and, on the basis of the evidence revises the assumption. By evolving thus from day to day truth is ultimately disclosed. Still later, when attending the lectures of Dr. Hu Shih, I discovered that the historical method consists in the apprehension of a given event from every conceivable angle and in every possible relationship——no event being regarded as having sprung up independently of other considerations. To be perfectly honest, these are the only features of the scientific method that have impressed themselves upon me.

What I want now to do is to apply these fragmentary concepts to the reorganization of our scattered and highly disordered historical materials; that is to say, by analysis, classification, comparison, and experimentation discover the laws of cause and effect that made them what they are. Above all, I want to make bold use of hypothesis and induction, assembling evidence in support of new postulates, and so be in a position to put forth new theories. To speak somewhat presumptuously, perhaps, these are the methods that I regard as having received the baptism of modern science. Whatever doubts I have concerning the validity of these methods, all relate to their extraordinary simplicity——can it be that by such a few simple concepts one can attack problems in every field of study? With such doubts in my mind I have not the courage to give an affirmative answer. For this reason I intend, when time permits, to make a thorough survey of the methods employed in the physical sciences, and apply the results to a searching criticism of my own thoughts and writings, so that I may be said to have actually acquired those methods and not merely proclaim an empty slogan.

We see from the above quotation that Ku pursues his investigations, not merely as a critic of others, but also as his own critic. It is a mark of true humility of the scholar himself that he is willing to abide by this principle. Hypotheses may be bold, but never final.

Theologians and philosophers proudly say to the scientist: 'Your outlook on life is limited to physical phenomena, how can you compare with us, who are in touch with the Creator and with the ultimate principle of things?' Such language sounds plausible enough, if one did not ask by what methods they arrive at their conclusions. Do they not proceed entirely from their imaginations? Those souls, who fancy themselves in direct communion with the Creator, still lack the positive evidence which can be adduced by scientists who, after years of investigation, apprehend the truth that underlies some minute physical object. The methods of the theologians would be justified if they did not claim to be promoting scholarship; but if they want to be characterized as scholars, they must be willing to begin with minute things first. Research may be compared to the gradual piling up of earth to make a mound, the higher one wishes to build it, the broader one must plan the foundations. But no matter how high the mound may be reared, it is useless to expect that it will ever brush the stars or touch the Great Dipper——and this despite the fact that it is possible to raise the level a little higher each day. The realization of this truth caused my over-exuberant spirit to rest with more tranquility. I realized that there is no need for us to expend our energies in the vain search for ultimates. If each of us pursues his own task with industry and care, like the husbandman who slowly and painfully sets out one rice shoot after another, or like the workman who laboriously piles basket after basket of earth on the mound, then each may be said to be filling his function in life....

Above all, the scholar needs the constant encouragement of criticism for his own work to be fruitful in the endless pursuit of truth:

> I can ask for no better fortune than that I may always have friends who will criticize me so unsparingly, spurring me on to probe other hidden channels, thereby giving me a sense of the inadequacy of my knowledge which I may thus continue to enlarge. In the realm of the physical world we are wont to pray for peace and quiet, but we know that in the realm of knowledge there can be no tranquility; and, if there were, it would only connote decadence and decay. I suspect, therefore, that to the end of my days I shall be exploring new avenues to knowledge, never experiencing the joy of being able to say, 'Truth has at last revealed herself to me, hereafter there will be nothing left to do.'

To this modern Chinese historian the problem of scientific truth is vital for honest scholarly work. Ku recognizes that, in the end, perhaps, the historian cannot solely do analytical work, and that a synthesis of historical materials under a definite viewpoint is also valuable and necessary. He himself feels that he will never come that far. We, who live nearly 40 years later, know that the work of reconstruction and re-evaluation of Chinese history has by no means been finished. On the mainland, persistent attempts are now being made to build up a new picture of China's past, following the dictates of a Marxist-Leninist scientific foundation. Outside the mainland, Chinese historians are scattered wide and far, and there are some attempts at reaffirming traditional viewpoints discarded long ago by Ku Chieh-kang and his age. The task in front of the Chinese historian remains in all its gigantic proportions, to be undertaken by many generations of scholars who, it can only be hoped, will be as passionately truthful in their pursuit of learning as the historian whose ideas we introduced here.

A final quotation from this instructive Preface reveals the trying and chaotic circumstances under which it was written; an image of China in turmoil, which is itself characteristic of the violent process of change which the Chinese people are undergoing in the transition from Empire to modern nation:

> Just as I am completing the first draft of this preface, the military situation in North China is extremely tense——for days on end Peking was surcharged with consternation. In the daytime aeroplanes dropped bombs over the city, at night time the roar of cannon deafened our ears. The lagoons of the Winter palace, and the pagoda on Coal Hill (near which my residence is), ordinarily spots of rare beauty, became targets of aerial warfare. As bombs fell into the lagoon, the jade-green waters seemed to splash as high as the White Dagoba, and the sills of my windows shook as if there had been an earthquake. When the aeroplanes made their daily round, the populace had visions that demons of death were circling over the city. Members of my household were so frightened that the mere clanking of covers on water-jars, or the slamming of doors in the court-yard created illusions of hissing bombs and cannon's roar. After the booming ceased, the marketplaces became quieter than ever. Smaller shops, in fear of robbery by disbanded soldiery, barred their doors under the pretext of 'clearing up accounts;' wine shops and restaurants ceased to do business under the pretence that 'cooking stoves are under repair;' while yet more ostentatious establishments kept intruders at bay by posting the sign, 'This iron door is electrified!' In fact, business was more systematically interrupted than it is at the time of our New Year holidays.

> During those months the Peking National University issued but fifteen percent of my salary, without indicating when or at what discount other payments would be made. When friends met each other they could only knit their brows, take long sighs or find relief in tears. Everything that had any bearing on my existence seemed suddenly to terminate; even the publishing houses, because of interrupted communications and scarcity of paper, no longer importuned me for manuscript material. In a sense it was a relief to bury oneself in study and do, day after day, without interference, just what one likes to do best. For two months on end I wrote what came to my mind, and the result is this preface---the longest single article that I have ever written! It was a relief to give expression in this way to long pent-up feelings. And now that the work is completed

my wife stands at my side and laughs and says, 'Your Introduction, which covers everything in the universe, has long ago ceased to be a preface to a Symposium on Chinese History!' Nevertheless, I wanted to seize this opportunity to clarify the methods I employ in my study of ancient history, and the steps by which I have arrived at my conclusions. Since one fact cannot stand by itself, I was compelled, in order to make clear the connection, to discuss innumerable other facts along with it. Whether or not the result corresponds to what is ordinarily considered a preface is really of little consequence.

HISTORY AND
RELATED DISCIPLINES

E VER SINCE AUGUSTE COMTE outlined his 'new science' of social physics, many people have regarded history either as itself a social science or as intimately related to sociology, anthropology, psychology and economics. For some of these, history was thus by marriage related to the more respectable family of the natural sciences. Durkheim, following Comte, had brought the vast field of the 'history of religions' (*Religionsgeschichte—Religionswissenschaft*) into the same gross family by making this new discipline a branch of sociology. He defined theology as the projection of the social consciousness and of its ideal self interpretation. From the side of Protestant Liberalism, for quite other reasons, theology had been since Kant divorced from science and natural philosophy in order that it might be the more firmly rooted in history. At the beginning of our century all these several disciplines were the daughters of history.

During the past century, however, it has become increasingly clear to historians, social scientists and theologians that the precise pedigree of history as a science is difficult if not impossible to define. Social scientists have come to despair of a scientific history—sometimes because they are no longer sure that sociology can synthesize its own many detailed samplings of complex phenomena into any general principles that would be of use to the historian. Some have been frankly skeptical of the value of history as a science because they are skeptical of law as a historiographic concept. The sociological historians such as Durkheim, Levy Bruhl, Hubert, Mauss and E. B. Tylor do not, from contemporary standards, appear to have been either good historians or good anthropologists. Many sociologists are convinced that the time has not yet come even for social theory, and they are quite sure that in the meantime it is not the historian who should formulate the principles of explanation of social phenomena.

However indirectly sociological studies in the last half century have helped to form the mind of historians, the writing of history in this period has shown surprisingly little direct response either to the data or the perspectives of the social sciences. It is of course the case that only in the recent past have sociological studies been available to the historian, and these by their nature have little direct bearing upon a past more remote than the first quarter of this century. They do, however, have implications. They have pointed out some new lines of enquiry that the historian may find significant.

The historian differs from the sociologist in his interest in the unique individual and the unique event in all their concrete richness rather than the general pattern of human behaviour abstracted from the total life of the individual and his society. Biography lends itself to historical narrative. The Kinsey Report does not. Best-seller novelists could make use of Kinsey's statistics in the writing of historical fiction—but that is not history. The statistical probability is not 'what did happen' based upon actual events and particular persons. To know what 79% of the housewives of America in 1950 thought about a particular brand of toothpaste does not guarantee the fact that Mrs. John Doe of Kalamazoo used that brand on the morning of December 26, 1928, when she decided to divorce her husband. In the natural sciences the same laboratory experiment is repeated over and over again with precisely the same results. A sampling of human behaviour made in the same locality, using the same people, is likely to be quite different in 1950 from what it was in 1928. The social scientist is forced to deal with history because men have none other than an historical existence. Social studies are however snapshots that represent the look of something from a particular angle at a particular moment. An album of such snapshots is not history.

History differs from social science in that it describes what appears in events of importance. It pictures the landscape of the past and centers upon its predominant features. The center of gravity of social phenomena lies beneath the surface of events. The historian creates out of the tangible stuff of factual evidence the historical image of a colourful individual. He can examine his speeches and letters, check through his bank statements, review the opinions about him expressed by others. He can describe the part he played in some particular event. He can even suggest the social background of his views and his manner of action. But he cannot write a history of social change involving the complex and subtle motions of a culture that go beneath the surface of events. Social phenomena are too diffuse and hidden for the historian. They are like the unseen pressures that build up down below the crater of a volcano. Only rarely does their unnoted presence over long periods force itself upon attention in an eventful eruption. The historian deals with the event; the sociologist with the hidden pressures. Hence political history has a greater appeal both to the historian and to his readers than the social process. The public figure is articulate. He leaves behind him in the sands of time rather more footprints than either his contemporaries or the historian might consider to have been really necessary to his getting to wherever he thought he was going! The more important the figure (presidents, admirals and generals or the literate artist) the more he will give the historian to get on with. His many contacts with all manner of people and affairs in his time leads to the assumption that he is a key figure, i.e. a classical and representative type (as, for example Leonardo da Vinci—'the man of the Renaissance'). Social studies can suggest to contemporary and future historians that such an assumption, if not misleading, is at best only partially valid. To understand America in the 1860's through the lives of Lincoln, Seward, Lee and Grant is to miss a great deal—and even a great deal that is essential to the understanding of these men themselves. Of real importance is the highlighting and backlighting of the great events of that decade that come from the lives of the little people—the preachers who spoke Sunday after Sunday from rural pulpits in the South and in New England and on the frontier across the Ohio River, the mayors of towns and cities: the judges in the county courts, the businessmen and the planters, Social studies could suggest such bed-rock samplings. Yet as monographic efforts they would not be history until they were, like the threads on the wrong side of the tapestry, interwoven according to a pattern that could explain the texture of the top side of history. Such tracing o. the many threads cannot be the work of the lone historian. This fact leads to another suggestion which social science can offer to the historian: that historians may need to follow the lead of sociologists toward a wider use of group work. Yet here again there is a qualificationf the writing of history, the ultimate task, is properly the work of one man who has the rare powers of sympathy, insight and constructive creation together with a mastery of the art of narration.

Historians may continue to adapt certain of the techniques and interests of the social scientist to the study of history. Panel enquiries, career-line analyses, patterns of familial structure and child rearing, analyses of mass political behaviour and of response to mass communications media are some of the suggestions of two contemporary historians who are keenly interested in social phenomena and keenly aware of the difference between social science and history (Thomas Cochran and Richard Hofstadter). Both sociologists and historians have noted some areas of common interest that could lead to a reconstruction of the remote past as well as to the writing of the history of the recent past. Among these are a more precise enquiry into the role of the successful leader in terms of the social evaluation of types and qualities of leadership. It is interesting and instructive to compare the kinds of explanation in a recent study in cultural anthropology, *Plainville, U.S.A.*, with the classic written by the Nineteenth Century historian, Fustel de Coulanges on *The Ancient City*. Such social-economic studies as *The Organization Man* can be a clue to the bearing of the economy of mid-Nineteenth Century America upon the culture of that era; for the organization man is the 'son' of the new 'captain of industry' of the 1880's and the 'grandson' of the new industrial entrepreneur of the 1850's. Grandsons do reveal something, even in their rebellion, of the character and pedigree of their grandparents. In turn, these new insights derived from contemporary studies applied to the developments of the Nineteenth Century may fill out with further detail Max Weber's study of the role of Protestantism in the development of the capitalist society, and provide a fuller account of the economic and sociological aspects of Puritanism. In such studies there could be, to the profit of all, a closer cooperation among economists, sociologists, historians and theologians.

The social sciences, including psychology, on the other hand, have profited by a sense of history. Social change is not a new phenomenon. Its contemporary expressions may sometimes be better understood in the perspective of change in the past and of the character of the adjustments which men have shown themselves capable of making The historian, furthermore, provides the setting in which all sociological phenomena have actually occurred. Without that setting, social and psychological explanations have, in Hofstadter's phrase, only a 'flat time dimension.'

Finally, a sense of history can remind the social scientist that he too is rooted in history, that he stands within a tradition. He does not discover a project, devise the method of his survey, collect his data, derive his categories, or explain his statistics in a vacuum. Indeed his very choice of vocation and his notion of his task have a vital relation to his judgment of history. Without a sense of history his own presuppositions are likely to be more apparent to others than to himself. When you know that your presuppositions are showing, you are more likely to be a bit less sure of the correctness of your own image and thus save yourself from a more serious embarrassment.

Despite some important differences, history is closer to social science when it most narrowly restricts itself to monographic research. Laboratory experiments, social studies and historical monographs can at times focus a bright if narrow beam that sweeps like a beacon through a wide circle of knowledge. But such flashes are momentary. Monographic studies do not illumine the past any more than a beacon lights up the whole landscape. They are flickering and broken lights in the night, not the full light of day. In sober realism most contemporary historians have concluded that there is no such thing as scientific history. History is something essentially different. Nor is social science scientific history. Nor is it likely that either the historian or his readers shall ever be content with history as simply the setting of 'problems of social enquiry in their integral relations and in their totality.' The concluding paragraphs from 'The Sister Disciplines of History' in Jacques Barzun and Henry F. Graff, *The Modern Researcher* are a good summing up of the lessons all have learned in the century since Comte's *Course on Positive Philosophy*.

(The social sciences, after an assertion of their youthful independence, have come home to brood.) It is clear they still belong in part to their nurturing mother---they are historical by origin and necessity, and they can never be wholly something else. A hundred years ago Ernest Renan, a French philologist, predicted that in a few decades there would be no need of art, literature, ethics and philosophy. There would be only curious histories of these antiquated pursuits, because by that time we would *know*. Later the social sciences were ready to get rid of history on the same ground. For when we know the laws, it was supposed, what interest will there be in particular events?

As far as we now see, the need for description reports on human behaviour will continue, and hence the ways of history will also be in demand. Its ways, as is clear from the historian's method of attaining truth, correspond to two realities that we are not likely to get rid of in a hurry---one is the dramatic (constructive or story-telling) habit of thought; the other is the diversity and---as we often say---the irony of life. The interest that human beings take in history, therefore, springs from some of our least changeable tendencies. As a modern historian puts it: 'Historical inquiry has its deepest impulse in the lust for life.'

(This is not to say that the social sciences lack the same impulse. On the contrary, their method puts the researcher very much in the midst of life and, if it affects the historian, forces him out into the open from his imprisonment in the dusty archives. Yet it is clear that the main interest of the social sciences is in the regularities which can be charted. Hypotheses are then erected upon these at the risk of distortion. In this respect the social sciences are closer to the physical sciences, which assume——rightly for their purpose——the complete uniformity of nature and its laws. Can this assumption be made about human nature whose fixity is still to be demonstrated?) Physical science can in its domain generalize from a very few instances. The subjects called 'humanities,' so named because they deal with man and his life, record variety, vagueness, and an infinite play of nuance. The social sciences try to bridge the gap between the other two by reducing the variety to regularity. Hence arises the trouble these sciences meet both in making assumptions and in studying instances. A chemist uses a purified sample of a substance and argues after a few tests that under the same conditions all samples will behave alike. The sociologist in imitating the chemist, samples mankind, which is hard to purify, and he seldom reaches the same result twice. Often, he knows how inadequate his 'instances' are, but is helpless. A scientific theory, as a noted economist points out, 'is always simpler than reality. Even when it seems terribly complex, it is still simplicity itself as compared to the range of factors operating as conditions, as means, or as ends, in any actual, concrete situation.' It is a great temptation to the theorist to work from a few premises....It makes it easier for him to reach definite and precise answers.

There can be no question, then, of social science displacing history as a mode of understanding reality, any more than of history producing theory in the scientific sense. There should accordingly be no conflict between the two. History and the social sciences interpenetrate and cannot afford to ignore or condemn one another. The very form of modern culture requires study to be many-sided. Social science and history are true sister disciplines. The best histories today are written with the results of surveys, statistics and conclusions of the social sciences and the best social scientists adopt a historical attitude toward their material and handle it by the methods of research originally devised by historians. The historian's presentation of the facts is narrative and concrete, and the social scientist's is abstract and, so to speak, additive. But there is no proof that one or the other is more instructive and useful to mankind. An imaginative combination of both in the study of man and society may be yet the most powerful in effect.

Something of the issues and details of that task are discussed in the following essay by Joan Ho.

History as a Discipline in The Social Sciences by Joan Ho

From the dawn of his existence down to the present day, man has been interested in himself — his origins, his dreams, his possibilities. This interest traditionally found academic expression in the discipline of history. In the modern era, history has given birth to the social sciences, a group of studies designed to make perpetually fascinating man the object of exact scientific investigation.

We would expect to find resemblances between a mother and her children and we are not disappointed when we look for them here. The techniques of footnoting, making references, and compiling bibliographies which the social scientist uses in his research and reporting have all been inherited from history. Any report given by the social scientist insofar as it seeks to present facts is necessarily historical. It is a record of the past. Its arguments are based on what has been happening, what is over.

These rather obvious resemblances between history and the social sciences are supplemented by more fundamental bonds. Some of the basic beliefs and methods of approaching problems in the social sciences have been derived from history.

At the time of the birth of the social sciences in the eighteenth and nineteenth centuries, many historians conceived of history as a progressive process governed by general, discoverable laws. Mankind was assumed to be capable of change for the better. It was believed that the increase and diffusion of knowledge about history would enable men to determine and, to some extent, to control its future direction and, in doing so, to improve themselves. These views were absorbed by the young social sciences. Note Auguste Comte's theory of progress, his law of three stages, and his confidence in the possibility of social reconstruction on the basis of sufficient knowledge. Such notions have retained footholds in the social sciences. The hope of finding general laws operating in the development of at least some aspects of human societies remains very much alive. The belief that societies and individuals can change for the better is a basic and virtually unquestioned assumption, and knowledge of the past is an important tool to be used in the accomplishment of this change. Social engineering is considered a goal and a possibility.

Against the background of these general perspectives, let us turn to some particular illustrations of the place of historical insights and methods in specific social sciences. One of the oldest and most interesting children of history, is psychology, which hovers on the borderline between the natural and the social sciences, running to the former in some endeavors (as when the biological machinery of behavior is the object of study) and to the latter in others (as in the work of the social psychologist). One of the major groups of methods used by the psychologist in his attempts to understand man is taken directly from the historian. This group consists of the life-history methods which can be divided into three basic varieties: the daybook method, the biographical method, and the case history method. The use of any of these involves the intensive study of the lives of individuals in an effort to discover and to understand the factors responsible for particular forms of behavior.

The daybook method is especially popular among psychologists who are studying the behavior of children. The child's development is carefully observed and recorded. When did he first lift his head, smile, roll over, sit, stand, clap? A sufficient number of such observations and records can lead to the formulation of criteria for normal development.

The use of the biographical method entails tracking down important psychological facts about people from accounts of their lives written either by themselves or others. This method has obvious limitations since relevant information may be omitted in such accounts and since the authors are liable to be biased. Nevertheless, biographies are helpful when the subject cannot be examined directly.

The psychologist employing the case-history method collects information about the previous experiences of the client, usually through interviewing the client himself. When this is put in the context of an overall theoretical framework, it enables him to understand more clearly the client's behavior and to render treatment which will result in constructive change in the behavior. The information obtained may also contribute to the fund of knowledge about general types of human behavior. The following case furnishes us with an example of this method as it is used within the framework of Freudian psychology:

> '—a young woman was deathly afraid of touching anything made of rubber. She did not know why she had this fear; she only knew that she had had it as long as she could remember. Analysis brought out the following facts. When she was a little girl, her father had brought home two balloons, one for her and one for her younger sister. In a fit of temper she broke her sister's balloon, for which she was severely punished by her father. Moreover, she had to give her sister her balloon. Upon further analysis it was learned that she had been very jealous of her younger sister, so much so that she secretly wished her sister might die and leave her the sole object of her father's devotion. The breaking of her sister's balloon signified a destructive act against her sister. The ensuing punishment

and her own guilt feelings became associated with the rubber balloon. Whenever she came into contact with rubber, the old fear of the wish to destroy her sister made her shrink away.

A second child of history, anthropology, also has inherited important characteristics. Dr. Wm. Duncan Strong, Professor of Anthropology at Columbia Universiy, argues that although much of recent anthropology has emphasized the functional approach more than the historical approach, anthropology in both its biological and its socio-cultural aspects has been and continues to be fundamentally conditioned by history which is defined as 'recorded change through time and space.'

Physical anthropologists, in their concern with biological man, must obviously lean heavily on evolutionary theory and on human history. S. L. Washburn states flatly, 'The interpretation of the genetic situation demands an understanding of history.' The work of the physical anthropologist is unthinkable apart from the contributions of archaeology which is by its very nature an historical tool.

It is in the realm of cultural anthropology that problems of methodology and the question of the links of anthropology with history have come most clearly to the fore. Here the interest is centered in man as distinctly human, i.e., possessing qualities and characteristics which are not shared to any significant extent by other forms of life. This interest tends to draw the anthropologist toward the province of the historian who is also primarily interested in this aspect of man.

E. B. Tylor, who may be regarded as the founding father of cultural anthropology, L. H. Morgan, and other important scholars in the nineteenth century took as their objective the discovery of the psychological laws which underlay and determined human history. They believed that cultures developed progressively in time and followed essentially the same pattern of development everywhere. Morgan constructed a scale of seven stages or statuses through which culture was alleged to advance beginning with a low status of savagery and ending with civilization. This pattern was not actually applied to culture as a whole but to certain aspects of it such as the family, art, and religious belief. As a specific scheme, the pattern has been largely discredited in twentieth century anthropological theory except in the U. S. S. R.

Nevertheless, a broad historical approach to anthropology continues to be important. Contemporary anthropologists may be roughly divided according to the way in which they deal with data, i.e., whether their approach is primarily scientific or historical. The first group, including such men as Malinowski and A. R. Radcliffe-Brown, emphasize a non-historical, generalizing approach. Malinowski attempts to explain culture by reference to biological considerations and makes substantial use of the concept of 'function.' Culture is seen as an organization designed to accomplish particular aims. Radcliffe-Brown is concerned with the unambiguous description of social structures, the systematic classification of social phenomena, and the formulation, by scientific means, of general laws or principles which underlie social phenomena and which can be applied without reference to historical period or geographical distribution.

These men may be contrasted with a second group of which W. D. Strong and Evans-Pritchard are examples. Members of the latter group are interested in organizing data in a way which will bring out important historical relationships. This approach is frequently identified with an effort at 'descriptive integration,' in which prehistory and the historical emphases of such fields as ethnology, linguistics and physical anthropology are utilized in an attempt to reconstruct and preserve reality in the contexts of unique positions in space, time, and quality and in which validity is tested by determining the degree to which the phenomena reported fit into the totality of the conceptual findings. Adherents of this approach generally engage in cultural history. In the minds of most, such history involves more than the collection of masses of historical materials and the use of historical safeguards. Interpretative elements are also important. The bright optimism of the unilinear evolutionary theory of Tylor and Morgan has vanished, but the search for limited patterns of development remains. For example, recent anthropological research in Peru has led to an outline of six roughly sequential cultural eras including: '(1) the prehorticultural (2) the incipient horticultural, (3) the formative (of local civilization); (4) the florescent, (5) the fusional, and (6) the imperial.'

Linguistics is a discipline closely allied with anthropology and sometimes considered part of it. Linguists, like anthropologists, employ two basic kinds of analysis: descriptive and historical. The first is formal and deals with individual languages. The languages are dissected into their essential parts: sound systems, lexicons, and grammatical principles and are then classified on the basis of structural principles.

The second kind of analysis seeks to establish genetic connections between known languages, to trace developments within languages, and to reconstruct languages of the past which are the forerunners of present dialects. Reconstruction is done with the help of specialized techniques frequently developed first in descriptive linguistics. Edward Sapir (1883-1939) formerly Sterling Professor of Anthropology and Linguistics at Yale University, in a classic paper on 'The History and Varieties of Human Speech' delineates both of these kinds of analysis. The following excerpt from this paper illustrates the use of historical analysis:

'...grammatical developments on the basis of phonetic changes have occurred with great frequency in the history of language. In the long run, not only may in this way old grammatical features be lost and new ones evolved, but the entire morphologic type of the language may undergo profound modification. A striking example is furnished again by the history of the English language. It is a well-known feature of English that absolutely the same word, phonetically speaking, may often, according to its syntactic employment, be construed as verb or as noun. Thus, we not only *love* and *kiss,* but we also give our *love* or a *kiss,* that is the words *love* and *kiss* may be indifferently used to predicate or to denominate an activity. There are so many examples in English of the formal, though not syntactic, identity of noun stem and verb stem that it may well be said that the English language is on the way to become of a purely analytic or isolating type, more or less similar to that of Chinese. And yet the typical Indo-germanic language of earlier times, as represented say by Latin or Greek, always makes a rigidly formal not merely syntactic, distinction between these fundamental parts of speech. If we examine the history of this truly significant change of type in English, we shall find that it has been due at last analysis to the operation of merely phonetic laws. The original Anglo-Saxon form of the infinitive of the verb *kiss* was *cyssan,* while the Anglo-Saxon form of the noun *kiss* was *cyss*. The forms in early middle English times became dulled to *kissen* and *kiss*, respectively. Final unaccented -*n* later regularly dropped off, so that the infinitive of the verb came to be *kisse*. In Chaucer's day the verb and the noun were still kept apart as *kisse* and *kiss*, respectively; later on, as a final unaccented -*e* regularly dropped off, *kisse*, became *kiss*, so that there ceased to be any formal difference between the verb and noun. The history of the Anglo-Saxon verb *lufian* 'to love' and noun *lufu* 'love' has been quite parallel; the two finally became confused in a single form *luv*, modern English *love*. Once the pace has been set, so to speak, for an interchange in English between verbal and nominal use of the same word, the process, by the working of simple analogy, is made to apply also to cases where in origin we have to deal with only one part of speech; thus, we may not only have a sick *stomach*, but we may *stomach* an injury (noun becomes verb), and, conversely, we may not only *write up* a person, but he may get a *write up* (verb becomes noun). It has, I hope, become quite clear by this time how the trivial changes of pronunciation that are necessitated by the very process of speech acquirement may in due course of time, profoundly change the fundamental characteristics of language. So also, if I may be pardoned the use of a simile, may the slow erosive action of water, continued through weary ages, profoundly transform the character of a landscape. If there is one point of historic method rather than another that the scientific study of language may teach other historical sciences, it is that changes of the greatest magnitude may often be traced to phenomena or processes of a minimal magnitude.

The work of Max Weber, the German sociologist and political economist, is perhaps the most striking example of the meeting of historical and scientific methods in modern social science. Weber was interested both in specific historical problems and in comparative sociology of a generalizing character. He was sensitive to the multiplicity and uniqueness of concrete social and historical situations, but he considered this uniqueness to be the consequence of particular combinations of general factors which could be isolated and quantified. He developed the notion of 'ideal types,' logically precise general concepts constructed from certain elements of reality, e.g., 'democracy' as 'minimization of power.' If his interest in a particular research project centered on the reconstruction of an historical object, he could approximate the many sidedness of the specific historical situation by bringing various type concepts to bear on it. Where the emphasis was on comparative studies, history furnished him with examples of general type concepts. He took the descriptive materials of history as his raw material and prepared them for comparative analysis with the tools of ideal types and quantification.

One of the historical phenomena which Weber found especially interesting was the development of western bourgeois capitalism. He was dissatisfied with the Marxist explanation of this solely in terms of changes in the character of the economic environment. He was willing to grant that economic conditions in sixteenth and seventeenth century Europe were, in many respects, favorable to the growth of capitalism, but he pointed out that similar conditions had existed at various times in the past without leading to capitalism. Thus, this was clearly not an adequate explanation. What other factors had been involved? Weber advanced the theory that the development of Western bourgeois capitalism had been necessarily preceded by Protestant religious movements, particularly Calvinism. The bourgeoisie of the time had found in Calvinism a new conception of religion in which the pursuit of wealth was regarded not as a vice, but as a virtue and a duty. This conception had given them the vigor they needed in the fray with the established aristocracy and had enabled them to emerge triumphant.   In a famous essay on 'The Protestant Ethic and the Spirit of Capitalism' (1904), Weber showed that there was a high degree of congruence in the occurrence of these two phenomena.   He then plunged into a comparative study involving many other civilizations in an attempt to validate his original theory.   He found that although many conditions favorable to the growth of capitalism in the Western sense were present in other cultures, such capitalism failed to emerge.   He concluded that the type of personality produced by the 'worldly ascetic' ethic of Protestantism should be numbered among the conditions sufficient for the appearance of capitalism.

Many other specific examples of the use of historical method and ideas in the social sciences could be found.   It is hoped that the few suggested will spur the interested reader on to make further investigations for himself.

Perhaps partly because they share common characteristics, children and parents often encounter common questions and difficulties.   Such is the case for history and the social sciences.   A number of intriguing questions of concern to both are currently in the air: Are all propositions about society as a whole or about historical institutions ultimately reducible to propositions about the actions or dispositions of individuals? If not, what is the ontological status of 'societal' or 'institutional' facts? What is the scope of precise quantitative research techniques? Can these be applied only to relatively simple and limited problems or are they suitable for the exploration of broader issues as well? Is it possible to do justice to the fullness of concrete cases and at the same time to formulate abstract, general principles applicable to many specific instances? How can empirical data gathered in one discipline be illuminated by concepts from a second? How can concepts from one area of knowledge be used to spark new research and suggest new viewpoints in another?

History and Science

The first thing to be said about science is that it too is a human activity. In part because it has drawn a sharper line between its officiants and its laymen, in its early stage as alchemy and astrology as well as in its modern form as mathematics, science has preserved its aura of mystery and magic long after art and history have suffered disenchantment. Nonetheless, science, too, is a human activity, and it is, like history, a construction of the world in terms of human intelligence.

When Huxley defined science as sitting down before the facts like a child he was nearer to the truth than he deserved to be because his misunderstanding of science was cancelled out by his misunderstanding of children. Science is not a carbon copy of nature and children are the most imaginative and creative people. The scientist like the artist and like the historian creates a world in the image of human understanding. The truth of Huxley's aphorism is not that nature speaks for itself or even that the 'facts' of nature are any less the raw materials of science than the 'facts' of the past are the raw stuff of history. All knowledge is both an ordering and an interpretation of facts.

The second thing to be said about science is that it has a history and that it is itself a form of history—the record of events in the physical universe. It too is the application of thought to action—the action that is 'nature.' History is a reconstruction of the past. Science is a reconstruction of events that have occurred and will recur. Science emphasizes the universality of event in nature. History seizes upon the uniqueness of the events of human action. Science in our time has, however, moved from the ancient mythologies of an immutable cosmological order that excludes all novelty, all uniqueness, to the notion of an open-ended universe which also has its history—which is not the same as it was in the remote past and will not be the same as it is now in a remote future.

From the time of the Greeks to the end of the Eighteenth Century, science and history appear to have been two different and opposing ways of looking at the world. The classical study of nature cancelled out what the Christian faith understood to be the soul of history, and Christian thought for the most part chose history rather than nature as the area of God's significant self-disclosure. The physical world was in orthodox theology little more than the stage upon which the divine drama of salvation was enacted. The conflict of religion with science that arose in the Seventeenth Century continued in part to be the conflict of history and the study of nature, the opposing emphases upon the general and the specific, the mass and the individual, the inevitable and the unique, necessity and freedom. History guarded the notion of the unique occurrence conceived either in humanist fashion as the miracle of human creativity or in religious fashion as divine intervention. Seventeenth and Eighteenth Century science reinforced the notion of nature as a fixed and unalterable order after the analogy of fate in Greek thought and the structure of the primitive folk society in general.

The philosophy of nature continued through the Eighteenth Century as a projection into the physical universe of the closed system of tribal society with its unalterable custom, its denial of individual expression. The concepts of Eighteenth Century science centered upon the immutable and the static and were not essentially different in perspective than the cosmological myths of primitive man. The philosophies of Plato and Aristotle were profound treatments of primitive mythology which pictured the universe as a two-storied building: earth and heaven, the home of men below and the abode of the gods above, the fate-bound, tragedy-laden realm of human existence and the eternal, perfect realm of absolute truth, beauty and goodness. Primitive science pictured the unit of reality as some irreducible substance, imperishable and unchanging out of which all things were made. For the most part romantic history in the latter part of the Eighteenth and the first half of the Nineteenth Century developed the concept of the unique, the highly individual expressed in images of the heroic individual and the spirit of the age. Since von Ranke and Croce, history has come nearer to science not only as method but also conceptually. A good deal of the best contemporary historical writing could be described as a thinking out of Croce's mature conclusion that 'the universal must be incarnate in the individual,' and that it is this divination of the structure and dynamic of process incarnate in individual events which is the real task of the historian.

Science also has moved nearer to history. In the work of Dalton, Becquerel, the Thomsons and Rutherford, of Planck and Einstein, the notion of the universe as consisting of masses in a static pattern in space was overthrown. The new physics deals with the atom not as substance but as event. Next to mathematics the most appropriate description is, poetic: 'an atom is a tiny planetary system, a merry-go-round in miniature.' And these tiny plants, the electrons, are not substances. They have been pictured as 'particles of negative electricity,' as 'points of energy or response.' The description of an atom is an interpretive *report* of activities in relationship; and that of a molecule is the *story* of a larger event involving the relation of relations of activities.

The hypothesis of organic evolution undermined the notion of a static two-storied universe from another perspective. Biology was the first of the physical sciences to devise the notion of emergence and novelty as a necessary explanation of some stubborn facts of science. The concept of relativity and the quantum theory in the recent past have pointed to an open-ended universe in which natural law becomes simply statistical averages and in which the position of viewing anything is as significant as the object to be viewed.

The definite boundary between nature and history exists neither for the historian nor for the theoretical scientist. From the point of view of these new hypotheses, nature is something happening—*nature is history*. Whitehead presses the notion of event as the unit of natural occurrence toward universal applicability for all circles of learning in his philosophy of organism. Here there is no divorce between nature and life, nature and man or the circles of art, history and science.

In modern thought, history is the mediating circle between the circles of art and science. Historical method structures the studies of the several departments, and history in any field is a significant way of seeing theory in perspective. Historical study is thus a community effort. Equally important is the role of history as pontiff—the bridge builder between science and art. There can be no study of human action in the modern world (from the Seventeenth Century onward) that does not take account of science. Looking backward, Professor Butterfield can criticize the notion held by historians in the very recent past, that the modern world was the product of the Renaissance. What was begun in the Seventeenth Century, he sees as an altogether new kind of civilization, one that 'could cut itself away from the Graeco-Roman heritage in general.' He concludes his essay on 'The Place of the Scientific Revolution in the History of Western Civilization' with the judgment that 'since the rise of Christianity, there is no landmark in history worthy to be compared with this.'

The student in history requires a broad knowledge of science not only for his telling of the story of human affairs since the Seventeenth Century but also in understanding himself, his own perspective and the point in time from which he must view the whole of the past. And the science student needs history. There are several facets to the insight with which Collingwood concludes his *Idea of Nature*—'that natural science as a form of thought exists and has always existed in a context of history, and depends on historical thought for its existence'. History is the key to an adequate grasp of sientific theory. It is also the key to an understanding of experimental science and that essential attitude toward laboratory procedure that makes physics and chemistry and biology university subjects. The 'scientist' who knows nothing of the history of the great experiments which he repeats in the laboratory does not really know what he is doing and why he is doing it. Apart from history a science student's lab work is little more than a higher grade of manual labour performed in a factory that produces nothing—not even—especially not—a scientist!

History in Eastern culture today is even more important than it is in the West. For the modern East, living at random under the impact of technology, Western science, taught apart from its history, is indeed a dangerous thing. It is then all that the East has feared of it, a new white magic at every moment threatening to turn black, a harsh thing, giving so little in reparation for so much that it has destroyed.

From medieval times into the very recent past, Aristotle's logic served as the meeting place for doctor and mathematician, philosopher and theologian. For the modern world, one meeting place is the history of science.

The history of science is a quite new yet rapidly growing area of special study. It is of two types and serves two purposes. The first is history as a division of university science that undertakes to collect and set in order a record of the development of studies in a specific area of research. Such history is a kind of digest of science abstracts organized in a developmental scheme. It supplies a kind of background case study manual for the research scientist, informing him of what has been attempted and accomplished in the past and advising him as to the present frontier.

The second type of the history of science centers upon the history of ideas—scientific theory. It attempts to tell how determinative insights were discovered, how they were related to seminal ideas of the age, and how new achievements in theory and technology have, in turn affected human life and thought. Both scientists and historians are today writing histories of science. There are as yet no canons relating either to goals or methods. Of many problems that are just coming to the surface, the issue of biography in the history of science, may be of general interest.

Are biographies important to a history of science? The obvious answer would be that the lives of scientists are in no way relevant to a history of scientific theory. Science is a body of demonstrable and mathematically expressed propositions, discoverable, illustrated and proved by precise experiment and the success of wider applications. Such propositions have nothing to do with personalities, historical occasions, or even cultural presuppositions.

It may be important for the student of poetry to know in detail the date when a poem was written, the background and life of the poet, and the confluence of external circumstance and internal disposition at the moment of his writing. Many would say that the study of history involves a study of historians, that sociological theory reflects the heredity, environment and personality of the sociologist. Some people are convinced that a final proof of theological fallacies is to be sought in the maladjustment of theologians. On the other hand, who would suggest that the merits of the wave and corpuscular theories of light should be determined by a comparison of the psychographs of Hugyens and Newton. It is argued that scientific theory has no relation whatsoever to the temperment or experiences of its authors or, indeed, even to culture. Yet great men, particularly great scientists, are heroes whose lives are of interest quite apart from any question of the relation of persons and principles. It is one of the curious facts of the history of science that until quite recently 'historians' have dealt with biographical materials as though scientists were chiseled cameos—rare materials finely wrought. Some science trained 'historians' are eager to prove by biographical details that scientists too are people. Exalted and mysterious, majestic and miraculous though their achievements have been, we should see them as people—warm, generous, humane geniuses 'who really lived.'

More recent studies take biography more seriously. The historian of science is prepared to ask why Copernicus could not question the doctrine of circular planetary motion—why Galileo rejected rectilinear motion and why he did not take Kepler's work into account or consider the relation of the forces of inertia and gravity. Men like Collingwood press the historian of science to ask of the men behind the documents of the Seventeenth and Eighteenth Centuries why the analogy of a machine was more congenial than that of organism as a basic perspective in the interpretation of nature.

Equally important is the question of the bearing of the mentality of a Copernicus, a Kepler, a Galileo and a Newton upon what they did achieve. Freudian analyses of Shakespeare, Luther and Marx have not proved very helpful, and there is little reason to suppose that the clue to the frontiers of modern science will turn out to be a matter of case studies of the 'jet propelled couch'. Physical science as an intellectual venture is no more reducible to the experimental categories of social science than it is to semantics or even to mathematical logic. The point to be made is that science too is a human activity, and as a profoundly significant aspect of modern culture, deserves the serious attention of the historian who looks at all manner of men and movements with an equal eye.

History and Religion

History in relation to the study of religion involves not only such questions of enquiry and method that have been raised in our discussion of the social and physial sciences. It involves also the dimension of ultimate judgment concerning human nature and its destiny. Theologians have during the past century been keenly interested in the whole range of historical studies, and they have found in history the most significant source of religious knowledge. Contemporary theological literature examines in detail the technical problems of historicity and historicism, of the nature and use of historical fact, and of the nature and meaning of myth. Many of the pioneers in academic and technical history in the Nineteenth Century were Biblical scholars. Many also of the more astute critics of historical theory were constructive theologians and historians of dogma. To the neglect of the physical sciences and of metaphysics, theologians for a full century have identified their own critical and constructive tasks with those of the historian. We have, however, chosen a study of history and religion not from this vast literature of theology but from the writing of a contemporary professional historian, Herbert Butterfield, sometime Vice-Chancellor of the University of Cambridge, Master of Peterhouse, and Professor of Modern History. In the following review of his *Christianity and History*, the abstracts and excerpts that appear as quotations were made by Philip Shen and Joan Ho.

In his *Christianity and History* Professor Butterfield holds a conversation with himself *qua* historian and *qua* Christian. He approaches his broad subject with two questions: 1. How does a professional historian's summing up of the great themes of history compare with the Christian understanding of history; and 2. does Christianity contribute any essential perspectives to the interpretation of history? Points of view and 'ground rules' are clarified in the 'Introduction' and in the first chapter, 'Historical Scholarship and its Relation to Life.'

(First of all Professor Butterfield makes an important distinction between history in the strict academic sense and history in the sense of an overall interpretation of the human drama. Historical judgments in the first sense are 'interim judgments' and cannot be final. They may be changed by new facts and revised in a different interpretation. Moral judgments on moral issues in history are of this type in so far as they fall within the competence of the historian. But history in the second sense requires a personal, religious decision, and for that every man is responsible. Because it has to do with the meaning of life and destiny, it is the most sovereign decision that he can make. Nevertheless, it remains a 'historical' decision because it is informed by one's study of history and is not made outside of history itself. It must be made, in other words, in the fullness of historical existence and it shares the particularity and finiteness of history itself. To deny this is to deny our human nature, its significance and its limitations.)

History must deal with some things which can only be discovered and verified by insight, sympathy and imagination——for example, the reconstruction of historical characters——but it is extremely hazardous for the historian to make unnecessary speculations. In respect of points which are established by the evidence, or accepted by the judgment of common sense, history has a certain validity of its own, a certain minimum significance that is independent of philosophy, race or creed. Technical history is a science because it studies the very concrete and tangible things, such as can be tested and attested by a definite kind of evidence. It examines the observable or demonstrable connections between things. If it demonstrates that a man did live and die in a certain period it does so for all men regardless of what they believe. But this matter-of-fact policy in technical history does not provide people with the meaning of life. It is a habit of mind which is only adopted for the purpose of a particular technique.

(Yet there are reasons to suggest that this approach to history as a science is a specifically Christian one.) It does not deny providence. It does not hold that events will form a self-explanatory system without any necessity for the idea of God. It relegates scientific history to a humble role, certainly not assuming that it will suffice either to answer the question whether the hand of God can be found in history, or to explain why man exists, or to settle ultimate philosophical problems. And certainly it does not assume, as the Marxists and so many other secularist thinkers seem to do, that when we have learned the history of a thing we shall have achieved its final and total explanation.

If men have found no philosophy or religion in their actual experience of life, it can hardly be claimed that the academic study of history will itself provide the remedy, or that the attempt to learn more scientifically when things happened or how they happened can solve the whole problem of human destiny or achieve anything more than a better statement, a better laying-out, of the essential riddle. Technical history and historical research only comprise a specialised part of our attitude to the past, and their realm is restricted by the character of the apparatus which they use and the kind of evidence which is available. They provide us with a reasonable assurance that certain things did happen, that they happened in a certain order, and that certain connections exist between them, independent of any philosophy or creed of ours.   But for the fullness of our commentary on the drama of human life in time, we have to break through this technique to stand back and see the landscape as a whole.   And for the sum of our ideas and beliefs about the march of ages we need the poet and the prophet, the philosopher and the theologian.

Indeed we decide our total attitude to the whole of human history when we make our decision about our religion——and it is the combination of that history with a religion, or with something equivalent to a religion, which generates power and fills the story with significance.   We may find this in a Christian interpretation of history, or in the Marxist system or even perhaps in H. G. Well's *History of the World.*   Our interpretation is a thing which we bring to our history and superimpose upon it.   However, we cannot say that we obtained it as technical historians by inescapable inferences from the purely historical evidence.

The cry for an interpretation of the human drama is a cry not for technical history but for something more like 'prophecy'.   Those who complain of the aridity of technical history which strands itself in petty discussions about the date of a dispatch or the mechanical operation of a constitutional device, while evading the majestic issues that relate to man's larger destiny, are crying out for precisely the thing which the Biblical writers were doing with the human drama, and to the dignity of which the academic historian could not pretend to reach.

On the decisive question of the posture one should adopt towards life or the interpretation one would give to the whole human story, it would be unwise to surrender one's judgment to a scholar, any more than one would expect a scholar by reason of his technical accomplishments to be more skilled than other people in making love or choosing a wife.   Neither should one be guided in the great decision by the spirit of an age——for, concerning the spirit of any age, even technical history can find many disillusioning things to say.   Our final interpretation of history is the most sovereign decision we can take, and it is clear that every one of us, as standing alone in the universe, has to take it for himself.   It is our decision about religion, about our total attitude to things, and about the way we will appropriate life.   And it is inseparable from our decision about the role we are going to play ourselves in that very drama of history.

After these introductory remarks about history and historians, Butterfield deals with three major themes: 1. human nature in history, 2. judgment including cataclysm and tragic conflict in history, 3. providence and the historical process.

The Christian view of man is best stated paradoxically: man is made in the *image of God and* man is a *sinner*. Made in the image of God means that man enjoys the endowments of intelligence, value discrimination, and the freedom to be active and creative within the limits of his capacities. Apart from the limitations of his historical existence itself, man is free and active not passive and determined.

The vitality of man, his creation of empires, institutions, systems of law and social structures, his strength in the face of terrible odds, his courage in defending what he cherishes and attacking what he fears and deplores, his capacity for self-sacrifice, for suffering even unto death for what he believes or for those whom he loves, his soaring imaginative genius and his artistic expression usually in fealty to his dream of beauty, goodness, and truth—this huge vitality that man has demonstrated in history would appear from the historian's point of view to correspond to the Christian doctrine of the *Imago Dei*. Put more bluntly, the Islamic doctrine of man which pictures man as the puppet of Allah, as the passive pawn in the chess game of his God, or the Hindu view of human experience as the illusive or sportive play (*lila*) of Brahma, projecting, as it were, a shadow of his partial self upon the distorting screen of duality (the phenomenal world) cannot do justice to the fact of human nature in history—its vitality, its goodness and its evil. The historian is obliged to regard man as sentient, purposeful, vital, and creative.

> The kind of history which has developed in our civilization and was handed down to the 20th century has clustered around personalities, and we have tended to think of it as organizing itself into the form of narrative. It resurrects particular periods, reconstitutes particular episodes, follows the fortunes and discusses the decisions of individual people, and rejoices to recover the past in its concreteness and particularity. It does not limit its interests to the things that can be reduced to law and necessity——a project more feasible to those who direct their studies upon the materialistic side of human beings and human purpose. It is more interested in what is free, varied and unpredictable in the actions of individuals; and the higher realms of human activity—the art and the spiritual life of men are the essential substance, not a mere fringe to the story. The play of personality itself is not a mere ornament in any case—not a kind of cadenza or violin obligato —but is itself a factor in the fundamental structure of history. The historian does not regard personality as a mere 'thing,' to be studied as other external things ars studied. He does not deal with events as though they were things which could be mechanically and externally explained but as they come out of personalities and run into personalities; so that the insides of human beings are brought into the discussion—mind, and motive, hope and fear, passion and faith have to come into the question. The

story cannot be told correctly unless we see the personalities from the inside, feeling with them as an actor might feel the part he is playing—thinking their thoughts over again and sitting in the position not of the observer but the doer of the action.

Traditional historical writing emphasises the importance of sympathetic imagination for the purpose of getting inside human beings. We may even say that this is part of the science of history for it produces communicable results—the insight of one historian may be ratified by scholars in general, who then give currency to the interpretation that is produced.

(This attitude to history is particularly congenial to our Christian civilization with its high view of personality. It is particularly appropriate for the Christian who happens to be a historian.) It implies a telling of the story which has the effect of doing justice to freedom as well as necessity, and in which the spiritual (as well as the material) is organic to the theme—not a mere added ornament. It is typified in the flexibility of narrative, and is to be contrasted with the kind of history which sets out rather to schematise the centuries or turn everything into a process. The traditional historian has shown an interest in individuals for their own sake, and in a bygone generation as an end in itself, which we in our civilization have perhaps too easily taken for granted. It is possible that a grossly materialistic civilization, too intent upon utilitarian purposes, would not see the point of these things and would not produce the kind of fabric that we call history. The Christian must defend it however; for this is a kind of history in which—in a certain sense at least—personalities are the irreducible things. [The last three paragraphs are taken mainly from *History and Human Relations* (1951), by the same author.]

The sense of the all-importance of personality is ingredient in our civilization. It denies that the world of history is merely an extension of the world of nature, that man is merely the last of the animals, or that his story is mainly that of the development of the species as a whole, the individual himself having no significance in the end. The historian envisages a world of human relations standing over against nature, a universe in which every human being is a separate well of life, a separate source of action, and every human being, so far as mundane things are concerned, has his aspect as an end in himself....There is a new order superimposed on nature, and personalities are the crowning blossom of creation, though vast masses of blind matter may have to roll round for immeasurable astronomical years to make this possible.

But this does not mean that man is good. The Christian doctrine of man is that he is a sinner—that he is constantly tempted and constantly yielding to the temptation to pride and pretention that he is more than he is (that he is God), that he has the right, not only for himself but for others, to make absolute judgments of value and to enforce these judgments to the limit of his power. It is the Christian view of man as sinner that his basic sinfulness is not a function of his weakness (being prey to instinctive desires—sex, food, etc.) but rather a function of his strength: exercising his creativity, his intelligence, conscience, and will to the fullest extent of his powers not only as an image of God but in rebellion against God or in usurping the place of God. The worst face of man's sinfulness is his self-righteousness, his tendency to make his own notion of goodness so sacred that it is not open to criticism. So man makes idols of his notions of beauty, goodness and truth, and worships and serves these idols in place of God.

From the historian's point of view this concept of man accords best with the facts. Everyman, tested in history, seems to exhibit aspects of the demonic. No man is perfect and those who have claimed perfection beyond their fellows under the strong light of historical research may be charged with contributing more than others to the injustice, misery and coruption of their times.

A second paradox of the Christian understanding of man relates to man in society. Government (social structure) is a punishment for sin *and* a divinely ordained institution for the welfare of mankind.

If man were not a sinner he would not need government, and the irksome restraints of being subject to the will of others, and hence the customs and orders of society are a just punishment for his sinfulness. Augustin, and to an extent, Luther, even justified tyrannical and unjust government on the basis that it was deserved by sinful men, or that it was a constant reminder to man of his sinfulness.

On the other hand, government is regarded as a divinely ordained institution for the benefit of man. Again both sides of this paradox seem to be evidenced in history. All social institutions are imperfect. All governments are imperfect. Their imperfections are sources of injustice enforced upon individuals. Governments tend to be ends in themselves rather than simply means toward an end. The injustice embedded in institutions is persistent. Individuals win through to new and higher concepts of justice long before institutions. Society as a whole tends to perpetuate its wrongs—sometimes in the name of right. These observations led an American theologian, Rheinhold Niebuhr, to write a book entitled: *Moral Man and Immoral Society*. Many citizens are far in advance of their governments and frequently governmental reform lags behind even a majority opinion.

But there is another side to this problem. Government is for the

most part a resolution of the selfish interests of the various elements
of the society over which it rules. In resolving conflicting selfish
interests, simply for the sake of order and peace within the country,
government serves as an instrument for cancelling out forces of cupidity
which might otherwise be ruinous to everyone. So-called advances
in social and economic justice are frequently simply the result of the
most practical resolution by government of various selfish pressures,
none of which had in itself a good purpose.

(Having begun with a high estimate of personality, the historian proceeds
to a lower view of human nature than the one current in the 19th and
20th centuries. Lord Acton said that all great men were bad men and that
hardly any public reputation survived the exposure of private archives.
He could well have said that *all* men are sinners. As he pointed out,
much evil in history is the result of sin, not mistakes. More often than
people generally recognize it is true that a moral element—pride or wilfulness
or a tendency to wishful thinking, for example, enters into the constitution
of even our intellectual mistakes.

Some of us have become so accustomed to a humane form of society
that we imagine its virtues to spring straight out of nature with no more
cultivation than the wild flowers on the bank of a stream.) [The virtues of
modern society are in reality the product of] much education, tradition and
discipline; they needed centuries of patient cultivation. (Certain subtle
safeguards in society keep the surface of life comparatively respectable;
down below there slumbers all the time the volcano that lies in human
nature, and an unexpected cataclysm may bring it into activity. In normal
times these safeguards work so quietly that the superficial observer may
miss them altogether. These are the things that differentiate between
civilization and barbarism; they are the different conditions for the same
human nature. If these safeguards were to be removed many men who
had been respectable all their lives would be transformed by the discovery
of the things which they could now do with impunity. The weak ones
would take to crimes for which they had lacked the courage before. The
strong ones, with no check on their power, would proceed on large scale
exploitation. The seamy side of men is exposed by such events as a great
and prolonged police-strike, a continuing revolutionary situation in a nation,
and the exhilaration of conquest in an enemy country. The atrocities of
Nazi barbarism in the last war on such a wide scale were not so much of
a proof of German wickednss but rather a good indication of what human
nature basically is like all along. Only the conditions were slightly altered.)

Society caters for human cupidity in all of us and secures its ends by
making a skilful use of human nature, so that when all things are nicely
balanced men may be doing their duty without realising that their self-
interest has come into the matter at all—they may hardly be conscious of

the neat dove-tailing of public service and private interests.

Nobody may pretend that there has been an elimination of the selfishness in human nature, and the self-centredness of man. And nobody may pretend that egotism is a thing which belongs, for example, to social classes as such rather than to human beings. If we eliminated the conflict between horizontal layers in society—if we got rid of that 'class-conflict,' which has certainly been a great feature of human history—there would still be room for vertical conflicts, cut-throat battles between coal-miners, railwaymen and teachers, each thinking that they have a right to a higher share in the total sum of benefits which are open for distribution in a given society.

(Since sin is always present, history is not a black-and-white affair.) Nothing more completely locks the human race in some of its bewildering dilemmas and predicaments than to range history into a fight of good men, pure and righteous, against the diabolically wicked, instead of seeing initially that human nature—including oneself—is imperfect generally. In reality events tie themselves into knots because of the general cupidity; situations becoming more frantic and deadlocks more hopeless because of man's universal presumption and self-righteousness; and some men may even be goaded to greater wickedness by the exasperating conduct of the stiff-necked.

(There is a tragic element in the wars and struggles of mankind, which would obviously not have occurred if all men had been perfect saints or had been competing with one another in self-sacrifice.) Yet—as in the great struggles between Protestant and Catholic in the 16th century—it has often happened that both of the parties carrying on the warfare have devoutly felt themselves to be in the right. It is even true that many of the inhuman conflicts of mankind would probably never have taken place if the situation had been one of completely righteous men confronted by undiluted and unmitigated crime. One can hardly fail to recognise the element of tragedy in many conflicts which take place between one half-right that is perhaps too wilful, and another half-right that is perhaps too proud. It is even possible that great wars should come about because idealists are too egotistical concerning their own plans of salvation for mankind, and because the righteous are stiff-necked.

(It seems to me at this point even in the realm of observable historical happenings the historian must join hands with the theologian.) The truth of the fact becomes patent when conflicts are bitter and times are desperate. In the kind of world that I see in history there is one sin that locks people up in all their other sins, and fastens men and nations more tightly than ever in their predicaments—and that is—the sin of self-righteousness.

(I cannot say that in history statesmanship works differently with a Christian in power. Neither can I say that the clergy has always been right—in modern times the unbeliever has sometimes fought against the churchman for a higher ethical objective, the one that most corresponds with the deeper influences of Christianity.) In one fundamental sense, however, it seems to me that Christianity alone attacks the seat of evil in the kind of world we have been considering, and has a solvent for the intellectual predicaments which arise in such a world. It addresses itself precisely to that crust of self-righteousness which, by the nature of its teaching, it has to dissolve before it can do anything else with a man.

The more human beings are lacking in imagination, the more incapable men are of any profound kind of self-analysis, the more we shall find that their self-righteousness hardens, so that it is just the thick-skinned who are more sure of being right than anybody else. And though conflict might still be inevitable in history even if this particular evil did not exist, there can be no doubt that its presence multiplies the deadlocks and gravely deepens all the tragedies of all the centuries. At its worst it brings us to that mythical messianic hoax of the 20th century which comes perilously near to the thesis: 'Just one little war more against the last remaining enemies of righteousness, and then the world will be cleansed, and we can start building Paradise.'

One's picture of history will be seriously distorted if his programmes and philosophies begin by assuming a world of normally wise and righteous men. What I have described in history is very different. It amounts to an historical equivalent—I think it is a valid equivalent—to the usual theological assertion that all men are sinners, and I am saying that this is the way we must look at human nature in history.

It is necessary for me to emphasise the fact that what I have been outlining in this lecture is not merely a Christian idea—it is not dependent on the truth of any super-natural religion. We are concerned for the moment not with theology but rather with anthropology, with our ordinary doctrine concerning man; and the view that is here presented is supported by non-religious as well as by religious thought. It means that we ought to consider very carefully our doctrine on the subject of human beings as such in the first place; and it is a mistake for writers of history and other teachers to imagine that if they are not Christians they are refraining from committing themselves, or working without any doctrine at all, discussing history without any presuppositons. Amongst historians, as in other fields, the blindest of all the blind are those who are unable to examine their own presuppositions, and blithely imagine therefore that they do not possess any. It must be emphasised that we create tragedy after tragedy for ourselves by a lazy unexamined doctrine of man which is current amongst us and which the study of history does not support. And now, as in Old Testament days, there are false prophets who flourish by flattering and bribing human nature, telling it to be comfortable about itself in general, and playing up to its self-righteousness in times of crisis.

It is essential not to have faith in human nature. Such faith is a recent heresy and a very disastrous one.

JUDGMENT IN HISTORY——CATACLYSM AND TRAGIC CONFLICT

The lives of men and nations seem in a large measure to work themselves out according to an intricate and sometimes delicate and elastic process of checks and balances. Man as an individual and as a member of a society both as dreamer and as sinner seems by this system of checks and balances to be gently pushed and tenderly pulled toward the kinds of solutions to his problems that are at any given time nearly satisfactory to the majority of individuals involved.

There are, however, not infrequently in history occasions when either the process seems to go haywire, when some cog slips and the spring recoils with great violence or when some definitely demonic element seems for a time to hold sway. Butterfield illustrates this building up of insensitive, coercive force with his account of the Prussian militaristic regime which he traces back to the comparatively gracious court of Frederick the Great and the relatively acceptable aggressiveness of Bismarck. Only sometimes is the judgment of God upon the great pretentions of men so swift that it is unmistakable. Napoleon's meteoric career is a striking example. But the judgment upon German militarism waited for a hundred years.

The Christian view of divine judgment is one of waiting, sometimes patiently and sometimes anxiously. The more profound and realistic Hebrew and Christian thinkers have not been so naive as to suppose that there is a one-to-one correlation between wrong doing and the sure judgment of God—at least not within a single generation. One of the prophets observed that while it was the fathers who ate the sour grapes, it was the children's teeth that were set on edge.

> Precisely because all men are sinners and precisely because the rest of the truth about the matter cannot be disentangled short of the Judgment Day, the vindication of the moral element in history neither requires nor permits the separation of the righteous from the evil men by the technical historian. Precisely because the issue is so important and precisely because life is a moral matter every inch of the way (while no historian can keep his ethical vigilance continuous or trouble to be making moral judgments absolutely all the time)—precisely for these reasons the occasional dip into moral judgments is utterly inadequate to the end it purports to serve. (For one thing, the historian is apt to select unconsciously the moments when it is fit to raise the moral issue. His selection is apt to be determined by his own political bias. History thus becomes polemical. Further

pursuit of it leads to propaganda. The historian then assumes the solemn role of moral arbiter as history is staged into an epic of the righteous against the unrighteous. To ask for moral judgment in history is to tempt the historian to a dangerous form of self-aggrandisement. The role of academic history is a much more humble one.)

It is not often remembered that there is such a thing as a sheer historian's zeal, a passion for the past which does not subordinate itself to militant causes. Besides the ardour for the Whig or Tory or Socialist programme, there can be another kind of flame which is simply a compassion for human beings. Historians who pursue questions belonging to this order of thought may make discoveries that are equally valid for opposing parties; they may reach something of that deeper kind of truth which embraces and helps to explain even the antitheses. Such historians are drawing together again the torn fabric of historic life, and healing the wounds of mankind and deepening our insight into human destiny. We are right if we wish to see human history in moral terms, but we are running to myth if we mount the story on the pattern of the conventional war for righteousness.

In view of the universal sinfulness of man, righteous indignation itself tends to corrupt those who have it and it does not improve those to whom it is directed. It is actually a demand for an illegitimate form of power—the power to sit in judgment and condemn one's fellowmen, as though they are worse men than oneself. It is true that we must punish crimes, however direct or certain their moral implications are (they are as a rule never so direct and certain as most self-righteous citizens think). But they are punished on the grounds of a legal verdict which in no case may be expanded into a final judgment on personality. Only God holds that authority, not human beings.

Some passages of history seem, at least in retrospect, to have offered to the nations in question some clear chance to make amends for past sins and to seek new directions. This certainly is the experience of individuals. Each of us has the sure sense that he has 'not been dealt with after his sins nor rewarded according to his iniquities.' I, personally, am not sure that Butterfield is justified in dealing with German militarism as a separate instance of national arrogance apart from the whole complexion of European history in the Nineteenth and Twentieth Centuries. I would be inclined to see the two world wars, and the broken waters beneath their great falls, as part of a dynamic reorganization of Western Civilization involving drastically changing social structures and increasing demands of interdependence among nations. While Germany was attempting to control by expansion its markets in Europe, upsetting English diplomacy in its strategy of balance of power on the continent,

Great Britain was herself attempting to control, with no less show of coercion and pretention, the markets of the Far East. America had its own vast land to exploit and was hence not so fatally exposed to empire fever. It would seem to me that the industrial revolution, fostering intense urban devvlopment and opening the way for a disorganization of mores, traditions and even social structures, while it forced a new interdependence of nations both in terms of sources of raw materials and markets for industrial output, presented European nations with a demand for a re-conception of nationalism and internationalism for which they were not prepared. The solution to this immense problem is not yet in sight. Further, since the middle of the Nineteenth Century the Western World has been obliged to face a radical development in scientific knowledge, which, while it tended to weaken older beliefs, had not yet developed any controlling motif. Our own time is part of a tumultuous and challenging age of which the past century and a half constituted the first movement.

If the study of history, according to the Christistian doctrine of sin, does not allow us to condemn our fellowmen, neither does it permit us to put our final trust in any human institution or system, for both are acts of pride, or a covert expression of self-righteousness, which is *the* original sin of man according to traditional Christian theology. This is another way of stating that morality itself is part of the structure of history, a thing as real and as drastic in its operation as the material strength of principalities and powers. The judgment that is visited upon nations and empires and all human systems is not an arbitrary declaration of the historian but rather inherent in the process of history itself. The historian can clearly observe this in operation in, say, the case of Prussian militarism.

The moral judgments that lie in the very nature of history are often long-term affairs, so that one gets the impression that the sins of the fathers are visited on the children to the third and fourth generation: though on further analysis we may have to recognize that the later generations suffered rather for allowing the sins to go on uncorrected. In the case of Prussia the time-period was undoubtedly extended as a result of the prudence or the virtue of Frederick the Great and Bismarck themselves; for instead of becoming Napoleons they provided perhaps the two most remarkable examples in modern history of men who called a halt to careers of conquest, precisely because they had a curious awareness of the importance of the moral element in history. They so realized the danger of nemesis that for long decades in the latter part of their lives they stood out as conservative statesmen, not only pacific themselves but anxious to see that nobody else in Europe should disturb the peace. Nevertheless judgment came to Prussian militarism in our century (whether we say in 1918, 1933, or 1945), which could have been avoided if it was not in excess. It was a judgment that fell not on Frederick the Great and Bismarck personally but on the Hohenzollerns as a dynasty and on the Germans as a people. On the other hand, in the case of ancient Rome and the Norman Conquest of England it is shown that judgment is not inevitable upon all conquerors. Heaven often gives men a chance to redeem the effects even of their own violence and to turn the evil they have done into later good.

(It is easy to see the downfall of others as the result of moral retribution. But the same observation may be made concerning ourselves.) We are hoaxing ourselves if we think that because judgment came upon Germany through the victory of our arms, we—being the instruments of God in this matter—may count ourselves as having qualified for virtue; or as having even found special favour in His sight. If such an argument were valid, God must have a great and unusual favour for Communism, which besides being the chief beneficiary in two world wars, could outbid us in the claim to have been the most terrible instrument of Divine judgment in our generation. But the truth is that a God who could use even the Philistines in order to chastise His chosen people may similarly use us for the purpose of chastening Germany, while still reserving for us a terrible judgment later. It is not too much to say that if Germany is under judgment so are all of us. If once we admit that the moral factor operates in this way in history at all, then we today must feel ourselves to be living in one of those remarkable periods when judgment stalks generally through the world, and it becomes a question whether the orders and systems to which we have been long attached can survive the day of reckoning....Some advantage is achieved if men can be persuaded at least to think of their disasters as a judgment of God and make them the occasion for a deeper kind of self-questioning.

We can hardly avoid the conclusion that moral defects have something to do with the catastrophes that take place. The processes of time have a curious way of bringing out the faultiness that is concealed in a system which at first seems to be satisfactory....Whether we think of the Greek city-state or the Roman Empire or the medieval idea of the Church's relation to society; whether we have in mind the cultural system of the modern humanist, or the ideals of secular liberalism or the principle of the nation-state—all these have a way of turning sour with the lapse of time, and when they come to an end it is not the case that they are merely unfortunate. In the realm of the relatively good we may admit that all of these things were good in their beginning and that for a period they had a valid claim upon human loyalty....The men who have lived under one or other of these various systems have even come to regard their own order as the best that could be imagined, and have felt—that, if that particular organization of the world collapsed, there would be nothing left to make life worth living either in their own day or in all the future. Yet the river of time is littered with the ruins of these various systems, and we can hardly understand why those who lived under them should have even wished them to go on forever or valued them so much.

Judgment comes upon these orders and systems; and what is judged, of course, is not this man or that but the system as a whole. Or rather we may say that, though it is the system that perishes, it is not quite the system as such which has come under condemnation—for all the ones which I have mentioned are virtuous enough in themselves, virtuous enough if we only consider them in the abstract. At bottom it is an inadequacy in human nature itself which comes under judgment; for in the course of time it is human nature which finds out the holes in the structure, and turns the good thing into an abuse.

That this form of judgment exists in history is a thing which I believe can hardly be denied, though it is important to note that its verdict is an interim affair and not a final judgment on anything. What many would deny of course is the view that this form of judgment is a judgment of God. It is embedded in the very constitution of the universe, but those who do not believe in Christianity will hardly admit that it is there by any providential and purposeful ordination.

In general, Butterfield's chapter on judgment in history is consonant with the formula with which Amos introduces his oracle against Israel: 'For three transgressions...yea for four (more).' The point here is that God's judgment is not arbitrary nor does it follow wrong as the night and day—for three, yea and for four, (seven altogether) means that in each instance the judgment of God came only after repeated wrongs, persistent arrogance. The second point here is that all nations were involved (Ammonites, Edomites, Moabites, Philistines, Syrians, Phoenicians) both the great nations and the small ones. The prophet's own people were involved in transgression, both Judah and Israel. Finally, in each instance the punishment came through the aggression of a nation which was in no way more righteous than the nation it defeated.

A second contribution to our understanding of judgment in history is the caution of the *Book of Jonah*. The spokesmen of 'the right side' are frequently impatient to see God's judgment executed against their enemies. That God is not so eager to destroy as is man would appear to be true, both from the Bible and from the historian's notebook. Perhaps from God's vantage point the 'right side' and the 'wrong side' are not so easily distinguished.

The conclusion of the matter would appear to be this: history leaves little room to believe that demonic expressions of power, arrogance, greed and brutality are foundations upon which stable, happy and prosperous nations can be built. The meteoric rise and fall of such nations seems almost to suggest that they served only a limited and tragic purpose in the large history of mankind. They were rods picked up to chasten other evil doers and then broken themselves as a parent might break a switch after whipping a child.

But history does not, nor does the Bible, present any clear case for believing that the 'wicked' will always be punished when and as the 'righteous' would dictate. History is too dynamic, and human freedom too much a part of it; and any one historical event is far too complex to permit any sober person to believe that the righteous in his judgment will be rewarded and the wicked in his judgment will be punished. Indeed, the Christian faith would strongly suggest that punishment is not a purpose of God anymore than it is a purpose of a good parent. Nor should we believe that happiness in terms of prosperity, peace and progress is the assured reward of goodness.

The notion that there is a judgment of God involved in the very processes of history is older than Christianity. It is a product of the Hebrew prophetic view of history. It sprang from a reflection on national cataclysm, a wrestling with destiny and tragic history at its worst, and we can appreciate it better if we realize that their history was fundamentally of the same texture as our own, characterized by tragic conflict. 'The day of the Lord,' announced Amos the prophet, was not one of triumph and exultation for the nation but a dark, terrible day of reckoning. The modern world has been in a similar position, imagining itself on the very threshold of utopia, of progress and prosperity, and then suddenly awaking to the fact that it was really on the edge of an abyss. The Hebrew people had a very short period of political independence and were engulfed in the conflicts between the vast empires in their neighbourhood. And yet by virtue of inner resources and unparalleled leadership, they turned their tragedy, their very helplessness in the international struggle for power, into one of the half-dozen creative moments in world history. By the sheer grimness of suffering men are sometimes brought into a profounder understanding of human destiny.

The problem that the Hebrew nation faced was the meaning and purpose of national disaster. Why should it happen to them, the chosen people of God? The first answer, given by Amos and those who followed him, was that national catastrophe was the personal wrath of God, His judgment on men's sin, on social evils current at the time. This was to vindicate the moral character of history and God's righteousness itself, which tolerates no evil. Thus every threat of destruction raised the question 'What are the sins of Israel?' and became an occasion for repentance, a test of character and an inner discipline. From the prophetic point of view God's judgment falls heaviest upon those who put their trust in man-made systems and worship the work of their own hands, or those who say that the strength of their own right arm gives them victory. Hebrew historiography was unique in that it ascribed the successes of Israel not to virtue but to the favour of God—God elected them not on account of their superiority to other people. Instead of narrating the glories or demonstrating the righteousness of the nation, like our own patriotic histories, it denounced the infidelity of the people as a constant feature of their history, even to the extent of saying that the sins of Israel were worse, their hearts more hardened, than those of other nations around them. So it was that other nations were instruments of God's judgment on Israel.

Cataclysm and tragic conflict in history may be not so much the judgment of God as occasions for profound experience which only the righteous can appropriate. This is the genius of the Old Testament prophetic movement. Israel was battered 'by the shocks of doom into shape and use'—into a deeper understanding of destiny and a purer notion of faith. From a naive and somewhat sanguine notion of 'a God mighty in battle' and of the man of God as a dauntless and sometimes merciless soldier (e.g. the champions of Israel in the *Book of Judges*) they were led to the notion of a law-abiding, just and peaceful people, hospitable to the stranger and tender-hearted to the poor (*Deuteronomy*) and hence were led to put their hope (when the nation as a whole failed to live up to this ideal) in a righteous remnant which, by persuasion of its goodness rather than coercion by its power, would win the nation as a whole to deeper loyalty than mere patriotism and a higher sense of God's favour than mere prosperity. Finally, cataclysm and tragic conflict provided the occasion for divining that the destiny of Israel was that of a suffering servant of its Lord, willingly subject to injustice, yet by its purity able to bear and somehow to redeem the wrongs of the nations round about.

This leads to another paradox in the understanding of history: 1. justice emerges as the resolution of largely selfish pressures. 2. Insight into higher concepts of justice is bought at the price of sacrificial dedication—vicarious suffering.

Men are forced into practical concessions to justice for the sake of their own selfish ends, but they come to an intentional commitment to justice sometimes only by the glimpses of goodness presented to them by suffering saints. The pull of purpose supplies comprehension and commitment to that which grudgingly emerges from the push of progress. Aeschylus, the first great Greek dramatist, came close to this. Intentional sacrifical suffering undertaken in purity and charity he did not reach, but know did he the uses of adversity:

God, whose law it is that he who learns must suffer,
And even in our sleep, pain that cannot forget, falls, drop by
    drop, upon the heart,
And in our own despite, against our will,
Comes wisdom to us by the awful grace of God.

Israel suffered for all mankind—so that when the Gentiles should hear of it and realize it themselves, even that knowledge alone would move them and exert a redeeming influence upon them—the very spectacle would move the nations to penitence. And behind the whole argument is the assumption that if Israel as a nation could realize that this was her role in the world, she would become reconciled to her suffering and see some meaning in it, and would no longer cry out against God or complain against the apparent injustice of it.

The picture of the Suffering Servant, unlike the more superficial political messianism of the ancient Jews, takes in the tragedy as it actually exists and embraces it with both arms. The writer does not complain now that the catastrophe of the nation is against the rules, but accepts it as part of the game, recognising that it has its place in the scheme of things. He even goes further and induces us to see that, far from being meaningless, it provides the nearest thing to a clue for those who wish to make anything out of the human drama. And that dim clue, even if we only take it at the ordinary human level, is left, like all important things in life, for each person to follow up in his own way.

Nobody can pretend to see the meaning of this human drama as a god might see it, any more than one could hope to foresee the future—what one acquires is a vision for working purposes in the world, and one gains it by adopting an attitude, assuming a certain role within the drama itself....Ultimately our interpretation of the whole human drama depends on an intimately personal decision concerning the part that we mean to play in it. It is as though we were to say to ourselves: 'There is dissonance in the universe, but if I strike the right note it becomes harmony and reconciliation—and though they may kill me for it they cannot spoil that harmony.'

And here is where the thought of the ancient Jews goes one note higher than the top of the piano, so to speak, and meditation upon history drives on into ultra-historical realms—the interpretation of human drama is thrown back into the intimate recesses of our personal experience. Here is also the place where the Old Testament most gives the impression that it is trying to break into the New. It has often been pointed out that you cannot moralize history or achieve a reconciliation with it except by some development of a doctrine of vicarious suffering. ..Though it might be a remarkable thing to find an example of the Suffering Servant existing in its absolute purity—though there may have been only one perfect fulfilment of it in history—it is impossible to deny this picture its place as the pattern or the working-model of ideas which do in fact operate throughout the ages, helping to reconcile man with his destiny. (Vicarious suffering, especially the idea of one man taking on himself the sins of others, implies the solidarity of the human race not on the level of the herd but by a principle of love and even by a heightened conception of personality. In a world of tragic conflict, by taking the judgment and the suffering into oneself man can measure the heights and depths of love and reach the finer music of life. Because there is tragedy in history love itself is brought to burn with an intenser flame in human experience. This is how, in the Christian conception of man, life may be in the end redeemed, and good brought out of evil.)

PROVIDENCE AND THE HISTORICAL PROCESS

Neither the historian nor the Christian will regard providence (the working of God in history) as the hand of the puppeteer who pulls strings from above so that the figures on the stage seem to move their heads and hands and feet. The Christian view of providence is that of a structure of purpose within the historical process which creates new alternatives at every turn of human choice and action. Providence indeed may be said to be a force within history which constantly re-creates freedom when men by their own folly tie themselves up into knots from which they could not themselves get out.

The emphasis in Christian theology is upon the immanence of God. He is not the big boss who lives upstairs in a second story universe and runs things from up there. He is a persuasive and pervasive working within the process (nature, history, and personality), gently structuring what would otherwise be brute and chaotic force, channelling it into constructive and creative occasions. There is a sense in which God is transcendent. He is not one being among other beings. He is the ground, the condition, of all being. In a sense God is so transcendent that properly speaking we cannot say that God exists. If he existed, he would be just one thing among other things—perhaps the biggest and the best. But he does not exist as beings exist. He is not a being. He is the ground of being, the condition of being, the very structure productive of 'all being. He is not a person but he is the condition and ground and source of all personality. Yet to us his working in history is most closely analogous to the working of a person. That is to say, his working is not mechanical, not like a machine that grinds on forever doing the same thing in the same way. Butterfield uses the happy analogy of a composer who writes the score even as it is being played—transmuting dissonance into melody, modulating from one key to another while preserving and enriching the theme.

(The pattern of history-making, however, is not the product of anybody's will but the product of many actions and purposes.) [Much of this process] goes on, so to speak, over our heads, now deflecting the results of our actions, now taking our purposes out of our hands, and now turning our endeavours to ends not realized. Indeed one may be carried to such depths in one's analysis of this, that, however many things the historian may say about the processes of time, he can never feel that he has uttered the last word on the subject—never feel that by the technique of his particular science he has really got to the truth that lies at the bottom of the well.

We might say that this human story is like a piece of orchestral music that we are playing over for the first time. In our presumption we may act as though we were the composer of the piece or try to bring out our own particular part as the leading one. But in reality I personally only see the part of, shall we say, the second clarinet, and of course even within the limits of that I never know what is coming after the page that now lies open before me. None of us can know what the whole score amounts to except as far as we have already played it over together, and even so the meaning of the passage may not be clear all at once—just as the events of 1914 only begin to be seen in perspective in the 1940's. If I am sure that B flat is the next note that I have to play I can never feel certain that it will not come with surprising implications until I have heard what the other people are going to play at the same moment. And no single person in the orchestra can have any idea when or where this piece of music is going to end.

Even this analogy is not sufficiently flexible to do justice to the processes of time; and to make the comparison more authentic we must imagine that the composer himself is only composing the music inch by inch as the orchestra is playing it; so that if you and I play wrong notes he changes his mind and gives a different turn to the bars that come immediately afterwards, as though saying to himself: 'We can only straighten out this piece of untidiness if we pass for a moment from the major into the minor key.' Indeed the composer of the piece leaves himself room for great elasticity, until we ourselves have shown what we are going to do next; although when the music has actually been played over and has become a thing of the past we may be tempted to imagine that it is just as he had intended it to be all the time—that the whole course of things had been inevitable from the first.

Here the modern historian is in agreement with the new science. The older view of the divine providence which was described under the category of natural law (a klnd of inexorable working out of a pre-arranged course) was in keeping with the mechanistic notions of the older physics. The new physics uses such phrases as 'the principle of indeterminacy,' 'emergence of novelty,' and 'open ended universe.' God as the structure of creativity, the ground of freedom, and the source of novelty is one side of Divine Providence. This is the aspect of God which Alfred North Whitehead describes as his 'Primordial Nature.'

Butterfield speaks of another aspect of Providence—a working within history of 'something like the collective wisdom of the human race.' Another way of getting at this force in history is by reference to the preservation of experience—the handing on of accumulated wisdom (See the book of *Malachi*). Whitehead refers to this as the 'Consequent Nature of God.' He can speak of God as preserving in himself and hence, to a degree being modified by, all that has been actualized in the universe, and providing new ways of making this available at new junctures of human experience.

(If there is progress in history it is the work of Providence.) For men did not just decide that history should move—so far as concerns certain particular matters—either as an ascending ladder or as a spiral staircase or as though it were a growing plant. They did not say to themselves: 'Now we will establish progress.' On the contrary they looked back and discovered to their amazement that here was a thing called progress which had already been taking place—in other words they arrived at the idea by post-rationalization. Millions of men in a given century, conscious of nothing save going about their own business, have together woven a fabric better in many respects than any of them knew. And sometimes it has only been their successors who have recognized that the resulting picture had a pattern, and that that particular period of history was characterized by an overarching theme—Here is one of the bases of a kind of progress which comes from no merit of ours and implies no necessary improvement in our essential personalities, but is part of the system of things, part of the providential order. (There is progress in the development towards larger organizations—from the city-state and inter-municipal trade, to the nation-state and international trade, and finally to our vast imperial systems and a world economy.) In these cases men have cupidities and, as we see them in history, they are engrossed in the task of pushing their private business on. But they are agents of deeper processes than those of which they are aware, instruments of a providence that combines their labours and works them into a larger pattern. Whenever we see anything like an evolutionary development we should be wrong to imagine that this takes place because an individual has consciously tried to give that particular turn to the future history of the species.

But, as we have seen, Providence does not guarantee progress——does not promise an ascending course no matter how human beings behave for there is also in the dispensation of Providence a judgment which falls on our orders and systems. In any case there are regions where such progress cannot be regarded as having effective play. In those cases where the most intimate parts of human wisdom and experience are concerned, each generation, each individual, has to start, in a certain sense, at the beginning again. [These instances demand that we look upon each generation as, so to speak, an end in itself, a world of people existing in their own right], equidistant from eternity.

(There is then another meaning of Providence which has to do with what we might call the collective wisdom of the human race.) It is as though, once the history has happened, with all its accidents and tragedies, it is further worked upon by the reflecting activity of an ordaining and reconciling mind; or as though, once a handful of chance notes have been struck together on the piano, some person refuses to let the matter lie there and sets out to resolve the discord. This is a providence, in fact, which moves over history with the function of creating good out of evil. (The Fire of London, for example, made it possible to rebuild the city on a superior plan, when its dwellers got over grieving for their losses. The loss of the American colonies in the reign of George III was a mistake but without it there would not have been a United States of America. In many similar ways the disasters of a given generation may be somewhat redeemed when another by an after-reflection profits by it.)

(All this is merely an analysis of the way in which history happens and should hold true for Christian or non-Christian alike.) Even this limited view of the Providence that lies in the very structure of history, however, ought to affect our conception of human action and of the role of human beings in the world; and even at this mundane level we reach a stage higher in human consciousness and we improve our relations with the universe if we conceive ourselves not as sovereign makers of history but as born to co-operate with Providence. It is useless to say that you will achieve a particular purpose in the world or impose a certain condition of things in the course of your lifetime. You may succeed in committing this or that action, but you are working on material which is alive and which may rebel against you, and there is a Providence which complicates the effects of your action. It is this Providence which in fact has the last word to say about the results.

All of these essays in Butterfield point to a flexibility in the patterns of history and the need of a flexible and open minded interpretation of events. Butterfield is disposed to reject iron clad categories of the good and the bad, the righteous and the wicked. Rather he suggests that if there be sheep and goats to be identified by the historian, he would be inclined to use the simple criterion of those who have exhibited in their lives a childlike quality as over against those who have insisted upon inflexible notions—absolutes in politics, ethics and religion.

If history is of the texture which I have described, then men can calculate the immediate consequences of their actions. and they are heavily responsible for those consequences. But their remoter consequences, and the effect on the distant future, are matters which always lie in other hands. The hardest strokes of heaven fall in history upon those who imagine that they can control things in a sovereign manner, as though they were kings of the earth, playing Providence not only for themselves but for the far future—reaching out into the future with the wrong kind of far-sightedness, and gambling on a lot of risky calculations in which there must never be a single mistake.   And it is a defect in such enthusiasts that they seem unwilling to leave anything to Providence, unwilling even to leave the future flexible, as one must do....It is agreeable to all the processes of history, therefore, that each one of us should rather do the good that is straight under our noses. We cannot postpone living the good life until the world is better. Nor can we put aside all the arts until the great victory is won. If men in the past had taken that attitude there would never have been a civilization. The only good that man ever has is attained 'now' or never.

(The subtlety and delicacy of the texture of history forbids us to look upon it as a closed and interlocking system.) When we look back upon the past we see things fixed and frozen as they happened, and they become rigid in our minds, so that we think they must always have been inevitable —we hardly imagine how anything else could have happened. But when we look to the future, while it is still fluid, we can hardly fail to realize its unspeakable liquidity. (No overall pattern in the interpretation of the course of history is adequate because it is bound to be too inflexible. Instead of searching for this or that pattern, it is better to rely on personal symbols, after the analogy of human intelligence, unpredictable and full of surprises. History is like the work of a person in that its course is both free and open and at the same morally reliable. Is is as though an intelligence were moving over the story, taking its bearings afresh after everything men do, and making its decisions as it goes along—decisions sometimes unpredictable and carrying our purposes further than we wanted them to go, or changing its course in order to make the best of everything —as in the picture of the composer presented before.)

(To a religious mind all this work of Providence and is divine and it is the ordering of God Himself in the course of men. In the workings of history the believer sees the movement of a living God.) Perhaps a better picture of our situation would be that of a child who played her piece very badly when she was alone, but when the music-teacher sat at her side played it passably well, though the music-teacher never touched her, never said anything, but operated by pure sympathetic attraction and by just being there. Perhaps history is a thing that would stop happening if God held His breath, or could be imagined as turning away to think of something else. (We cannot demand too great a security for the future; neither can we believe that divine Providence is going to cease its care for the world whatever the next turn may be.)

I do not think that any man can ever arrive at his interpretation of the human drama by merely casting his eye over the course of the centuries in the way a student of history might do. I am unable to see how a man can find the hand of God in secular history, unless he has first found that he has an assurance of it in his personal experience. If it is objected that God is revealed in history through Christ, I cannot think that this can be true for the merely external observer, who puts on the thinking-cap of the ordinary historical student. It only becomes effective for those who have carried the narrative to intimate regions inside themselves, where certain of the issues are brought home to human beings. In this sense our interpretation of the human drama throughout the ages rests finally on our interpretation of our most private experiences of life, and stands as merely an extension to it. At the same time I am not sure that any part of history has been properly appropriated until we have brought it home to ourselves in the same intimate way, so that it has been knit into one fabric continuous with our inner experience.

The epilogue ('Christianity as a Historical Religion' and 'History, Religion and the Present Day') deals with the special problem of the historicity of those events upon which the Christian religion is founded— the life, death and resurrection of the Christ. Christianity has for the most part been content to rest its assurance of salvation upon the saving act in history of the man, Christ Jesus. Does this mean that Christianity can be proved or disproved by the historian? The answer is no—in part because of the nature of history itself.

Even in the earliest Church, during the time that the New Testament was being written, there was a conscious distinction between the 'Christ known after the flesh,' and the 'Christ known after the Spirit.' This is the distinction between the Jesus of History and the Christ of Faith. Every event is made up of two elements: 1. fact and 2. reception. An historical event is the impact of something that happened upon someone. The fact was the Jesus of history—the man who lived and died in Palestine almost 2000 years ago. His impact upon his disciples— their reception of him as the Christ, as The Saviour known after the Spirit, i.e. 'The Christ of Faith.'

We cannot recover the Jesus of history. We cannot know what

words he actually said or what deeds he actually did. Almost a whole
century of scholarship was devoted to that task before it became
apparent that it is not within the power of the historian to discover
what actually happened. Indeed, this historical study of the Bible led
to a new concept of history in our century. Most historians today,
because of this, would regard von Ranke as naive and his optimism
about writing presuppositionless history as unrealistic. As Professor
Oakeshott has put it: 'Historical truth is not what really happened but
what the evidence obliges the historian to believe.' Or as Toynbee
has written: 'The proper categories of historical explanation are not
those of cause and effect but of challenge and response.' Event is fact
plus meaning or fact represented in terms of its meaning.

Therefore the irreducible element of the stuff of history is not some
hard little nugget of clearly proveable fact It is occurrence *and*
meaning. History is thus a far more subtle search for truth than the
Nineteenth Century could have understood. It is the historian and the
man of faith—or rather the historian as the man of faith—who can give
us the best answers. This does not mean that either the historian or
we who read his history ought to develop a large and easy swallow so
that we can ingest whole chunks of incredible things. It does mean
that God's work in history is far more complex and comprehensive
than the Nineteenth Century could understand. It means that he is
involved both in the fact and in the reception of the fact: in the word
spoken and in the moment of hearing and understanding. It means
that the real issue for the historian is not the Jesus of history but
rather the Christ of Faith. That is the phenomenon with which he
has to deal. His task is then to tell us as precisely and as vividly as
he can what it meant to be a believer in the Early Church, what it
meant 'to live in Christ' and to be 'in the Spirit of Christ,' what it
meant to recall in the preaching of the Gospel and in the liturgy of
the Eucharist the sign of the cross and the symbol of the resurrection.

Butterfield's closing remarks are a comment upon the force of
Christianity in history. He suggests that, true to his own observations
and to the Christian view of human nature which includes ecclesiastical
human nature (a variety that may be even worse than the ordinary
kind), one should not look to find the power of Christianity in terms
of a pure and righteous religious institution (The Church) battling the
world for the sake of social justice, charity or even tolerance. Those
gains have come mostly through secular pressures and often despite
the opposition of the Church. The force of Christianity is rather to

be sought in the silent, unobtrusive working within the minds and hearts of men and women who hear from time to time the kindly words of the Gospel and who may at times even glimpse some aspect of the spirit of Christ enshrined in the smiles, the tears, the words and gestures of some one of their fellowmen.

THE SELF EXAMINATION

OF THE

CONTEMPORARY HISTORIAN

WHEN LORD ACTON wrote in his notebook: 'The great point is the history of history,' the rethinking of the main lines of Nineteenth Century historiography had already begun. Like Moses, Acton looked across from his own mountain of achievement toward the new world of historical thought into which he could not himself enter. In his note there is a fundamental distinction, and it raises the central issue debated by Twentieth Century historians. He made the distinction between history and historiography, and he thereby raised the question of the nature of historical thought. The academic historians had been primarily interested in history as 'the totality of past human actions.' The history of history points to a different concern—one that centers in the kind of account of the past which historians have written. The history of history examines the historian's task and the nature of historical knowledge.

Dilthey

It was the lonely genius, Wilhelm Dilthey (1833-1911), whose re-examination of the nature of historical knowledge raised the question of what it means to be an historian. Dilthey began his career as a theological student whose sense of vocation led him into philosophy rather than the parochial ministry. But philosophy thrust him into history as the most significant discipline leading to man's self interpretation and understanding. He had, during his student days, a great interest in von Ranke's documentary approach, and he had also a deep respect for the famous professor as a conscientious and competent workman.

Dilthey's own studies in philosophy, however, would not let him rest content with the prevailing notion that science could answer the deeper questions either of philosophy or history. He sensed that the secret of philosophical thought lay in history, and he became convinced that academic history was a peripheral concern—that the center of the historian's task was something more than von Ranke and his students had grasped.

Throughout his professional career in philosophy (first at Basle in 1867 and then from 1882 in Berlin) Dilthey struggled with the problem of the nature of historical thought. In its concrete form this question led him to an agonizing reappraisal of the several roles of philosophy, science and history as expressions of man's intellectual and moral experience. Much of his thought grew out of and thrust him into self examination—the difficult and painful analysis of his inner life, of the experience behind expression, of the nature of human understanding and the meaning of human existence. Dilthey had something of Augustin's genius for profound introspection but not his ease or mastery of expression. Something of the painful and rigorous self judgment of Kirkegaard is in Dilthey, but not that great theologian's gift for sure and vivid insight. Dilthey struggled throughout his career against the grain both of the mood of his times and his own doubts and inner compulsions. In 1883 he published his *Introduction to the Sciences of the Mind*. He defined human science as parallel but distinct from physical science not only in method but also in purpose. Human science aims at a different kind of understanding which can be gained only through an inward experience of its object.

> Side by side with the natural sciences, a group of studies linked together by their common subject matter has grown naturally from the problems of life itself. These include history, economics, law, politics, psychology, and the study of religion, literature, poetry, architecture, music and philosophic world views and systems. All these studies refer to the same great fact: mankind. It is mankind which they describe, recount and judge, and about which they form concepts and theories.

Historical understanding, based upon an inward experience of its object, cannot be achieved by the spectator. The task of the historian demands involvement. Von Ranke's trust in documentary materials and 'scientific' rules of evidence was therefore misleading. Understanding of the kind of objects that are the substance of history presses the historian toward a psychological interpretation.

In the humanities we are dealing with states, churches, institutions, customs, books and works of art, in such facts, as in man himself, there is always the reference from an outer sensuous side to one withdrawn from the senses and, therefore, inner. In history we read of productive labour, settlements, wars, foundations of states. They fill our souls with great images and tell us about the historical world which surrounds us. But what moves us, above all, in these accounts is what is inaccessible to the senses and can only be experienced inwardly; it is inherent in the outer events which originate from it and which, in turn, react on it.

It is thus not primarily as an object of sense perception, but insofar as man experiences human states, gives expression to his experience and understands these expressions that he becomes the subject of the humanities. Understanding is not a purely conceptual procedure, but is rather an imaginative rediscovery, reconstruction and re-living of a mental state or experience in which we first become aware of the unity and significance of the whole in light of which we then interpret the details. Here life grasps life, and the power, with which this procedure is carried out, preconditions the adequacy of the human studies in all their branches.

Life has an historical character. History is, indeed, life under the aspect of continuity and universality. History is a live concern. It deals with life and it serves life. Like life, history is a living and restless thing.

What we grasp in experience and understanding is life as the context which embraces mankind. Life is the fullness, variety and interaction within a continuous flow of events experienced by individuals. Its subject matter is identical with history. At every point of history there is life. And history consists of life of every kind in the most varied circumstances. History is merely life viewed in terms of the continuity of mankind as a whole. Life is the fundamental fact which is the starting point for the humanities. It is that which is known from within, that behind which we cannot go.. .The life peculiar to man shows distinctive characteristics in its individual aspects such as relations, attitudes, conduct, the shaping of things and people and the suffering caused by them.

The historian is therefore called to be something more and other than a disinterested scholar engaged in academic research. He is summoned not to record but to revive the past. His task is that of imaginative reconstruction. He bears in himself an aweful responsibility and he confronts an awesome task.

We understand ourselves and others only by putting what we have actually experienced into every kind of expression of our own and others' lives. So, mankind becomes the subject matter of the humanities only because the relation between experience, expression and understanding exists. The human studies are thus based on the relationship which provides their distinctive criterion. A discipline belongs to these studies only when its subject matter becomes accessible to us through the procedure which is founded on the connection between life, expression and understanding.

The development of the humanities depends on the deepening of experience and on the increasing tendency to bring its content to the surface....We notice an overall difference between the natural sciences and the humanities. In the first, scientifc thinking...has become detached from our practical contact with the external world, but, in the latter, a connection between life and science is retained so that thought arising from life remains the foundation of scientific activity. The direct relationship in which life and the humanities stand to each other leads in the latter to a conflict between the tendencies of life and the scientific goals of the humanities. Because historians, economists, teachers of law and students of religion stand in the midst of life, they want to influence it. They subject historical personages, mass movements and tendencies to their judgment which is conditioned by their individuality, the nation to which they belong, and the age in which they live. But, in every science as such the demand for general validity is implied. If the humanities are to be sciences in the strict sense of the word they must aim at validity more consciously and more critically.

Only in the actual construction of the humanities is the conflict settled ....Life, and the experience of it, are the ever freshly flowing sources of the understanding of the social-historical world. Starting from life, understanding penetrates into ever new depths. Only in reacting on life and society do the humanities achieve their highest significance and this is constantly growing. But the road to such effectiveness must pass through the objectivity of scientific knowledge....I find the principle for the settlement of the conflict within these studies in the understanding of the historical world.

History deals with objective expressions of experience (documents, relics, ruins) which become evidence only as interpreted by experience— only through the imaginative reconstruction of the historian. But history itself objectifies human experience. History is thus 'objective anthropomorphism'—a kind of cultural introspection and analysis. Man cannot know himself simply by direct and personal introspection. He can know himself only through history and only by participation in it as historian. History is liberation. It releases man from the fetters of the purely subjective, from the idols of a particular age and a particular culture.

The manifest meaning of history must, first of all, be sought in what is always present, in what always recurs in the structural relations, in the patterns of interactions, in the formation of values and their purposes, in the inner order in which they are related to each other, i.e., in everything from the structure of the individual life up to the last all-embracing unit.

This is the meaning which history always has. It rests on the structure of the individual existence and reveals itself through the objectifications of life, in the composite patterns of interactions.

The historical consciousness of the finitude of every historical phenomenon, of every human or social condition and of the relativity of every kind of faith, is the last step towards the liberation of man. With it man achieves the sovereignty that allows him to enjoy every experience to the full and surrender himself to it unencumbered, as if there were no system of philosophy or faith to tie him down. Life is freed from knowledge through concepts; the mind becomes sovereign over the cobweb chains of dogmatic thought. Everything beautiful, everything holy, every sacrifice re-lived and interpreted, opens perspectives which disclose some part of reality. And equally, we accept the evil, horrible and ugly, as filling a place in the world, as containing some reality which must be justified in the system of things, something which cannot be conjured away. And, in contrast to relativity, the continuity of creative forces asserts itself as the central historical fact.

We are open to the possibility that meaning and significance arise only in man and his history.

Benedetto Croce

Dilthey's probings into the nature of historical knowledge and the task of the historian stimulated the historians of the next generation. There is a fairly direct line of development from Dilthey through Benedetto Croce to Collingwood. All three were philosopher-historians. Dilthey and Collingwood were professors of philosophy whose studies drove them into history. Croce (1866-1952) was a classical scholar and antiquarian who moved through history to a philosophy of history in the modern sense of the study of historical knowledge as criticism and explanation. Like other historians, Greek and Chinese, whom we have met in this broad survey, Croce began his career as a man of action. For a time he served as a Senator and then later as Minister of Education in the Italian Government. But his active role ended with the rise of fascism. The champion of liberty then turned from action to thought. We have already reviewed the earlier work of Croce (Part I) in which he at first defined the historian's task to lie within the realm of art rather than science. Later he identified history with the ultimate task of philosophy. He then saw history as primarily the history of thought (as did also Collingwood), and considered that its chief end was judgment—the judgment of the shape of past events. His final view, and his most important contribution, came from his study of the history of historiography in which he concluded that all history is contemporary history. The real source of history is not documentary evidence or the relics of the past. History has its *being* in the mind of the historian as a present interest. The historical past can only be the past that is known to us and as it is known to us. Mere records, though they represent much labour and expert scholarship, can never be even the foundation for history. They constitute only testimony and testimony is simply chronicle. That distinction, he considered fundamental; for it not only distinguishes history from science, it also points up what is true historical knowledge.

True history is contemporary history. 'Contemporary history' is usually considered to be the history of a passage of time, looked upon as a most recent past, whether it be that of the last fifty years, a decade, a month, a day, or indeed of the last hour or of the last minute. But if we think and speak rigorously, the term 'contemporaneous' can be applied only to that history which comes into being immediately after the act which is being accomplished, as consciousness of that act: it is, for instance, the history that I make of myself while I am in the act of composing these pages.... 'Non-contemporary history' would on the other hand, be that which finds itself in the presence of a history already formed, and which thus comes into being as a criticism of that history, whether it be thousands of years or hardly an hour old.

But if we look more closely, we perceive that this history already formed, which is called or which we would like to call 'non-contemporary' or 'past' history, if it really is history, that is to say, if it means something and is not an empty echo, *is also contemporary*, and does not in any way differ from the other. As in the former case, the condition of its existence is that the deed of which the history told must vibrate in the soul of the historian....History is never constructed from narratives but always from documents, or from narratives that have been reduced to documents and treated as such. Thus if contemporary history springs straight from life, so too does that history which is called non-contemporary, for it is evident that only an interest in the life of the present can move one to investigate past fact. Therefore this past fact does not answer to a past interest, but to a present interest, in so far as it is unified with an interest of the present life.

Croce illustrates his point by contrasting our historical knowledge of Greek sculpture with our chronicle evidence of Greek painting. We have a truly historical knowledge of Greek sculpture. We have a present aesthetic experience of the marbles of Phidias and Praxiteles. We have only a record, a testimony to the fact that such and such a Greek was a painter. We cannot enter into any experience of his work for none survives. We may accept the authority of the records that tell us that there were Greek painters, but we cannot have any historical knowledge of Greek painting because we can have no present aesthetic experience of it. The real foundation of history is thus not testimony but present experience. If history not be contemporary it has no being at all. Yet there is one justification for testimony or chronicle. Chronicle is the corpse of the past. Chronicle sometimes survives history—when history has lost its meaning for the present, or when man has lost his capacity to respond as a present experience to the things of the past. Archives should be kept in view of future possibilities of a renewed capacity to respond.

What is the object of these acts of will which go to the preservation of what is empty and dead? Perhaps illusion or foolishness, which preserves a little while the worn-out elements of mortality....by means of the erection of mausoleums and sepulchres? But sepulchres are not foolishness and illusion; they are, on the contrary, an act of morality, by which is affirmed the immortality of the work done by individuals. Although dead, they live in our memory and will live in the memory of times to come. And that collecting of dead documents and writing down of empty histories is an act of life which serves life. The moment will come when they will serve to reproduce past history, enriched and made present to our spirit. For dead history revives, and past history again becomes present, as the development of life demands. The Romans and the Greeks lay in their sepulchres until awakened at the Renaissance by the new maturity of the European spirit. The primitive forms of civilization, so gross and so barbaric, lay forgotten, or but little regarded, or misunderstood, until that new phase of the European spirit, which was known as Romanticism, 'sympathized' with them —that is to say, recognized them as its own proper present interest. Thus great tracts of history which are now chronicle for us, many documents now mute, will in their turn be traversed with new flashes of life and will speak again.

These revivals have altogether interior motives, and no wealth of documents or of narratives will bring them about; indeed it is they themselves that copiously collect and place before themselves the documents and narratives, which without them would remain scattered and inert. And it will be impossible ever to understand anything of the effective process of historical thought unless we start from the principle that the spirit itself is history, maker of history at every moment of its existence, and also the result of all former history.

> Do you wish to understand the true history of a Ligurian or Sicilian or Peking neolithic man? First of all try if it be possible to make yourself mentally into a Ligurian or Peking man; and if it be not possible, or you do not care to do this, content yourself with describing and classifying and arranging in a series the skulls, the utensils, and the inscriptions belonging to those neolithic peoples....This leads to the idea from which I started in making these observations about historiography, as to history being contemporary history and chronicle being past history.

Croce warns against the misunderstanding of his point, whereby, when it is accepted that mere scholarship (chronicle) is not history, someone may think that history is pure feeling, the passing pulsation of this moment's passion. He still retained to the last the distinction he had in his first essay, written at the age of twenty-seven, made between art and history. Art holds before us all that is aesthetically significant in the possible. But history must limit itself to what has really happened. History must ignore all that which is merely possible or even merely probable.

Hence history is not literature or poetry or drama any more than it is chronicle. History is, in the most profound sense of the phrase, purely practical. It responds to the present character of importance. In his *History as the Story of Liberty* written in 1938, Croce gave these answers to his question: 'What makes a History Book History?'

> A history book is not to be judged as literature or eloquence in the sense that was customary to the old humanistic men of letters, who when not otherwise occupied, used to translate ancient Roman poets, or produced some erudite notes of literary merit on some historical incident to which they were quite indifferent but which they deemed a suitable subject for a literary exercise....When the Abbe de Vertot was given some documents which could have helped him to revise the current story of a battle, he refused them with the comment: 'My battle is over.' (By this he meant that he had completed his account of the incident in victorious prose which he did not now intend to alter, since any change would mar its present perfection.)

> Neither is an historical work to be judged by the greater or less number and correctness of the facts it contains. Anthologies of information are chronicles, notes,, memoirs, annals, but they are not history. And even if they are critically put together, and every item has its origin quoted

or its evidence shrewdly sifted, they can never, on the plane on which they move, however hard they try, rise above unceasing quotation of things said and things written. They fail to become truth to us just at that point where history demands an assertion of truth arising out of our intimate experience....Exactitude in any case is a moral duty, but in theory and in fact chronicle and history are different....and neither the dull metal of the chronicles nor the highly polished metal of the philologists will ever be of equal value with the gold of the historian even if that is concealed in dross.

Finally, an historical book should not be judged by how much or how little it stirs the imagination, is moving, exciting, or amusing, because dramas and novels can make a similar impression but a history book need not.

An historical work should be judged solely on its practical merit. What constitutes history may be thus described: it is the act of knowing and understanding prompted by the requirements of practical life....It may be a moral requirement, the requirements of understanding one's situation in order that inspiration and action and the good life may follow upon this. It may be a merely economic requirement, that of discernment of one's advantage. It may be an aesthetic requirement, like that of getting clear the meaning of a word, or an allusion, or a state of mind, in order fully to grasp and enjoy a poem; or again an intellectual requirement like that of solving a scientific question by correcting and amplifying information about its items, through lack of which one had been perplexed and doubtful. History....in all its detailed elaboration exists for the purpose of maintaining and developing the active and civilized life of human society.

The Nature of the Historical Past

Twentieth Century historiography has been quite clear about the difference between the real past and the historical past. There is only one thing that can be said about the real past. It is dead and can never be recovered. It was a figment of the imagination of Eighteenth and Nineteenth Century positivists and 'scientific' historians. We can never know all that actually happened or how it actually happened, let alone why it happened. The only past we can know at all is the historical past and it is known to us only because other people considered certain things important enough to record and write opinions about. Not even the archaeologists can recreate the actual past. The stones they excavate can tell us something. We can judge from them concerning the size and relative importance of houses and temples, markets and palaces. We can judge the technical knowledge, the skill of their architects and builders. We can on the basis of material ruins, hazard some guesses as to their concept of art and artistry. But the stones of the past can tell us very little. They cannot speak for the people. They cannot repeat the words exchanged by king and priest within the chambers they enclosed, nor tell us of the inner problems of state and personal ambition that sent out the soldiers who left their signatures of destruction in the broken and charred ruins. Certainly they do not remember the glances exchanged by young men and maidens in their presence so many centuries ago, let alone the inner lives of the people who walked and talked and laughed and sang and wept and worried so nearby in the streets and in the poorer houses that have long since disappeared without a trace of stone or pottery. The only past there is has chance to thank for its existence—relics that survived by chance, documents that often unintentionally were preserved—the chance that someone, for some reason, or no reason at all, found something worth preserving or worth mentioning. It is the historian who creates the only past we know or can ever know.

Two possibilities of approach to this task of creation have marked the efforts of historians. One is the historian's attempt to make himself as nearly as possible a contemporary of the events he desires to reconstruct. Some historians have insisted (the school of von Ranke and Acton) that the historian must make every sacrifice of personal viewpoint in order to become, as nearly as possible, a contemporary spectator through the aid of documents and relics of past events. James Moffatt vividly describes the aim and end of the historical imagination as it was understood from this point of view. It was to put oneself 'as far as possible in the position of those to whom the words of the documents were first written....We must create their world afresh for ourselves, with its far-off colour and shape, its environment and its atmosphere.' This is the invitation extended by the poet William Morris in the prologue to his *Earthly Paradise:*

> Forget six counties overhung with smoke,
> Forget the snorting steam and piston-stroke,
> Forget the spreading of the hideous town:
> Think rather of the pack-horse on the down,
> And dream of London, small and white and clean,
> The clear Thames bordered by its gardens green;
> Think, that below the bridge, green lapping waves
> Smite some few keels that bear Levantine staves
> And cloth of Bruges, and hogsheads of Guienne
> While nigh the thronged wharf Geoffrey Chaucer's pen
> Moves over bills of lading.

'That is, he asks and helps the reader to go back to the latter half of the Fourteenth Century, in order to understand his poem. So with the historical method; it invites us to forget the intervening centuries, and to imagine with the aid of research, the far-off conditions of life in which First Century Christianity arose, as these are represented or implied in the (documents of the) New Testament.' Fustel de Coulanges was, still in the latter half of the Nineteenth Century, optimistic about the possibility and the results of this flight from the present into the past. 'It is not I who speak,' he wrote once in a parody of St. Paul, 'but the past that speaks through me.' For the most part, however, this approach was abandoned. Its most articulate critics were the Biblical scholars who had themselves given so many years of expert and conscientious effort to its testing. We have already noted the conclusion of Albert Schweitzer concerning the failure of *historicism* in his *Quest of the Historical Jesus* (see above Chapter V). Moffatt in his essay on 'The Limitations of Historical Method' from which we have just quoted, went on to conclude: 'I want to admit candidly that such an effort of the historical imagination cannot yield us all we might expect. We have not the materials for reconstructing the outer or the inner world of the New Testament with any completeness. Unfilled spaces remain in any synthesis we draw up—Let this then be my last word about the historical method which would set our feet upon the road to the New Testament: in moving towards this great literature we are not fully enlightened if we fail to be moved by it as we approach it.'

By this conclusion is suggested the other possibility open to the historian in creating the historical past—to make the past his contemporary. But this approach immediately raises another set of problems: What is the nature of historical evidence in and of itself? Is the historical past then any thing more than a subjective fantasy? What indeed is the value of the historical past to any one other than the individual historian who creates it? Is there any truth in history? What is the nature of a historical fact? In the following medley of quotations some answers are given to these questions by contemporary historians—Professors W.H. Walsh (*An Introduction to the Philosophy of History*), Jacques Barzun and Henry F. Graff (*The Modern Researcher*, 1957) and Fritz Stern (*The Varieties of History*, 1956).

Mr. Walsh reminds us that historical facts are not simply given. 'They have in every case to be established—historical evidence is not an ultimate datum to which we can refer to test the truth of historical judgments.' Barzun and Graff similarly insist that no matter how it is described or classified, 'no piece of evidence can be used for historiography in the state in which it is found....'

It is invariably and necessarily subjected to the action of the researcher's mind, and when that action is methodical and just, what is being applied is known as the critical method. Faced with a piece of evidence, the critical mind of the searcher for truth asks the fundamental questions:

Is this object or piece of writing genuine?
Is its message trustworthy?
How do I know?

These questions lead to an unfolding series of subordinate questions:

1. Who is its author or maker?
2. What does it state?
3. What is the relation in time and space between the author and the statement, overt or implied, which is conveyed by the object?
4. How does the statement compare with other statements on the same point?
5. What do we know independently about the author and his credibility?

In history no truth may be accepted without evidence. What does this mean? It means that the report cannot be supported by a hunch, no matter how possible or plausible the author's conjecture may be. What would be more than adequate for village gossip does not begin to be enough for history. The historian cannot say: 'Since there is nothing against my view; since on the contrary, certain facts can be made to support my view, therefore, my view is proved.' This is a common fallacy. Proof demands decisive evidence, that is, evidence which *confirms* one view and *denies* its rivals. For in history, as in life critically considered, truth rests not on possibility nor on plausibility but on probability.

Probability is used here in a strict sense. It means the balance of chances that, given such and such evidence, the event it records happened in a certain way; or in some cases, that a supposed event did not in fact take place. This balance is not computable in figures, as it is in mathematical probability; but it is no less attentively *weighed* and *judged*. Judgment is the historian's form of genius, and he himself is judged by the amount of it he can muster.

The grounds on which he passes judgment are again the common grounds derived from, and applicable to life: general truths, personal and social experience (which includes a knowledge of previous history), and any other kind of special or particular knowledge that proves relevant.

What is plausible or implausible, no matter how impressive, ought not to have anything to do with thehistorian's judgment. To him, a chain of probabilities is worth all the plausibility in the world. There are many things in history that seem quite unbelievable but nevertheless they are held by historians to be true because of reliable evidence.

Probability is determined by a critical review of the evidence. In this review the question of plausibility does enter. Namier once defined the historical sense as 'an intuitive understanding of how things do *not* happen.' Against such intuition probability must far outweigh plausibility. Even historical facts determined by strong probability are not facts of the actual past. But this skepticism, Barzun and Graff point out, can work two ways. When the skeptic protests:

'But you were not there. All you know is what others choose to tell you. How can you be sure? Most people are notoriously bad observers; some are deliberate or unconscious liars; there is no such thing as a perfect witness. And yet you naively trust any casual passerby, and on his say-so you proclaim: 'This is what happened.'

Except for the words 'naively trust' everything said above is true. But it proves too much. Even if we were there, what then? Just a few more imperfect witnesses on the scene. We might be convinced that what *we* saw, remembered and understood was right, but other witnesses would still feel equally certain about their evidence.

To put it differently, every observer's knowledge of the event doubtless contains some exact and some erroneous knowledge, and these two parts, multiplied by as many observers as may be, are all the knowledge there can be. This is important to grasp and remember; it makes one both humble and grateful about the known and knowable past. There is no such thing as a real past that is a solid entity hidden from us like a mountain hidden by a mist. This is a figment of the skeptic's imagination. The only available past is like the past we have—a thing of opinions and reports, of memory and interpretation, of belief and judgment.

But if thoroughly attested proof of the kind science depends upon is lacking in history this fact is itself, Fritz Stern urges, 'a challenge to the responsibility of the historian....Even if the existence of historical Truth be problematical, truthfulness remains the measure of (the historian's) intellectual and moral achievement. Amidst temptations he will remember William James' proud complaint: 'I have to forge every sentence in the teeth of irreducible and stubborn facts.'

One of the more profound conclusions as to the nature of

historical knowledge from a historian's self examination is R. G. Collingwood's definition of history 'as the re-enactment of past experience.' Collingwood, like Dilthey, was a lonely man. He lived at Oxford largely in retirement from all but a few students and a few close friends. Like so many historians, he was out of step with his contemporaries. In promise he was beyond them. In performance he waged a weary war against both the enemies of his thought and his health. Before middle age he was an ill man, struggling against the indifference of many to a broad humanism in an age of analysis and specialization.

In his latter years, Collingwood turned more and more from philosophy, which was his first love, to history; and what he sought was not a philosophy of history but a kind of philosophical historiography based upon the conviction that 'the chief business of Twentieth Century philosophy is to reckon with Twentieth Century history.' On the other hand he was as firmly convinced that 'thought is the fundamental concept of historical enquiry.' Like Croce, his chief contribution lay in his humanity—in the insights into many things of a first rate British mind—art, science, history of philosophy and the history of history. It was his passionate belief that it was the whole duty of man to know himself in the 're-enactment of past experience.'

How, or on what conditions, can the historian know the past? In considering this question, the first point to notice is that the past is never a given fact which he can apprehend empirically by perception. The historian is not an eyewitness of the facts he desires to know. Nor does he fancy that he is; he knows quite well that his only possible knowledge of the past is mediate or inferential or indirect, never empirical.

The second point is that this mediation cannot be effected by testimony. The historian does not know the past by simply believing a witness who saw the events in question and has left his evidence on record. That kind of mediation would give at most not knowledge but belief, and very ill-founded and improbable belief. And the historian, once more, knows very well that this is not the way in which he proceeds; he is aware that what he does to his so-called authorities is not to believe them but to criticize them. If then the historian has no direct or empirical knowledge of his facts, and no transmitted or testamental knowledge of them, what kind of knowledge has he: in other words, what must the historian do in order that he may know?

The historian must re-enact the past in his own mind.
Suppose a historian is reading a passage of an ancient philosopher.

Of course he must know the language in a philological sense and be able to construe; but by doing that he has not yet understood the passage as an historian of philosophy must understand it. In order to do that, he must see what the philosophical problem was, of which his author is here stating his solution. He must think that problem out for himself, see what possible solutions of it might be offered, and see why this particular philosopher chose that solution instead of another. This means re-thinking for himself the thought of his author, and nothing short of that will make him the historian of that author's philosophy.

Categories of Explanation and Interpretation

Related to the question of the nature of historical knowledge is the issue of the meaning and validity of the basic categories or concepts of explanation and interpretation. We shall consider three of these (cause, pattern, progress) as they have been discussed in recent historiographic literature. Mr. Walsh approaches the problem of cause in history by asking 'whether there are any pecularities about the way the historian explains or attempts to explain the events he studies—What sort or sorts of 'why' are involved in history?'

CAUSE

We can best approach this question by considering the way in which the concept of explanation is used in the natural sciences. It is a commonplace that scientists no longer attempt to explain the phenomena with which they deal in any ultimate sense: they do not propose to tell us why things are what they are to the extent of revealing the purpose behind nature. Given any particular situation, their procedure is to show that it exemplifies one or more general laws, which can themselves be seen to follow from, or connect with, other laws of a wider character. The main features of this process are, first, that it consists in the resolution of particular events into cases of general laws, and secondly that it involves nothing more than an external view of the phenomena under consideration. It can thus be said to result in an understanding which is properly described as abstract. Now it has been claimed by many writers on history that historical understanding is not thus abstract but is, in some sense, concrete.

It is clear that the question whether there is anything in this contention depends upon whether historians explain their facts in the same way as natural scientists explain theirs, or whether they can be shown to possess some peculiar insight into their subject matter enabling them to grasp its individual nature.

There are some philosophers who have only to pose such a question to answer it in the negative. Explanation, they hold, is and can be of only one type, the type employed in scientific thinking. A process of explanation is essentially a process of deduction; and at the center of it there is always something expressable in general terms.

(To answer the question we must begin by examining) the steps historians actually take when they set out to explain an historical event or set of events. And when we do we are immediately struck by the fact that they do not seem to employ generalizations in the same way as scientists do. Apparently at least, historians do not attempt to illuminate particular situations by referring to other situations of the same type. Thus when asked to explain a particular event, e.g., the British general strike of 1926, they will begin by tracing connections between that event and others with which it stands in inner relationship (in the case in question, certain previous events in the history of industrial relations in Great Britain). The assumption here is that different historical events can be regarded as going together to constitute a single process, a whole of which they are all parts and in which they belong together in a specially intimate way.

Barzun and Graff similarly point up the distinction between the concept of cause in history and the notion of cause in the natural sciences.

A practical distinction about causality made in physical science may be adopted here, namely between causation that occurs in a long chain of events of various kinds and causation that occurs within a closed system. An example of the first is: a cloud forms, the sun darkens, temperature drops, people move, a thunderstorm bursts, a man takes cover under a tree and lightning strikes and kills him. What is the cause of death? The chain of 'causes' is miscellaneous and each event in it unpredictable, not because it is not determined by other preceding events, but because it occurs outside any controllable limits.

As against this, in a physics laboratory, an elastic body of known stresses and strains goes through a series of evolving states, at any moment a single definite distribution of measured stresses and strains is the effect of the previous moment, which may therefore be regarded as its complete cause, as *the* cause. The difference is that in the first case there is no restriction on the events that may be related—that belongs to the choice of the observer. He selects not the causes (in the sense of the laboratory causes) but the *conditions* that belong to the chain and are interesting to him and his audience. They will judge whether he is making sense to them in the way they are used to judging life situations in general.

(The historian) is supposed to think and choose, and he is judged by the intelligence and honesty with which he does both. Again, the objection that history cannot be true because it has to be rewritten every thirty years appears as a sign of the usefulness of history: it not only should respond to the demands made upon it but it *can* respond. The successive revisions of the past do not cancel each other out, they are additive: we know more and more about the past through history.

PATTERN IN HISTORY

Every piece of historical writing is the result of the historian's selective, intelligent judgment about the past, organized in an intelligible pattern or a suitable narrative sequence. Without a pattern of meaningful relations of events, history does not make sense, Some years ago a publisher planned to issue a book on the 'Hundred Greatest Moments of History.' A number of 'distinguished historians and journalists' were asked to choose among a list of 150 events those that were really great. This illustrates a common misunderstanding of what history is. Without some principle of organization and an intelligible pattern a mere accumulation of names and dates is useless.

In the study of nature the facts do not arrange themselves. A formula implies the selection of certain phenomena which experiment has related, first to a scale of measurement, and then to other facts in fixed or variable connections. The choice of facts and of relation is dictated by human interest as well as by nature. It is human curiosity and need that seek to ascertain the relation between the molecules of a gas and the phenomena of heat and pressure. The facts, moreover, are seen through ideas (e. g. the idea of a molecule itself) which are not immediately visible and ready to be noted down. They are searched out with a purpose in mind, The facts once ascertained are meaningless until there is the action of a mind that frames an hypothesis in order to achieve a total view of related events which is properly called a theory.

The purpose of the historian is to portray events intelligibly. Therefore he must 'relate' in the ordinary sense of recount life-like sequences. He presents human affairs as in a story, describing conditions and complications, and reaching climaxes and conclusions so as to permit understanding.

He can of course measure time, and chronology supplies a natural order among his facts. But chronology is long and it includes everything. It too needs a pattern. That is why the historian carves out manageable periods—reigns, centuries, eras. He also adopts popular labels for certain constellations of historical phenomena like 'Gothic,' 'Neo-Confucianism,' 'Afro-Asian Nationalism,' etc.

Now it may be asked, what elements of thought and observation go into the making of any 'constellation' that unites the loose particles of fact? The first element in a historical pattern is obviously a comparison of some sort, natural or artificial. The first rule of pattern making is this: To be successful and appropriate, a selection must face two ways: it must correspond to the mass of evidence, and it must offer an intelligible design to the beholder.

THE CONCEPT OF PROGRESS
(From R.G. Collingwood, *The Idea of History*—'Progress as Created by Historical Thinking')

The term 'progress', as used in the Nineteenth Century when the word was much in people's mouths, covers two things which it is well to distinguish: progress in history, and progress in nature. For progress in nature the word 'evolution' has been so widely used that this may be accepted as its established sense; and in order not to confuse the two things I shall restrict my use of the word 'evolution' to that meaning, and distinguish the other by the name 'historical progress.' 'Evolution'is a term applied to natural processes in so far as these are conceived as bringing into existence new specific forms in nature.

But progress in nature, or evolution, has often been taken to mean more than this: namely the doctrine that each new form is not only a modification of the last but an improvement on it. To speak of improvement is to imply a standard of valuation. This, in the case of breeding new forms of domestic animals or plants, is intelligible enough: the value implied is the new form's utility for human purposes. But no one supposes that natural evolution is designed to produce such utilities; the standard implied, therefore, cannot be that. What is it?

The conception of a 'law of progress,' by which the course of history is so governed that successive forms of human activity exhibit each an improvement on the last, is a mere confusion of thought, bred of an unnatural union between man's belief in his own superiority to nature and his belief that he is nothing more than a part of nature. If either belief is true, the other is false: they cannot be combined to produce logical offspring.

Nor can the question, whether in a given case an historical change has or has not been progressive, be answered until we are sure that such questions have a meaning. Before they are raised, we must ask what is meant by historical progress, now that it has been distinguished from natural progress; and, if anything is meant, whether the meaning is one applicable to the given case we are considering. For it would be hasty to assume that, because the conception of historical progress as dictated by a law of nature is nonsensical, the conception of historical progress itself is therefore nonsensical.

As a first attempt to define its meaning, we might suggest that historical progress is only another name for human activity itself, as a succession of acts each of which arises out of the last. Every act whose history we may study, of whatever kind it is, has its place in a series of acts where one has created a situation with which the next has to deal. The accomplished act gives rise to a new problem; it is always this new problem, not the old problem over again, which the new act is obliged to solve. If a man has discovered how to get a meal, next time he is hungry he must find out how to get another, and the getting of this other is a new act arising out of the old. His situation is always changing, and the act of thought by which he solves the problems it presents is always changing too.

The idea of historical progress, then, if it refers to anything, refers to the coming into existence not merely of new actions or thoughts or situations belonging to the same specific type, but of new specific types. It therefore presupposes such specific novelties, and consists in the conception of these as improvements. Suppose, for example, a man or community had lived on fish, and the fish-supply failing, had sought food in a new way, by digging for roots: this would be a change in the specific type of situation and activity, but it would not be regarded as progress, because the change does not imply that the new type is an improvement on the old. But if a community of fish-eaters had changed their method of catching fish from a less to a more efficient one, by which an average fisherman could catch ten fish on an average day instead of five, this would be called an example of progress.

But from whose point of view, is it an improvement? The question must be asked, because what is an improvement from one point of view may be the reverse from another; and if there is a third from which an impartial judgment can be passed on this conflict, the qualifications of this impartial judge must be determined.

At the present day we are constantly presented with a view of history as consisting in this way of good and bad periods, the bad periods being divided into the primitive and the decadent, according as they come before or after the good ones. This distinction between periods of primitiveness, periods of greatness, and periods of decadence, is not and never can be historically true. It tells us much about the historians who study the facts, but nothing about the facts they study. It is characteristic of an age like our own, where history is studied widely and successfully, but eclectically. Every period of which we have competent knowledge (and by competent knowledge I mean insight into its thought, not mere acquaintance with its remains) appears in the perspective of time as an age of brilliance: the brilliance being the light of our own historical insight. The intervening periods are seen by contrast as, relatively speaking and in different degrees, 'dark ages': ages which we know to have existed, because there is a gap of time for them in our chronology, and we have possibly numerous relics of their work and thought, but in which we can find no real life because we cannot re-enact that thought in our own minds. That this pattern of light and darkness is an optical illusion proceeding from the distribution of the historian's knowledge and ignorance is obvious from the different ways in which it is drawn by different historians and by the historical thought of different generations.

The same optical illusion in a simpler form affected the historical thought of the eighteenth century, and laid the foundations for the dogma of progress, as that was accepted in the nineteenth. When Voltaire laid it down that 'all history is modern history,' and that nothing could be genuinely known before about the end of the fifteenth century, he was saying two things at once: that nothing earlier than the modern period could be known, and that nothing earlier deserved to be known. These two things came to the same thing. His inability to reconstruct genuine history from the documents of the ancient world and the Middle Ages was the source of his belief that those ages were dark and barbarous. The idea of history as a progress from primitive times to the present day was, to those who believed in it, a simple consequence of the fact that their historical outlook was limited to the recent past.

The old dogma of a single historical progress leading to the present, and the modern dogma of historical cycles, that is, of a multiple progress leading to 'great ages' and then to decadence, are thus mere projections of the historian's ignorance upon the screen of the past.

Can we speak of progress in happiness or comfort or satisfaction? Obviously not. Nor does it mean anything to ask whether there is progress in art. The artist's problem, so far as he is an artist, is not the problem of doing what his predecessor has done and going on to do something further which his predecessor failed to do. There is development in art, but no progress: for though in the technical processes of art one man learns from another, Titian from Bellini, Beethoven from Mozart, and so on, the problem of art itself consists not in mastering these technical processes but in using them to express the artist's experience and give it reflective form, and consequently every fresh work of art is the solution of a fresh problem which arises not out of a previous work of art but out of the artist's unreflective experience.

In one sense, there is or may be moral progress. Part of our moral life consists of coping with problems arising not out of our animal nature but out of our social institutions, and these are historical things, which create moral problems only in so far as they are already the expression of moral ideals. A man who asks himself whether he ought to take a voluntary part in his country's war is not struggling with personal fear; he is involved in a conflict between the moral forces embodied not merely in the ideal, but in the equally actual reality, of international peace and intercourse. Similarly the problem of divorce arises not out of the whims of sexual desire, but out of an unresolved conflict between the moral ideal of monogamy and the moral evils which that ideal, rigidly applied, brings in its train. To solve the problem of war or of divorce is only possible by devising new institutions which shall recognize in full the moral claims recognized by the State or by monogamy, and shall satisfy these claims without leaving unsatisfied the further claims to which, in historical fact, the old institutions have given rise.

The same double aspect appears in the economic life. So far as that consists in finding from moment to moment the means of satisfying demands which spring not from our historical environment but from our nature as animals with certain desires, there can be no progress in it; that would be a progress in happiness or comfort or satisfaction, which we have seen to be impossible. But not all our demands are for the satisfaction of animal desires. The demand for investments in which I can put my savings to support me in old age is not an animal desire; it arises out of an individualistic economic system in which the old are supported neither statutorily by the State nor customarily by their families, but by the fruits of their own labour, and in which capital commands a certain rate of interest. That system has solved a good many problems, and therein lies its economic value; but it gives rise to a good many others which as yet it has failed to solve. A better economic system, one whose substitution for this would be progress, would continue to solve the same problems which are solved by individualistic capitalism, and solve these others as well.

The same considerations apply to politics and law, and I need not work out the application in detail. In science, philosophy, and religion the conditions are rather different.

Progress in science would consist in the suppression of one theory by another which served both to explain all that the first theory explained, and also to explain types or classes of events or 'phenomena' which the first ought to have explained but could not. I suppose that Darwin's theory of the origin of species was an example. The theory of fixed species explained the relative permanence of natural kinds within the recorded memory of man; but it ought to have held good for the longer stretch of geological time, and it broke down, too, for the case of selectively-bred animals and plants under domestication. Darwin propounded a theory whose claim to merit rested on its bringing these three classes under one conception. I need hardly quote the now more familiar relation between Newton's law of gravitation and that of Einstein, or that between the special and general theories of relativity. The interest of science, in relation to the concept of progress, seems to be that this is the simplest and most obvious case in which progress exists and is verifiable. For this reason, those who have believed most strongly in progress have been much in the habit of appealing to the progress of science as the plainest proof that there is such a thing, and often, too, have based their hope of progress in other fields on the hope of making science the absolute mistress of human life. But science is and can be mistress only in her own house, and forms of activity which cannot progress (such as art) cannot be made to do so by subjecting them, if that phrase meant anything, to the rule of science; whereas those which can must progress by finding out for themselves how to improve in doing their own work.

Philosophy progresses in so far as one stage of its development solves the problems which defeated it in the last, without losing its hold on the solutions already achieved. This, of course, is independent of whether the two stages are stages in the life of a single philosopher, or are represented by different men. Thus, suppose it true that Plato grasped the necessity for an eternal object, the world of Ideas or Idea of the Good, and also for an eternal subject, the soul in its double function of knower and mover, as solutions for the problems with which his predecessors' work had left him confronted: but was baffled to say how those two were related; and suppose Aristotle saw that the problem of the relation between them, as Plato had stated it, or rather as he himself saw it in his long apprenticeship to Plato's teaching, could be solved by thinking of them as one and the same, pure intellect being identical with its own object, and its knowledge of that object being its knowledge of itself; then, so far (though conceivably not in other respects) Aristotle's philosophy would mark a progress on Plato's, granted that by that new step Aristotle sacrificed nothing that Plato had achieved by his theory of Ideas and his theory of soul.

In religion, progress is possible on the same terms. If Christianity, losing no jot or tittle of what Judaism had won by its conception of God as one God, just and terrible, infinitely great over against man's infinite littleness, and infinitely exacting in his demands on man, could bridge the gulf between God and man by the conception that God became man in order that we might become God, that was progress, and a momentous one, in the history of the religious consciousness.

In such senses and in such cases as these, progress is possible. Whether it has actually occurred, and where and when and in what ways, are questions for historical thought to answer. But there is one other thing for historical thought to do: namely to create this progress itself. For progress is not a mere fact to be discovered by historical thinking: it is only through historical thinking that it comes about at all.

If Einstein makes an advance on Newton, he does it by knowing Newton's thought and retaining it within his own, in the sense that he knows what Newton's problems were, and how he solved them, and, disentangling the truth in those solutions from whatever errors prevented Newton from going further, embodying these solutions as thus disentangled in his own theory. He might have done this, no doubt, without having read Newton in the original for himself; but not without having received Newton's doctrine from someone. Thus Newton stands, in such a context, not for a man but for a theory, reigning during a certain period of scientific thought. It is only in so far as Einstein knows that theory as a fact in the history of science, that he can make an advance upon it. Newton thus lives in Einstein in the way in which any past experience lives in the mind of the historian, as a past experience known as past—as the point from which the development with which he is concerned started—but re-enacted here and now together with a development of itself that is partly constructive or positive and partly critical or negative.

THE VOCATION OF THE HISTORIAN
(From Fritz Stern, 'Introduction' to *The Varieties of History*)

'—The historian must serve two masters, the past and the present. And while his obligation to the past, his complete, unassailable fidelity to it, must always claim his first loyalty, he must accept the fact that the choices he makes as a historian are not of consequence to him alone, but will affect the moral sense, perhaps the wisdom, of his generation. And since he knows that his own being, his intellectual capabilities and his critical faculties as well as his deeper sense of righteousness and love, are engaged in the writing of history, he knows that his work, too, is a moral act.

Some seventy years ago, F.W. Maitland repeated what a historian had said long before: 'In truth, writing this history is in some sense a religious act.' The deeper sense of the image remains with us, and Miss Wedgwood is right that 'it is as important for the historian today to be a good, and if possible a great, man as it was for the high dignitaries of the Medieval Church.' From these admonitions the historian can derive pride and abiding humility: his is a serious task, for which great predecessors have prepared him. As he deals with men and their lives in society, both past and present, he touches on the ultimate questions of human existence, as does religion itself. And as he deals with men and their creations, he will alternately feel pride and exultation, awe and sorrow, at how varied, complex, unpredictable, wretched and glorious is human life.'

HISTORY AND SOCIETY:

A SUMMARY

MAN HAS BEEN INTERESTED in his past when the need arose to define and interpret the foundations of society. Both Chinese (Ssu-ma Chien) and Israelite (*J*) historiography began with empire. Greek historiography began with the sense of destiny. The importance of the present always raises the question of the character of importance and it is history that answers that question in the dialogue between the present and the past. Again historiography has been a major effort of a society faced with the loss of meaning, a society in transition, a suffering society with the courage to be—the will to survive. Israel's Deuteronomist and priestly historians were convinced that cultural survival in exile depended upon remembrance. The exile became a time of hope after it had become a tryst with history. The writing of history has been the vocation of individuals who have been released, most often against their wills, from the pressures of action that they might pursue the tasks of thought.

Historical study is a discipline. The historian and his readers must be willing to listen to the speaking of the past if the past is to become the kind of mirror that reflects a sharp image of the present. If the mirror is itself defective the image will be distorted. Above all, history is the speaking of man to man, and speaking of man for man. When a society has lost its sense of history it hasl ost its humanity; yet a stricken society, if it has a sense of history, though it be dead, yet shall it live again.

History is the mediator between poetry and science. It has at various times been closely associated with the social sciences as the fundamental discipline upon which these are built—as mathematics is the foundation of physical science. Since the middle of the Nineteenth Century, history and social science have developed together. The new disciplines of archaeology, philology, anthropology, sociology and psychology have been the help-meets of history; and history, in turn, has been the method basic to social studies. Comte at the middle of the Nineteenth Century described useful and reliable knowledge as consisting of five sciences: astronomy, physics, chemistry, physiology and *social physics*. The term is significant. Societies and social institutions in Comte's view have also a nature which can be observed and measured and described as well as, and in the same way as, physical phenomena. Social physics, is in Comte's words to be a subject henceforth reducible to definite laws, 'enabling us to base action upon sure knowledge.' Thus the two poles of explanation in the age of science are clearly marked. Science is the study of nature. History is the study of human affairs or of the human significance of things. Science studies man as a part of his physical environment. History views man as distinct from his physical environment. History studies man as a being that seeks not only to know and to live but to express his life—to create, to act not only in accordance with his environment but upon it, to create for himself in the midst of the perpetually perishing and over against the inexorable laws of nature a dimension of immortality and freedom. Over against what nature is, stands what man has done. It was the insight of the Israelites that the real distinction between man and all else in creation was that man has a history. It is his history more than his nature that provides the significant data for the study of man. His destiny is a function of his history as well as his nature. His nature is the goal of his history.

Chinese and Greek thought, on the other hand, regarded history as a function of human nature, the function of the substance that is man. History could then also be the poetry of the past, not in the Cartesian sense of fiction, but as the concrete instance of universal law. But the poetry of reason was always more important for the Greek than the poetry of event. History, however conceived, has always exhibited an inner tension between the demand that it be a descriptive science and the demand that it be an interpretive discipline.

In the views of Comte, von Ranke, Dilthey and Croce three notions of history appear: history as art, history as method (scientific control in the testing of evidence and the scientific report of investigation) and history as judgment. The first observation to be made here is that history is indeed all these, and it is for this reason in part that it is the mediating discipline between poetry on the one side and science on the other. And the second observation is this: the excellence of art and the excellence of science do not, however, depend upon the degree of isolation which they may be able to achieve with respect to each other. The artist is not the greater artist because he is religiously ignorant of science or because his thought processes have the least in common with those of science. Nor is the scientist the better chemist or physicist because he has carefully filtered out of his working mind all artistic sensitivity and insight. Both artist and scientist are observers whose capacity for alert attention has grown with discipline; and in some notable instances the physicist and biologist have found in poetry and painting a significant detail of form or behaviour which they had themselves previously missed. Neither artist nor historian deals with a different set of the general laws of thought than is in force in science. We may in fact observe that the painter and poet were aware of the need to create for their own media symbols of the relation of relations before science had developed its post Euclidian mathematical symbols to describe the relation of relations in the physical world.

In all circles of contemporary learning a new concept of being, and of the relation of fact and thought to being, has replaced the former center. The center of each of these circles until the very recent past had been the notion of being as substance. The irreducible things of science, the atom as the elemental substance, could be compared to the irreducible fact—the hard, objective stuff of history. And the artist dealt with the essence of substances. Yet the basic difference between scientific and historical fact remains. A physical fact is the interpolation of statistical averages based upon observation either direct or controlled (experiment). When the physical events observed are of significance for science—that is, when evidence points to the conclusion that they may generally be expected to happen in a certain way—this knowledge is most precisely and adequately presented in the language of numbers and mathematical symbols. Historical fact, as Cassirer has pointed out, is of a different kind and is discovered in a different way. The historian has no laboratory in which an apparatus can enable him to observe with greater precision the events of the past. The most characteristic aspect of the past is that it is gone—gone forever. The chemist works with all the necessary materials at hand and with his apparatus he can reconstruct the event in which he is interested. If he is a competent chemist with reliable equipment his experiment will result in an accurate reconstruction of a physical event. The historian cannot so reconstruct the past. He can only remember it. With the

aid of all documents, artifacts and other materials at his disposal he
can picture what may have happened. An historical event is a million
times more complicated than a physical event. Historical events are
too complex to yield to scientific control. The historian can only
remember as best he can with the incomplete aids available. And his
conclusions will always be of the nature of memory which is partial
and selective. Memory reveals not all that happened or indeed what
did happen or the way something happened, but rather the character
of the importance of the past to somebody in some situation, as, for
example, the trade accounts of Venetian business men. Memory is
never a reconstruction. It is a re-creation, a resurrection from the
dead involving if not a new spirit at least a new body. Even
contemporary history can in no precise sense be 'scientific.' A fact in
the realm of human affairs is never a mere occurrence. Something
occurs and somebody responds to the occurrence, and this response is
the stuff of an historical fact. Historical fact is always occurrence and
reception. But the historian is himself not receiver. He works with
the testimony of others—people whom he has never known, with whom
he could not speak, whose ways of life he has not shared. Ancient
languages no longer spoken are no longer languages of direct
communication, and the things of history are no longer things. They
have ceased to be physical objects. They have ceased to be facts. They
are the material of symbols. The world of the historian is, in Cassirer's
words, a symbolic universe. The laboratory work of the historian is
thus not an analysis of molecules but an analysis of symbols. And
symbols have life — they are meaningful only in so far as they
participate in the life of the historian himself. He breathes into them
the breath of his own experience. History then is what the past means
to us at this moment and from this perspective. And so there is no
'fixed and finished past.'

Is history then simply the mirror in which we see ourselves, or, to
be more cynical, only the mirror in which the historian sees himself?

In a very real and important sense, this is true. The past is such
a mirror. History as the mirror of the human face and the posture of
man in the world means just the opposite, however, of subjective
portraiture. History objectifies human experience. It shows us man
as creator and victim and sinner. History is, in Cassirer's paradoxical
phrase, 'objective anthropomorphism.' It is not simply a series of
snap shots of individuals either candid or contrived but the portrait
of man, the portrayal of what man is in terms of what men have

done. History objectifies in that it corrects the distortions of the partial data of individual lives and of particular times; and the final work of the historian is not a series of generalizations about the average man or the conventional group picture but the 'real man'— man in terms of the potentialities of the species evidenced by what, across the ages, men have done. Without history, which reaches over the broken arches of our generations and our institutions and our cultures to span 'the opposite poles of time,' we would be simply creatures of a day. History enables us to see ourselves and to criticize ourselves at a distance. It is a kind of cultural introspection and psychoanalysis which goes deeper than individual experience could tolerate, and plumbs such depths as the single layers of particular ages could not provide.

So far what has been said of history binds it to art not only in terms of interest and of method but also of function and effect. History as a circle with the integrity of its own field and purpose seems to have become absorbed into the circle of arts so that it is itself not a whole circle but only that common area of the intersecting circle of art and of science. Its distinctive aspect is hence to be sought elsewhere. History is the knowledge of event as judgment and as vocation. Friedrich Schlegel described the historian as '*einen rückwarts gekehrten Propheten*' or as Cassirer translates, a retrospective prophet. Schlegel and Cassirer mean by this the prophecy of the past as 'revelation of its hidden life.' The historian as prophet can reveal a significance in men and movements which was not seen by their contemporaries. But this is not all, nor is it the important work that the historian does as prophet. History is the meaning of the past for the present, and thus 'all history is contemporary history.' The 'facts of history are present facts.' The Israelite prophet found in history God's way of pointing to the alternatives in the insistent present. History is not only a mirror in which we see ourselves in the depth and fulness of historic time. It is a word that is spoken to us. History supplies and supports the human sense of heritage and responsibility, of commission and stewardship, of command and destiny.

The great historians have in every age sensed that their vocation was a calling to prophesy. The poorer historians are those who speak without having been spoken to. The naive historians are those who have mistaken their sermons for objective accounts of what actually happened. Gibbon was an excellent example of the apostle who preached with fervour the gospel of those liberal virtues to which he had been so fully converted before he found them in the Antonine Age. All history is judgment. It is first of all judgment of what shall be studied; what are the questions to be asked and of whom the enquiries shall be made. It is judgment in respect of the kinds of evidence that shall be sought and the kinds of criticism to which collected evidence shall be submitted. It is judgment with respect to how evidence, so proved, shall be used. It is judgment in terms of interpretation, and it is judgment in terms of conclusions. And all this judgment, whether it be of matters small or great, follows from the historian's fundamental conviction as to the character of the importance of human life. History is the realm of the divination of goodness, the circle of the conscience, the science of the prophetic word. And this is also the oldest as well as the most persistent notion of history as a discipline. The *Han Shu* so describes the purpose of the *Spring and Autumn Annals:* It 'passes moral judgments on events and is the symbol of good faith.' In the West from the Hellenistic through the Medieval Ages the most frequently quoted definition of history was 'that philosophy that teaches by examples.' For Lord Acton, history was 'the record of truths revealed by experience.' Herbert Butterfield, latest of the great Cambridge historians, is even more straightforward: 'Our final interpretation of history is the most sovereign decision we can take, and it is clear that every one of us, as standing alone in the universe, has to take it for himself. It is our decision about religion, about our total attitude to things, and about the way we will appropriate life. And it is inseparable from our decision about the role we are going to play ourselves in that very drama of history.'

These are now years of exile for Chinese culture. As the Israelites of the Sixth to the Fourth Centuries before Christ had, after humiliating political and military defeat, fled to Egypt or lived as captives in Babylon, so Chinese culture today survives in exile. One Hebrew prophet was convinced, during the last days of Jerusalem, that cultural and spiritual bankruptcy was the real tragedy of that time and of the years before. But then Israel found in exile the opportunity to review its history and to weigh its values—to reconsider the character of importance in respect of defeat and destiny. In fulfilling that task of retrospective prophecy, it found the courage to go on. There are significant disparities in all historical parallels, and there are many in this comparison of the Chinese Diaspora in the mid Twentieth Century and the exile of Israel twenty-five hundred years ago. And yet the task of retrospective prophecy by the waters of this fragrant harbour offers the elements of realism and heroism that are lacking in the alternatives. By the waters of Babylon a community that remembered Moses and suffered deeply from conscience concerning its destiny did light a torch that was handed on from generation to generation of refugees and rebuilders. Chinese studies are the rightful heritage of those who care—not just for porcelains and calligraphy—but for China, for a people; and not in a sentimental way, or in the sad sweet sorrow that mourns a mistress of rare delight, but for the moments of greatness that God has vouchsafed to his people—for those moments of China's past that are eternal amidst the perpetual perishing of past and present.

Part Four

Readings in History

PEOPLE IN GENERAL read history for informative entertainment, adventure and pure delight. History, particularly for the banker or research chemist, can be the most rewarding holiday bringing the excitement of adventure and novelty into the few relaxed hours of a quiet evening at home. Faster than by jet flight he can be wafted away from his climatic surroundings. With the magic of a well told tale he will be bravely borne into other lands and under other skies.

The readings chosen for your pleasure provide a first class world tour. From Hong Kong you will fly westward 'through the malice of time and over the grave of a dream' to touch down where once a mighty city of great power and some splendor was filled with busy, earnest folk intent upon the affairs, as they rather simply called it, of 'real life.' There with C.W. Ceram you will make your own rediscovery of the Assyrian Empire. Then westward again, along the course of civilization, you will come to Greece, for a brief visit with George Santayana, before sailing to Byzantium with Gilbert Highet. Then northward to the meeting of past and present, East and West, in Russia with Sir Bernard Pares. Next comes a rest stop for 'Dinner at Four' in Eighteenth Century London with Arnold Palmer, before the flight across the Atlantic to the new world of the Puritans. Here you will be in the hands of a first rate contemporary historian, Perry Miller, writing about the age and the people with whom he has been content to live out a career of scholarship and sympathetic insight. Leaving the Puritans behind—as they themselves would insist, since you are bound for the theatre—you will hear Frederick Artz describe the 'Origins of Modern Drama.' Then at last, for everyone does at times profess an interest in 'real life,' Henry Steele Commager conducts you from Puritan realism to the wider context of 'American Nationalism.'

THE REDISCOVERY OF THE ASSYRIAN EMPIRE

By
C. W. Ceram

Flat was the land between the Euphrates and Tigris Rivers, but here and there mysterious mounds rose out of the plain. Dust storms swirled about these protuberances, piling the black earth into steep dunes, which grew steadily for a hundred years, only to be dispersed in the course of another five hundred. The Bedouins who rested by these mounds, letting their camels graze on the meager fodder growing at the base, had no idea what they might contain. Believers in Allah, and in Mohammed, his prophet, they knew nothing of the Biblical passages describing their arid land. A question was needed, a powerful intimation, to set in motion the solution of the mounds' layered secrets. This and an attack by an energetic Westerner who knew how to make bold use of pick and shovel.

Here evolved one of archaeology's greatest triumphs, if only for the reason that the land of mounds showed no visible traces of past greatness. There were no temples and statues to fire the archaeological effort, as on the classic earth of Greece and Italy. No pyramids and obelisks reared into the sky as in Egypt, and there were no sacrificial stone blocks to tell a mute story of the gory hecatombs of Mexico and the wilderness of Yucatan. The blank faces of Bedouin and Kurd failed to reflect their ancestral greatness. Local legends reached back little farther in time than the glamorous days of Harun al-Rashid. Earlier centuries swam in twilight and mist. The modern languages spoken in the land of mounds exhibited no intelligible relationship to the languages spoken thousands of years before.

Outside the mounds scattered over the dusty plain, the investigators had little to go on but some poetical descriptions from the Bible. That and some clay shards, covered with cuneiform characters which, as one early observer said, looked as if 'birds had been walking over wet sand.' and which many archaeologists at first mistook for mere ornament. For all these reasons the archaeological conquest in this arena was particularly memorable.

In the Old Testament the region between the Tigris and the Euphrates was called, simply, Aram-naharaim-Syria (land) between the two rivers—this being the Hebraic equivalent for the Greek 'Mesopotamia.' Here were located the famous cities on which the God of the Bible visited

His mighty wrath. Here, in Nineveh and Babylon, reigned terrible kings who had other gods besides Him and therefore had to be expunged from the face of the earth. Today it is called Iraq, and Baghdad is its capital. To the north the area is bounded by Turkey, on the west by French mandated Syria and Transjordan, on the south by Saudi Arabia, and to the east by Persia, or Iran in modern usage.

The two rivers called the Tigris and the Euphrates, which made the land a cradle of culture even as the Nile gave life to Egypt, arise in Turkey. They flow from the northwest to the southeast, come together a short distance above present day Basra—this was not so in ancient times—and empty into the Persian Gulf.

Assyria, the old land of Assur (Asshur), stretched out in the north along the rapidly flowing Tigris. Babylonia, the ancient Sumeria and Akkad, spread out in the south between the Euphrates and the Tigris as far down as the green waters of the Persian Gulf. In an encyclopedia of general information that appeared in 1867, under the heading of Mesopotamia, the following entry is found: 'The land reached its peak under the Assyrian and Babylonian rule. Under the rule of the Arabs it became a possession of the Caliphate, and again bloomed. But with the Seljuk, Tartar, and Turkish incursions, it began to decline, and at present is in part an uninhabited desert.'

Out of the deserts of Mesopotamia rise mysterious mounds, flat-topped, with steep, often eroded slopes, cracked open like the dried sheepmilk cheeses of the Bedouins. These curious mounds kindled the imagination of inquiring spirits to such a degree that it was in Mesopotamia that archaeology as an excavational art celebrated its initial triumphs.

As a young man Paul Emile Botta had already made a trip around the world. In 1830 he entered the service of Mohammed Ali as a physician, and in this capacity also accompanied the Egyptian commission to Sennar. In 1833 the French government made him consul in Alexandria, from which point he made a trip into Yemen, the results of which he comprehensively recorded in a book. In 1840 he was appointed consular agent in Mosul, on the upper Tigris. Evenings, at twilight, when Botta had fled the suffocating heat of the bazaars to refresh himself on horseback excursions out into the countryside, he would see the strange mounds that dotted the landscape everywhere.

But it is not fair to imply that he was the first to notice these startling prominences. Older travelers—Kinneir, Rich, Ainsworth—had already suspected that ruins lay beneath them. The most interesting of these earlier explorers was C. J. Rich, a prodigy like Champollion, who commenced to study the Oriental languages at the age of nine. At fourteen he was already dipping into Chinese. At twenty-four he was counsel for the East India Company in Baghdad. From that vantage point he made trips through the whole valley of Mesopotamia, bringing home valuable booty for the science of his day. Englishmen and Frenchmen, much more often than Germans, Russians, and Italians, have combined an interest in science and the arts with practical affairs. Often, in adventurous fashion, they have been shining representatives of their nationalities in foreign parts and are remembered as men who knew how to combine a high respect for the political necessities with scientific and artistic labors. Recent examples of this type of personality are Paul Claudel and Andre Malraux, the French authors, and Colonel T. E. Lawrence, the English soldier.

Botta was such a man. As a physician he was interested in natural science and as a diplomat he knew how to make the most of his social connections. He was everything, it would seem, but an archaeologist. What he did bring to his future task was a knowledge of native tongues, and an ability, developed during his extensive travels, to establish friendly relations with the followers of the Prophet. He also had a fine constitution and a boundless capacity for work, which even the murderous climate of Yemen and the swampy Nile flatlands could not dent.

Botta set to work without any plan or basic hypothesis to guide him. Vague hope, mingled with curiosity, carried him along. And when he was successful, no one was more surprised than he.

Evening after evening when he closed up his office, with wonderful persistence he reconnoitered the landscape about Mosul. He went from house to house, from hut to hut, always asking the same questions: Have you any antiquities for sale? Old pots? An old vase, perhaps? Where did you get the bricks for building this outhouse? Where did you get these clay fragments with the strange characters on them?

Botta bought everything he could lay hands on. But when he asked the sellers to show him the place where the pieces came from, they shrugged their shoulders, explaining that Allah was great and that such things were strewn about everywhere. One need only look to find them.

Botta saw that he was getting nowhere by quizzing the natives. He decided to try his hand with the spade at the nearest mound of any size, the one at Kuyunjik.

One must imagine what it meant to persist in such apparently fruitless activity; what it meant, particularly, when there was nothing to spur on the would-be digger but the ambiguous notion that the mound might contain something worth the effort of excavation; what it meant to go on day after day, week after week, month after month, without finding anything more re-warding than a few battered bricks covered with signs that nobody could read, or a few sculptured torsos, so badly broken that the original form was quite unrecognizable.

A whole year long!

Should we wonder, therefore, when Botta, after the year had run out, during which innumerable false leads had been brought to him by the natives, at first dismissed a talkative Arab who, in colorful language, reported a mound containing a rich store of all the things the Frank was looking for? The Arab gabbled on, ever more importunately, about how he came from a distant village, how he had heard about the Frank's search, how he loved the Franks and wanted to help them. Was it bricks with inscriptions that Botta wanted? There were masses of them where he lived in Khorsabad, right near his native village. He ought to know, for he had built his own stove out of these same bricks, and everybody else in his village had done the same since time immemorial.

When Botta found he could not rid himself of the Arab, he sent a couple of his workmen to look over the alleged site, some nine or ten miles away.

By sending off this little expedition Botta was eventually to immortalize his name in the history of archaeology. The identity of the Arab informant is forgotten, lost in the drift of the years. But Botta is still remembered as the first to disclose the remains of a culture that had flowered for almost two thousand years, and for more than two millennia and a half had slumbered under the black earth between the two rivers, forgotten by men.

A week later an excited messenger came back to report to his master. Hardly had they turned the first spadeful of earth, the man said, when walls came to light. These walls, when freed of the worst of the dirt that clogged them, proved to be richly carved. There were all kinds of pictures, reliefs, terrible stone animals.

Botta rode over to the site posthaste. A few hours later he was squatting in a pit, drawing the most curious figures imaginable—bearded men, winged animals, figures unlike any that he had ever seen in Egypt, and certainly unlike any sculptures familiar to European eyes. Shortly afterwards he moved his crew from Kuyunjik to the new site, where he put them to work with pick and shovel. And soon Botta no longer doubted that he had discovered, if not all of Nineveh, certainly one of the most splendid palaces of the Assyrian kings.

The moment came when, no longer able to keep this conviction to himself he sent the news to Paris, and so out into the world. 'I believe,' he wrote with pride, and the newspapers made headlines of it, 'that I am the first to discover sculptures that can be truly identified with the period when Nineveh was at its height.'

The discovery of the first Assyrian palace was not only a newspaper sensation. Egypt had always been thought of as the cradle of civilization, for nowhere else could the history of mankind be traced back so far. Hitherto only the Bible had had anything pertinent to say about the land between the two rivers, and for nineteenth-century science the Bible was a collection of legends. The sparse evidence found in the ancient writers was taken more seriously than the Biblical sources. The facts offered by these early writers were not entirely unbelievable, yet often they contradicted one another and could not be made to agree with Biblical dates.

Botta's finds, in consequence, amounted to a demonstration that a culture as old as the Egyptian or even older had once flourished in Mesopotamia—older if one cared to give credence to Biblical accounts. It had risen in might and splendor, only to sink, under fire and sword, into oblivion.

France was fired by Botta's revelations. Aid was mobilized on the most generous scale to enable Botta to continue with his work. He dug for three years, from 1843 to 1846. He fought the climate, sickness, the opposition of the natives, and the interference of the pasha, the despotic Turkish governor of the country. This greedy official could think of only one explanation for Botta's tireless excavations: the Frenchman must be looking for gold.

The pasha took Botta's Arab workmen away from him and threatened them with whippings and imprisonment to get them to tell him Botta's secret. He ringed the hill of Khorsabad with guards, he wrote complaining letters to Constantinople. But Botta was not the sort to be intimidated. His diplomatic experience now came in handy: he countered intrigue with intrigue. The result was that the pasha gave the Frenchman official permission to continue with his project, but unofficially he forbade all natives, on pain of dire punishment, to have anything to do with the Frank. Botta's diggings, he said, were nothing but a pretext for building a fortress to be used in depriving the Mesopotamian peoples of their freedom.

Undeterred, Botta pressed on with his work.

The palace was laid bare, rising up from mighty terraces. Archaeologists who had rushed to the site on reading Botta's original report of his find recognized the structure as the palace of King Sargon, the one mentioned in the prophecies of Isaiah. It was, in fact, a summer palace that had stood on the outskirts of Nineveh, a sort of Versailles, a gigantic Sans Souci built in the year 709 B.C., after the conquest of Babylon. Wall after wall emerged from the rubble, courtyards with richly ornamented portals took shape, public reception rooms, corridors, private apartments, a tripartite seraglio, and the remains of a terraced tower.

The number of sculptures and reliefs was staggering. At one swoop the mysterious Assyrian people were lifted out of the abyss of the past. Here were their reliefs, their household implements, their weapons; here they could be visualized in the domestic round, at war, on the hunt.

The sculptures, however, which in many cases had been made of highly destructible alabaster, fell apart under the hot desert sun after being removed from the protective covering of debris and earth. The French government then commissioned Eugene Napoleon Flandin to help Botta, and he went at once to the Middle East. Flandin was a draftsman of note, who in the past had gone with an archaeological expedition that explored Persian sites, and later had written books about his experiences, containing excellent drawings of ancient sculptures. Flandin became for Botta what Vivant Denon had been for Napoleon's Egyptian commission. But whereas Denon had drawn enduring structures, Flandin had to make hurried records of material that was falling apart under his eyes.

Botta succeeded in loading a whole series of sculptures on rafts. But the Tigris, here at its upper course, was a fast-flowing and tempestuous mountain stream. The rafts whirled about, spun like tops. They tipped to one side, and the stone gods and kings of Assyria, newly resurrected from oblivion, sank once more out of sight.

Botta refused to be discouraged. He sent a new load down-river, this time taking all imaginable precautions, and the trip was a success. At the river mouth the precious pieces of sculpture were loaded aboard an ocean-going vessel, and in due course the first Assyrian carvings arrived on European shores. A few months later they were on exhibition in the Louvre.

Botta himself continued to work on a large frieze, until eventually a commission of nine archaeologists took the task off his hands. One member of the commission was Burnouf, soon to be known as one of the most important French archaeologists—a quarter of a century later he became Heinrich Schliemann's oft-cited 'learned friend.' Another was a young Englishman named Austen Layard, whose later fame was to eclipse Botta's.

Yet Botta's ought not to be forgotten. He was the trail-breaker in Assyria, as Belzoni was in Egypt. Like Belzoni, he was a furious 'digger,' a determined seeker after booty for the Louvre. The role of 'collector' in Nineveh, corresponding to one played by Mariette in Cairo, was filled by another French consul, Victor Place. Botta's account of Nineveh: *Monuments de Ninive decouverts et decrits par Botta, mesures et dessines par Flandin,* is numbered among the classics of archaeological literature. The first two of its five volumes contain plates of architectural and sculptural subjects, the third and fourth the collected inscriptions, and the fifth the descriptions.

SANTAYANA IN GREECE

By
George Santayana

On the way from Beirut to Athens, we saw the coasts of Cyprus and Rhodes, and stopped at a small island and then at Samos. In these islands I first trod Hellenic ground, but without emotion: hardly a stone, hardly a head, reminded me of Hellas. Athens itself, for the most part, was uninspiring. I engaged a youngish man, a Cypriot journalist, as a guide and as a teacher of Greek; but in both respects, in my two months at Athens, I gathered little new knowledge. The social foreground was too cosmopolitan, and the material foreground too ugly and insignificant. We went on one excursion, intending to reach Delphi; but at Corinth we found that the steamer had been purloined by a private pleasure-party, and I had to be satisfied with a trip to Nauplia, for Tiryns and Mycenae, and to Epidaurus. This last, most remote point, proved the most inspiring. Whether it was the light and the solitude, the steepness of the pit, the completeness of the theatre (except for stage) or the somber wooded hills above, somehow all the poetry of early Greece seemed to flood the place:

small, heroic, silvan, open to sea and sky, lyric and divinely haunted.

In the Acropolis I had two or three unexpected intuitions. One regarded the vitality, the dash, the solidity of Greek architecture. The lion's head at the corner of the immensely projecting cornice in the Parthenon seemed to have all the picturesqueness of a gargoyle: and the entablature was not what its name and usual aspect imply, a wooden beam laid across posts: it was a great wall built up over a foundation of columns, like the wall of the Doge's palace in Venice, firmer if not so high. On the other hand, that bold cornice and those broad pediments lent it an even greater dignity. This effect, of the temple raised over peristyle, was new to me, and important. It removed the reproach, that pursues buildings of one storey, of lacking weight and height and being set up on stilts, propped up, rather than built. Here the burden carried seemed sufficient to ennoble the bearers, and to justify their stoutness, their number and their fidelity to one model, like hoplites in a phalanx. This architecture was not merely utilitarian and economical; it was religious and martial.

Beautiful beyond words seemed to me the door and the Ionic porch at the back of the Erechtheum. Byzantine, Saracenic, and Gothic cannot surpass such a thing in loveliness; their advantage lies only in allowing greater variety, so that in a larger and more complex world they could diffuse disparate beauties, more picturesque and romantic than those of Greek buildings.

I left Greece disappointed, not with Greece but with myself. I should have been young and adventurous, knowing the language well, both ancient and modern, and travelling alone, with infinite time before me. Then if the historical Ilyssus proved to be a rubbishy ditch in a dusty waste, I could have found another Ilyssus in some mountain gorge in which to bathe my feet like Socrates and pass in dialectical thought from sham rhetoric to rational love. But the foreground was a dreadful impediment, and I was the worst of impediments, with my middle-aged ignorance, my academic ties, and my laziness. Hellas must remain for me an ideal, a thing to recompose, as the Evangelists recomposed their idea of Jesus, so as to individualise and replenish their ideal of Christ. The real Greece is dead, pulverised, irrecoverable. There remain only a few words and a few relics that may serve to suggest to us a rational ideal of human life.

SAILING TO BYZANTIUM

By
Gilbert Highet

History is a strange experience. The world is quite small now; but history is large and deep. Sometimes you can go much farther by sitting in your own home and reading a book of history, than by getting onto a ship or an airplane and traveling a thousand miles. When you go to Mexico City through space, you find it a sort of cross between modern Madrid and modern Chicago, with additions of its own; but if you go to Mexico City through history, back only 500 years, you will find it as distant as though it were on another planet; inhabited by cultivated barbarians, sensitive and cruel, highly organized and still in the Copper Age, a collection of startling, of unbelievable contrasts.

There is one such world, one historically distant planet, which very few of us have ever visited. This is Byzantium. The city which was called Byzantium is now called Constantinople, or rather Istanbul, in modern Turkey. But the civilization called Byzantine was the Roman Empire: it was the eastern section of the Roman Empire, its oldest and its most culturally fertile area, the Greek part of the Graeco-Roman world. From another point of view, equally important, Byzantium was the Roman Empire refounded as a Christian empire. And do you know that it survived until just 500 years ago, until 1453—nearly 1000 years after the western Roman Empire had crumbled into fragments? It still existed, and it still called itself the Roman Empire, when Christopher Columbus was born—although it fell (as though by some secret logic of history) just before America was discovered. Historically it is closer to us than medieval Mexico; but it feels far away.

All that most of us know about it is that it was beautiful. Its center was one of the loveliest buildings in the entire world, something worthy to rank with the Taj Mahal and Notre Dame: the Cathedral Church of the Holy Wisdom, St. Sophia, with its enormous, airy dome. Some of us also know the strange unforgettable paintings and mosaics of Byzantium: when you enter a Slavic or Greek Church today, or look at an icon, what you see is Byzantine art: those tall thoughtful figures, with vast somber eyes. Connoisseurs know also that much of Byzantine art spread through the rest of Europe and the Middle East. So St. Mark's in Venice, St. Basil's Cathedral in Moscow, the legendary palace of Harun al-Raschid in Baghdad—all these are Byzantine. In fact, we are told that it was the beauty of Byzantium which converted the Russians to Christianity. They had been idol-worshipping pagans until the tenth century; but some of their leaders had been baptized; and their monarch Vladimir began to consider which of the great faiths they ought to adopt. He thought of Judaism; but he said, 'No, the Jews are scattered and powerless.' He thought of Mohammedanism; but that is a teetotal religion, and he said, 'To drink is a joy for the Russians, and we cannot live without drinking.' Then he sent envoys to Byzantium. They were taken to see the Christian services at St. Sophia. When they returned, they said, 'We did not know whether we were in heaven or on earth; for on earth elsewhere there is no such splendor. We know that there God dwells among men.' And so the Russians became Christians converted through Byzantium, and to this day their alphabet, and much of their art, their religion, even their way of life, is Byzantine.

We know, too, that it was a complicated and difficult civilization. If we have read Gibbon, we remember how contemptuosly he dismissed the Byzantines as a succession of priests and courtiers, and how unwilling he was to pay serious attention to their eager discussions of a God in whom he himself scarcely believed, and to their struggles against the barbarism which he believed had by the eighteenth century been largely exterminated. And if we have glanced into modern histories of Byzantium, we have still been bewildered by painfully complex dynastic disputes, and by almost impenetrably difficult and feverishly excitable arguments over what at first seem to us very tiny religious problems.

And the language of Byzantium is Greek—and not wholly classical Greek, but a special Greek of its own. Few translations of Byzantine Greek works are made, and few scholars study them; if it were not for the Dumbarton Oaks group in Washington, there would hardly be any Byzantine scholarship in the entire American continent. Even apart from the language, the literature is awfully hard: long highly elaborate histories, carefully wrought theological treatises, stiff and formal poems, together with wild folk-romances and epic poetry written in a fantastic blend of cultures and languages.

Perhaps Byzantium is too difficult for us? There might be a sound reason for this. You remember that Spengler said that all important cultures followed the same pattern of growth, maturity, and decay, although at different periods in history. Therefore the people of one culture might well sympathize with the people of another culture, although the two were separated by many centuries, provided they were both at the same stage in their development. For example, he called Mohammed a 'contemporary' of Cromwell. Now, if this is true, you see what follows? It follows that people cannot properly understand a stage of history which is later in development than they are—even if it happened a long time ago. Mohammed could have understood Cromwell perfectly, although Cromwell lived 1000 years after him; but he could not have understood Disraeli, or even Napoleon, because they inhabited a later stage of civilization. (We see this in our daily life: you know how hard it is for a youth of twenty to understand a man of fifty—much harder than it is for a man of fifty to understand a youth.) Well, supposing all that is reasonable and true, then we have not reached the stage of development in our own culture which will correspond to Byzantium, and therefore we cannot understand Byzantium fully—just as we cannot now foresee and understand the world our own great-grandchildren will inhabit.

This may be true. Byzantium has a grown-up, an almost elderly feeling, which we do not possess. As we look at the portraits of men and saintly or divine personages which have survived from Byzantium, and see their great thoughtful eyes, and the long powerful faces in which strength and the ability to feel pain are curiously intermingled, we realize that these people were wise with a wisdom which we have not yet attained; that they knew more about the world's problems, even to understanding that some of those problems cannot be solved. But we do not feel that they are behind us, or inferior to us. The difficulty of understanding them is more like the difficulty that young people have in understanding their elders. We are still young. They are mature, and growing old.

Perhaps that is why so little had been written about Byzantium. There are hardly any novels or plays about it: some failures, of course, but few successes. I can recall only Sir Walter Scott's *Count Robert of Paris* and John Masefield's *Basilissa* and *Conquer*. And all these books fail partially, because they are not written with sufficient gusto and richness. The two Masefields deal with the reign of Justinian, but they are supposed to be written by a dry official who has little sympathy with any of the wild passions which blazed through the empire. They are good reporting, but they are like black-and-white reproductions of a complex painting. The Scott novel takes us to Constantinople in the time of the First Crusade. Although it is full of fine ideas, they are not worked out: Scott was very tired when he wrote it. I remember one chapter in which Count Robert is entertained in the sumptuous palace of the emperors. He wakes late, because his wine the night before was drugged. As he wakes, the first thing he sees and hears in the darkness of his room is a tiger, with burning eyes and hungry roaring growls: it had been chained there so that when he moves he will either fall under its claws or else go mad with the effort to avoid it. Now, in his best days, Scott would have made the next half hour into a long splendid combat. But here Count Robert merely throws a stool at the tiger, and fractures its skull, 'which, to say the truth, was none of the largest size'; and then proceeds to escape, with the help of a blind prisoner in the next cell, who has been sawing his way out for years, and of a trained orangoutang which is an assistant warder. A pity that *Count Robert of Paris* was not written when Scott had more energy: it might have been as good as *Ivanhoe*.

Still, there are some fine non-fiction works about Byzantium. (And here, in Washington, we have one of the few great centers of Byzantine studies: the Dumbarton Oaks Library and Research Collection of Harvard University, which puts out a number of learned studies every few months, and is now established as a source of vital new ideas on the subject). The standard book is *Byzantium: An Introduction to East Roman Civilization*, edited by Norman Baynes and H. St. L. B. Moss. Mr. Baynes (of the University of London) is really the top scholar on the subject in the English-speakig world, and to make this introduction he has assembled a group of essays by over a dozen specialists, and has added some fine illustrations and a copious bibliography. Byzantine art can be glimpsed in a new and beautiful collection of reproductions of mosaics in Italy: *Byzantine Mosaics,* edited by Peter Meyer. Very recently the best history of the Byzantine Empire was published in this country, written by A. A. Vasiliev. (It was originally planned in Russia before the Revolution; and then—such are the trials and torments of scholarship—it passed through editions in French, Spanish, and Turkish before attaining its present English form.) It is a profoundly scholarly book with a stupendous bibliography; it may be too elaborate for the ordinary reader, but it will become a standard work.

Beginners like myself are more apt to be interested by enthusiastically appreciative studies of those odd and incomprehensible people. Such enthusiasm struck me first in Robert Byron's *The Byzantine Achievement,* a very youthful book issued in London in 1929; and, linked with wisdom, it appears in one of the most wonderful travel books—no, not travel books—one of the most wonderful books of appreciation, of travel and history, and human character and national psychology, and art and religion, one of the finest books written in our lifetime on apparently one of the least promising subjects, Rebecca West's *Black Lamb and Grey Falcon.*

It describes only one small part of the Byzantine empire, as it is today: the Slavic part of the Balkan Peninsula. It penetrates with unexampled sympathy and sensibility into the souls of those strange countries, Serbia, Montenegro, Macedonia, Bosnia, the lands where trouble grows like grass. Beauty and disease, poverty and courage, ignorance and heroism, narrow minds and broad epic spirits, these and many other contrasts are evoked in Miss West's beautiful and eloquent book. (It is written with love—like Browning's poems on Italy; or like a blend of Hemingway's books on Spanish courage and Sitwell's books on Spanish art.) Miss West has a superb style. Consider a sentence or two, which few others could have composed:

> These handsome peasant women bore themselves as if each wore a heavy invisible crown, which meant, I think, an unending burden of responsibility and fatigue.

And this:

> If during the next million generations there is but one human being in every generation who will not cease to inquire into the nature of his fate, even while it strips and bludgeons him, some day we shall read the riddle of the universe.

And this, the reason she wrote the book:

> If a Roman woman had, some years before the sack of Rome, realized why it was going to be sacked, and what motives inspired the barbarians and what the Romans, and had written down all she knew and felt about it, the record would have been of value to historians. My situation (in 1939-40), though probably not as fatal, is as interesting.

That is our situation at this present time, and it was the situation of the Byzantine Empire. We may not be overrun and sacked; but we could be; attempts have been made on us already, and others will be made. When they are, when we resist them and beat them off, we shall realize more of the mystery, the difficulty, and the preciousness of high civilization; and then we shall understand more of the Byzantine achievement. Byzantium is not only in the past. For us it is a possible world of the future. That is part of its power and remoteness. In 1928, W. B. Yeats published a book of poems about his own old age, called *The Tower*. Its first poem, 'Sailing to Byzantium,' distinguishes the temporary animal life of youth and passion, which Yeats saw himself leaving, from the stately permanent life of thought and art. He sees himself as a Christian saint, one of those

> sages standing in God's holy fire
> As in the gold mosaic of a wall . . .

or as a nightingale made by Greek goldsmiths

> Of hammered gold and gold enamelling
> To keep a drowsy emperor awake;
> Or set upon a golden bough to sing
> To lords and ladies of Byzantium
> Of what is past, or passing, or to come.

That is the world of art, and thought, and history which we inhabit when we gaze into the somber eyes of the Byzantine saints, or look at the sumptuous Byzantine buildings. Our own buildings look like *machines a vivre*, made for the present. Theirs seem to be homes of ceremony and prayer, intended to make the mind large enough to contemplate all that

> is past, or passing, or to come.

RUSSIA—EAST OR WEST?

By
Sir Bernard Pares

One great question runs right through Russian history—Tsars or Bolsheviks—and that is because it is one that Nature puts to Russia, and it runs not only through all her story, but through all her thought as well. Russia is at the boundary of Europe and Asia, straddling over half of Europe and an enormous part of Asia. Any line between the two must be imaginary: that adopted by the government of the Tsars did not correspond to our maps. In reality, the two continents are one, divided only by an idea; and the idea has nothing to do with geography—only with civilisation: but that is exactly what makes the question a difficult one.

The first Russia, that of Kiev, was undoubtedly European, and Kiev, even today, feels more European to one than any other of the large towns of Russia. There was no question in those first days. The Russians, of course, are a branch of that Indo-European stock to which most of the other nations of Europe belong. Their parent family, the Slavs, even in the ninth century, extended not only, as now, to the Adriatic, but to the neighbourhood of Hamburg; Berlin, Dresden, Leipzig are Slavonic place-names, and all the Slavonic languages are extraordinarily closely akin. Kiev was a Viking State, defending Christian Europe from the nomads of Asia. Her princes and princesses intermarried with half the thrones of Europe.

All this was broken off short by the Tartar conquest. Already the northern Russians had been blending with the non-European Finnish tribes, which they found in the forests, where they were seeking shelter from the nomad devastations. The conquest itself tore them away from the uniting influence of their great imperial waterroad and plunged them into a parochial life of small and divided communities in their new forest home. Quite cut off from their mother Europe, they learned the mind and habits of a subject people, the necessity of guile and manoeuvre, of adjournment of all challenge, of a policy of small moves and accumulation of small means, of waiting for life itself to alter all the existing conditions in their favour. No wonder that they became 'Asiatised,' for in all their own actions they had to follow on the purposes of their Asiatic masters. The very blood became mixed. Even the one great European asset that they retained with unfaltering faith, their Christianity, derived as it was from Constantinople, of itself separated them from nearly all the rest of Europe, and, in the darkness and ignorance into which they had been plunged, itself became another kind of parochialism, cutting them off from their natural fellows.

Yet it is no exaggeration to say that, by stemming the Tartar invasion, far the most formidable of the onslaughts of Asia, and slowly sucking all the life out of the Tartar domination, Russia saved Europe from one of the greatest dangers that ever threatened it and allowed it to grow up in its own way, without such a fundamental interruption as had befallen herself: and when the slow moving mills of historical processes, far more surely than any military opposition, had so ground down the conquerors' power that it broke of itself, Russia, who had

had the hard task of Europe's rearguard, was left with the heritage of leading the counter-stroke of Europe into Asia. In the end this came of itself—very rapidly, and almost imperceptibly. The Russian conquest of Kazan in 1552, the last great Tartar stronghold, opened what proved to be an almost unchallenged road to the Pacific.

Two hundred and forty years of subjection, that is a long break in the initiative and enterprise of a nation—and every one of the other Slavonic peoples, Poles, Czechs, Serbs and Bulgars, has suffered the same temporary elimination. And now the long task of catching up again—to re-attach herself to her natural affinity of race and religion—to Europe. This was an equally hard task, and an equally deep aspiration of the Russian people. The strongest element in its favour was Russian Christianity, which, if one looks right through Russian history, comes out as the most unifying and solidifying factor in it. Even today, there is not one essential difference between the accepted doctrine of the Orthodox Church and that of our own. But politically, even the Church itself had not been wholly able to escape the Asiatic inflection. And when Russia at last turned round and looked westward, she found all sorts of new obstacles in her way, sometimes created by religion.

On three sides—north, centre and south—new barriers had arisen, each of which, as it was attacked, seemed only to become more formidable. It was a veritable labour of Hercules, constantly extending and expanding. In the north were the German settlements on the Baltic which, when they at last broke up politically, only opened the door to a terrific struggle with Sweden at her strongest that occupied nearly the whole long reign of Peter the Great. In the south was the last remaining Tartar stronghold in Crimea, and when that began to fall to pieces, it was replaced by the far more formidable barrier of Turkey. But the longest duel of all was in the centre, with Poland, and that bitter feud, with nationality acerbated by religion, has run all through Russian history and is not finished yet. It began with a fight for the mastery of the disputed provinces which have come again into the limelight since the beginning of World War II, but were then united in a vast intermediate State known as Lithuania, stretching at one time almost from the Baltic to the Black Sea. Here Poland was at first the winner. She united 'Lithuania' to her under her own crown. She also did all she could to bring the Russian peasantry, who were the chief element in the population of that mixed State, under the authority of the Pope. On this side Russia was at

first and for a long time engaged solely in a policy of what we now
call 'self-determination,' very clearly understood as such—to use the
language of the time, the reassembling of all Russian population under
a Russian sovereign.   The life and death struggle came to a long
pause with the partition of Poland at the end of the eighteenth century.
Poland disappeared from the map.   Russia at that time did not annex
purely Polish territory, but in this peculiarly shameful deal, she
connived at its partition between Austria and Prussia.   The Napoleonic
Wars engaged Russia much further, making her mistress of Warsaw
itself.   That was nothing but a source of constant trouble to her, and
in the last wars she at first lost not only her hold on the heart of
Poland but most of the long-disputed provinces as well.

But it was not only territorially that Russia, throughout this long
period, was persistently straining westwards.   Against Poland she was
at least fighting under the flag of nationality, against Turkey under
that of Christendom, but also with a growing interest in the smaller
Slavonic nationalities of the Balkans, which ultimately heightened into
a national crusade and is commonly described, rather vaguely, by the
name of Panslavism.   It need hardly be said that Russia's treatment
of Poland has proved the greatest discouragement to minor Slav
peoples to trust themselves to her.   But that was one of the cardinal
follies of Tsardom which was vigorously opposed by most of the
Russian thinking public as soon as it found means of expressing itself.
In the north, on the Baltic coast, Russia's plea was neither national
nor religious.   It was first of all economic.   But it also had
a far-reaching political purpose.   She was trying to force her way
over small peoples, always so far in subjection to others, in order to
get an outlet of her own to Europe.   This was the main objective of
the three most enlightened statesmen of Russian history—John the
Terrible, Ordyn-Nashchokin, Minister of Tsar Alexis, and Alexis's
son, Peter the Great.   There is nothing surprising in the fact that
this struggle was completed first of the three, and that Peter, who
spent most of his reign on it, was also the outstanding workman in
the Europeanising of Russia.

But was Russia to imitate Europe at the cost of her own soul? She
was so far behind Europe that she might almost think so.   Thinking
Russians were poignantly conscious of this backwardness.   They were
like the schoolmaster close to the Urals who said to me, 'So good of
you to be interested in our Asia.'   It was at once a confession of
inferiority and an ironical protest.   In this remark we see at the same

time the germs of the rival instincts of the Slavophile and the Westerniser, the two great currents of Russian political thought. We English people have never realised how much more Europe is to them than it is to us, and how many painful heartsearchings it has given them.

If there was ever anything like the Renaissance in Russia, it was in the time of Peter's father, Alexis. Then all was happy and confident. Alexis was the most gentle and lovable of Russian sovereigns, and he found no difficulty in blending the new with the old. Sovereign, nobles and people would go forward hand in hand. They need not fear to move, and they need not hurry. They would be in no danger of ceasing to be themselves, and what they chose to absorb from the West they would digest at their own pace. But in the wilds outside the small court circle, the blackness was so abysmal that it would take a revolution to penetrate it, and the revolution came from the throne itself with Peter.

In Russia it was always a question between the slow way and the rapid, the peaceful progress and the storm of change. Klyuchevsky has said of another Russian statesman that he went so fast that he raised a wind against him, and Peter himself was like an elemental convulsion. The easy synthesis of Alexis was smashed to pieces. Everything was to go by order: a wholesale imitation of the West, entirely utilitarian and to the profit of the throne and the State.

There could be no better illustration than his foundation of St. Petersburg. It was not even in Russia but Estonia. It was a marsh— constantly flooded—on which no one was meant to live. It can hardly even be drained properly. It was a few miles from the Finnish frontier—an absurd position for the capital of so vast an empire. The government was thus isolated from the people, and every question had to come to this far corner to receive an official answer. This region could not grow its own food, let alone supply the capital; and the food supply of St. Petersburg had to be a firstclass achievement of transport, in a country of which transport was one of the weakest features. No one else had ever dreamed of putting the capital here. Yet, as human labour was the only source, masses of it were worn out in laying solid foundations in the marsh, watchtowers were set up to anticipate the flooding of the great river, and the building of stone or brick houses was stopped all over the empire until that of the new city had got well under way.

All sorts of moral values perished in this process of hurricane change. And the enthroned innovator himself had, so to speak, to feel his way gradually upward from the thing that he wanted to the way in which it could be produced for him. Europe had taken generations to create all these things, and there was no short-circuiting. First the object (say the weapon, for with Peter war came first), then the man who knew how to use it, the trainer for the man, and, last, the civilisation which could have inspired and produced the training. The natural order was completely reversed. And Peter himself, who was essentially an opportunist, was throughout learning his own way upward. And with civilisation throughout went conquest: conquest westward, for which Russia was culturally not qualified. Under Peter's one true successor, Catherine, this contrast became even more appalling. Poland partitioned, the Black Sea won, the door to Europe opened wide—and meanwhile the slough of serfdom more threatening than ever in the rear.

And at that moment blows through the open door the great storm of the French Revolution, and the wars that follow draw Russia into Europe as never before. She partakes in full of its common life. Indeed Russia—though in a curiously negative way, by the strength of resistance in her backward people—proved to be the main factor in the fall of Napoleon. To Europe it looked as if the old had triumphed after all, in the person of Russia. There is something like a paralysis of the intellect that overtakes even such a realistic historian as the Frenchman, Theirs, in the contemplation of this awful vengeance of the unknown.

Not so with Russia, where the new ideas already began their counterstroke with the widespread conspiracy of the Decembrists. We in England, satisfied with our own Revolution, had looked patronisingly at the first beginnings of revolution in France, and when they went beyond our measure and our interest, we turned aside with instinctive alarm and aversion. For Russia everything was yet to come; and Russians charted the whole story with all its diverse currents with an eagerness and accuracy as would never have occurred to us.

In the great slump that followed in Europe, largely under the influence of the Russian imperial power—with the old princes, more obstinately unintelligent than ever, restored everywhere, as if there had been nothing more than a bad dream—Europe was thinking hard, and Russia perhaps the hardest of all. No one with intellect could think that this was to be the end. The reaction was headed by the Russian sovereign and the first Minister of Austria; and as Europe slowly recovered, there came from time to time, again from Paris,

minute bells that marked the revival of the challenge. The reign of
Nicholas I (1825-55) was nothing else than one long rearguard action
against the new ideas, and every assertion of them in Europe was
followed by all-round and indiscriminate repression in Russia. As a
liberal Russian censor wrote, 'When they play tricks in Europe, the
Russian gets a smack.'

In this atmosphere, more than ever, rose again the old controversy of
East and West, this time, of Slavophile and Westerniser. Could Russia
produce a soul of her own? It didn't look much like it. Then must
she succumb wholesale to imitation of the West? What a complete
confession of failure! It began with the publishing of a private letter
without the knowledge of the writer. Chaadayev, who wrote it, was
isolated from both camps and had leanings toward Catholicism. Russia,
he said, as a distinctive moral force, had no past, present or future;
she had no contribution to make to the world. Nicholas I officially
declared him to be mad. Both Slavophiles and Westernisers were,
directly or indirectly, alike pupils of the great German thinkers. The
Slavophile, Kircyevsky, most fascinating thinker, found a basis for a
civilisation of Russia's own in her earliest teachers, the old Greek
ascetics. Intellect, logic are not everything. In the whole man, heart
and mind, intuition and reason should be working in complete harmony.
In the West, modern humanism had separated them, but not in Russia.
There the corporate consciousness was still entire, as witnessed by
Orthodoxy and the village community. By the way, Slavophilism is in
no way to be identified with Panslavism: the first is a sincere product
of Russian thought; the second is a weapon in the armoury of Russian
foreign policy. Belinsky and his Westernising friends would take
wholesale from the West, but were anything but clear as to what
they wanted to take. Most of them were attuned for secularism and
atheism, but, like the Bolsheviks who were to follow them, they turned
these into a religion. At bottom, every intelligent Russian is both a
Slavophile and a Westerniser, just as, after all, Russia continues to lie
between East and West.

The Crimean War was provoked by Panslavism, the imperial demand
for an extension of Russian influence. In the end it was a victory on
Russian soil of the West, almost at its most inefficient, over Russia,
which was worse. It was a war of the fighting man, and on the
Russian side, if we leave out the engineer general Todleben, all the
distinction that there was went to the Russian peasant soldier. Western
lessons were learned, even on the throne, and it was followed by the

Emancipation and the other great reforms. But their significance was almost entirely missed abroad, especially in England, who ought to have been the first to give them recognition. Our eyes were blurred by the bogey of Russophobia, an exaggerated fear for our hold on India, just as they are now obscured by an exaggerated fear of Bolshevism. In Russia itself the public mind was confused by the vaguest political theories, which monopolised all our sympathies.

Meanwhile Russia, as usual when humiliated in the West, recoiled into the far easier East, where she absorbed enormous new territories which brought her appreciably nearer to India. That was quite enough to frighten us, though the methods of advance were similar to those of our own empire-builders. When the misgoverned Balkans again took fire, we were not able to distinguish between the grasping imperialism of Nicholas I and the national and religious crusade that dragged his unwilling son into war with Turkey; which had to be explained to us too late by Turgenev. This time Russia won, but only to face another galling humiliation from the West in the settlement of Berlin. Alexander II was almost as much blamed by the Slavophiles for accepting this as he was by the 'Nihilists' for not further revolutionising the structure of the State. There was as yet no clearly formed Liberal public opinion. Of the last five Tsars, it has been the two who made concessions that did not perish by the hands of assassins.

As usual, and with doubly good reason, Russia, that is the Russian Government, retired into itself and sulked—and again set itself to find out what could be made of the easier road eastwards. At home, it was at first a case of just sitting tight. For Alexander III, a strong man with a narrow mind, his course of home policy was permanently set by the murder of his reforming father. Only for the peasants he made an exception; every manifestation of initiative in the educated public was kept under the harrow. Now that the bright hope of liberating the lesser Slav peoples and of perhaps replacing the Cross on Saint Sophia was gone, there seemed less reason than ever for treating the 'home aliens' of the Empire with anything like common decency. This was the worst time for the Poles and Germans—later for the Finns, and always for the Jews.

Imperialism instead of constitutions, Asia instead of Europe, those were the watchwords given from the throne to the Russian people. Yet all the time Russia went forward rapidly of herself. However persistently the Government might shut its eyes, the vast economic forces released by the Emancipation were always bringing Russia

economically, and therefore politically, closer into the common fold of
Europe. The eastern advance, which went so well with reaction, was
at first prosecuted with reservations and restraint, for Alexander was
clear that he did not want war. But when his weak–willed son Nicholas
II replaced him, all restraint and caution were dropped, and common
adventurers took charge of eastern policy. It was not possible to get
away from civilisation by plunging one's head into the depths of Asia.
In the perpetual search for sea outlets, the head peeped out on the far
side, only to receive a crushing blow from that Asiatic government
and people which had been most willing to learn all that Europe could
teach them. That was the lesson of the Russo-Japanese War, and it
set rolling a great wave of new vigour in the Russian people which,
after shaking the very foundations of the throne, at least gave Russia
a national representative assembly.

In this bankruptcy of the eastern policy, Russia, of course, turned
again towards Europe. In this new period, policy, economics, thought,
national aspirations, all combined to westernise Russia, and this time
the westernising went deeper than ever before. It ended in her playing
an outstanding part in the earlier years of a first-class European
struggle. But as so often with her contacts with the West, this one
too brought home convulsions on the same world-scale.

In all that follows, Russia does not and cannot escape this constant
antithesis of East and West. It speaks a new language, but it is there
just the same. Within the new framework, the early Bolsheviks are
the new Westernisers—who want to engage Russia in the promotion
of revolution all over Europe and in America. Lenin, almost as if
without concern, makes enormous sacrifices of territory. Stalin is the
national leader of the Soviet homeland, who recovers the lost territory,
plants his feet between Europe and Asia—that is, in the centre of
Russia—and faces both ways, in home organisation and home defence,
against the double menace of Germany and Japan.

DINNER AT FOUR

By
Arnold Palmer

The English of 1780 did not, of course, invent their day; they
inherited it, made their modifications, and passed it on, as is done by

every generation. They took over, with the rest, a steady tendency
which had persisted throughout the century and throughout the
centuries, a tendency for dinner, the main meal of the day, to become
later. They may well have been unaware of it, for the tendency,
having been very active during the reigns of the first two Georges,
was in a lull. But its progress, if irregular, was irresistible, or seemed
to be. A crisis—rebellion, revolution, war—usually gave it a little extra
push, but even in peaceful times it had its own gentle impetus. At
the beginning of the sixteenth century, Henry VII's England dined at
11 a.m. One hundred and fifty years later, Cromwell's England dined
at 1 o'clock. By the beginning of the eighteenth century the hour was
2, and still moving on. Steele, though he was only fifty-seven when
he died in 1729, noted that 'in my memory, the dinner hour has crept
from 12 o'clock to 3'.

Familiar and convenient in warmer countries farther south, a long
break in the middle of the day is ill-suited to our cooler, darker
atmosphere. Nobody, however, seems to have been troubled by the
waste of the daylight hours, the snapping of all continuity, the paralysis
of the broken-backed day. On the contrary, the changes were invariably
resented by the more responsible citizens, who saw in them nothing
but manifestations of restlessness and instability by their immature
and thoughtless juniors. A few years before his death Pope's friend,
Lady Suffolk, was dining as late as four; and the poet, now turned
fifty, came to the reluctant decision that he could not go the pace
and must absent himself henceforward from her table at Marble Hill.

That was 1740, that was smart and highbrow Twickenham. To
University Common Rooms and Cathedral Closes Pope, with his habit
of dining at 2, must have seemed no less skittish than the Countess.
John Richard Green tells us that when, in 1723, Queen Caroline sent
a buck to Magdalen, 'the dinner at which it appears is at 10 a.m.
Each advance was made amidst grumblings from the older and more
conservative members'. He goes on to quote from Hearne's diary of
the same year:

> Tis an old custom for the scholars of all houses on Shrove
> Tuesday to dine at 10 o'clock, at which time the little bell,
> called pancake bell, rings at St. Maries, and to sup at 4 p.m.,
> which was always followed in St. Edmund's Hall as long as
> I have been in Oxford till yesterday, when they went to dinner
> at twelve and supper at six. Nor were there any fritters at

dinner as there used always to be. When laudable old customs alter 'tis a sign learning dwindles.

Things moved, then, even at the Universities, and by 1767 Balliol had fixed the hour of dinner at 2 and of supper at 8. But the fashionable world kept its lead; by 1780 only the oldest inhabitants could remember Lady Suffolk's victory, only the most learned could be unaware of its consequences. The reader, on the other hand, if he pursues his way, will find his thoughts often returning to her, and to Pope. Behind and between all the pages of this book there is always a dashing hostess, there is always an ageing and discomposed celebrity. They are with us still; the struggle is constantly renewed, and no less regularly the lady wins. Perhaps it is as well that she should. But in the days just past, when Miss Burney had been scribbling away in secret at her *Evelina, or The History of a Young Lady's Entrance into the World*, she was clearly untroubled by the thought that that World had known any innovations up to a day some eighteen months before her narrative opens. It is precisely this unconcern that keeps her story perennially fresh.

So here, now, and at last, with ties straightened and throats well cleared, let us turn to the day as revealed not only in the Burney novels and diary but in the diaries and correspondence of her contemporaries also. There is plenty of confirmation.

Breakfast

Since the stomach, the English stomach, does not care to remain inactive for more than four or five hours, breakfast advanced with dinner, though more slowly. In 1780, both in and out of London, it was and for some while had been customary to defer the first meal of the day till 10 o'clock. Most people had by then been up for two or three hours, but there was, of course, no hard and fast rule. Country-dwellers probably rose earlier than town-dwellers—the heroine of Cecilia, after her first night in London, 'arose with the light' and found herself amid sleepy servants doing the fires. Whether or not Miss Burney intended it, such behaviour certainly suggests a dewy innocence. But in both town and country much was accomplished during the hours before breakfast. Letters were written, housekeepers interviewed, and walks taken, flowers picked and arranged, music practised and studies pursued, and calls, business or social, could be paid. When, for instance, a playwright arrived at Mrs. Thrale's

before breakfast with a play in his pocket, the ladies were more
flattered than amused or surprised. During the meal itself, visitors
would often drop in and set themselves at table; such calls could be
formal or informal, and their correct interpretation sometimes needed
address. A few mornings after her defeat by the servants Cecilia,
still the guest of the Harrels in their London house, found a Miss
Larolles at breakfast. She did not learn till later that Miss Larolles
had been 'waiting on her' and was gravely offended when Cecilia
failed to pay a return visit within the regulation three days.

Breakfast was a highly conversational meal and it could go on for
a long time—there is a breakfast in *Evelina* which lasts till nearly 1
o'clock—but usually it ended about 11. Nevertheless, it seems to have
been still a fairly light meal, not to be compared with some of the
breakfasts to be described in the following chapters. We read of a
gentleman plying a lady with 'cakes, chocolate, or whatever the table
afforded'. A Swiss pastor, C. P. Moritz, who spent a long and cheap
holiday in England in 1782, was given no more than tea and bread
and butter for his breakfast. 'The slices of bread and butter which
they give you with your tea are thin as poppy leaves. But there is
another kind of bread and butter usually eaten with tea, which is
toasted by the fire and is incomparably good. This is called 'toast.'
With breakfast at 10, elevenses were presumably not yet invented; but
Moritz makes it clear that twelveses, oneses, or twoses were already
a national habit. He noticed another national habit. 'I would always,'
he wrote, 'advise those who wish to drink coffee in England to mention
beforehand how many cups are to be made with half an ounce, or
else the people will probably bring them a prodigious quantity of
brown fluid.'

Some years before he could buy a cup of tea, the Englishman could
buy a cup of coffee; indeed, from the days of Charles II to the days
of George II, more coffee was bought and brewed by the Londoner
than by any citizen in the world. There is no evidence to show that
he ever learned or wished to learn the knack of making it, or knew
that there was one. Repeated efforts to instruct him have left him
almost unmoved, and the time is approaching when we should, perhaps,
acknowledge that he, like Lady Suffolk, has won.

Dinner

Dinner could be at any time between 3 and 5; by it, and not by
the sun, the day was divided. A man or woman, if at home, would

wear a housegown and undressed hair until 2 or 3 o'clock. This was especially true of the City, where there were fewer idlers and less thought for appearances than in St. James's It was 'morning' till one dined. 'Shall you be at home to-morrow morning?' asked Lord Orville; and, on Evelina's assurance that she was likely to be found, he added, 'About three o'clock?'

Our Swiss pastor, having few friends, dined at a coffee-house; he had no difficulty in finding one to suit him, a quiet, decorous place where clients read the newspapers and never dreamed of talking. There were coffee-houses for all tastes and purses, except those of the poorest classes. For them there were cook-houses, differentiated from the coffee-houses not only by their prices but also by their dirt and stench. Moritz, though he found a decent place, could not afford the better restablishments, and resigned himself to 'a piece of half boiled or half oasted meat; and a few cabbage-leaves, boiled in plain water; on which they pour a sauce made of flour and butter, the usual method of dressing vegetables in England.' But at least he could satisfy his intellectual appetite. In the higher.class houses, where gentlemen would not dine under a 'guinea, quarterlies and magazines were provided and newspapers were filed for a year; for the trades-man spending 2s., at the chop-house, newspapers were as customary as salt-cellars; and even the mechanic, carrying his half-pound of beef or ham to the ale house, found newspapers there for those who could read. Authority, regarding the coffee-houses with an inflamed eye, mistook them for the cause, when they were merely the occasion, of the arguments of the disaffected. Under the press restrictions of Charles II they were forbidden to sell reading matter; the managements, by providing it free of charge, added to the number and eloquence of their clients.

Four o'clock was the commonest hour. The Thrales at Streatham, Cowper and Mrs. Unwin in their retired Buckinghamshire village, and (for the most part) the hostesses of *Evelina*, all dined at 4. At about 3 o'clock reception rooms and gardens began to empty; for the costumes and *coiffures* of the age an hour was none too long. Lord Orville, then, timed his call at 3 o'clock with the express purpose of catching Evelina alone, and she was not for a moment deceived.

Keeping to the near side of 4 o'clock there were, as there always are, ancient bodies, like colleges and livery companies; and they were regarded then, as today, as picturesque at a distance but inconvenient at close quarters. In October 1876 Sir Joshua Reynolds scribbled a note to Boswell, offering to take him to dine with the painter Stainers 'in their Hall in the City. . .as you love to see life in all its modes, if you have a mind to go I will call on you about two o'clock, the blackguards dine at half an hour after.'

Similarly, there were the spiritual, or social, descendants of Lady Suffolk whose efforts though often premature and unsuccessful, were continual and, in the end, prevailing. A number of years had still to elapse before ordinary people, on ordinary occasions, dined later than 4; but century after century, always kept up and always in the same direction, the pressure on the dinner-hour goes on. This pressure, sometimes weaker, sometimes stronger, never entirely relaxes even when the unpredictable day arrives and the garrison gives way. Individuals may hold out, social upheavals may prove momentarily stronger; but the pressure goes on and, in the end, dinner is eaten a little later.

At the time with which we are dealing an invitation to dinner could be, in effect, an invitation to spend seven or eight hours in company, from 3.45 till 11 or midnight; and it covered more meals than one. Unallotted to one another in the reception room, unplaced at table, the party entered the dining-room in a polite mob, gentlemen bringing up the rear and at once manoeuvring for position, and ladies, in spite of their recognized and practised helplessness, possibly finding themselves not too tiresomely surrounded. When the up-start Morrice seated himself next to Cecilia, Mr. Monckton by the use of a little ingenuity made him stand up for an instant, when he immediately inserted himself into Morrice's chair. Except for Morrice's laugh there was no comment, not even of silence.

Ladies were for ever being handed in and out of coaches and sedan chairs, up and down steps, in and out of seats at the theatre, through doors and past obstacles; but their hands, though sometimes kissed, were never shaken, and as we have seen they entered the dining-room without a supporting arm.

When the long meal was drawing to a close, the tablecloth was removed for dessert and wine. The ladies now usually, but not invariably, retired; if they went, one or more of the men might accompany them without exciting remark unless the party was smallish or the host touchy about his port; and if it was, as of course it was, the general custom of the ladies to depart for coffee and the men to remain for wine, we should note that, in a period now regarded as highly formal, there was altogether greater freedom than at a set dinner-party today. Any man with a weak head or an engaged heart might quit the circulating decanter and wander into the drawing-room whenever he felt like doing so. If he was quick, he might be in time for the coffee with which the ladies were presently served. 'Tea-board, urn and cake bearers' arrived about 8.30 and the gentlemen, warned by the butler, arrived with them, their legs presumably a little stiff after four hours and more at table.

In modest households, and when no company was entertained, the whole programme was naturally curtailed and the family ready for tea at any time from 7 o'clock, dinner having been at 4. (Today, in thousands of modest homes, where the last set meal is high tea at 6 or 6.30, tea with cakes and sandwiches is similarly welcomed some three hours later.) From the succulent pages of the Reverend James Woodforde we receive the impression that he sometimes drank tea and coffee simultaneously. He may well have done so after one of those simple dinners alone with his niece—'boiled chicken and a pig's face, a bullock's heart and a rich plumb pudding.'

Supper

Those cups of tea, those cakes and sandwiches fulfilled their little mission of revival. But even with their help a repast, however large, at 4 o'clock could not support people, least of all people of the eighteenth century, through the night and into the middle of the following morning. A further meal, varying in splendour with the establishment but commonly substantial, came on between 10 and 11— cold meats, sweets, fruit, and wine on ordinary occasions, a choice of hot dishes when company was present.

A hearty man like Mr. Woodforde, his natural appetite sharpened by Norfolk air, did not care to wait till 11, even when the presence of four or five friends gave him an excuse for a less frugal repast than the one just mentioned. There was that October night, when they sat down six at table:

I gave them for dinner a dish of fine Tench which I had caught out of my brother's pond in Pond Close this morning, Ham, and 3 Fowls boiled, a plumb pudding; a couple of Ducks roasted, a roasted neck of pork, a plumb Tart and an Apple Tart, pears, Apples and Nutts after dinner; White Wine and red, Beer and Cyder. Coffee and Tea in the evening at six o'clock. Hashed Fowl and Duck and Eggs and potatoes etc. for supper. We did not dine till four o'clock—nor supped till ten.

Woodforde's high colour catches the eye, but eighteenth-century

England was not exclusively rubicund. There were paler households, like Cowper's, where supper was 'a Roman meal....a radish and an egg.'

Theatrical performances began at 7. People going to the play would thus have no difficulty in dining and supping at home. If the rendezvous was at the theatre, or if a man and his wife went by themselves, dressing might be deferred till 6 o'clock, after dinner.

The Day

In 1786, when she was fifteen years old, Lord Sheffield's daughter Maria Josepha Holroyd, wrote a letter. She was at home, at her father's house in Sussex; she had not much news; and it may be doubted whether even she supposed that her letter—schoolgirlish, high spirited, shrill, and rather breathless—was of the faintest importance. But because she had the habit of telling her friends what they knew already, subsequent generations have noted and quoted her.

I get up at 8, I walk from 9 to 10; we then breakfast; about 11, I play on the Harpsichord or I draw. 1, I translate, and, 2, walk out again, 3, I generally read, and, 4, we go to dine, after Dinner we play at Backgammon; we drink Tea at 7, and I work or play on the piano till 10, when we have our little bit of Supper and, 11, we go to bed....I think I have very near carried another point, which is to breakfast down stairs.

Precise and perfect, there is the story of one kind of day, and a far from uncommon one.

Evelina might doubt whether breakfast, compared with dinner and supper, 'may be called a *meal*', but its place in the middle of the morning made it one of the two main hinges of the day. Of this day there were three parts—before breakfast, between breakfast and dinner, and after—and for many months of the year the first and third divisions were, as often as not, spent indoors.

Between the end of breakfast at 11 and the beginning of dressing for dinner at 3, four hours were left for the day, or for the daylight. They were uninterrupted hours, or could be so for anyone prepared to forego the 1 o'clock snack at the pastry-cook's or the coffee-house; and for people of fashion, with plenty of servants to do the household shopping, they were apparently ample. But grumblings already were audible about a domestic crisis, a difficulty of obtaining servants or of paying their rising wages. In 1772 black servants, who had hitherto been slaves and unpaid, became free; some went home, while those who remained swelled the wage–list. To us, the crisis does not seem very severe; Mr. Woodforde, whose income was in the neighbourhood of £400, could keep five servants at a total cost, in wages, of £22. 10s. 6d. per annum. But everything is a matter of comparison, and wages had risen and the once endless supply of likely girls and boys was increasingly and noticeably being tapped by industry. The wives of men of good income were, moreover, accustomed at this time to a leisure which their mothers had not known. Admirable but strenuous, the days had gone by when households were self-supporting, when everything was made or provided at home. Shops and itinerant tradesmen were rapidly increasing, and the lady of fashion looked to her domestic staff to do the routine work of catering and upkeep. She was, therefore, very sensitive to even the shadow of a threat to the supply of labour, plentiful and cheap, and she easily grumbled. But, in fact, she was very far indeed from having much to grumble at, and we may leave her with her problem of filling in her four hours at a stretch, with no children to be taken to school, no queues to be joined, no one at home expecting a midday meal, no children to be fetched from school, no crockery and cutlery to be cleaned, no beds to be made, no absent charwoman to be wondered about. Perhaps I shall be expected to say that the pace, too, was slower, but anyone who has read *Evelina* and *Cecilia* must have his doubts on that point.

For the rest of the world four hours were not enough. We have seen that a certain amount of work, particularly correspondence, could be got through before breakfast; lawyers, politicians, civil servants (including the King and his ministers), the professional classes generally, all these often worked long hours after dinner. The equivalent of the modern business man, having an office in London and a house at Working, hardly existed; his prototype seldom had or saw the need to work. Yet shops, including shops in fashionable districts, were open as long as twelve hours a day; and if, from the nature of their business, we are sometimes led to wonder what customers they served at 8 in the morning or 7 at night, it is clear that dinner at 4 was by no means a signal for the shutters.

For that considerable proportion of the public which had nothing to do, it would be truer to say that the hour was a beginning. The previous hours had been filled by visits to or from the tailor or dressmaker, in leisurely and talkative patronage of the bookseller, in attendance at rehearsal of a play or opera, in watching the conjuring up Portland Place beneath the elegant wand of the Adam brothers, and everywhere and always in gossip—in brief, in collecting something smart to wear or talk about from 4 o'clock onwards.

In an age markedly social and sociable, the day was hardly long enough for all the little confabulations and forgatherings so dear to the hearts of the models for Backbites and Sneerwells and Surfaces. The calls which began before breakfast went on until supper-time. Men-about-town of assured position, men like Horace Walpole, would wander out after dinner in search of ever more friends and ever more conversation. 'New-dressed by seven, went to Madame Walpole's, and then supped at Lady M. Churchill's,' he noted, being then in his seventy-fourth year and rather proud of these 'feats of agility.' Invited or uninvited, he had no fear of being unwelcome; but other guests, especially if male and unattached, were frequently asked to come in for tea, cards, and supper, no slight being intended or felt by an invitation to join a party rising from the dining-table.

The dining club and the tavern are often indicated as promoters of still further sociability; but a French observer blamed them for 'the lack of society' which he found in London. In theory, and occasionally in practice, the *habitues* of such places passed the night in brilliant conversation. More often they were sunk, not an idea stirring, in the labours of digestion and the fumes of wine. Goldsmith, before ending up as a member of the most famous of all dining clubs, had experimented with other gatherings of less illustrious company. From the boredom of those evenings he extracted nothing save matter for a good essay.

THE PURITANS AND DEMOCRACY

By
Perry Miller

Although in the year 1740 some fairly flagrant scenes of emotional religion were being enacted in Boston, it was mainly in the Connecticut Valley that the frenzy raged and whence it spread like a pestilence to the civilized East. The Harvard faculty of that time would indeed have considered the Great Awakening a 'crisis,' because to them it threatened everything they meant by culture or religion or just common decency. It was a horrible business that should be suppressed and altogether forgotten. Certainly they would not have approved its being dignified as a starting-point in a series of great American crises.

As far as they could see, it was nothing but an orgy of the emotions. They called it—in the lexicon of the Harvard faculty this word conveyed the utmost contempt—'enthusiasm.' It was not a religious persuasion: it was an excitement of overstimulated passions that understandably slopped over into activities other than ecclesiastical and increased the number of bastards in the Valley, where already there were too many. And above all, in the Valley lived their archenemy, the deliberate instigator of this crime, who not only fomented the frenzy but was so lost to shame that he brazenly defended it as a positive advance in American culture. To add insult to injury, he justified the Awakening by employing a science and a psychological conception with which nothing they had learned at Harvard had prepared them to cope.

It was certainly a weird performance. Edwards delivered his revival sermons - for example the goriest, the one at Enfield that goes by the title 'Sinners in the Hands of an Angry God' and is all that most people nowadays associate with his name—to small audiences in country churches. In these rude structures (few towns had yet prospered enough to afford the Georgian churches of the later eighteenth century which are now the charm of the landscape) the people yelled and shrieked, they rolled in the aisles, they crowded up to the pulpit and begged him to stop, they cried for mercy. One who heard him described his method of preaching: he looked all the time at the bell rope (hanging down from the roof at the other end of the church) as though he would look it in two; he did not stoop to regard the screaming mass, much less to console them.

Of course, in a short time the opinion of the Harvard faculty appeared to be vindicated. In 1740 Edwards had writhing in the churches not only his own people but every congregation he spoke to, and he dominated the entire region. Ten years later he was exiled, thrown out of his church and town after a vicious squabble (the fight against him being instigated by certain of the first citizens, some of them his cousins, who by adroit propaganda mobilized 'the people' against him), and no pulpit in New England would invite this terrifying figure. He had no choice but to escape to the frontier, as did so many misfits in American history. He went to Stockbridge, where he eked out his last years as a missionary to a lot of moth - eaten Indians. Because of the works he produced under these—shall we call them untoward?—circumstances, and because he was still the acknowledged leader of the revival movement, he was invited in 1758 to become president of the College of New Jersey (the present - day Princeton), but he died a few weeks after his inauguration, so that his life really belongs to the Connecticut Valley.

One may well ask what makes such a chronicle of frenzy and defeat a crisis in American history. From the point of view of the social historian and still more from that of the sociologist it was a phenomenon of mass behavior, of which poor Mr. Edwards was the deluded victim. No sociologically trained historian will for a moment accept it on Edwards's terms - which were, simply, that it was an outpouring of the Spirit of God upon the land. And so why should we, today, mark it as a turning-point in our history, especially since thereafter religious revivals became a part of the American social pattern, while our intellectual life developed, on the whole, apart from these vulgar eruptions? The answer is that this first occurrence did actually involve all the interests of the community, and the definitions that arose out of it were profoundly decisive and meaningful. In that perspective Jonathan Edwards, being the most acute definer of the terms on which the revival was conducted and the issues on which it went astray, should be regarded—even by the social historian—as a formulator of propositions that the American society, having been shaken by this experience, was henceforth consciously to observe.

There is not space enough here to survey the Awakening through the vast reaches of the South and the Middle Colonies, nor even to list the intricate consequences for the social ordering of New England. The splintering of the churches and the increase of sectarianism suggest one way in which Americans 'responded' to this crisis, and the impulse it gave to education, most notably in the founding of Princeton, is another. Such discussions, however valuable, are external and statistical. We come to a deeper understanding of what this crisis meant by examining more closely a revelation or two from the most self-conscious—not to say the most literate—theorist of the Awakening.

The theme I would here isolate is one with which Edwards dealt only by indirection. He was skilled in the art of presenting ideas not so much by expounding as by vivifying them, and he achieved his ends not only by emphasis. In this case, it is entirely a matter of divining nuances. Nevertheless, the issue was present throughout the Awakening and, after the temporary manifestations had abated, on this proposition a revolution was found to have been wrought that is one of the enduring responses of the American mind to crisis.

I mean specifically what it did to the conception of the relation of the ruler—political or ecclesiastical—to the body politic. However, before we can pin down this somewhat illusive development, we are confronted with the problem of whether the Great Awakening is properly to be viewed as a peculiarly American phenomenon at all. It would be possible to write about it—as has been done—as merely one variant of a universal occurrence in Western culture. Between about 1730 and 1760 practically all of Western Europe was swept by some kind of religious emotionalism. It was present in Germany, Holland, Switzerland, and France, and in Catholic circles there was an analogous movement that can be interpreted as an out-cropping ot the same thing, and that the textbooks call 'Quietism.' And mos, dramatically, it was present in England with the Wesleys, Whitefieldf and Methodism.

Once this international viewpoint is assumed, the American outburst becomes merely one among many, a colonial one at that—and one hesitates to speak about it as a crisis in a history specifically American. What was at work throughout the Western world is fairly obvious: the upper or the educated classes were tired of the religious squabbling of the seventeenth century, and turned to the more pleasing and not at all contentious generalities of eighteenth-century rationalism; the spiritual hungers of the lower classes or of what, for shorthand purposes, we may call 'ordinary' folk were not satisfied by Newtonian demonstrations that design in the universe proved the existence of God. Their aspirations found vent in the revivals, and in each country we may date the end of a Calvinist or scholastic or, in short, a theological era by the appearance of these movements, and thereupon mark what is by now called the era of Pietism or Evangelicalism.

In this frame of reference, the Great Awakening was only incidentally American. It is only necessary to translate the European language into the local terminology to have an adequate account. In this phraseology, the Great Awakening in New England was an uprising of the common people who declared that what Harvard and Yale graduates were teaching was too academic. This sort of rebellion has subsequently proved so continuous that one can hardly speak of it as a crisis. It is rather a chronic state of affairs. And in this view of it, the uprising of 1640 belongs to the history of the eighteenth century rather than to any account of work only on this continent.

Told in this way, the story will be perfectly true. Because we talk so much today of the unity of Western European culture, maybe we ought to tell it in these terms, and then stop. But on the other hand there is a curiously double aspect to the business. If we forget about Germany and Holland and even England - if we examine in detail the local history of Virginia, Pennsylvania, and New England—we will find that a coherent narrative can be constructed out of the cultural developments in each particular area. The Awakening can be seen as the culmination of factors long at work in each society, and as constituting, in that sense, a veritable crisis in the indigenous civilization.

The church polity established in New England was what today we call Congregational. This meant, to put it crudely, that a church was conceived as being composed of people who could certify before other people that they had a religious experience, that they were qualified to become what the founders called 'visible saints.' The founders were never so foolish as to suppose that everybody who pretended to be a saint was a saint, but they believed that a rough approximation of the Covenant of Grace could be worked out. A church was composed of the congregation, but these were only the professing Christians. The rest of the community were to be rigorously excluded; the civil magistrate would, of course, compel them to come to the church and listen to the sermon, collect from them a tax to support the preacher, but they could not be actual members. Those who qualified were supposed to have had something happen to them that made them capable—as the reprobate was not—of swearing to the covenant of the church. They were able as the others were not, *physically* to perform the act.

The basic contention of the founders was that a church is based upon the covenent. Isolated individuals might be Christians in their heart of hearts, but a corporate body could not come into being unless there was this preliminary clasping of hands, this taking of the official oath in the open and before all the community, saying, in effect: 'We abide by this faith, by this covenant.' In scholastic language, the congregation were the 'matter' but the covenant was the 'form' of the church. They objected above all things to the practice in England whereby churches were made by geography; that a lot of people, merely because they resided in Little Willingdon, should make the church of Little Willingdon, seemed to them blasphemy. That principle was unreal; there was no spiritual participation in it—no covenant.

That was why they (or at any rate the leaders and the theorists) came to New England. On the voyage over, in 1630, John Winthrop said to them: 'For wee must Consider that wee shall be as a Citty vppon a Hill, the eies of all people are vppon us.' They had been attempting in England to lead a revolution; after the king's dismissal of Parliament in 1629 it looked as though there was no longer any hope of revolution there, and so they migrated to New England, to build the revolutionary city, where they could exhibit to Englishmen an England that would be as all England should be.

The essence of their conception was the covenant. As soon as they were disembarked, as soon as they could collect in one spot enough people to examine each other and acknowledge that each seemed visibly capable of taking the oath, they incorporated churches—in Boston, Charlestown, and Watertown, and, even in the first decade, in the Connecticut Valley. But we must always remember that even in those first days, when conviction was at its height, and among so highly selected and dedicated numbers as made up the Great Migration, only about one fifth of the population were found able, or could find themselves able, to take the covenant. The rest of them—with astonishingly few exceptions - accepted their exclusion from the churches, knowing that they were not 'enabled' and praying for the grace that might yet empower them.

From that point on, the story may seem somewhat peculiar, but after a little scrutiny it becomes an old and a familiar one: it is what happens to a successful revolution. The New Englanders did not have to fight on the barricades or at Marston Moor; by the act of Migrating, they *had* their revolution. Obeying the Biblical command to increase and multiply, they had children—hordes of them. Despite the high rate of infant mortality, these children grew up in New England knowing nothing, except by hearsay and rumor, of the struggles in Europe, never having lived amid the tensions of England. This second generation were, for the most part, good people; but they simply did not have—they could not have—the kind of emotional experience that made them ready to stand up before the whole community and say: 'On Friday the 19th, I was smitten while plowing Deacon Jones's meadow; I fell to the earth, and I knew that the grace of God was upon me.' They were honest people, and they found it difficult to romanticize about themselves—even when they desperately wanted to.

In 1662 the churches of New England convoked a synod and announced that the children of the primitive church members were included in the covenant by the promise of God to Abraham. This solution was called at the time the Halfway Covenant, and the very phrase itself is an instructive demonstration of the New Englanders' awareness that their revolution was no longer revolutionary. These children, they decided, must be treated as members of the church, although they had not had the kind of experience that qualified their fathers. They must be subject to discipline and censures, because the body of the saints must be preserved. But just in case the authorities might be mistaken, they compromised by giving to these children only a 'halfway' status, which made them members but did not admit them to the Lord's Supper.

This provision can easily be described as a pathetic, where it is not a ridiculous, device. It becomes more comprehensible when we realize that it was an accommodation to the successful revolution. Second and third generations grow up inheritors of a revolution, but are not themselves revolutionaries.

For the moment, in the 1660's and 1670's, the compromise worked, but the situation got worse. For one thing, New England suffered in King Philip's War, when the male population was decimated. Then, in 1684, the charter of Massachusetts was revoked, and after 1691 the colony had to adjust itself to the notion that its governor was imposed by the election of the saints. Furthermore, after 1715 all the colonies were prospering economically; inevitably they became more and more concerned with earthly things—rum, land, furs. On the whole they remained a pious people. Could one go back to Boston of 1710 or 1720—when the ministers were asserting that it was as profligate as Babylon—I am sure that one would find it, compared with modern Hollywood, a strict and moral community. Nevertheless, everybody was convinced that the cause of religion had declined. Something had to be done.

As early as the 1670's the ministers had found something they could do: they could work upon the halfway members. They could say to these hesitants: 'You were baptized in this church, and if you will now come before the body and 'own' the covenant, then your children can in turn be baptized.' Gradually a whole segment of doctrine was formulated that was not in the original theory—which made it possible to address these citizens who were neither outside the pale nor yet snugly inside, which told them that however dubious they might be as saints, visible or invisible, they yet had sufficient will power to perform the public act of 'owning the covenant.'

With the increasing pressures of the late seventeenth and early eighteenth centuries, the practice of owning the covenant gradually became a communal rite. It was not enough that the minister labored separately with John or Elizabeth to make an acknowledgement the next Sunday: a day was appointed when all the Johns and Elizabeths would come to church and do it in unison, the whole town looking on. It is not difficult to trace through the increasing re-enactments of this ceremony a mounting crescendo of communal action that was, to say the least, wholly foreign to the original Puritanism. The theology of the founders conceived of man as single and alone, apart in a corner or in an empty field, wrestling with his sin; only after he had survived this experience in solitude could he walk into the church and by telling about it prove his right to the covenant. But this communal confession—with everybody doing it together, under the urgencies of an organized moment—this was something new, emerging so imperceptibly that nobody recognized it as an innovation (or rather I should say that some did, but they were shouted down) that by the turn of the century was rapidly becoming the focus for the ordering of the spiritual life of the town.

The grandfather of Jonathan Edwards, Solomon Stoddard of Northampton, was the first man who openly extended the practice of renewal of covenant to those who had never been in it at all. In short, when these occasions arose, or when he could precipitate them, he simply took into the church and up to the Lord's Supper everyone who would come. He called the periods when the community responded *en masse* his 'harvests,' of which he had five: 1679, 1683, 1696, 1712, 1718. The Mathers attacked him for so completely letting down the bars, but in the Connecticut Valley his success was envied and imitated.

The Great Awakening of 1740, seen in the light of this development, was nothing more than the culmination of the process. It was the point at which the method of owning the covenant became most widely and exultingly extended, in which the momentum of the appeal got out of hand, and the ministers, led by Jonathan Edwards, were forced by the logic of evolution not only to admit all those who would come, but to excite and to drive as many as possible, by such rhetorical stimulations as 'Sinners in the Hands of an Angry God,' into demanding entrance.

All of this, traced historically, seems natural enough. What 1740 did was present a number of leading citizens, like the Harvard faculty, with the results of a process that had been going on for decades but of which they were utterly ignorant until the explosion. Then they found themselves trying to control it or censure it by standards that had in fact been out of date for a century, although they had all that while professed them in filial piety. In this sense—which I regret to

state has generally eluded the social historian—the Great Awakening
was a crisis in the New England society.

Professional patriots, especially those of New England descent, are
fond of celebrating the Puritans as the founders of the American
tradition of rugged individualism, of conscience, popular education, and
democracy. The Puritans were not rugged individualists; they did indeed
believe in education of a sort, but not in the 'progressive' sense; they
abhorred freedom of conscience; and they did not believe at all in
democracy. They advertised again and again that their church polity
was not democratic. The fact that a church was founded on a covenant
and that the ministers happened to be elected by the mass of the
church—that emphatically did not constitute a democracy. John Cotton
made the position of the founders crystal clear when he told Lord Say
and Seal that God never ordained democracy as a fit government for
either church or common-wealth; although at first sight one might
suppose that a congregational church was one, in that the people chose
their governors, the truth was that 'the government is not a democracy,
if it be administered, not by the people, but by the governors.' He
meant, in short, that even though the people did select the person, the
office was prescribed; they did not define its functions, nor was it
responsible to the will or the whim of the electors. 'In which respect
it is, that church government is justly denied. . . .to be democratical,
though the people choose their owne officers and rulers.'

The conception ran through every department of the social thinking of
New England in the seventeenth century, and persisted in the eighteenth
up to the very outbreak of the Awakening. The essence of it always
was that though officers may come into their office by the choice of
the people, or a number of people, nevertheless the definition of the
function, dignity, and prerogatives of the position does not depend upon
the intentions or wishes of the electorate, but upon an abstract, divinely-
given, absolute prescription, which has nothing—in theory—to do with
such practical or utilitarian considerations as may at the moment of the
election, be at work among the people.

The divine and immutable pattern of church government was set,
once and for all, in the New Testament; likewise, the principles of
political justice were given in an eternal and definitive form. The
machinery by which a particular man was chosen to fulfill these
directives (as the minister was elected by the vote of a congregation,
or as John Winthrop was made governor of the Massachusetts Bay
Company by a vote of the stockholders) was irrelevant. The existence

of such machinery did not mean that the elected officer was in any sense responsible to the electorate. He knew what was expected of him from an entirely other source than their temporary passions; he knew what he, upon becoming such a being, should do—as such!

The classic statement, as is widely known, was the speech that John Winthrop delivered before the General Court on July 3, 1645. He had been accused by the democracy of over-stepping the limits of his power as a magistrate, and was actually impeached on the accusation. He was acquitted, and thereupon made this truly great declaration. He informed the people that the liberty of the subject may sometimes include, as happily it did in Massachusetts, the privilege of selecting this or that person for office, but that it did not therefore mean the right to tell the officer what he should do once he was installed. The liberty that men enjoy in civil society, he said, 'is the proper end and object of authority, and cannot subsist without it.' It is not a liberty to do what you will, or to require the authority to do what you want: 'It is a liberty to do that only which is good, just, and honest.' Who defines the good, the just, and the honest? Obviously, the authority does.

In other words, the theory of early New England was basically medieval. Behind it lay the conception of an authoritative scheme of things, in which basic principles are set down once and for all, entirely before, and utterly without regard for, political experience. The formulation of social wisdom had nothing to do with the specific problems of any one society. It was not devised by a committee on ways and means. Policy was not to be arrived at by a discussion of strategy—for example (in modern terms), shouldn't we use the atomic bomb now? This sort of argument was unavailing, because the function of government was to maintain by authority that which was inherently—and definably—the true, just, and honest.

In Hartford, Connecticut, a colleague of the great Thomas Hooker, the most comprehensive theorist of the Congregational system, summarized the argument by declaring that Congregationalism meant a silent democracy in the face of a speaking aristocracy. There might be something which we call democracy in the form of the church, but the congregation had to keep silent when the minister spoke. And yet, for a hundred years after the death of Hooker, this strange process went on inside the institution. The official theory remained, down to the time of Edwards, that the spokesman for the society—be he governor or minister—told the society, by right divine, what it should or should

not do, without any regard to its immediate interests. whether emotional
or economic. He had laid upon him, in fact, the duty of forgetting
such wisdom as he might have accumulated by living as a particular
person in that very community or having shared the hopes and qualities
of precisely these people.

What actually came about through the device of renewing the covenant,
was something that in fact completely contradicted the theory. (We must
remember that the church was, during this century, not merely something
'spiritual', but the institutional center of the organized life.) Instead
of the minister standing in his pulpit, saying: 'I speak; you keep quiet,'
he found himself, bit by bit, assuming the posture of pleading with
the people: 'Come, and speak up.' He did not know what was happening.
He began to find out only in the Great Awakening, when the people
at last and multitudinously spoke up.

The greatness of Jonathan Edwards is that he understood what had
happened. But note this carefully. He was not Thomas Jefferson;
he did not preach democracy, and he had no interest whatsoever in
any social revolution. He was the child of this aristocratic, medieval
system; he was born to the purple, to ecclesiastical authority. But he
was the man who hammered it home to the people that they *had* to
speak up, or else they were lost.

Edwards was a Puritan and a Calvinist. He believed in predestination
and original sin and all those dogmas which college students hold to
be outworn stuff until they get excited about them as slightly disguised
by Franz Kafka. Edwards did not submit these doctrines to majority
vote, and he did not put his theology to the test of utility. But none
of this was, in his existing situation, an issue. Granting all that, the
question he had to decide was: What does a man do who leads the
people? Does he, in 1740, say with the Winthrop of 1645 that they
submit to what he as an ontologist tells them is good, just, and honest?

What he realized (lesser leaders of the Awakening, like Gilbert
Tennent, also grasped the point, but none with the fine precision of
Edwards) was that a leader could no longer stand before the people
giving them mathematically or logically impregnable postulates of the
eternally good, just, and honest. That might work in 1640, or in
Europe (where to an astonishing extent it still works), but it would not
work in Northampton. By 1740 the leader had to get down amongst
them, and bring them by actual participation into an experience that
was no longer private and privileged, but social and communal.

In other words, he carried to its ultimate implication—this constitutes his 'relation to his times,' which no purely social historian can begin to diagnose—that slowly forming tendency which had been steadily pressing through enlargements of the ceremonial of the covenant. He carried it so far that at last every body could see what it really did mean. Then the Harvard faculty lifted its hands in horror—because this ritual, which they had thought was a segment of the cosmology of John Winthrop, was proved by Edwards' use to flow from entirely alien principles. For this reason, his own Yale disowned him.

In the year 1748 Edwards' revolutionary effort-his leadership of the Awakening must be seen as a resumption of the revolutionary thrust that had been allowed to dwindle in the Halfway Covenant—was almost at an end. The opposition was mobilizing, and he knew, even before they did, that they would force him out. When the fight had only begun, his patron and friend, his one bulwark in the civil society, Colonel John Stoddard, chief of the militia and warden of the marches, died. There was now no civil power that could protect him against the hatred of the 'river gods.' Out of all New England, Stoddard has been really *the* outstanding magistrate in that tradition of aristocratic leadership which had begun with Winthrop and had been sustained through a massive succession. As was the custom in New England, the minister gave a funeral sermon: Edwards preached over the corpse of the town's greatest citizen—who happened, in this case, to be also his uncle and his protector. Those who were now certain, with Colonel Stoddard in the ground, that they could get Edwards's scalp were in the audience.

Edwards delivered a discourse that at first sight seems merely one more Puritan eulogy. He told the people that when great and good men like Stoddard are taken away, this is a frown of God's displeasure, which indicates that they ought to reform their vices. This much was sheer convention. But before he came, at the end, to the traditional berating of the populace, Edwards devoted the major part of his oration to an analysis of the function and meaning of authority.

It should be remembered that Winthrop had commenced the New England tradition by telling the people that they had the liberty to do only that which is in itself good, just, and honest; that their liberty was the proper end and object of authority thus defined; that the approbation of the people is no more than the machinery by which God calls certain people to the exercise of the designated powers. And it should also be borne in mind that these powers are given apart from any consideration of the social welfare, that they derive from ethical, theological—*a priori*—considerations.

Jonathan Edwards says that the supreme qualification of a ruler is that he be a man of 'great ability for the management of public affairs.' This is his first and basic definition! Let us follow his very words, underlining those which carry revolutionary significance. Rulers are men 'of great *natural* abilities' who are versed in discerning 'those things wherein the *public welfare or calamity consists*, and the proper *means* to avoid the one and promote the other.' They must have lived among men long enough to learn how the mass of them disguise their motives, to 'unravel false, subtle arguments and cunning sophistry that is often made use of to defend *iniquity*.' They must be men who have improved their talents by—here are his great criteria—'*study, learning, observation*, and *experience*. By these means they must have acquired 'skill' in public affairs, a great understanding of *men and things*, a great *knowledge of human nature*, and of the way of *accommodating* themselves to it.' Men are qualified to be rulers if and when they have this 'very extensive knowledge of men with whom they are concerned,' and when also they have a full and particular understanding 'of the *state and circumstances* of the country or people that they have the care of.' These are the things—not scholastical articles—that make those in authority 'fit' to be rulers!

Look closely at those words and phrases: skill, observation, men and things, state and circumstances—above all, experience! Is this the great Puritan revivalist? It is. And what is he saying, out of the revival? He is telling what in political terms the revival really meant: that the leader has the job of accommodating himself to the realities of human and, in any particular situation, of social, experience. No matter what he may have as an assured creed, as a dogma—no matter what he may be able to pronounce, in the terms of abstract theology, concerning predestination and original sin—as a public leader he must adapt himself to public welfare and calamity. He cannot trust himself to *a priori* rules of an eternal and uncircumstanced good, just, and honest. There are requirements imposed by the office; authority does indeed consist of propositions that pertain to it, but what are they? They are the need for knowing the people, the knack of properly manipulating and operating them, the wit to estimate their welfare, and the cunning to foresee what may become their calamity.

When we are dealing with so highly conscious an artist as Edwards, we not only are justified in submitting so crucial a paragraph to close analysis, we are criminally obtuse if we do not. Most of my effort in my recent studies of him comes down to persuading people to read him. So it becomes significant to note what Edwards does immediately after his radically new definition of the ruler. Following his own logic, he is prepared at once to attack what, in the state and circumstances of the Connecticut Valley, constituted the primary iniquity from which the greatest social calamity might be expected.

He does it without, as we might say, pulling punches: a ruler must, on these considerations of welfare, be unalterably opposed to all persons of 'a mean spirit,' to those 'of a narrow, private spirit that may be found in little tricks and intrigues to promote their private interest, (who) will shamefully defile their hands to gain a few pounds, are not ashamed to hit and bite others, grind the faces of the poor, and screw upon their neighbors; and will take advantage of their authority or commission to line their own pockets with what is fraudulently taken or withheld from others.' At the time he spoke, there sat before him the merchants, the sharp traders, the land speculators of Northampton; with the prompt publication of the sermon, his words reached similar gentlemen in the neighboring towns. Within two years, they hounded him out of his pulpit.

The more one studies Edwards, the more one finds that much of his preaching is his condemnation, in this language of welfare and calamity rather than of 'morality,' of the rising and now rampant businessmen of the Valley. It was Edwards's great perception—and possibly his greatest value for us today is precisely here—that the get-rich-quick schemes of his contemporaries were wrong not from the point of view of the eternal values but from that of the public welfare. The ruler, he said, must know the 'theory' of government in such a way that it becomes 'natural' to him, and he must apply the knowledge he has obtained by study and observation to 'that business, so as to perform it most advantageously and effectually.' Here he was, at the moment his protector was gone, and he knew that he was lost, telling those about to destroy him that the great man is he who leads the people by skill and experiential wisdom, and not by making money.

It is further revealing that, after Edwards had portrayed the ruler in this frame of utility and calculation, when he came to his fourth point he then for the first time said that the authority ought to be a pious man, and only in his fifth and last did he suggest the desirability of a good family. For Winthrop these qualifications had been essentials of the office; for Edwards they were radically submitted to a criterion of utility. 'It also contributes to the strength of a man in authority—

when he is in such circumstances as give him advantage for the exercise of his strength, for the public good; as his being a person of honorable descent, of a distinguished education, his being a man of estate.' But note—these are all 'useful' because they add to his strength, and increase his ability and advantage to serve his generation.' They serve 'in some respect' to make him more effective. It had never occurred to John Winthrop that the silent democracy should imagine for a moment that the elected ruler, in church or state, should be anyone but a pious, educated, honorably descended person, of adequate economic substance. Edwards (who was pious, educated, and very well descended, but not wealthy) says that in some respect these advantages are helps to efficiency.

From one point of view, then, this was what actually was at work inside the hysterical agonies of the Great Awakening. This is one thing they meant: the end of the reign over the New England and American mind of a European and scholastical conception of an authority put over men for the good of men who were incapable of recognizing their own welfare. This insight may assist us somewhat in comprehending why the pundits of Boston and Cambridge, all of whom were rational and tolerant and decent, shuddered with a horror that was deeper than mere dislike of the antics of the yokels. To some extent, they sensed that the religious screaming had implications in the realm of society, and those implications they—being businessmen and speculators, as were the plutocracy of Northampton—did not like.

Again, I would not claim too much for Edwards, and I have no design of inscribing him among the prophets of democracy or the New Deal. What he marks—and what he alone could make clear—is the crisis from which all the others (or most of them) dealt with in this book depend, that in which the social problem was taken out of the arena of abstract morality and put into the arena of skill, observation, and accommodation. In this episode, the Americans were indeed participating in an international movement; even so, they came—or Edwards brought them—to sharper formulations of American experience. What the Awakening really meant for Americans was not that they too were behaving like Dutchmen or Germans or Lancashire workmen, but that in the ecstasy of the revival they were discovering, especially on the frontier, where life was the toughest, that they rejected imported European philosophies of society. They were now of themselves prepared to contend that the guiding rule of this society will be its welfare, and the most valuable knowledge will be that which can say what threatens calamity for the state.

THE ORIGINS OF MODERN DRAMA

By
Frederick B. Artz

Both the Greek and the medieval drama developed out of religious ceremonies, though the medieval—and ultimately the modern—drama had an independent development and were not derived from Greek and Roman drama. In the early Middle Ages the church disapproved of plays, since they were too much a part of the paganism that the church was fighting. Among the people their place was taken by wandering minstrels and acrobats, commonly called 'mimes.' These entertainers often traveled with trained bears or other animals and sometimes with a troupe of children. They performed in castle halls or on the village street; such entertainment supplemented the recitation of narrative or lyric verses. The survival of these 'mimes,' and the survival of traditional dances, kept alive types of dramatic characterization and the traditions of pantomime and acting that reappear later in the medieval drama. At the same time there were a number of dramatic elements in the Latin services of the church. The mass itself is a sort of symbolic drama of the death and resurrection of Christ with chanting by the priest and responses by the choir. Sometimes two priests would give a sermon, either in Latin or in the vernacular, in dialogue form; hymns were occasionally arranged for two choirs. As early as the tenth century, and perhaps earlier, short dramatic pieces (tropes), began to to be introduced, especially in monastic churches, in connection with the great festivals of Easter and Christmas.

One of the earliest surviving tropes, the *Quem Quaeritis*, is hardly more than a series of stage directions for a brief play inserted into the mass of Easter. All the parts were in Latin and were chanted.

The original play included a scene between the angels and the Marys at the tomb of Jesus, followed by a responsive chant between the Marys and the choir. In the course of time, tropes like *Quem Quaeritis* were extended by the addition of dialogue and of more dramatic action, producing plays with several different scenes. In time, tropes were arranged in series, the resurrection story was extended backwards to include the Crucifixion and then other events of the last days of Jesus. On Good Friday, for example, a swathed cross would be laid away in some part of the choir with lamentations, and then on Easter morning it would be taken out with appropriate words and action.

A second step in the development of the drama was to move it out of the church. Comic elements which crept in made the plays seem out of keeping with the church services. Moreover, the crowds, who wished to see such presentations could not be accommodated in the dark and narrow interiors of the church. So it gradually became the custom to give the plays outside, in front of the church. Many new incidents from both the Old and New Testaments were added. Other changes that came in were the use of laymen as actors and the use of the vernacular instead of Latin. A number of transitional plays survive in which the dialogue is written partly in Latin and partly in the vernacular. All this meant a growing secularity in the drama and a growing dramatic effectiveness, for plays given by laymen in the church encouraged acting that was more varied and more realistic. And new scenes and incidents were invented. Noah's wife became the typical nagging shrew; Herod was now a typical bully, and to 'out-herod Herod' furnished a great opportunity for dramatic action. The life of Mary Magdalene before her conversion offered the chance to present scenes of profligacy.

In some towns the remains of a Roman theater or arena were used for plays; in others booths were built on a public square or in a field outside the town wall. Here the central structure, in three levels, represented paradise, this earth (with the walls of Jerusalem, Herod's palace, Noah's Ark, the hill of Golgotha, and the Garden of Eden), with Hell below. The scenery was very crude; the costuming was elaborate but completely unhistorical, as it was in medieval painting. God's traditional costume was of white with a gilt wig and beard. This was, likewise, the costume for Christ though he usually wore red shoes as one who 'had trod the winepress'. Saints also wore gilded wigs, angels had gilt wings, and the Virgin wore a crown. The saved were dressed in white; the damned, in black or black and yellow. Herod was often clothed as a Saracen. The devil and his attendant demons wore grisly masks, were dressed in suits covered with horsehair, and wore horns and forked tails. Sometimes, in such a setting, a series of sets would be arranged side by side and the actors would move from one set to another. The common method of presenting plays in England was to mount them on a series of wagons or 'pageants,' on each one of which one important Bible story could be acted. Usually one of these platforms with wheels had two sections or floors; the lower, hung with curtains, supplied a dressing room, and the upper, covered with a canopy open on four sides, was the stage. So arranged, the plays could be repeated at several points as they were moved through a town. The juxtaposition of a series of sacred scenes, and in the scenes the mixing of sacred, profane, and even farcical elements, created a sprawling confusion of incidents and personages exactly as they were presented in medieval romances or in the huge and cluttered Gothic tapestries and paintings. The settings of both medieval and Renaissance theaters were derived from the architecture, the painting, and the sculpture of the period, and many of the effects striven for were to turn into living pictures the conceptions of the plastic art of the time. Noah's ark was represented as a ship, and a dragon's mouth stood for the gates of hell. Into these gates the devil would throw a sinner; there would then be groaning and a great rattling of pans, and smoke would belch forth. Parts of the play were often given on the ground in front of a set; it was a common feature for devils to run about the audience and torment some of the spectators to the delight of the other onlookers. It was now possible to introduce real dramatic action both comic and tragic into the plays.

In many towns the guilds took over one scene or another in the long cycles of plays that were presented on important feast days. Sometimes there was a real appropriateness in all this; the wine merchants presented the Marriage at Cana, and the fishmongers either the story of Jonah or the miracle of the miraculous draught of fishes or the feeding of the five thousand. In the York Cycle, the plasterers' guild presented the building of the ark, and the bakers' guild put on the Last Supper. Whole cycles of plays were given which covered the main stories in the Bible from the fall of man in Eden, through the Crucifixion, to the Last Judgment; one cycle from York in England includes forty eight plays. The actors were all amateurs who, for a time, would set aside their labors to perform the sacred stories. They did not look on their work as a regular profession, though the guild would usually pay them for their services. Account books speak of paying '29 pence to God, 21 pence to the demons, 3 pence to Fauston for cock crowing, and 16 pence to two worms of conscience.' Sometimes plays were put on by companies of students or of townsmen, independent of the guilds. The plays and their performance were the creation of the townsmen. The first regular company with its own establishment was probably the *'Confrerie de la passion'* which began in Paris about 1402.

From the thirteenth century on, it became the custom to refer to plays based on the Bible as mysteries, a designation probably derived from, *misterium*, meaning a liturgical ceremony; in Italy, mystery plays, which became common in the fifteenth century, were called *sacre rappresentazione*. Those based on saints' lives were called miracle plays. Often comic insertions with improvised antics and farce with some mockery of the clergy crept in. Students in the cathedral schools and universities dramatized romances and other stories, but no examples of their efforts have survived. In the fourteenth century morality plays became common; here the actors represented virtues and vices and other abstractions like the characters in the *Roman de la Rose*. The favorite theme of the morality plays was the pursuit of Everyman (mankind) by evil forces and his rescue by Conscience or Wisdom. The morality plays, which continued to flourish into the sixteenth century, always inculcated some lesson. They were much longer than earlier mystery and miracle plays, and they show more ecclesiastical influence and, sometimes, a more aristocratic tone; it is known that they were frequently presented in castle halls. The peculiar paradox is that in seeming to draw drama away from realism into allegory the writers of morality plays succeeded in linking drama closer to actual life and to contemporary types. The comic scenes provided by the Devil and Old Vice, a buffoon, have in them the sort of humor which supplied the authors of the interlude with certain subjects and methods. In the tragic figures the authors discovered the secret of showing the development of character and the delineation of conflicting passions. In addition, the morality plays have more unity and show more skill in construction than was shown in the mystery or miracle plays. Thus, they form an important link between the earlier medieval and the modern drama. The most famous of the morality plays, *Everyman*, exists in a number of languages of which an English fifteenth—or early sixteenth-century version is the best. Of all serious plays of the Middle Ages, it has still the greatest power on the stage.

The final stage of the medieval drama is represented by the development of the interlude. This was originally put between the parts of a sacred play, but it came to be developed for itself. The first good interlude is one of Adam de la Halle, the *Jeu de Robin et de Marion*, written in French, and first presented about 1283 at the Court of Naples. The spoken dialogue, which is charming and sprightly is interspersed with songs and dances; with some exaggeration it has been called 'the first comic opera,' though it has no historical connection with this later form. The wittiest interlude that has survived is *Patelin*, a fifteenth-century French farce, which is still occasionally performed. Sometimes interludes were performed by puppets; sometimes they were done in pantomime, or had merely a few general directions and the actors had to make up their speeches. Out of this last came the Italian *commedia dell' arte*. In the interlude the plot and the action were freer than in the religious plays, and there was more opportunity for humor and realistic treatment. No great writer appeared to handle the drama during the Middle Ages, but out of the morality play and the interlude came the great drama of the age of Shakespeare and Lope de Vega.

THE NATURE OF AMERICAN NATIONALISM

By
Henry Steele Commager

There had been nations long before the American and the French Revolutions but the rise of self-conscious nationalism, of cultural and and linguistic as well as political nationalism, is largely a product of the last century and a half. Into the vexed and perhaps insoluble question of the origins and antiquity of nationalism in the Old World, I do not propose to enter. Even those most insistent on the early, perhaps the medieval, origins of modern nationalism will, I think, readily concede that the nationalism of the late eighteenth and nineteenth centuries represented something new, and that much of what we now think of as nationalism is a product of this modern period. Beginning with the French Revolution, older nations—France herself, for example, or the Denmark of Grundtvig, or Norway, experienced a new birth of nationalism. And all through the nineteenth century, nations struggled towards birth as states, and states disintegrated into nations, as people conscious of a common language and culture and history strove to transform that cultural-social-religious nationalism into political nationalism, or sought to give older and artificial organizations new and more meaningful form. Thus Greece and Serbia in the early years of the century; the states of Latin America in the second and third decades; Belgium in the 1830's; Germany, Italy, Rumania, Finland, Norway, Bohemia, in subsequent years. The culmination of all this—

in the opinion of many, a regrettable culmination—was the doctrine of self-determination sponsored by President Wilson and written into the World War I settlements.

Against this background of renascent or of emergent nationalism, the American experience after 1776 appears familiar and unexceptional, and historians have customarily interpreted it as an harmonious part of an harmonious pattern. In a sense this is proper enough; after all, the same impulses of nationalism and romanticism and reform that quickened the mind and spirit of the peoples of Old World nations moved and quickened the American people, and the same immeasurably important forces of economy—the industrial revolution, the railroads, the corporate device, electricity and the dynamo—that emerged in eighteenth and nineteenth century Europe, operated in America with redoubled force.

Yet in a very real sense the American experience differed from that of the Old World, differed from that of all other continents. In a very real sense it can be said that the American experience, far from being harmonious with past history, reversed the processes of history.

This was the view of one of the most sagacious of American statesmen, John Adams, and we may take as our point of departure what he wrote to his friend Hezekiah Niles in 1818:

> The colonies had grown up under constitutions of government so different, there was so great a variety of religions, they were composed of so many different nations, their customs, manners and habits had so little resemblance, and their intercourse had been so rare, and their knowledge of each other so imperfect, that to unite them in the same principles in theory and the same system of action, was certainly a very difficult enterprise. The complete accomplishment of it, in so short a time, and by such simple means, was perhaps a singular example in the history of mankind. Thirteen clocks were made to strike together—a perfection of mechanism which no artist had ever before effected.

Because thirteen American states hugging the Atlantic seaboard became a single nation spanning a continent, we take American nationalism for granted. But there was nothing foreordained about that triumph. Why, after all, did not the United States go the way of Europe, of Latin America, of Asia? The most elementary foundations

for the new nation remained to be laid, and to many contemporaries
the forces that threatened their security far more formidable than the
forces that protected it. Thus the Earl of Sheffield observed in 1783 of
the then American West that 'the authority of Congress can never be
maintained over those distant and boundless regions, and her nominal
subjects will speedily imitate and multiply examples of independence.'
Turgot too, thought the forces of disintegration stronger than the forces
of integration.   'In the general union of the provinces among themselves,'
he wrote to Dr. Price, 'I do not see a coalition, a fusion of all the
parts, making but one body, one and homogeneous.   It is only an
aggregation of parts always too much separated, and preserving a
tendency to division, by the diversity of their laws, their manners,
their opinions....still more by the inequality of their actual forces.   It
is only a copy of the Dutch Republic;   but this Republic had not to
fear, as the American Republic has, the possible enlargement of some
of its provinces.'   And the clerical economist, Dean Josiah Tucker,
was even more sweeping in his rejection of American nationalism;
he wrote:

As to the future grandeur of America and its being a rising
empire under one head....it is one of the idlest visionary notions
that ever was conceived, even by writers of romance....When
those immense inland regions beyond the back settlements, which
are still unexplored, are taken into account, they form the highest
probability that the Americans never can be united into one
compact empire, under any species of government whatever.
Their fate seems to be—a disunited people till the end of time.

The creation of a single great nation out of disparate elements, the
making first thirteen clocks strike as one, and then forty-eight, was
indeed, as John Adams put it, 'a singular example in the history of
mankind.'

For how did it happen, after all, that that people which confessed
the most heterogeneous racial stocks, the most varied soil and climates,
the most diverse and contrasting economic interests, the most variegated
religious pattern, achieved a stable and enduring national character
with an ease that confounded not only the expectations of her critics,
but history and experience as well?   In the Old World, with its age-old
traditions of feudalism and nationalism, the particular triumphed over
the general.   In the New World, the general triumphed over the
particular.   In the Old World, territory was fragmented, and economies,
cultures, languages and religions followed divergent and often conflicting

paths. In the New World the fragmentation under way in the seventeenth and eighteenth centuries was partially arrested, and then succeeded by concentration and unity.

Nor is it sufficient to remark that the United States developed after the industrial revolution. That was important but Latin America, too, came to maturity after the industrial revolution, without consequent unification, and even twentieth-century economic and technological forces have not induced the tiny states of Central America to unite. In Europe, too the industrial revolution appears to have accentuated rather than mitigated national fragmentation; Scotland adhered to England before the industrial revolution, but the most pressing economic considerations have not induced Northern and Southern Ireland to drop their differences. Nor is there as yet any evidence that the industrial revolution will make for the unification of Asia; so far the tendency is rather in the other direction.

What is the explanation of this phenomenon, so astonishing that to Americans and perhaps to others, it has always appeared providential? For in a very real sense President Lincoln's description of the event was correct: the Fathers brought on this continent a new nation. American nationalism was a creative act, the product of the deliberate application of will and intelligence by statesmen, jurists, soldiers, scholars, men of letters, scientists, artists, explorers and others. For where, in almost all Old World countries, the social, cultural and psychological foundations of nationalism were laid before the political superstructure was constructed, in America the political fabric came first, and the rest had to be added. The United States started as a national state, and was confronted at once with the task of vindicating the political and constitutional decision—vindicating it first on the field of battle, then in the arena of the social, the economic, the cultural and the emotional.

When the long traditions of English, French, Danish or Swedish nationalism—of language, law, tradition—are compared with the American situation, the contrast is clear enough. For even in those countries where political nationalism was very old, the nation grew out of well-cultivated soil, out of a century-long process of cultural integraton. And the newer nations of the nineteenth and twentieth centuries— Norway, Belgium, Serbia, Italy, Germany, Poland, Czechoslovakia—all had long traditions of cultural nationalism (and sometimes of political) stretching back into the dim past, before their final crystallization in the modern state.

Instinctively, and consciously, Americans of the Revolutionary generation set about to create a new nation, to furnish a common body of laws, language, literature, education, history, heroes, myths and traditions, with all those things supposedly conducive to nationalism. As Thomas Paine said—Paine who himself contributed so much to the making of the new nation—'a new era for politics is struck, a new method of thinking hath arisen.'

Thus young Noah Webster, hot for thoroughgoing independence, pointed out that 'America is an independent empire, and ought to assume a national character. Nothing,' he added, 'can be more ridiculous than servile imitation of the manners, the language, and the vices of foreigners.' And in 1788 he exhorted his fellow countrymen: 'Unshackle your minds, and act like independent beings. You have been children long enough, subject to the control....of a haughty parent....You have an empire to raise and support by your exertions, and a national character to establish and extend by your wisdom and virtue.' Thus Alexander Hamilton not always enthusiastic for homespun, confessed to Rufus King that 'we are laboring hard to establish in this country Principles more and more *national*, and free from all foreign ingredients, so that we may be neither Greeks nor Trojans, but truly Americans.' Thus his great rival Jefferson agreed with Webster that 'the new circumstances under which we are placed, call for new words, new phrases, and for the transfer of old words to new objects. An American dialect will therefore be formed.' Thus the doctor-educator Benjamin Rush wished American youth to be taught 'that there can be no durable liberty but in a republic, and that government, like all other sciences, is of a progressive nature.' 'Fortunately,' he added, 'the chains which have bound this science in Europe are....unloosed in America. Here it is open to investigation and improvement.'

Improvement, too, was in the mind of the mathematician Nathaniel Pike, who pointed out in the preface to his *Arithmetic* of 1788; 'As the United States are now an independent Nation, it was judged that a system might be calculated more suitable to our Meridian than those heretofore published.' Even geography was to be given a national slant, and one Robert Davidson was moved to flaunt his national pride in verse:

Having cross'd the Pacific, we'll now take our stand, On this happy, prolific, and widespreading land, Where Nature has wrought with a far nobler hand. No more let the Old World be proud

of her mountains, Her rivers, her mines, her lakes and her
fountains—Tho' great in themselves—they no longer appear to
be great—when compar'd to the great that are here.

How did Americans achieve nationalism, achieve it and preserve it,
even through the great crisis of the 1860's? This is, indeed, the subject
of these lectures, and I can do no more today than suggest some of
the broader aspects of the enterprise. What we must understand is
that the achievement was by no means foreordained, and that it was
far from easy. Scholars are not yet agreed on what are the essential
ingredients of nationalism, but it is reasonably clear that effective
nationalism requires a common body of traditions and history, a common
language, a common territory. (Even these are not quintessential;
the Swiss manage to maintain nationalism without a common language,
the Jewish people have not until now had a territorial basis.) America
became a nation, or claimed to be one, with only language as a firm
ingredient, with the territorial basis uncertain and the people
heterogeneous and the traditions yet to be established.

It is not necessary to remind you that for a century and a half
America was part of an empire, and that common loyalties were rather
with the mother country than with other American colonies:

Though we feast and grow fat on America's soil
Yet we own ourselves subjects to Britain's fair isle;
And who's so absurd to deny us the name,
Since true British blood flows in every vein.

wrote the author of *Virginia Hearts of Oak* in 1766, with a good
deal of exaggeration as far as 'true British Blood' was concerned.
That same year young Francis Hopkinson, later to sign the Declaration
of Independence, observed rhetorically in a commencement essay that
'We in America are in all respects Englishmen, notwithstanding that
the Atlantic rolls her waves between us and the throne to which we
owe our allegiance.' And Franklin observed—somewhat disingenuously,
to be sure—that 'their jealousy of each other is so great that, however
necessary a union of the colonies has long been....and how sensible
soever each colony has been of that necessity; yet they have never
been able to effect such a union among themselves, nor even to agree
in requesting the mother couutry to establish it for them.'

It is necessary neither to belabor this point, nor to exaggerate it.

There were intercolonial rivalries and jealousies; there were elements of unity. During the contest with the mother country, Benjamin Franklin had argued that the thirteen colonies were so abandoned to suspicion that they never could unite; the Revolution almost proved him right, and it is relevant to recall what Americans themselves tend to forget, that John Adams estimated the 'patriots' and the loyalists at the same number, and that perhaps fifty thousand Americans fought in the ranks of the King and seventy to eighty thousand fled the country after independence had been won.

There was, as yet, no common body of tradition, nor a common loyalty, both were in the making: that habit of deliberately creating a tradition overnight, as it were, which gives such pain to Europeans, is a very old one. Every poet, every orator, every statesman, exhorted his fellow countrymen to rejoice in their national character, to abjure the Old World and look to the New. Almost every American was conscious that he was embarked upon a great experiment, one of interest not to America alone but to mankind. It will be sufficient to cite one poet, one preacher and one statesman. Thus that Francis Hopkinson who was a judge when he was not a poet:

> Make room, oh! ye kingdoms in hist'ry renowned—
> Whose arms have in battle with glory been crowned,—
> Make room for America—another great nation
> Arising to claim in your council a station.

Thus Timothy Dwight, in a commencement address of 1776, at Yale College:

> You should by no means consider yourselves as members of a small neighborhood, town or colony only, but as beings concerned in laying the foundations of American greatness. Your wishes, your designs, your labours are not confined by the narrow bounds of the present age, but are to comprehend succeeding generations, and to be pointed to immortality.

And thus Washington, in his circular letter of 1783:

> (The Americans) are, from this period, to be considered as the Actors on a most conspicuous Theatre, which seems to be peculiarly designated by Providence for the display of human

greatness and felicity....This is the time of their political probation, this is the moment when the eyes of the whole world are turned upon them, this is the moment to establish or ruin their national Character forever....

The traditions were still to be made, but (as we shall see) within a single generation, they had been born or created, and had been nourished. What of the second ingredient: the territory? There was an American land, to be sure, but by 1783 it was immense, it was largely a void, it was still in the making, and it was in the end to be but a small part of the whole. What, after all, was the territorial basis of the new nation? Was it the land that was actually settled—as in the old world the land of England or France or Denmark was that which had been subdued to the needs of society? If so, it was a comparatively small area, for even the Atlantic seaboard was not properly settled by the end of the Revolutionary War. Was it the immense domain acquired by the Treaty of Paris, doubled, and more, by the Louisiana purchase, almost doubled again by the acquisition of Florida, of Texas, of California and Oregon? Such a territory was rather an invitation to dispersion and fragmentation than an encouragement to national unity; this was what Henry Adams had in mind when he wrote of the situation in 1800 that:

> No prudent person dared to act on the certainty that when settled government could comprehend the whole; and when the day of separation should arrive, and America should have her Prussia, Austria and Italy as she already had her England, France and Spain, what else could follow but a return to the old conditions of local jealousies, wars and corruptions which had made a slaughter house of Europe?

Yet territorial growth more rapid than any other nation has experienced (with the dubious exception of Russia) did not make for disunity but rather strengthened unity. Instead of fragmenting the nation, it diffused nationalism; instead of contributing to particularism, it encouraged the generalization of patriotism and loyalty. Thus, American love of country had always been a curiously general affair, almost an abstract one. Few Americans have that passionate attachment to a particular soil, a particular county or region, that is so common in England, Sweden, France or Switzerland. We have a regional literature, but it is rather a tribute to the passing of genuine regionalism than an expression of it, and we have no literature comparable to the English literature of county and village, the loving study of field and wall and brook, the curious histories of village cricket or of fishing, the voluminous studies of local dialects and of place names. Boys and girls in prairie states or in the arid Southwest can sing with rapture, 'we love thy rocks and rills, thy woods and templed hills,' with no sense of incongruity because they take for granted that these things belong to them as truly as the prairie or the desert. Perhaps the most truly national of our patriotic songs is 'America, the Beautiful,' which carefully embraces in its catholic affections all landscapes and all regions.

'We have so much country,' wrote Nathaniel Hawthorne to Longfellow in the thirties, 'that we really have no country at all.' It was an exaggeration, but some foreign obsevers came to the same conclusion. Thus the Scotsman Charles Mackay observed in 1857 of the American that 'his affections have more to do with the social and political system than with the soil which he inhabits. The man whose attachments converge upon a particular spot of earth is miserable if removed from it, but give the American his institutions, and he cares little where you place him.' Thus the German Francis Grund wrote, in the same year, that 'an American's country is his understanding; he carries it with him wherever he goes, whether he emigrates to the shores of the Pacific or the Gulf of Mexico; his home is wherever he finds minds congenial to his own.'

Much of this was the product of the pioneering experience, of the habit of using up land and moving on, of large-scale immigration, or of the later urban movement and the mobility encouraged by good roads and easy transportation. The pioneer learned to cherish whatever land he cultivated, while he cultivated it, but could not afford to develop lasting sentiment about it. (Perhaps—we may say parenthetically— that is why he was all the more vociferous about it while he was there, as if he had to reassure himself of a devotion which was faintly artificial, just as the American college student who moves so easily from college to college, often makes a career of articulate and ostentatious college loyalties.) The pioneer learned, as Stephen Vincent Benet puts it, to wander with the wind—and like it. He learned to think of whatever place he occupied as Eden or New Babylon—until he found a better one. As for the immigrant, if he could not truly love the slums of Boston or Pittsburgh or Gary, Indiana, or the stockyards of

Kansas City (or the mines of Scranton and Wilkes-Barre), he might sincerely love the whole country. Mobility, too, is something of an explanation of this generalized affection for the whole country, a mobility that began with the movement from the Old World to the New, the trek from Virginia and Massachusetts Bay inland, and which continues to our own day: ten million people moved to the Pacific Coast in the last decade—it is as if the whole of Sweden should have moved to Spain. Americans are the most restless of people and the most traveled; it is no accident that while they put up with housing that Scandinavians or the Dutch would regard as a disgrace, they have the most comfortable trains, and that by and large their automobiles and their highways are the most efficient in the world.

What, finally, of the third major ingredient in modern nationalism: people and language. Most (not all) Old World nations rejoiced in a homogeneous population, speaking the same language and worshiping at the same church. But even before the Revolution, the American population was very heterogeneous, racially, linguistically, and religiously, and heterogeneity persisted throughout the first half of the nineteenth century. The American people has been a constantly changing thing, buffeted, one might say, by continuous invasions. The number of immigrants in the generation before the Civil War seems small by comparison with the vast influx after 1880, but immigration was actually on as large a scale in the earlier as in the later period: roughly five per cent of the total population in 1830, ten per cent in 1840 and 1850; not until 1900 was there any substantial proportionate increase. These figures, it is proper to add, take no account of the Negroes who were imported as slaves, but they, too, were destined to contribute to the heterogeneity and to the richness of the American social fabric.

Americans did have a common language, and this though a substantial part of the colonial population was of non-British origin. That they were able to retain a common language—a language with fewer variations in accent and idiom than is to be found in England, in Sweden, in France, in Austria—is one of those things always taken for granted but actually astonishing, and even unprecedented. No other colonial people has retained its language so largely intact: compare Mexican with Spanish, the French of Quebec with that of Paris, the Portuguese of Brazil with that spoken in Lisbon; compare even the vicissitudes of Danish or Norwegian with those of English, in the New World.

These crucial ingredients, then—the traditions, the loyalties, the land, the people, even the language—had still to be mastered and developed. But one feature of this development cannot but arrest our attention: its democratic character. In the United States, nationalism was not the creation of a monarch, of an aristocracy, of an army, of an intellectual elite even, as it was in almost all Old World countries. It was created by the people themselves. Everybody participated, in one way or another, everybody who was white in any event, and in a curious fashion even those who were not, for the Negroes have given us much of our music, our folklore, our social and cultural habits. Immigrants contributed as well as the native born, women as well as men, the poor and humble—because there were more of them—more than the rich and the wise and the wellborn. They all participated—in the westward movement, through the public schools, in the political party, in labor unions, in all those ways of working together that were encouraged by the most pervasive of all our institutions, the voluntary association.

In its democratic and equalitarian character, then as in its lack of dependence upon national antipathies, the development of American nationalism offers interesting departures from the Old World norm. In one other respect, too, the contrast is sharp: the interrelations of nascent nationalism with romanticism.

Everywhere in the Old World the emergence of nationalism was associated with romanticism. The Age of Reason had been a cosmopolitan one, one that took dynastic struggles in its stride as it were, that distinguished between necessary quarrels by monarchs and their mercenaries and the universal community of science and art and letters, and of the aristocracy, too. It was an age in which Frederick the Great could honour French philosophers even while fighting the French; in which George III of England could welcome the American painters Benjamin West and John Singleton Copley to his court during the Revolution; and in which a Trumbull even in prison, could command the sympathy and support of English artists; in which Turgot could instruct the French navy not to bother Captain Cook whose work was 'one of the glories of civilization'; in which artists and philosophers went undisturbed from one warring country to another. I need not remind you how all this has changed.

It was, in short, difficult to develop genuine nationalism in the Age of the Enlightenment which was by its very nature, suspicious of every thing that was local, parochial, traditional, and emotional, and that was suspicious of nationalism itself.

But the new nationalism came in on a tide of romanticism, and nationalism has always associated itself with emotion rather than with Reason.   And romanticism—I need not elaborate on anything so familiar as this—looked to the past, to some golden age of the past, or to the actual Middle Ages; romanticism cherished origins, traditions, myths and legends; romanticism addressed itself to recovering the past, by recovering the tales, the ballads, the early laws and customs of society. Romanticism not only recovered the past but conserved it and celebrated it.

In America, perhaps alone in America, romanticism did not need to look backwards—could not indeed do so—but addressed itself to the present and the future.   Thus the Reverend Jacob Duche, chaplain to the Continental Congress, wrote as early as 1770 that, 'I tread the hallowed soil (of America) with far higher pleasures from *anticipation* than your classic enthusiasts feel from *reflection*.'   Thus, a generation later, Fenimore Cooper observed that:

> The moral feeling with which a man of sentiment and knowledge looks upon the plains of your (Eastern) hemisphere, is connected with recollections;   here it should be mingled with his hopes. The same   effort   of   the   mind is as   equal to the one as to the other.... But   the   speculator   on   moral   things   can   enjoy   a satisfaction here that he who wanders over the plains of Greece will seek in vain.   The pleasure of the latter....is unavoidably tinged   with   melancholy   regrets;   while   here   all   that   reason allows may be hoped in behalf of man.

It was no accident that so many European romantics looked to the New World for their utopia, their Eden, their golden age: that the French court should adore Franklin for his rustic simplicity rather than his sagacity; that Chateaubriand should set his romance in the wilds of Florida; that Southey could idealize the Pennsylvania forests and rejoice in the music of the word Susquehanna; that Coleridge should draw on America for inspiration for 'Kubla Khan'; that even so clearheaded a pair of observers as Beaumont and Tocqueville should have bathed themselves in the romanticism of the forest, Beaumont writing a bad novel about it, Tocqueville reveling in its letters and essays.

For in America romance could feed on reality; the romantic was, indeed, the real, and the real the romantic, and the lines between them were hopelessly blurred. America naturalized romanticism, as it were, took it away from the romantics and restored it to the realists. We see this curious blend of the two in much of American literature, in art, even in politics. We can see it most simply in the treatment of the Indian and of Nature—a simple matter for the European romantics, but a very complicated one for a Cooper or an Irving, an H. H. Breckenridge or a William Gilmore Simms; a very complicated matter, too, for the artists and ethnologists like Catlin and Schoolcraft, for painters like Church or Moran, Miller or Bierstadt.

It was in part at least for this reason that American romanticism did not, except in the South, connect itself irretrievably with the past, with reaction, with class consciousness, or with the military. That it did so in the South will be admitted, and furnishes support to the general thesis, for the South was the one nondemocratic part of the country. Outside the South—and not wholly outside even there— America could be romantic and democratic, romantic and equalitarian, romantic and progressive. As James Madison put it as early as 1788:

Happily for America, happily I trust for the whole human race, they (the Americans) pursued a nobler course (than that which animated the past). Is it not the glory of the people of America that while they have paid a decent respect to the opinions of former times and other nations, they have not suffered a blind veneration for antiquity, for custom, for the names, to overrule the suggestions of their own good sense, the knowledge of their own situation and the lessons of their own experience.